INTERNATIONAL TRADE, FACTOR MOVEMENTS, AND THE ENVIRONMENT

International Trade, Factor Movements, and the Environment

MICHAEL RAUSCHER

Clarendon Press · Oxford
1997

Oxford University Press, Walton Street, Oxford OX2 6DP

Oxford New York
Athens Auckland Bangkok Bombay
Calcutta Cape Town Dar es Salaam Delhi
Florence Hong Kong Istanbul Karachi
Kuala Lumpur Madras Madrid Melbourne
Mexico City Nairobi Paris Singapore
Taipei Tokyo Toronto
and associated companies in
Berlin Ibadan

Oxford is a trade mark of Oxford University Press

Published in the United States
by Oxford University Press Inc., New York

British Library Cataloguing in Publication Data
Data available

Library of Congress Cataloguing in Publication Data
Rauscher, Michael
International trade, factor movements, and the environment /
Michael Rauscher.
Includes bibliographical references and index.
1. International trade—Environmental aspects. 2. Commercial
policy—Enivronmental aspects. 3. Environmental policy. I. Title.
HF 1379. R38 1996 333.7—dc20 96–19523
ISBN 0–19–829050–0

Typeset by Alliance Phototypesetters
Printed in Great Britain
on acid-free paper by
Bookcraft (Bath) Ltd., Midsomer Norton, Somerset.

Preface

This monograph is the result of several years of research on foreign trade and the environment. The subject attracted economic scientists for the first time in the mid-1970s and there was an extensive literature in this field at that time, but then came the oil crisis followed by periods of stagflation and unemployment. Subsequently, the scarcity of jobs and the slowdown of productivity were regarded as being more important than the scarcity of resources and the decline of natural capital. Only in recent years has there been a revival of environmental economics. Probably, this was fostered by the insight that environmental problems become increasingly global and that the standard prescriptions of economic theory may not work very well in this case. In this context, it is often argued that these environmental problems are aggravated—if not caused—by free trade and by the globalization of international commodity and factor markets. Therefore, it seems to be desirable to reconsider the relationship between international trade and the environment. Compared to the literature of the mid-1970s, two additional aspects have to be taken into account. One of them is the global nature of the environmental problems that are of predominant concern nowadays. The other one is the development in the international trade literature in the 1980s. Major achievements have been made by abandoning the assumption of perfect competition underlying the traditional models. Increasing returns to scale and imperfectly competitive market structures have been introduced and it has been shown that some of the policy implications of the traditional approach, that have in general been pro free trade, are altered dramatically. This new view on international trade may have important consequences for the evaluation of environmental polices in open economies and for the assessment of the whole subject of trade and the environment.

Before I start talking about negative externalities that constitute the environmental problem, I wish to mention the positive externalities that I have profited from during the time I was preparing the manuscript. I discussed my ideas with numerous colleagues and friends. Among those who contributed to this study with their remarks, suggestions, and critique are Kym Anderson, Claude D'Aspremont, Richard Baldwin, Ed Barbier, Scott Barrett, Elga Bartsch, Richard Blackhurst, Lans Bovenberg, Joanne Burgess, Carlo Carraro, Klaus Conrad, Henk Folmer, Horst Herberg, Arye Hillman, Michael Hoel, Sebastian Killinger, Gernot Klepper, Jean-Jacques Laffont, Karl-Göran Mäler, Petros Mavroides, Ernst Mohr, Rüdiger Pethig, Richard Portes, Jim Poterba, Jim Rollo, Günther Schulze, Albert Schweinberger, Horst Siebert,

Ingo Thomas, Angelica Tudini, Henry Tulkens, Tony Venables, and Alan Winters. I wish like to thank all of them. To two of them, I am particularly indebted. The first one is my academic teacher, Horst Siebert, who stimulated my interest in issues of environmental economics and international economic relationships. His comments and critique saved me (at least to some extent) from over-emphasizing theoretical curiosities and paradoxes at the expense of the practically relevant issues. The other one is Horst Herberg. His detailed critique and suggestions on an earlier version of the manuscript led to significant improvements. Of course, all errors, shortcomings, and misconceptions that have remained in the manuscript in spite of all this help and advice are my own responsibility.

Travel grants which enabled me to participate in the international academic discourse on workshops and conferences were provided by the University of Kiel, the Beijer Institute of Ecological Economics at the Royal Swedish Academy of Sciences in Stockholm, the Centre of Economic Policy Research in London, the Fondazione ENI Enrico Mattei in Milan, the Center of Economic Research at Tilburg University, the Deutsche Forschungsgemeinschaft, and the European Science Foundation. Last but not least, I wish to thank the Kiel Institute of World Economics for providing the intellectual atmosphere that has been the fertile ground on which my ideas could develop and grow.

Finally I wish to mention the negative externalities connected with the work on this book. Most of them were borne by my family, Karin, Steffen, and Marten. Their patience gave me the time and contemplation I needed to elaborate my ideas; their impatience made me write them down in the end.

Contents

Figures

Tables

1

Introduction

1.1 Trade and the Environment: An Awkward Relationship

Starting with Adam Smith (1776) and David Ricardo (1817), economists have always viewed free international trade as a source of wealth and welfare gains. The voluntary exchange of commodities induces favourable patterns of specialization and, therefore, leads to an improvement in the international division of labour. Since each country is driven to utilize its comparative advantage and to produce what it can produce most efficiently, the global output is increased and gains from trade accrue to all countries. This optimistic view of free trade has been challenged both from inside the body of mainstream economic theory (e.g. the optimal-tariff and infant-industry arguments) and by outsiders like dependencia theorists. It has survived these critiques, albeit with some qualifications. Knowing that there are some exceptions to the rule, most economists now accept the general validity of the free-trade principle, at least as a good rule of thumb e.g. see Krugman (1987). This view is now being challenged again, this time by environmentalists. 'Free Trade: The Great Destroyer' is a title of a recent article by Morris (1990) in the *Ecologist*.

Environmentalists are sceptical about international trade for several reasons.[1] First of all, there are the specialization effects. Some countries specialize in the production of pollution-intensive goods and this tends to increase environmental disruption there. These countries may experience welfare losses and in the case of transboundary pollution other countries too may be worse off with free trade than without. Second, the mainstream economic theories predict that international trade raises global output and consumption. With increased output, waste-management problems will also be increased. Third, there is a factor-mobility problem. Everything else being equal, mobile factors of production will move to countries where the pollution abatement requirements can be met relatively easily and cheaply, i.e. to the world's pollution havens. This environmental capital flight can have severe consequences. Since all countries are interested in attracting mobile factors of production, they may wish to adjust their environmental regulation. Ultimately, so the argument goes, there will be a disastrous competition among jurisdictions, which results in undesirably low levels of environmental regulation worldwide and the whole

---

[1] See Cobb and Daly (1989), Ekins (1989), Goldsmith (1990), Morris (1991), Shrybman (1991, 1991/92), Arden-Clarke (1991, 1992), Batra (1993, chs. 11–12), Daly and Goodland (1994), and Røpke (1994) for instance.

world will be turned into a pollution haven. The fourth problem area is that of international trade in hazardous waste. Waste importers are said to be less well-prepared than the exporters to store or process hazardous substances. Moreover, it is often argued that the possibility to export problems reduces the incentives to solve them, i.e. to employ sound environmental policies that reduce the quantity of toxic waste created. The fifth argument is the transport problem. Trade requires transport, transport requires energy, and energy utilization damages the environment. A sixth argument is the impact of free trade on Third World countries. It is argued that the dependence of these countries on imports will be increased, be it due to the behaviour of multinational corporations, or to declining terms of trade. This would prevent them from adopting sound environmental policy measures.

Besides potential environmental problems created by international trade, additional disputes arise from the impact of environmental regulation on international trade. Not only are free-trade policies attacked by green lobbies, there is often also no less resistance of trade lobbies against sound environmental policies. It is now widely agreed upon that environmental problems should be solved by applying the polluter-pays principle, i.e. by a policy that assigns the social cost of pollution to those who produce the damages. In theory, this provides the correct signals for the economic utilization of the environment and leads to an efficient allocation of scarce environmental resources. However, whenever it comes to an implementation of such environmental policies, the idea tends to be undermined by trade-related concerns. In particular, it is feared that domestic industries will not remain competitive if environmental standards are higher than those in other countries. Firms may to have to close down or move to pollution havens. Concerns like this tend to dilute the polluter-pays principle in practical environmental policy-making. I believe that low levels of environmental regulation can in many cases be explained by the impact of trade lobbies on the political decision-making process.

This book is an attempt to investigate the ticklish relationship between international trade and the environment. In the following paragraphs I will try to identify the major problem areas in the field of foreign trade, factor movements, and the environment.

As has been mentioned before, international trade in goods and factors have an impact on environmental quality and this is one of the reasons why environmentalists are concerned about trade and factor movements. To the economist the question arises whether there are still positive gains from trade if its environmental consequences are taken into account. A substantial part of the following analysis is devoted to this problem and conditions are established under which this is the case.

If trade has an effect on the environment, its regulation has an impact as well. If one believes that free trade and a high level of environmental quality are antagonisms and that environmental quality is more important as an objective of public policy than free trade, then trade restrictions are the appropriate solution. In some situations, these interventions may also appeal to people who generally do not share the green-protectionist view. Consider for instance a country which wants to do something against the greenhouse effect by imposing a substantial tax on CO_2 emissions. As a consequence, the relative prices of energy-intensive goods tend to rise. It becomes more attractive to import these commodities from abroad. Foreign production is increased and so are foreign CO_2 emissions. This is the so-called carbon-leakage effect. It reduces the effectiveness of the domestic CO_2 tax. The tax may even have a negative effect on environmental quality if the foreign production is more energy-intensive than the domestic production. One way out of this dilemma would be to restrict the import of CO_2-intensive goods in order to avoid the relocation of production. The second function of barriers to trade in the solution of international pollution problems is their use as sanctions. A country which does not behave co-operatively in an international environmental agreement can be punished by being excluded from exchanging goods in international markets. Credible threats of this kind can promote co-operation.

An example is the Montreal Protocol on Substances that Deplete the Ozone Layer (hereafter: Montreal Protocol), signed in 1987 by the major emission source countries.[2] It contains the possibility to punish non-compliant countries by banning their exports of goods containing chlorofluorocarbons (CFCs) and other ozone-depleting chemicals. The CFC content can be implicit, i.e. the goods banned do not have to contain these substances physically. It suffices if they have been produced in an unsustainable way. These trade restrictions serve two purposes. They help to discipline non-compliant parties and they deal with leakage effects.

From the point of view of free traders, international environmental agreements like the Montreal Protocol open a Pandora's box of green protectionism. The general problem with environmentally motivated trade interventions is the definition of the borderline between environmental protection and environmental protectionism. Green arguments can easily be abused to justify trade restrictions that are in reality only protectionist measures and it is often difficult to discriminate between true and pretended environmentalism. This delicate issue may be one of the reasons as to why the GATT has been sceptical about using trade restrictions as instruments of environmental policy. Now the issue is on the agenda again, now under the auspices of the World Trade Organization (WTO). One of the major future issues in the field of international relations is to find a way in which international environmental agreements and the international trading system can be made mutually consistent.

The problem of drawing a borderline between environmental protection and environmental protectionism arises also in the case of process and product standards. Product standards are applied in situations where the consumption of the imported good or its utilization as a factor of production causes

---

[2] For a survey of the Montreal Protocol see Enders and Porges (1992).

environmental damage in the importing country. Products not complying to these standards are excluded from trade. The use of environmental process standards in international trade goes even a bit further. Not only the characteristics of the commodity itself are decisive but often also the way in which it has been produced. If the foreign production of the traded goods is environmentally harmful, the importing country may be tempted to enforce its process standards on imported goods as well. Is this extraterritorialist policy economically sensible? Moreover, one is led to ask whether products with particular characteristics should be excluded from trade and, if they should, how the characteristics of the products are to be specified. Practical experience shows that product and process standards are often defined such that they discriminate against foreign firms and distort foreign trade. In addition, one may ask whether an international harmonization of standards is desirable.

In the wat that trade policy measures can be used to achieve environmental goals, environmental policies can be used to achieve trade-related policy objectives. For instance, a country may improve its terms of trade or it may support particular sectors of its economy by designing its environmental policy appropriately. This is attractive particularly in situations where the traditional instruments of trade policy (tariffs, quotas, and subsidies) are not available. This applies to most countries since they are members of free-trade zones like the NAFTA or the EU or they are signatories to the GATT. This limits the possibilities to use trade restrictions. Policy-makers look for other than the traditional instruments of trade policy, and environmental regulation is one of the candidates.

In this context the term 'environmental dumping' has been coined in the public discussion. It characterizes a situation in which the government imposes too low environmental standards on domestic producers. This reduces their costs and hence is a kind of hidden subsidization. Domestic producers are then able to dump their goods on world markets at prices that do not reflect the full cost of production. The interesting question is in which circumstances politicians have incentives to adopt environmental policies which result in environmental dumping. In this study we will look at terms-of-trade considerations, at the impact of lobbies, and at objectives of industrial policy. Moreover, there is the problem of environmental capital flight. Everything else being equal, footloose industries will locate in jurisdictions where abatement requirements are relatively low. One may ask in which circumstances a lax environmental policy that attracts these industries is a rational strategy.

If environmental dumping were a purely national phenomenon, then there would not be much to be concerned about. Either such a strategy is in the interest of the people or they should vote for a new government. However, environmental dumping also has an international dimension. If one country relaxes environmental standards, other countries may wish to retaliate. An interjurisdictional competition may be induced and this competition can have undesirable consequences. Environmentalists often argue that there will be a race to the bottom in terms of environmental regulation. The first question to be asked in this context is in which circumstances this is a realistic scenario. The second question then is which measures should be taken if one wants to avoid the race to the bottom.

Besides the problem of the strategic use of lax environmental standards, there exists perhaps also the converse. In the recent discussion on environmental policies in open economies, it has frequently been argued that tight environmental standards rather than lax standards enhance competitiveness and the performance of firms in international markets.[3] The underlying argument is that these standards force firms to produce better goods and to develop new environmentally friendly techniques. In the longer term, these firms may expect a competitive edge in international markets. The question arises whether this is only green rhetoric or whether such considerations should be considered a serious basis for the use of environmental regulation to achieve industrial-policy objectives.

Many of the issues raised here can be dealt with in a static framework. However, such an investigation would lack the important dimension of time. Many of the environmental problems that concern us nowadays are to an even larger extent problems of our children and grandchildren. This applies to climatic changes and to the destruction of the ozone layer where there are time-lags of decades between the cause (emission) and the effect (atmospheric change). Closely related to this is the accumulation of environmental disruptions over time. In many cases, the capability of the environment to regenerate is a function of the stock of remaining environmental resources. Moreover, there are irreversibility problems, as in the cases of the destruction of the ozone layer and of biodiversity loss. The major questions arising in this context are what kind of incentives an open country has to conserve its resources and what kind of action can be taken to improve the allocation of scarce environmental resources. An issue of particular interest here is the effect of trade measures such as boycotts of tropical timber or of commodities whose production involves CFCs. These issues will, however, not be dealt with in this monograph. Some of the results derived from the static model framework can be transferred to dynamic models where it is not the contemporary environmental damage that matters but the present value of future damages.[4]

Another intertemporal problem arises from the intertemporal nature of foreign trade. Commodities are not always traded in direct exchange for each

[3] In the US literature, this has been termed the Porter hypothesis after the publication of Porter's (1991) stirring article in the Scientific American.

[4] However, intertemporal environmental models generate some particularities like cyclical resource extraction paths which cannot be discussed in a static-model framework. See Rauscher (1994b). Additional models concerned with trade-related aspects of renewable resources use are Barbier and Rauscher (1994), Chichilnisky (1994b), and Brander and Taylor (1995a, b). Moreover, there exists a substantial literature on trade in exhaustible resources which provides some results concerning the relationship between foreign trade and the exhaustion of natural resources. See Kemp and Long (1984), Siebert (1985b), and Withagen (1985).

other; in many cases, commodities are given away in exchange for the promise of the trading partner to deliver commodities in the future. There are borrowers and lenders and when intertemporal trade does not work well, we experience debt crises: debtor countries are unable or unwilling to service their debt. It has been argued that the pressure to exploit environmental resources is closely related to the indebtedness situation of a country. A highly indebted country, so the argument goes, will do almost anything in order to earn foreign currency—including ruining its own future by overexploiting resources.[5] The question is whether this fear is justified and, if it is, what can be done to solve the problem of over-exploitation of environmental resources.

The questions addressed up to here can be dealt with on four levels. The first one is the level of positive analysis. We look at the effects of changes in exogenous variables on the values of endogenous variables. Typical subjects of the analysis are the effects of trade policy on the environment or of environmental policies on the patterns of trade. The second level is the normative one of how these policies should be designed if one wishes to achieve certain objectives, e.g. the maximization of welfare. This provides us with economic-policy recommendations. In a third step, we can then ask why these policy recommendations are not followed and why the world does not look the it could. This is the political-economy aspect of the problem.[6] Policy-makers are not benevolent and environmental policies in open economies are subject to protectionist pressures. This explains deviations of real environmental policies from the optimal ones. Finally, the fourth level is the institutional and constitutional one. Which kind of institutions help us to reduce regulatory capture and how can the world trading system be designed such that we can enjoy not only the gains from trade and factor mobility but also the benefits of a clean environment and a sustainable future?

The relationship between international trade and the environment is a multidimensional one, and the following chapters of the book will be devoted to the investigation of this complex issue. This will be done in a purely theoretical framework. But before the theoretical investigation starts, we will have a look at the data. What kind of results do we obtain from empirical studies? Are they compatible with our prejudices concerning what is going on in the world or do we obtain unexpected results that deserve further explanation?

1.2 The Empirical Evidence: A Survey of the Literature

In their recent survey on environmental economics, Cropper and Oates (1992) argue that there is not much evidence that environmental regulation has a

---

[5] See Adams (1991), George (1992, ch. 1), and Miller (1991).

[6] The term 'political economy' is used here in the sense of an analysis of the political dimension of economic problems.

significant impact on international trade and that, therefore, environmental
economists should not care too much about international competitiveness.[7]
This is good news to both the producers and the environmentalists. It means
that the producers are too pessimistic when they argue that environmental
legislation negatively affects their competitiveness. Environmentalists can now
easily reject the objections against tough environmental standards that are
raised by producers' lobbies. Matters would also become simple for the economic theorist since designing environmental policies for an open economy as
if it were a closed economy would be a good rule of thumb. But matters are not
that simple. First of all, it is far from clear that the impact of environmental
regulation on the patterns of trade and international factor movements is
negligible. There are important measurement problems, in particular in comparing environmental laws in different countries and assigning numbers that
quantify environmental regulation. It may be true that statistical insignificance
just reflects this measurement problem. And second, even if trade is not affected by environmental regulation, there are other interesting questions that
still remain to be settled, particularly the one concerning the impact of trade on
the environment. The following paragraphs will summarize the empirical evidence on the relationship between international trade and the environment and
collect some stylized facts that will provide the background of the theoretical
treatise of the following chapters.

The largest problem of any empirical assessment of the relationship between
trade and the environment is the measurement of the environmental variables.
Given the hypothesis that changes in environmental regulation have an impact
on international trade, one first needs a measure of the toughness of environmental standards. This becomes the more difficult, the more aggregated the
model is. It may be possible to solve this problem for certain sectors of an economy, or better for certain production processes, but finding a measure for the
restrictiveness of the regulation of an aggregate country amounts to measuring
the unmeasurable. Crude proxies, albeit not satisfactory, seem to be the only
solution. A similar problem occurs if the impact of trade on environmental
quality is to be investigated. How can one construct an index of the environmental quality in a country? Again, there are two ways out of this dilemma.
The first one is to do case-studies and to look at particular aspects or dimensions of environmental quality. Unfortunately, the results are not necessarily
generalizable. The second method is to construct proxy variables, which is unsatisfactory as well. This measurement problem is an inherent weakness of any
empirical study and it may explain why a uniform view of the empirical evidence has not yet been established.

If the mainstream economic theories are true, differences in environmental
regulations should affect the international division of labour and the allocation of factors of production. Tight environmental taxes and standards raise

---

[7] For surveys of the empirical evidence, see Ugelow (1982) and Dean (1992).

the costs of production in emission-intensive industries and this can lead to two kinds of factor-relocation effects. On the one hand, the patterns of special-ization may be affected. Under the assumption that factors of production are mobile across sectors, a country with tough environmental standards will specialize on the production of 'clean' commodities and a country with laxer regulations will increase its output of environmentally intensive goods. The first country exports the 'clean' products and the other country exports the 'dirty' products. On the other hand, there may be a relocation of production capacities from countries with restrictive environmental policies to countries with relatively lax regulations. Both hypotheses can be tested. In the first case, one has to look at trade figures, in the second at foreign direct investments. This has been done in several studies.

Before starting to look at relocational effects of environmental regulation, one may wish to consider the effects of environmental regulation on costs and factor productivities. Do changes in environmental taxes and standards have significant effects in this respect? Empirical studies like those of Barbera and McConnell (1986), Conrad and Morrison (1989), and Gray and Shadbegian (1993) suggest that this, is indeed the case. The next question then is whether this has induced the changes in the international division of labour predicted by foreign-trade theory.

One of the first studies trying to assess the role of environmental policy in international trade is the one by Walter (1973). His approach is based on Leontief's (1954) famous model. Walter approximates the costs of pollution abatement and other environmental-protection activities for all sectors of the US economy. Using an input–output analysis, he determines the so-called 'overall environmental-control loadings', i.e. the ratio of environmental-control cost, including those of the intermediate inputs, to the final price of the output. This is then multiplied by the value of US exports and imports to ob-tain the environmental-cost component of US trade.[8] It is shown that, on aver-age, the abatement-cost content of US exports is slightly higher than that of US imports. This suggests that the United States are relatively well endowed with environmental resources compared to the rest of the world.[9] The impact of international differences in environmental regulation is not analysed. This is a shortcoming not only of this but also of the other studies published in the 1970s. see Ugelow (1982) for a survey).

Robison (1988) uses a closely related approach. He incorporates more recent data and takes account of the abatement costs that are implicit in the capital

---

[8] Like in Leontief's (1954) study, the environmental-cost component of US imports is estimated by using US data. This is based on the heroic assumption that the trading partners use the same technologies and the same factor intensities to produce their export goods as the US economy. This is one of the crude approximations that have to be made due to a lack of data.

[9] The same method has been applied by Kim (1990) to determine the pollution content of Korean trade. The result of this study is that the environmental-control loadings of imports slightly exceed those of exports. Kim concludes that on average there is no significant difference be-tween the pollution contents of imports and exports.

stock used in the production process. Moreover, the investigation is carried out for several years. The abatement-cost contents of output, exports, and imports have risen from 1973 to 1982 due to increased pollution-abatement requirements. It is shown that the change in the abatement-cost content of imports is larger than that of exports and output. This indicates a shift in US imports from goods with relatively low-abatement requirements towards goods subject to relatively tough regulation. This is what one should have expected as a result of a change in environmental policy—however under the proviso that trading partners of the US have not changed their environmental policies themselves. Unfortunately, changes in environmental laws elsewhere are not considered by Robison due to a lack of data.

Sorsa (1994) comes to different conclusions in a study incorporating more recent data. Sorsa looks at trade flows in environmentally intensive goods and environmental expenditures in seven industrialized countries. It is shown that in most cases changes in exports in environmentally intensive goods and changes in environmental expenditures were uncorrelated. The exception was Austria with a positive correlation. In general, countries have maintained their comparative advantages during the period 1970–90 despite significant changes in environmental regulation during this period. Only Japan has experienced a drastic reduction in its environmentally intensive exports. Austria and Finland, in contrast, have become slightly more competitive in environmentally intensive products.

There are two problems intrinsic to the Leontief approach. First, the analyses are only bivariate, i.e. other factors than environmental costs that may explain patterns of specialization are neglected. Secondly, pollution-abatement data are taken into account only for the country under consideration but not for its trading partners. Tobey (1989, 1990) has overcome these problems. He uses a Heckscher–Ohlin–Vanek model[10] of international trade to address the question whether environmental policy affects trade. In a first step, he identifies pollution-intensive sectors by using 1977 US data and an input–output matrix to calculate the ratio of total environmental-control cost to the output price. These sectors are then subject to the econometric analysis. It tests the hypothesis that net exports of a sector's output are affected by the environmental regulation in a country in a way predicted by the theory. Thus, net exports are regressed on the factor endowments of different countries in 1975. The set of factor-endowment variables includes an index measuring the stringency of pollution control measures based on a 1976 UNCTAD survey.[11] In none of the five industries under consideration does the environmental-policy variable

[10] This model is a multifactor, multicommodity extension of the Heckscher–Ohlin–Samuelson model, which translates the imports and exports of goods into the imports and exports of the factor services contained in these goods. In recent years, it has been used frequently to test the theories of international trade. See Leamer (1984), for instance.

[11] This survey resulted in a partition of countries into seven categories ranging from 'tolerant' to 'strict'. Tobey (1990) quantified this variable by assigning the values 1 to 7. For a detailed description of the data, see Walter and Ugelow (1979).

turn out to be significant. An omitted-variables test reveals the same result.[12] This lack of empirical evidence, however, does not necessarily mean that there is no impact of environmental regulation on foreign trade. The Heckscher–Ohlin model represents a long-run view of international trade and specialization. It assumes that factors of production are relocated between sectors. This takes time and, therefore, changes in environmental policy that have been made during the seventies in response to the increased concern about environmental damages having an impact on international trade only with a lag of several years. To take account of this, Tobey also regressed changes in net exports on the stringency of environmental policy and finds a significant impact only for one out of five sectors—albeit with the 'wrong' sign.

Murrell and Ryterman (1991) also use an omitted-variables test in a Heckscher–Ohlin–Vanek model framework. Their analysis is based on 1975 data and their main result is that the hypothesis that trade is not influenced by environmental policies cannot be rejected. Of course, as in the previously discussed papers, the choice of the year of observation may explain this result. Tough environmental standards came into effect during the 1970s in some of the major industrialized countries and the induced adjustment processes should be expected to exhibit substantial lags.

International trade and specialization provide one channel through which differences in environmental regulation have an impact on the international division of labour. The other channel is foreign direct investment. Other things being equal, pollution-intensive production processes should move to countries with lax environmental standards, where abatement costs are relatively low. Walter (1982) evaluates data on the sectoral and firm levels and comes to the conclusion that generally there is no evidence that pollution-intensive industries have moved to less regulated countries and regions. This has happened only in special cases, when major projects have been obstructed for environmental reasons. Similar results are obtained by Bartik (1988) and Leonard (1988). Levinson (1994), using US data, also does not find much evidence that environmental regulation affects plant location. Only in the case of new branch plant of large enterprises do the coefficients have the expected sign and are significant. Rowland and Feiock (1991), in contrast, come to the conclusion that environmental regulation does affect locational decisions of investors. They use data on the chemical industry and consider the allocation of new capital across federal states of the USA. Some of these states differ substantially from each other in their environmental regulations of the chemical industry. The relationship found by Rowland and Feiock (1991) is highly non-linear: there is threshold value of pollution-abatement costs below which dislocation effects of environmental-policy changes cannot be observed.

---

[12] The omitted-variables test is based on the following idea. If the stringency of environmental regulation has a negative impact on the net exports of a certain commodity and if this variable is omitted in the regression analysis, then the residuals should systematically deviate from zero. They should be negative for the countries with tough regulations and positive for the pollution havens.

Introduction

Introduction

11

Hettige *et al.* (1992) and Lucas *et al.* (1992) report that there has been a re-location of environmentally intensive industries to developing countries. They infer this from the fact that low-income countries have experienced higher growth rates of pollution intensity per unit of output than high-income countries. This relationship, however, is not constant through time. In the 1960s, the pollution intensities of output grew more rapidly in high-income countries than in low-income countries. This was reversed in the 1970s and 1980s, i.e. during the period in which industrialized countries tightened their environmental standards. From these results, one can, however, not infer that patterns of specialization and trade have been changed in a way consistent with economic theory. Trade patterns have been considered by Low and Yeats (1992), who use data covering the period from 1965 to 1988 and show that the share of 'dirty' industries in exports has increased for some developing countries whereas it has declined for the industrial countries.

Hettige *et al.* (1992) and Lucas *et al.* (1992) also address the second of the two central questions, which concerns the impact of free trade on the environment. They find evidence in favour of the hypothesis that the pollution intensity of production has grown much more for high-growth inward-orientated developing countries than for high-growth outward-orientated economies. According to their explanation, this is due to differences in the investment behaviour between industrializing countries. In open economies, they argue, there are incentives to expand labour-intensive production, which is relatively clean, whereas closed economies tend to develop their capital-intensive dirty industries. This seems to support the hypothesis that free trade is good for the environment. However, if this is true for developing countries, one may argue that just the opposite is true for industrialized economies since they should follow the opposite pattern of specialization. Unfortunately, due to a lack of data, the authors are unable to present results on the effect of outward orientation on the cleanliness of production in industrialized countries.

The impact of international trade on emissions in industrialized countries is addressed by van Bergeijk (1991) by means of a simple regression model. He uses a pooled set of data for OECD countries from two years (1980 and 1985). The emissions of three pollutants (SO_2, CO_2, and NO_x) are regressed on a set of explanatory variables, including a trade variable. In the cases of SO_2 and NO_x, van Bergeijk finds a significant negative impact (albeit only at the 90 per cent confidence level), and for CO_2 emissions the sign is also negative but not significant. This suggests that openness is good for the environment. One explanation for this result may be that increased openness leads to increased specialization and pollution-intensive industries move to countries that are not in the data set. However, most of the trade of the OECD countries is amongst each other and, therefore, positive and negative specialization effects tend to cancel out. The alternative explanation is that gains from trade raise the income and, with a positive income elasticity of the demand for environmental quality, the environmental policy becomes tougher.

This is one of the arguments that Grossman and Krueger (1993) put forward in their analysis of the environmental effects of the North-American Free-Trade Association. They find that pollution in medium-income industrializing countries is negatively correlated to income and conclude that Mexico may be driven to employ a more-restrictive environmental regulation after having experienced the gains from NAFTA.[13] Similar findings concerning the relationship between income and emissions are reported by Holtz-Eakin and Selden (1993).

Birdsall and Wheeler (1992) examine Latin American countries to find out whether increased openness has led to increased environmental damage. They use a pooled cross-section for time-series for twenty-five countries and regress the toxic intensity of production on a set of explanatory variables including an index of openness.[14] They find a negative impact of openness on the toxicity of production. Using the Chilean economy as a case-study, they try to identify the reasons underlying this relationship. It is argued that the positive effect of free trade can be explained by the fact that increased openness gives a country access to new, modern technologies that are available on world markets. And modern equipment designed in and for industrialized countries is constructed to meet the pollution-abatement requirements prevailing there. Thus, cleanliness is embodied in these advanced technologies and it is bought by the industrializing country unintendedly. Although this explanation is plausible at a first glance, it does not explain the result obtained by Birdsall and Wheeler in their econometric study. The econometric model uses a pollution intensity index derived from 1987 US data, i.e. it is based on the assumption of a constant technology. Thus, the results of the econometric model can only be explained by changes in the allocation of factors across sectors.

Wheeler and Martin (1992) look at the international diffusion of clean technologies in more detail. For the case of the pulp industry, they find that the adaptation lag for the introduction of new, clean technologies is significantly raised if countries are inward-orientated.

The effect of free trade on agricultural production is investigated by Anderson (1992a,b). Markets for agricultural products are distorted in many countries due to huge subsidies to farmers and/or their protection by high trade barriers. Anderson shows that there is a high correlation between domestic prices and the utilization of fertilizer and pesticides. Differences in domestic price levels for identical products can only be caused by the existence of barriers to trade. Abolishing these barriers to trade would result in a relocation of production from highly protected industrialized countries (the EC and EFTA countries and Japan) to less developed countries. It is argued that the

[13] Another finding in this study is the significant negative impact of openness on SO_2 pollution in cities. The authors are unable to give an explanation for this non-intuitive result. Other pollutants are not significantly affected by openness.

[14] It should be noted that the data they use are crude proxies. The pollution-intensity figures are based on US data, not on country-specific data, and the openness index is a kind of a dummy variable ranging from 1 to 5.

corresponding reduction in the use of fertilizers and pesticides in the industrialized countries would outweigh the increase in the less developed countries, since the less developed countries tend to use more labour-intensive methods of production that require less chemicals. Thus, the net effect of trade liberalization would be a reduction in the use of pesticides and fertilizer. Similar results are obtained by Harold and Runge (1993) who find a significant positive effect of agricultural subsidies on the intensity of fertilizer use. It should be noted, however, that it is rather unlikely that there will be a uniform reduction in the use of fertilizer and pesticides in all countries. If trade liberalization induces increased production of agricultural goods in developing countries, their demand for fertilizer and pesticides will rise. Moreover, the incentives to convert tropical forests into agricultural land may be increased in some countries.

Positive effects of trade liberalization on the environment have also been established for the case of the coal market (see Burniaux *et-al* (1992)). They show with the OECD computable general-equilibrium model that the removal of existing distortions in energy markets, which predominantly take the shape of subsidization for protectionist reasons, would result in a drastic reduction of CO_2 emissions on a global scale.[15]

It may be true that the global effect of trade liberalization on environmental quality is positive for some markets like coal and agricultural products. For other markets, the negative effects of free trade may dominate the positive effects. There are even cases in which there are no positive effects on the environment at all. As an example consider the trade in endangered species. As a result of trade liberalization, exploitation of these species is increased in the exporting countries but it usually cannot be reduced in the importing countries since it has always been zero there. As an example consider exports of ebony from Africa to Japan and Hong Kong. Barbier (1991) analyses the demand for ebony in these countries and comes to the conclusion that, notwithstanding that there may be policy instruments that are more effective than barriers to trade, tariffs, quotas, and trade bans can contribute to the objective of preserving endangered species.

An issue that has long been overlooked in empirical studies is that of transportation. Gabel and Röller (1992) examine the effects of trade liberalization on international transportation for a set of European countries. They explain the volume of trade amongst these countries as a function of a number of variables including a measure of non-tariff barriers to trade. This variable has a significant negative impact. Removing these barriers would therefore result in an increase in the volume of trade of around 25 per cent. The corresponding increase in demand for international transportation would be even larger since the increase in long-distance trade exceeds the increase in medium-distance trade.

---

[15] It should be noted that computable general-equilibrium models are no tools to test theories. They are based on the assumption that some underlying theory is correct and can be used for policy simulations. They are useful to identify the direction of change of a dependent variable if the results obtained by theoretical reasoning are ambiguous.

As mentioned above, not all trade is direct exchange of commodities at one point of time. There is also intertemporal trade that resulted in a debt crisis in the 1980s. One may ask whether it is true that, as some authors argue, environmental disruption is increasing with foreign debt. Regression results based on a sample of 109 countries are presented by Diwan and Shafik (1992). The dependent variable is CO_2 emissions per capita. It is shown that per-capita foreign debt has a positive significant effect on emissions. This is explained by the need of indebted countries to raise their production in order to be able to service their debt.

Summarizing, the empirical studies seem to suggest the following stylized facts:

- The evidence concerning the relocation of dirty industries from industrialized to less developed countries is mixed. Some studies claim to find results pointing in this direction, other studies produce no significant result at all. This is true for both kinds of relocational effects, i.e. for specialization effects and for international capital movements. It is very difficult to identify the impact of environmental regulation on the aggregate level since, in general, environmental costs are only a small fraction of the total cost of production.[16]

- The impact of free trade on the environment is positive for some countries and some commodities. But there are other countries that lose in terms of environmental quality since they specialize in environmentally intensive goods. The interesting question of whether the traditional gains from trade are sufficient to offset the loss of environmental quality has not been addressed in the empirical studies. On the global level, the effect of openness on environmental quality is far from clear. It may be positive for some groups of commodities but negative for others.

- Environmental quality benefits from free trade if new technologies that are imported and adopted for reasons of efficiency are relatively clean. It is obvious that not all new technologies have this desirable property.

- The increased demand for international transportation may offset positive effects of liberalization.

- Highly indebted countries tend to use their resources more intensively than other countries.

There are a lot of ambiguities and there is no clear-cut evidence as to whether environmental quality is positively or negatively affected by international trade and as to whether environmental regulation has an impact on the patterns of trade or not. Additional research is necessary to improve our knowledge about the relationship between international trade and the environment. Empirical evidence is necessary to test the various theories that do not only offer differing

---

[16] The average expenditure on pollution control in OECD countries was well below two percent of GDP during the eighties. See OECD (1990, p. 40).

explanations of real-world phenomena but also have policy implications that are often highly sensitive to parameter changes and, in some cases, even contrary to each other. These theories are the subject of the remainder of this study.

1.3 Organization of the Book

As the introductory chapter has shown, the relationship between international trade and the environment is complex and multidimensional. Pollution can be caused by production, transportation, and consumption activities. Moreover, different types of international economic relationships are considered. We will deal with international factor movements, with trade in pollutants (e.g. toxic waste), and trade in final goods. We will look at static and dynamic aspects of the problems of the impact of international trade on the environment and of environmental policy on international trade, derive positive and normative results, and discuss the political-economy aspect of trade policy in open economies. All these problems will be looked at both from the perspective of a single open economy and from a global point of view where the interdependence of the decisions of individual countries is taken into account. This programme is organized as follows.[17]

Chapter 2 introduces the concepts that will be used in the theoretical section of the books. It is the section where the definitions of the terms are given that will be used in the following chapters. For example, we will define what is meant by 'endowment of a country with environmental resources' and by 'environmental dumping'. We will discuss the basic principles of environmental economics. Finally, the general framework of the theoretical model that is used in the following chapters will be introduced.

In Chapter 3, we will deal with international capital movements. Everything else being equal, mobile capital tends to move to the location where environmental standards can be met at relatively low costs, i.e. to pollution havens. The question arises whether this environmental capital flight can be welfare-improving and under what conditions. The major part of this chapter will, however, deal with the impact of environmental policy on international factor movements. Can environmental regulation be used to influence the international allocation of factors and, if so, should it be used? Will there be a competition for mobile capital amongst countries which leads to suboptimal levels of environmental allocation? Then the question arises whether it is desirable to intervene in international markets to achieve environmental objectives. Can one design 'green' barriers to factor mobility? Finally, we will try to find out how market power of the foreign direct-investor affects the results.

Chapter 4 deals with international trade in hazardous wastes. The reason to devote a separate chapter to this issue is predominantly an analytical one. Toxic

[17] Table 1.1 at the end of this chapter summarizes the contents of this study.

waste trade can be investigated within the framework of a simple one-sector model of the economy in which the service to store these substances is traded against aggregate final goods. The consideration of toxic waste trade in a standard two-sector trade model is possible theoretically but in our case turns out to be rather difficult since both consumption and production externalities are considered. Thus, this chapter on trade in toxic waste and the chapter on trade in final goods have been separated. Trade in hazardous waste raises a number of interesting questions. Producers in countries with tight environmental standards face high costs for the storage or treatment of toxic waste. Thus, there may be incentives to transport these substances to other countries with less stringent environmental standards. The first question in this context is what determines the willingness to accept toxic waste. In a second step, one may look at the welfare effects of trade in toxic wastes. This is perhaps the most controversial issue. Free-traders argue that all kinds of international trade are welfare-improving whereas environmentalists prefer strict regulations if not a complete ban of trade in waste. The question arises of whether trade in hazardous substances should be regulated or whether the issue of environmental regulation may be left to the sovereignty of the trading partners. It will be shown that trade restrictions can be beneficial to all the countries involved. Moreover, we look at the impact of environmental policy on the international trade in hazardous substances and address the question of whether suboptimal policies will be chosen in the absence of international policy co-ordination.

Chapter 5 is devoted to the analysis of trade and the environment in a modified Heckscher–Ohlin-Samuelson model. Factors are now mobile across sectors within an economy (but perfectly immobile between countries). Patterns of trade are explained by international differences in endowments with factors of production. In a first step, the impact of free trade on the environment and welfare is analysed. Afterwards, we will be concerned with the impact of changes in environmental policies on the allocation of the factors of production, on the patterns of trade, and on world market prices. We will than analyse the impact of barriers to trade on environmental variables: is there something like a 'green' tariff that can be justified on environmental grounds? Finally, more complicated versions of the simple model will be discussed which allow for the existence of non-traded goods and more than two countries, factors of production, and goods. A special case is that of non-traded goods that can be used as a reference point for the identification of ecological dumping.

The assumption of perfect competition in all goods and factors markets on which the Heckscher–Ohlin–Samuelson approach is based is not always realistic. The new trade theory literature, which was established in the 1980s, has shown that some of the results and policy recommendations of the traditional model have to be modified substantially when this assumption is dropped. This will be done in Chapter 6. Several types of imperfect competition can be thought of. We start with the simple monopoly model and look at the appropriate environmental policies for regulating domestic and foreign firms that trade their outputs internationally. Then the locational decision of the monopolist will be endogenized and we will address the question of whether there will be a race to the bottom in the area of environmental policies when many countries compete against each other for the foreign investor. The second class of imperfect-competition models involves oligopolies. Environmental regulation may be used to achieve trade-related economic policy goals. An example is its strategic use to give domestic industries a cost advantage in international markets and shift rents from the foreign country to the home country. This is the static, strategic environmental-policy model. Another aspect of the strategic use of environmental policies is the use of product-quality standards. It is sometimes claimed that tight environmental product standards can be used to increase the competitiveness of particular industries. We will explore in which circumstances this may be the case. The final issue is intra-industry trade and the model framework is that of monopolistic competition. In the extreme case, commodities produced with identical technologies are traded between countries that are identical with respect to their factor endowments and demand conditions. The questions arise whether this trade is still beneficial if environmental deterioration matters and what effects changes in environmental regulation have on the patterns of trade.

Chapter 7 is devoted to the political economy of environmental policies in open economies. The benevolent-politician model used in Chapters 3 to 6 will be abolished and a more realistic approach of modelling environmental-policy decisions will be used. This can be done for the cases of direct and representative democracies. In a direct democracy, the median voter decides on the policy to be made and, since the median voter is not always the mean voter, there may be deviations from the socially optimal policy. In a representative democracy, the policy-maker has some discretion and there will be lobbyists with idiosyncratic interest who try to influence the policy-making process. Two areas of public policy are of concern here. One of them is trade policy and one may ask how trade policy is affected by green lobbies. The other policy area is that of environmental regulation and the main question concerns the impact of protectionist interest groups that demand indirect subsidies in the shape of low pollution-abatement requirements. A partial-equilibrium model is considered where both environmentalists and industry-specific interest groups exert their influence on the government in order to achieve favourable conditions of environmental and trade regulation.

Chapter 8 deals with intertemporal trade, i.e. we look at the exchange of commodities against the promise of making or receiving a payment in the future. Thus, foreign debt will be addressed. The relationship between foreign debt and environmental disruption will be addressed and possible ways out of the debt-and-environment trap will be discussed. Among these are unconditioned debt reliefs, debt-for-nature swaps, and other kinds of side-payments.

In Chapters 3 to 8, I merely derive results from theoretical models. They are briefly summarized at the end of each chapter, but no policy implications are drawn there. This is deferred to the end of the book. Chapter 9 summarizes the results of the previous parts of the book in a more general context and derives economic-policy implications. Besides looking at policy instruments we will also deal with institutions. Which principles should a national trade law be based on if environmental issues are considered to be important? How can the capture of environmental policy by protectionist interests be prevented? We then move from national to international institutions and look at international environmental agreements and foreign-trade agreements. Some of the existing agreements that are relevant in this context will be reviewed. Finally, the question will be addressed if and how the world trading system should be amended in order to be capable of taking environmental issues into account appropriately. The central question is: how can developed and developing countries reap both the benefits from the improvement of environmental quality and the gains from trade?

The book is organized such that Chapters 3 to 8 can be read independently of each other although there are several linkages. Chapter 2, which develops the basic concepts and introduces a large part of the notation, is essential for the understanding of the other chapters.

TABLE 1.1: Contents of the Book

Chapter	2	3	4	5	6	7	8	9
Definitions and basic concepts	X							
Int. factor movements		X						
Impact of trade on the environment			X	X	X	X	X	
Impact of environmental regulation on trade			X	X	X	X		
Perfect competition			X	X	X		X	X
Imperfect competition			X	X		X	X	
Normative analysis			X	X	X	X		X
Political-economy analysis						X		
Static model			X	X	X	X	X	
Dynamic model							X	
Institutional issues								X

2

Basic Concepts

2.1 Externalities, Property Rights, and Market Failure

Neoclassical economists view environmental disruption as a problem of negative externalities.[1] A negative externality occurs whenever an agent has to bear a part of the cost of another agent's activity without being compensated. The agent causing the externality does not take this into account. She bears only the private costs of the activity. The social costs, i.e. the total costs that are borne by society, exceed the private costs. Since a part of the social costs is external and does not enter the agent's optimization calculus, too much of the activity is performed. Too much pollution is generated and environmental disruption exceeds its socially acceptable level. This is illustrated by Figure 1.1 where a market of a commodity is considered whose production causes environmental damage.[2] Thus, the social costs exceed the private costs of production. Let p and q denote the price and quantity of the commodity under consideration, and let D be the demand curve. The private and social supply of the good are given by the private and social marginal cost curves, PMC and SMC. The social marginal cost exceeds the private marginal cost since damages that accrue to the rest of society are not taken into account by the individual supplier. There is a private equilibrium, P, and a social equilibrium, S. It is obvious that the equilibrium supply and demand are smaller when the total cost of production is taken into account by the producer. Moving from equilibrium P to S causes losses of consumer and producer surplus equalling the area of the triangle b. On the other hand, there is a welfare gain $a + b$ due to improved environmental quality. The net effect is positive, i.e. the internalization of external effects is beneficial to society as a whole. Those who gain from internalization can compensate the losers without spending the total gains.

The question arises why external effects are not internalized in free-market economies. There are two potential reasons: ill-defined property rights and the absence of perfect markets. They will be discussed briefly.

---

[1] The concept of externality was introduced by Sidgwick (1883, book 3, chs. 2 and 4) in the nineteenth century. Negative externalities are of concern not only in environmental economics but also in consumer theory (envy, demand for social status), international trade theory (optimal tariffs and strategic trade policy), public choice (rent-seeking games), industrial organization (oligopolies, patent races), and many other fields. For an overview see Cornes and Sandler (1985a).

[2] Similar illustrations can be found in many textbooks on environmental economics, e.g. in Baumol and Oates (1988), Pearce and Turner (1990), and Siebert (1995).

The classical example is of ill-defined properties is the commons (see Hardin (1968)). The commons is an open-access resource which is owned either by no one or collectively by a community. By using the commons, an agent reduces the yields that other users derive from the commons. For example, if the commons is an open-access fishery, each additional fishing-boat will reduce the catches of the other fishing-boats. If all boats belonged to the same person, these reductions would be private costs and they would be taken into account perfectly by her. However, in the case of open access these costs are borne by other persons, they are social costs that are external to the individual adding the new boat to the fishery. As a result, too many new boats will be added and the resource will be overexploited. The tragedy of the commons takes its course.

Overexploitation can be avoided if property rights are defined. Coase (1960) has shown that under certain conditions this yields an efficient allocation of resources which is independent of the initial distribution of property rights. If the pollutee is given the property right, she has to be compensated by the polluter who wants to discharge. If the polluter has the property right, she has to be compensated by the pollutee for reducing the environmentally damaging activity. In Figure 2.1, the compensation payment is TS per unit of output. If the pollutee is the owner of the property right, the polluter will have to pay in order to obtain the permission to produce q^s. If the polluter initially has the right to pollute, the compensation payment is made by the pollutee. She bribes the polluter to reduce the output from q^p to q^s by paying TS per unit of output reduction.

The practical applicability of the Coasian bargaining solution is rather limited. High transaction costs often impede the bargaining process. Moreover, free-rider problems arise in cases where many agents are involved. If, for example, there is a large number of pollutees, an individual pollutee has no

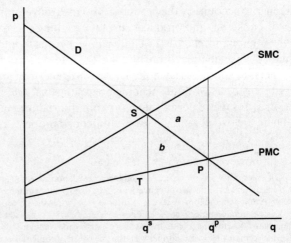

FIG. 2.1 Private and Social Costs

incentive to compensate the polluter for the cost of reducing emissions. In such a situation, the individual would provide a public good since the other pollutees also profit from improved environmental quality without paying compensation. Thus, the incentive to pay compensation is low and there is a prisoners' dilemma where the pollutees free-ride on each other. Compensation payments will be insufficient and the level of pollution will be too high. The dilemma may be solved by co-operation among interested agents, but in reality there are often high co-ordination costs that impede a co-operative solution.

If externality problems cannot be solved by the agents themselves via a Coasian bargaining process, an efficient solution may be achieved by the government. There are basically three different kinds of government intervention.

- The first one is the command-and-control approach where the government uses a rationing scheme to distribute pollution rights among interested parties. In Figure 2.1, this means that q^s is fixed and allocated to producers. There will be a scarcity rent of q^s times TS which accrues to the producers. The allocation of pollution rights is usually achieved by means of product or process standards.
- The second one is to use Pigouvian taxes or subsidies.[3] The producers either have to pay a tax of TS per unit of output, and the rent accrues to the state in terms of tax revenue. Or they receive subsidies for reducing output and emissions. In this case they appropriate the scarcity rent and the subsidy payment.

- Finally, there is the tradable-permits solution. The state defines the maximum level of emissions and sells or distributes tradable emission rights to the population. In a perfect market the price TS will be established by supply and demand. The scarcity rent is appropriated by the state if emission rights are sold by auction or by the initial owners of emission rights.

In a static and deterministic world without transaction costs, the three approaches are equivalent. In a more realistic setting, this is generally not true.[4]

In the following chapters, the concepts developed here will be incorporated into models of international trade. Private costs and social costs will be separable during most of the analysis. Private costs are merely those of buying consumption goods or hiring factors of production. There will be no private costs of pollution. This is due to the assumption that there are many polluters and each polluter's contribution to the environmental problem is practically zero. Therefore, the environmental cost that an individual polluter inflicts on herself is zero. This will, however, be different in the case of non-competitive market structure.

---

[3] The idea of using taxes to internalize external effects is due to Pigou (1920).
[4] Risk e.g. may lead to a ranking of instruments. See Weitzman (1974). Moreover, issues of dynamic efficiency, enforcement costs, and political aspects have to be taken into account. See Bohm and Russell (1985) for a broad overview.

The environmental-policy instruments to be considered are taxes (subsidies) and product standards. Since there is no uncertainty in most of the models that will be discussed, the tradable-permits scheme and the Pigouvian tax approach yield the same results.

2.2 Co-operative and Non-co-operative Environmental Policies

When optimal solutions have been derived for single countries, one can look at the interaction of environmental policies in different countries. This is usually done by using the concept of Nash equilibrium, which is due to Nash (1951)[5]. Each country determines its own optimal environmental policy for a given policy in the other country. A variation in the other country's environmental policy shifts the optimal emission level of the country under consideration. A continuum of variations in foreign policies yields the domestic reaction curve, i.e. the best response of a government to the environmental policy of the other country.[6] In the same fashion, a reaction curve can be derived for the other country. The intersection point is the Nash equilibrium. In this point, both countries have chosen their optimal responses given the other country's policy. The question arises how these reaction functions look like, whether there is a unique equilibrium and how it is affected by parameter changes.

A Nash equilibrium for the case of transfrontier pollution is depicted in Figure 2.2. The graphical representation is based on the assumptions that have been made for the construction of Figure 2.1. The demand function is declining and the marginal damage due to pollution, i.e. the difference between social and private marginal costs of production, is an increasing function of output. This marginal damage does not only depend on domestic output but also on foreign production. Consider a situation in which the foreign country raises its output (and emissions). The marginal environmental damage in the home country will be raised. The marginal social-cost curve is shifted upwards. The optimal response of the home country is to raise its environmental tax rate and to reduce emissions (and output). In the diagram depicting domestic and foreign output, q and Q respectively, the domestic reaction curve, $r(Q)$, is a declining function of foreign production. The same reasoning applies to the adjustments of foreign environmental policy to domestic output changes, and the foreign country's reaction curve, $R(q)$, has a negative slope as well. In the graphical representation, we assume that the foreign-reaction curve is steeper

---

[5] For modern approaches to Nash equilibria, see Friedman (1989: 22–66) and Fudenberg and Tirole (1991: 11–35).

[6] I follow the convention to use the term "reaction function" here although it is a bit misleading. The game considered here is a simultaneous one-shot game and in such a game there cannot be reactions in the literal sense of the word.

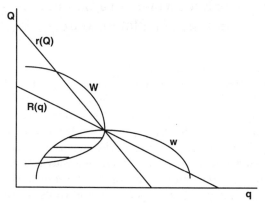

FIG. 2.2 Transfrontier pollution and the Nash Equilibrium

than the domestic-reaction curve.[7] The intersection point of the two curves is the Nash equilibrium in which each country has chosen the optimum response to the other country's policy.

The concave curves are the domestic and the foreign iso-welfare curves. Since transboundary pollution is a negative externality, each country would benefit from a reduction of the output in the other country. The shaded area represents the potential of Pareto improvements. If countries reduced their emissions, they could both attain iso-welfare curves representing a higher level of welfare. This can be achieved by international environmental negotiations during which both countries agree to reduce their outputs and emissions. Additional improvements may be achieved by means of side-payments. They are particularly useful if gains and losses of the improvements in environmental quality are unevenly distributed. For example, the downstream country may compensate the upstream country for improving water quality and both countries are better off. Unfortunately, the welfare gains cannot be represented graphically since side-payments change the locations of the systems of iso-welfare curves.

Finally, one can derive comparative-static results. For instance, consider an increase of environmental concern in the home country. This results in a shift of the domestic reaction curve to the left. It can be seen that the equilibrium changes its location such that the home country reduces its output of the pollution-intensive good whereas the foreign country raises its production. The impact on environmental quality depends on the slope of the foreign country's reaction curve and is ambiguous.

---

[7] This is the condition for stability of the Nash equilibrium. See Fudenberg and Tirole (1991: 23–6).

2.3 The Endowment of a Country with Environmental Resources

Trade theory usually explains trade flows as a result of differences in the factor endowments of countries. According of the Heckscher–Ohlin theorem, a country exports the goods that use the abundant factor intensively in their production. Applying this to the case of environmental resources, one should expect that a country which is well endowed with environmental resources exports commodities that are produced environmentally intensively. Here the question arises what is meant by 'well endowed with environmental resources'.

In standard international trade theory, there are two variables that define the endowment of a country with a particular factor: (i) its physical availability, e.g. the area of land and the number of workers and machines, and (ii) the demand for the goods that are produced by means of these factors. If there is a large demand for commodities that are produced labour-intensively in one country, then labour will be scarce there compared to a country which has the identical physical endowment but a population which rather prefers capital-intensive products. There will be price differences between these countries and there is an incentive to internationally exchange commodities.

The same considerations apply when environmental resources are concerned. First, there are physical characteristics of a country including for example the assimilation capacity of its natural environment, its population density, and the availability of international environmental media that can be used to get rid of emissions. The following examples may illustrate the importance of these variables. Scandinavian rocks and soils are substantially less alkaline than rocks and soils in other parts of Europe. Therefore, only a smaller share of the acidity of acid rain can be buffered by these soils and acid rain produces greater damage. In this respect, Scandinavian countries are less well endowed with environmental resources than other countries. On the other hand, Scandinavia is not densely populated and hence the area available to dispose of the waste is very large per capita. In this respect, these countries are well endowed. Finally, a country which has access to transfrontier environmental media like rivers and meteorological or oceanic currents can discharge its pollutants into these media such that they are deposited somewhere else. This is the 'advantage' that islands like Great Britain enjoy. Secondly, there is the demand side: if goods that are environmentally intensive in their production are preferred to other goods, environmental resources are scarce compared to other countries where preferences are the other way around. In these respects, the endowment of a country with environmental resources is governed by the same principles like those of all other factors.

In the case of environmental resources, however, two additional aspects have to be taken into account in the determination of a country's endowment. The first of them is also a demand-side variable: the preferences of a country's citizens for environmental quality. These preferences, together with the budget constraints, determine the demand for environmental quality. On the one hand, there are subjective value judgements. For example, it is often said that Scandinavians are more concerned about environmental quality than people living in Mediterranean countries. If this is true, then Scandinavian countries are, *ceteris paribus*, less well endowed with environmental resources. On the other hand, there is an income effect. If the willingness to pay for environmental quality is an increasing function of per-capita income, then environmental resources will be scarcer in rich countries than in poor countries.[8] This implies that poor countries tend to specialize in the production of environmentally intensive goods, whereas the rich countries import these goods and restrict themselves to the production of relatively 'clean' commodities.

The final and ultimately determining factor for a country's endowment with environmental resources, however, is the government. By deciding on the environmental policy, a government sets a price (implicit or explicit) for a country's environmental resources and thus fixes a scarcity measure. The resource endowment set by the government may differ from the endowment that would be inferred from the physical characteristics of the country and the preferences of its people. Although a government should act on behalf of its electorate, its policy decisions do not necessarily represent the will of the people. This has a number of reasons that range from the influence of powerful lobbies to inefficiencies in the bureaucracy of the public administration. In this context, we may distinguish the true and the *de facto* endowment of a country with environmental resources. The true endowment is determined by the three factors mentioned above: physical characteristics and preferences concerning consumption goods and preferences concerning environmental quality. The *de facto* endowment is the result of the legislational process during which physical characteristics and references are translated into practical environmental policies.[9]

Definition 2.1
The 'true' endowment of a country with environmental resources is the optimal supply of environmental resources, determined by an environmental policy which internalizes all domestic externalities.

---

[8] It is difficult empirically to determine the relationship between income and the demand for environmental quality, in particular in a cross-country comparison. Walter and Ugelow (1979) construct an index of the toughness of a country's environmental regulation and it can be seen that this index is positively correlated with national income. See also Kriström and Riera (1994) for empirical evidence suggesting a positive income elasticity of the demand for environmental quality.
[9] Chichilnisky (1994a) makes a similar distinction. She distinguishes private and public comparative advantage. Private comparative advantage is based on the private costs of resource use only whereas public comparative advantage results from the internalization of the social costs. She then constructs a resource-supply function where resource supply depends on the degree of internalization. This resource-supply function with incomplete internalization is equivalent to the concept of *de facto* endowment used in this study.

Definition 2.2
The 'de facto' *endowment of a country with environmental resources is the supply of environmental resources which is determined by the environmental policy of the government.*

Of course, if the government is benevolent and maximizes social welfare, then the true and the *de facto* endowment are identical—but this is rarely the case.

Which of the two concepts is more relevant? If the optimal division of labour among countries is the subject of the investigation, the analysis should be based on the concept of true endowment. If, however, we are interested in explaining the actual patterns of trade, a measure of the existing availability of environmental resources is needed. Since this is the case for the most of the remainder of this study, the *de facto* endowment will usually be meant, when the endowment of a country with environmental resources is mentioned.

It should be noted that the definitions as well as the choice of the *de facto* endowment as the more relevant concept involve some value judgements. Three issues have to be raised in this context:

- The first problem is that by using the concept of *de facto* endowment to define a country's endowment with environmental resources, the prevailing environmental policy is taken as given. Nevertheless, it will be taken into account in this study that the actual environmental policy is not necessarily the socially optimal one and it will be seen that this is the source of potential welfare losses in a trading economy.
- The second issue is the definition of the true endowment which takes into account the domestic external effects only. A country which has the opportunity to pollute its neighbours rather than itself is viewed as being well endowed with environmental resources according to this concept. One may argue, that the true endowment of a country with environmental resources should be defined by taking into account all external effects, including the damage imposed on other countries. However, this approach will not be taken here. Nevertheless, the problem of transfrontier pollution will be addressed in the following investigation. It will be seen that the consideration of merely domestic damage in the environmental-policy decisions can lead to substantial welfare losses and that co-operative solutions are mutually beneficial for all parties.
- The third issue is that the endowment of a country with environmental resources depends on its wealth. It has been said earlier that the endowment of a country with environmental resources depends *inter alia* on the willingness of its inhabitants to pay for environmental quality. However, willingness to pay is bounded from above by ability to pay. Here the issue of the international distribution of wealth turns up. Since people living in low-income countries cannot afford to spend much on the preservation of the environment, demand for environmental quality will be low and, as a consequence, the environmental laws of these countries will not be as

tough as those of wealthier countries. Hence, environmentally intensive industries tend to move from rich to poor countries and exports of toxic waste will go the same way. Thus, international trade tends to reduce environmental quality in poor countries and people in these countries are subject to higher health risks and mortality.[10] Nevertheless, neoclassical economists call this an optimal allocation.[11] The underlying problem is the exogeneity of wealth. It is not asked whether the distribution of wealth is fair or equitable, it is just taken as given. As in general-equilibrium theory, where the initial endowments of individuals are taken as given, voluntary exchange of commodities provides for a Pareto-optimal outcome of the market process. We follow this tradition and take initial endowments as given and do not call them into question.

2.4 Ecological Dumping[12]

One of the questions to be raised in the following chapters is in which circumstances international trade will lead to too low levels of environmental regulation. Economic theory has established the result that the polluter-pays principle induces individual producers and consumers to internalize the social cost of environmental disruption and therefore is an efficient instrument of environmental policy. Although this is now widely agreed upon, not only by economic theorists but also by voters and policy-makers, real-world environmental policies are still far from applying this principle. One of the underlying reasons is the transfrontier pollution problem that has been mentioned above. Another explanation is given by the public-choice approach. A single producer who uses pollution-intensive technologies is usually much more affected by changes in environmental regulation than a consumer of clean air and water, since the negative external effects of production are widely dispersed. Since, additionally, the interests of producers are much more homogeneous than those of the consumers, they are easier to organize. Thus, they are able to form powerful lobbies that can influence the policy-making process. Of course, powerful counter-lobbies like green parties and non-governmental organizations have been established in the recent past, but it takes time for their activities

[10] This line of arguing is based on the premises that environmental policies in low-income countries remain unchanged after trade has commenced. However, there are gains from trade and the section on the empirical evidence in the previous chapters has revealed that environmental standards tend to be tightened when these gains from trade are realized. The following chapters will show the underlying rationality analytically.

[11] In an internal memo, parts of which have been published in *The Economist* (1992), the chief economist of the World Bank, Lawrence Summers, has carried this line of arguing to extremes: 'The measurement of the costs of health-impairing pollution depends on the forgone earnings from increased morbidity and mortality. From this point of view a given amount of health-impairing pollution should be done in the country with the lowest cost, which will be the country with the lowest wages.'

[12] This chapter is based on the introductory parts of my Rauscher (1994a) article.

to produce results in terms of changes in environmental policies.[13] The third reason for a lack of application of the polluter-pays principle is the international-competitiveness argument. To an individual firm, rigid environmental standards mean high costs. If foreign firms face lower pollution-abatement requirements, then the competitiveness of the domestic firm tends to be reduced. It is argued that this is not only of concern to single firms but also for industries or the domestic economy as a whole. If this argument is given large weight in the policy-making process, environmental regulations tend to be too lax. In this context the catchword of 'ecological dumping' or 'environmental dumping' has been coined. It is used to characterize situations in which a country uses lax environmental policies to help domestic exporters sell their products at low prices in international markets. This is viewed as a practice of unfair trade and it is often argued that fair trade can be achieved by applying the same environmental standards in different countries.

The term 'ecological dumping' will be taken up in this study and will be used to describe some of the phenomena that occur in environmental-policy decisions of open economies. Before this can be done, a definition of the term is needed. Loosely speaking, ecological dumping is an activity that gives domestic firms an unfair advantage in international markets by applying too low environmental standards. It is, however, unclear what is meant by 'unfair' and by 'too low environmental standards'. One could argue that a too lax environmental regulation is laxer than the socially optimal one. According to this definition, environmental dumping would never occur if a government maximized social welfare. However, even a benevolent government may be led to use lax environmental policy to influence trade and this is what we call ecological dumping. The following pages will try to define this subject and relate it to the current discussion on classical dumping in commodity markets. First, one should note, however, that, in contrast to normal dumping, ecological dumping is an activity performed by the government and not by an individual firm. Moreover, it does not in the first place affect the price of a tradable commodity but that of a factor of production which is internationally immobile: nature's capability to provide environmental resources.

In public opinion, the term 'ecological dumping' characterizes a situation in which the environmental standards in one country are lower than those in other countries. By undercutting the environmental standards of other countries, a government reduces the production costs of domestic firms. They can

[13] Another deficiency of real-world environmental policies which can be explained by the public-choice approach is the wrong choice of the policy instruments. Usually, command-and-control approaches are chosen instead of market-orientated instruments like emission taxes. These rationing approaches to the allocation of environmental resources are advantageous to incumbent producers because entry is deterred, to the public bureaucracy since jobs are created in the public sector, and even to green interest groups, many of whom have a socialist background and a deep mistrust in markets. For these and additional arguments see Buchanan and Tullock (1975), Dewees (1983), Hahn (1989), Maloney and McCormick (1982), Hoekman and Leidy (1992), and Leidy and Hoekman (1994).

produce at lower costs than their foreign competitors and this is considered to be unfair. A desirable world of fair trade would then be characterized by complete harmonization of environmental policies: all countries should use the same environmental standards. This view of ecological dumping corresponds in a sense to the traditional definition of dumping in commodity markets. It is an activity which violates the law of one price for a traded commodity. The good is sold at a lower price in the foreign than in the domestic market (see Viner (1923) and von Haberler (1936)). In the case of ecodumping, it is not the price of the final good but that of a factor of production which differs between countries.

There are two objections against applying this concept to international differences in environmental regulations. First, if one believes in factor-price equalization, the implicit prices of environmental resources should be the same in all countries if there is trade. To detect eco-dumping activities, one would have to use the autarky prices. The second critique is more important. To a trade theorist, it does not make much sense to postulate that all countries should use the same level of environmental regulation. International differences in the endowments with environmental resources do exist, be it because of differences in physical characteristics of the countries, or to differences in the tastes of the people. The removal of the endowment differences by means of harmonization is equivalent to a partial removal of the basis of gains from trade (see Hansson (1990) for instance). Thus, ecological dumping by employing lower environmental standards than the rest of the world can be a good thing and there is no need to rack one's brains about it as a problem.

None the less, I think that ecological dumping is a problem. With another definition of the subject, this becomes obvious at once. The definition is related to the modern view of dumping in commodity markets which defines the subject of its analysis as pricing at less than marginal cost (see Davies and McGuinness (1982) and Ethier (1982)). Correspondingly, eco-dumping can be defined as pricing the activities that affect the environment at less than the marginal social cost of environmental degradation. Or more generally, ecological dumping occurs when, due to international trade, a country's government does not fully internalize domestic environmental externalities. Of course, this may be considered as a practice of unfair trade since domestic producers do not have to pay the full cost of production: they receive hidden subsidies. It is now obvious that eco-dumping is a problem which deserves investigation into its origins and into the appropriate policy measures to cope with it.

However, useful as it may be for the academic researcher, the definition is still not very helpful in real-world applications. There are many reasons for lax environmental regulation. Thus, laxity in environmental policy is not always motivated by trade issues. In order to identify trade-related motives, one may compare the sectors producing tradable and non-tradable goods. The underlying hypothesis is that trade-related measures of environmental policy are primarily targeted at the sectors of the economy that produce traded goods, i.e.

the import-competing and the export sectors, but not at the industries that do not have to compete in international markets. This implies a third definition of eco-dumping. Eco-dumping occurs whenever the (explicit or implicit) price of environmental resources is lower in the tradables than in the non-tradables sector. A prerequisite for this to be possible is that the government has the power to use sector-specific instruments of environmental policy. Anecdotal evidence tells us that this is indeed the case. There are even plant-specific differences in pollution abatement requirements, as is vividly testified by the electricity generation sectors in various countries.

Given that the public opinion view does not provide a sensible definition of eco-dumping, there remain two definitions:

Definition 2.3
Ecological dumping is an environmental legislation which does not fully internalize the domestic social cost of pollution and, thereby, gives domestic producers an advantage in international markets.

or, alternatively,

Definition 2.4
Ecological dumping is the discrimination of the non-traded goods sectors against the exporting sectors in terms of higher pollution-abatement requirements for the same pollutants.

Of course, these definitions are not mutually exclusive. The incomplete internalization of domestic social cost may be accompanied by a discrimination of certain sectors of an economy against other sectors. In the following sections, we will try to find theoretical arguments as to why ecological dumping is a strategy that a rational policy-maker is sometimes willing to follow. Since ecological dumping according to Definition 2.4 involves non-traded goods, the standard models of international trade have to be extended in this respect.

2.5 Emissions as a Factor of Production

Throughout this book, emissions will be modelled as an input into the production process. At a first glance, this seems to be counter-intuitive. We are used to thinking about pollution as a joint output of production: new substances are generated and discharged into the ambient. But these emissions only reflect the fact that the environmental resources that have entered the production process as inputs have been used up. Thus, the quantity of emissions may be taken as a measure of the consumption of environmental resources in the production process. Each unit of emissions indicates that a unit of environmental resources has been depleted in the process of production.

If this still seems implausible, an analogy may help. Labour is usually modelled as an input into the production process. However, each unit of labour allocated to production implies a loss of one unit of leisure. Thus, instead of modelling labour as an input, one may also model the destruction of leisure as a joint output of production. The same choice arises for all production factors, including environmental resources.

The properties of production processes involving environmental resources can be derived from the following considerations. In a first step, I model emissions in the usual way, i.e. as a joint output of production which can be abated by using a capital-intensive abatement technology, e.g. a filtering device. Then I show that after the elimination of some variables the production technology can be described by a function with emissions as an input. This function has the usual properties of a normal production function.[14] Let k^e and κ be the quantities of the capital goods needed for emission abatement and for the production of a final good. If we assume that these capital goods are malleable, i.e. production capital can be turned into abatement capital and vice versa, the total capital stock, k, is the sum of k^e and κ.

$$k = k^e + \kappa. \tag{2.1}$$

Let output, q, be an increasing function of production capital exhibiting non-increasing returns to scale.[15] The inverse production function is $\phi(.)$. Then the capital stock needed to produce q units of output is

$$\kappa = \phi(q). \tag{2.2}$$

with $\phi'(q) > 0$ and $\phi''(q) \geq 0$. Finally, let the emissions, e, be a joint output of production. Increasing output leads to an increase in emissions. Emissions can be avoided by using abatement capital. Let us assume that the abatement technology exhibits constant returns to scale. A 1 per cent increase in abatement capital is necessary to avoid a more than 1 per cent increase in emissions if output is increased by 1 per cent. Let emissions, e, be a function $\psi(.,.)$ of output and abatement capital:

$$e = \psi(q,k^e) \tag{2.3}$$

with the properties $\psi_q(q,k^e) > 0$, $\psi_{qq}(q,k^e) > 0$, $\psi_k(q,k^e) < 0$, $\psi_{kk}(q,k^e) > 0$, $\psi_{qk}(q,k^e) < 0, \psi(q,0) < \infty$, where the subscripts denote partial derivatives. The signs of the first derivatives are intuitive. ψ_{qq} is positive since an increase in output leads to a more-than-proportional increase in emissions if the stock of abatement capital remains unchanged. The positive sign of ψ_{kk} represents a declining productivity of capital in the abatement of emissions. The more emissions are already abated, the more difficult is it to abate an additional unit of emissions. The negative sign of the cross-derivative ψ_{qk} follows from the Euler equation (see the appendix to this chapter). Finally, one cannot generate infinite

[14] For a similar line of arguing, albeit without an explicit derivation of the production function involving emissions as a factor of production, see Gronych (1980: 16–20).
[15] It is assumed here that other factors like labour are used in constant quantities or, alternatively, that k can be interpreted as an aggregate factor consisting of capital and labour.

emissions by producing a finite quantity of output even if no abatement capital is used. One may think of a linear relationship between e and q in this case. This is a materials-balance relationship: matter can neither be destroyed nor created in a production process.[16]

Combining (2.1) to (2.3) yields

$$e = \psi(q, k - \phi(q)) \tag{2.4}$$

The partial first and second derivatives of q with respect to k and e are

$$\frac{\partial q}{\partial e} = \begin{cases} \dfrac{1}{\psi_q - \psi_k \phi'} > 0 & \text{if } \kappa > 0 \\[2mm] 0 & \text{if } \kappa = 0 \end{cases} \tag{2.5a}$$

$$\frac{\partial q}{\partial k} = \frac{-\psi_k}{\psi_q - \psi_k \phi} > 0 \tag{2.5b}$$

The marginal impact of capital on output is strictly positive, whereas that of the environmental resource may be zero.[17] For each k, there exists an e such that additional emissions do not raise output. This follows from the materials-balance assumption: with a given quantity of input, κ, it is physically impossible to generate infinite emissions. Thus, even if no capital is used for abatement purposes, emissions are finite and nothing can be gained raising them beyond this level. As a consequence, emissions will not go to infinity even if their price, the emission tax rate, is zero.

The second-order conditions for the case where strict positivity holds in (2.5a) are:

$$\frac{\partial^2 q}{\partial e^2} = \frac{\psi_k \phi'' + 2\psi_{kq}\phi' - \psi_{qq} - \psi_{kk}\phi'^2}{(\psi_q - \psi_k \phi')^3} \tag{2.6a}$$

$$\frac{\partial^2 q}{\partial k^2} = \frac{\psi_k^2(\psi_k \phi'' + 2\psi_{kq}\phi' - \psi_{qq} - \psi_{kk}\phi'^2)}{(\psi_q - \psi_k \phi')^3} - \frac{\psi_{kk}}{\psi_q - \psi_k \phi'} < 0. \tag{2.6b}$$

$$\frac{\partial^2 q}{\partial k \partial e} = \frac{\psi_k \psi_{qq} - \psi_q \psi_{kq} + \phi'(\psi_q \psi_{kk} - \psi_k \psi_{kq}) - \psi_k^2 \phi''}{(\psi_q - \psi_k \phi')^3} \tag{2.6c}$$

Equation (2.6c) can be rewritten using the results (2.A6) and (2.A7) from the appendix:

$$\frac{\partial^2 q}{\partial k \partial e} = \frac{-\psi \psi_{kq}\left(\dfrac{1}{q} + \dfrac{\phi'}{k^e}\right) - \psi_k^2 \phi''}{(\psi_q - \psi_k \phi')^3} \tag{2.6c'}$$

It is obvious that $\dfrac{\partial^2 q}{\partial k \partial e} > 0$ if ϕ'' is not too large. If ϕ'' is large, then there are

[16] See Pethig (1975: 101–2).

[17] Algebraically this can be established if the non-negativity constraint for the stock of abatement capital, $k^{e,}$ is taken into account.

strong decreasing returns to scale and the cross-derivative of q with respect to k and e may be negative.[18]

In what follows, we will assume that the technology either exhibits constant returns to scale or the impact of ϕ'' is small compared to the other effects on the right-hand side of equation (2.6c′) such that the cross-derivative still is positive. This implies that a laxer environmental regulation, i.e. a higher emission standard for the individual firm, leads to an increase in the marginal productivity of capital. This is a plausible assumption. Using the results derived above, output can be expressed as a function of capital and emissions:

$$q = f(k,e) \tag{2.7}$$

with

$$f_k > 0, \; f_e > 0, \; f_{kk} < 0, \; f_{ee} < 0, \; f_{ke} > 0, \; f_{kk}f_{ee} - f_{ke}^2 \geq 0.^{[19]} \tag{2.8}$$

Marginal productivities are positive if the materials-balance condition does not bind. In the last condition, equality holds if the production function $f(.,.)$ is constant-returns-to-scale (see the appendix to this chapter). The condition that $f_{ke} > 0$ will be of major importance for many of the results that will be derived in the remainder of the book. f_{ke} measures the impact of a change in emissions on the marginal productivity of capital, which determines the rate of interest. Thus, the magnitude of f_{ke} is decisive for the capital-relocation effects of environmental policy. The larger f_{ke}, the larger are the relocational effects. How can this be explained? For a constant-returns-to-scale production function, the elasticity of substitution is defined as

$$\zeta = \frac{f_k f_e}{f f_{ke}}. \tag{2.9}$$

See Burmeister and Dobell (1970: 11). Thus, if f_{ke} is small, the potential to substitute capital and emissions for each other are good and there is not much need for a relocation of capital after a change in environmental policy. A larger value of f_{ke} implies reduced substitutability and, therefore, increases the need to relocate capital from one sector to another or from one country to another country.

---

[18] It is known that constant returns to scale in a production function with two arguments are a sufficient condition for the cross-derivative to be positive. See equations (2.A3) and (2.A4) in the appendix. If the production function is not linearly homogeneous, then the Euler equation (2.A2) is changed. The sign of the cross-derivative becomes ambiguous if the degree of homogeneity is less than one.

[19] Consider the following example. Let emissions be $e = \psi(q,k^e) = \left(2q^{1/2} - \left(k^e\right)^{1/2}\right)^2$ and let the original inverse production function be $k = \phi(q) = 4_q$. Then the output can be expressed in terms of k and e as:

$$q = f(k,e) = \frac{k + \sqrt{(2ek - e^2)}}{8}.$$

This function is homogeneous of degree 1 and its partial derivatives have the properties described in (2.8) for economically meaningful values of k.

Finally let us assume that some Inada-type conditions hold, i.e. that the marginal productivity of a factor becomes 'sufficiently large' if the the input of this factor goes to zero and that the productivity goes to a 'sufficiently small' value if the input goes to infinity.[20] This implies that for any realistic value of the marginal productivities a non-negative input vector can be determined and the equilibria determined by conditions involving marginal productivities do exist.

Results similar to those derived here can be obtained if additional inputs, e.g. labour and intermediate products, are introduced into the production function. The approach of modelling emissions as an input into the production process will be used for the remainder of the book.

2.6 Elements of a Model of Environment and the Economy

During the first chapters of the book, a two-country two-factor model of international factor movements and trade will be analysed. The next chapter starts with a model with only one good in which international capital movements are discussed. Then a second good will be introduced and the international exchange of final goods will be addressed. Afterwards the model will be augmented by the consideration of additional commodities. This present section serves the purpose of outlining the basic features of the interaction between the environment and the economy. This will be done for the case of n commodities where n can be any finite integer. The countries under consideration are the home country and the foreign country. Let the variables of the home country be characterized by lower-case letters and the variables of the foreign country by the corresponding upper-case letters. The outline of the model starts with the home country.

There are three potential sources of environmental disruption: production, consumption, and transport.[21] Let output and consumption of the ith commodity be q^i and c^i, respectively. Exports are then $x^i = q^i - c^i$. e^i are the emissions due to production activities. Let the environmental impacts of emissions differ across sectors: different sectors discharge different types of pollutants. Define

[20] The normal Inada condition requires that the marginal productivity goes to infinity or to zero, respectively. In our model, this is possible only if the function is convex. If it is linear, f_k is bounded from above and below.

[21] It is implicitly assumed here that intranational and international transport are different matters. Compared to the environmental cost of international transport, the impact of intranational transport is assumed to be negligible. Of course, this is a crude simplification since in many cases the relationship is just the other way around, e.g. its is probably more expensive to transport commodities from St Petersburg to Vladivostok than to Helsinki or from Seattle to Miami than to Vancouver. None the less, one may argue that these are just counter-examples and that on average international trade involves higher transport costs than intranational trade, especially for smaller economies. In the framework of standard trade models this is taken into account by the implicit assumption that countries are points of zero dimension. Only recently has this view been challenged by introducing spatial aspects into trade models e.g. by Krugman (1991).

the impact factor as a^i. Emissions due to consumption are modelled in a similar fashion. The impact coefficients are b^i. Now, let us introduce transfrontier pollution spillovers. Let s be the share of pollutants that remains in the home country. $(1-s)$ is the share which is driven to the foreign country by environmental media. The same considerations apply to the foreign country albeit with upper-case variables. Finally, the environmental impact of transfrontier transport of commodities is $2\gamma^i$. For simplicity, it is assumed each country causes half of the emissions of transboundary transport, that there are no country-specific transport costs, and that the pollution due to transport emissions is shared equally among the countries. Using the assumption that the environmental impacts of the activities can be simply added up, the levels of pollution in the home and the foreign country are z and Z, respectively:

$$z = s \sum_{i=1}^{n}(a^i e^i + b^i c^i) + (1-S)\sum_{i=1}^{n}(A^i E^i + B^i C^i) + \sum_{i=1}^{n}\lambda^i \left|q^i - c^i\right|, \qquad (2.10)$$

$$Z = (1-s)\sum_{i=1}^{n}(a^i e^i + b^i c^i) + S\sum_{i=1}^{n}(A^i E^i + B^i C^i) + \sum_{i=1}^{n}\lambda^i \left|q^i - c^i\right|, \qquad (2.10')$$

where n denotes the number of commodities. Global pollution then turns out to be

$$z + Z = \sum_{i=1}^{n}\left(a^i e^i + b^i c^i + A^i E^i + B^i C^i + 2\lambda^i \left|q^i - c^i\right|\right). \qquad (2.11)$$

Equations (2.10) and (2.10′) define the impact of the economic activities on the environment. The assumption that the impacts of different types of pollution can be added up is a major simplification. In reality, there may be non-linearities and interactions between different types of pollutants. This problem will not be neglected here to keep the model tractable.[22]

What remains to be determined is the impact of the environment on the economy. Environmental disruption causes negative external effects on the users of environmental resources. Two types of effects can be distinguished. On the one hand, the quality of the environment as a public consumption good is deteriorated; for example, diminishing air quality causes disease. This is the kind of environmental disruption we usually have in mind when talking about environmental problems. On the other hand, environmental quality is used as a public input of production. As an example take the fishing industry, which suffers from water pollution, or forestry, which is negatively affected by acid rain.

The first effect can be modelled via the social-welfare function, which is the representative individual's utility function:

$$w = u(c^1, c^2, \ldots, c^n; c^{n+1}), \qquad (2.12)$$

where the $(n+1)$st consumption good is environmental quality which we define as the negative value of pollution:

[22] For models dealing with non-linear interactions between pollutants, see Beavis and Walker (1979) and Endres (1986)

$$c^{n+1} = -z. \tag{2.13}$$

The welfare function is a normal utility function with the standard properties (positive partial derivatives, strict quasi-concavity).

The second effect is introduced via the production function. Again, $(-z)$, is environmental quality.

$$q^i = g^i(-z)f^i(k^i, e^i). \tag{2.14}$$

$f^i(.\,,.)$ is a usual production function having the properties (2.8). $g(.)$ is an increasing and concave function of environmental quality: $g'(.) \geq 0$, $g''(.) \leq 0$, $g(0) > 0$. $g(.)$ is external to the individual firm.[23] If the number of firms is sufficiently large, i.e. in the case of perfect or monopolistic competition, the individual entrepreneur takes $g(.)$ as a given parameter of the production technology. She will not consider the impact of her own activities on $g(.)$.

Although this is already a simplified model of a world with international trade and pollution, it will turn out to be rather difficult to handle. In particular, the external effects on production will lead to major algebraic complications. In order to keep the model tractable, some additional simplifications will have to be made during the following analysis:

- In some sections, the external effects on production will be assumed to be negligible or equal for all sectors of the economy.
- On some occasions consumption and transport externalities will be neglected.
- In some sections, particular assumptions on shape of the utility function will be made, e.g. additive separability or homotheticity.
- Finally, in some sections it turns out to be useful to assume that all sectors have the same production functions and, therefore, differences in the environmental intensity of production can be represented by the pollution-impact coefficients.

2.7 The Dual Approach

On several occasions, it will be useful to turn from the traditional representation of technology and preferences in terms of utility and production functions to a more modern approach in which expenditure and cost or revenue functions are used. There are two major reasons for doing this. First, the algebraic representation of a multisectoral economy is simpler with the dual approach. Secondly, for the graphical treatment partial-equilibrium models, we need demand and supply functions that follow directly from expenditure and cost

[23] It should be noted that this specification implies that production becomes zero at a finite level of environmental disruption. However, it is assumed here that the level of environmental disruption causing this fatal decline in production is unrealistically large. Therefore, this case will not be considered here.

functions. Moreover, we will address the problem of environmental product quality standards. Although these can be introduced into a production function without any problems, it appears to be more intuitive to use them as arguments of the cost function: the more environmentally friendly the good, the higher the cost of production. The notation of the dual approach will be introduced here.[24]

Consider first a single firm in sector i of the economy. Its production technology can be described by means of a production function as in the previous section or by a cost function. The cost function has as its arguments the factor prices, i.e. the emission tax rate, $t^{e,i}$ and the interest rate, r^i, the product quality standard, b^i, and the quantity of the output. Moreover, the level of environmental disruption, z, may affect the cost of production. Here, this can be expressed by

$$\tilde{c}^i = \tilde{c}^i \, (t^{e,i}, r^i, b^i, q^i, z). \tag{2.15}$$

Its derivatives with respect to $t^{e,i}$, r^i, q^i, and z are positive and the derivative with respect to b^i is negative since environmentally unfriendly goods have lower production costs. Factor demands follow from Shephard's lemma:

$$e^i = \tilde{c}^i_t(t^{e,i}, r^i, b^i, q^i, z). \tag{2.16a}$$

$$k^i = \tilde{c}^i_r(t^{e,i}, r^i, b^i, q^i, z). \tag{2.16b}$$

Moreover, the cost function is homogeneous of degree one and concave in factor prices.[25] In the case of constant returns to scale it is homogeneous of degree one in output, i.e.

$$\tilde{c}^i = q^i \hat{c}^i(t^{e,i}, r^i, b^i, z), \tag{2.17}$$

where $\tilde{c}^i = q^i \hat{c}^i(t^{e,i}, r^i, b^i, z)$ is the unit cost function.

The dual approach will be used in situations where demand and supply functions are used in a partial-equilibrium framework, i.e. in Chapters 6 and 7. In Chapters 3, 4, 5, and 8, the standard approach with utility and production functions will be employed.[26]

---

[24] See Varian (1992) for the application of duality theory to microeconomic problems in general and Dixit and Norman (1980) and Woodland (1982) for its use in international trade theory.

[25] Linear homogeneity means that a doubling of input prices implies a doubling of costs. Concavity follows from the substitution possibilities. If only one factor price is doubled, then this factor is substituted by other ones such that the increase in costs is less than twofold.

[26] The general-equilibrium trade model in Ch. 5 could also be solved by means of the dual approach like in Dixit and Norman (1980) and Woodland (1982). However, I found that in most situations this did not simplify the analysis substantially.

Appendix: Properties of Linear Homogeneous Functions

Let $f(k,e)$ be a linear homogeneous function, i.e.

$$f(\beta k, \beta e) = \beta f(k,e). \tag{2.A1}$$

This function satisfies the Euler equation (subscripts denoting partial derivatives):

$$f_k(k,e)k + f_e(k,e)e = f(k,e). \tag{2.A2}$$

Differentiation with respect to k and e yields

$$f_{kk}k + f_{ke}e = 0. \tag{2.A3}$$

$$f_{ke}k + f_{ee}e = 0, \tag{2.A4}$$

where the arguments have been dropped for convenience. Combining these two equations gives:

$$f_{kk}f_{ee} - f_{ke}^2 = 0. \tag{2.A5}$$

Combining equations (2.A2), (2.A3), and (2.A4) yields.

$$f_e f_{kk} - f_k f_{ke} = -\frac{f_{ke}f}{k} \tag{2.A6}$$

$$f_k f_{ee} - f_e f_{ke} = -\frac{f_{ke}f}{e} \tag{2.A7}$$

3

Environmental Policy and International Capital Movements

3.1 Introduction

Before we turn to issues of foreign trade, the problem of international factor mobility will be addressed. One reason for dealing with this issue first is the simpler model framework. International factor mobility can be dealt with in a one-good model whereas the consideration of international trade in final goods requires at least two commodities. Thus, it is easier to derive results and to develop an intuition of what happens in models involving environmental resources and international economic relationships. It will be seen in the following chapters that similar results are obtained in models with international trade in final goods but these results will in many cases be not as unambiguous as those derived in the factor-mobility model.

The other—more important—reason to consider international factor movements here is their relevance. In the standard model framework which perfect competition and absence of scale economies, international trade and factor movements are substitutes.[1] Trade in final goods occurs when factors of production are internationally immobile. The specialization effects that are induced by foreign trade in final goods require the intersectoral relocation of the factors of production. Thus, there has to be some mobility of factors of production. In many cases, however, this assumption of intersectoral mobility and international immobility is not particularly realistic. Often it is easier to move sector-specific capital and know-how to other countries than to other industries. Thus, if we considered only trade models we would neglect an important and topical issue in international economics.

The basic problem in the context of environmental issues and international factor movements is that of environmental capital flight. The international mobility of capital is considered to be higher than that of other factors of production. This implies that capital tends to react more sensitively to cross-country differences in environmental policies. Tight environmental standards raise production costs and cause the delocation of environmentally intensive

---

[1] Situations in which trade and factor movements are complements have been considered by Markusen (1983) and Wong (1986).

production to less regulated countries. This causes a number of problems. If harmful production is located in pollution havens, its emissions tend to be under insufficient control. Besides the regulatory laxity, there are often serious enforcement deficits, particularly in developing countries. Environmentalists are concerned about the environmental consequences of such capital relocation. Moreover, it is feared that interjurisdictional competition for mobile capital leads to a mutual undercutting of environmental standards and causes a prisoners' dilemma where environmental regulation is too lax everywhere. This leads to the question as to whether international factor movements should be restricted for reasons of environmental preservation. These and other issues will be addressed in the following sections. The ultimate objective of this chapter is to derive policy implications for single countries and to identify scenarios under which rationality on the country level leads to undesirable results on the global level.

The analytical framework of this chapter is the standard model of international factor mobility developed by Jasay (1960), MacDougall (1960), and Kemp (1964, ch. 13).[2] Extensions of this model that include environmental variables have been considered by Merrifield (1988), Rauscher (1995a), and Wang (1995).[3] The second of these models will be modified here by the introduction of consumption externalities and external effects on production.

The chapter is organized as follows. Section 2 will outline the model. The third section deals with the determinants of international capital mobility. The next section then is devoted to welfare effects of international capital movements. Is free factor mobility always better than autarky? In Section 5, the effects of changes in environmental policy on foreign direct investment, consumption, and environmental quality will be discussed. It will be seen that international capital movements may reduce the efficacy of a country's environmental policy. Section 6 addresses the question of optimal environmental policies under conditions of free factor mobility. In this context, conditions for ecological dumping will be derived. In Section 7, the problem of conjectural variation will be discussed and it will be seen that the choice of the policy instrument in one country may affect the environmental policy in the other country. Section 8 is devoted to co-operative versus non-co-operative strategies. The central question is in which circumstances optimization by individual governments leads to unacceptably high levels of emissions and pollution. Section 9 will discuss the use of interventions into international factor markets for environmental reasons. Can barriers to mobility be a useful vehicle of environmental policy? In Sections 10, 11, and 12, the model will be extended into three directions. First, the assumption of benevolent government will be abolished. Then, we look at monopolistic supply of foreign capital. And finally, the

---

[2] For a survey including this and other approaches, see Ruffin (1984).

[3] In Merrifield's (1988) and Wang's (1995) models, trade and factor movements occur simultaneously. This is possible since they have two factors besides the environmental resource in their models.

question of the impact choice of the instruments of environmental policy will be addressed. A short summary of the main findings concludes the chapter.

3.2 The Model

Consider a world consisting of two countries, the home country and the foreign country. We look at the aggregated economy, i.e. there is a single commodity which is produced and consumed. There is no trade in this commodity. The same notation is used as in Chapter 2; since there is only one good, the superscripts can be dropped. $g(.)$ and $G(.)$ are functions denoting the impact of environmental quality on production. $f(...)$ and $F(...)$ are neoclassical production functions and e and E are the emissions in the home and the foreign country. Let k_0 and K_0 be the capital stocks owned by the citizens of the home and the foreign country. They are given exogenously and they are fixed.[4] Foreigners have moved a part of their capital, I, to the home country. k and K are the capital stocks that are actually employed in the home and the foreign country:

$$k = k_0 + I. \tag{3.1}$$

$$K = K_0 - I. \tag{3.1'}$$

A negative value of I means that domestic citizens own a part of the capital stock which is employed in the foreign country. I will be referred to as 'foreign direct investment' in the following text. Nevertheless, one should note that I is a stock and not a flow variable.

Since in this simple model only factors but not goods are internationally mobile, there will be no transport activities that are detrimental to the environment. Thus pollution turns out to be

$$z = s(ae + bc) + (1 - S)(AE + BC) \tag{3.2}$$

$$Z = (1 - s)(ae + bc) + S(AE + BC) \tag{3.2'}$$

Income is domestic output plus the return on capital invested abroad or minus interest payment made to the owners of foreign capital. Let r be the international rate of interest. The whole income is consumed; thus, the consumption possibilities of the two countries are:

$$c = g(-z) f(k_0 + I, e) - r I, \tag{3.3}$$

$$C = G(-Z) F(K_0 - I, E) + r I \tag{3.3'}$$

Two policy instruments will be considered: an emission tax and a barrier to international capital mobility. In accordance with most of the rest of the literature, it is assumed that the tax revenues generated by the emission tax and the

---

[4] Issues of capital accumulation will be discussed in Ch. 8.

tax on mobile capital are redistributed in a lump-sum fashion.[5] Thus, the redistribution of tax revenues not does distort the allocation of factors. The economy is assumed to be perfectly competitive. This implies that factors are paid their marginal products.

- If there is an emission tax, the optimal-allocation rule in the case of a perfectly competitive economy is:

$$g(-z)f_e(k,e) = t^e, \tag{3.4}$$

$$g(-Z) F_E(K,E) = T^e. \tag{3.4'}$$

- The barrier to international factor mobility may take the shape of a quantitative restriction or of a capital income tax. In a perfectly competitive world, these instruments are equivalent. If there is a quantitative restriction, one can always derive the tax equivalents, t^k and T^K, as the wedges between the marginal productivity of capital and the world market rate of interest, r.

$$g(-z)f_k(k,e) = r + t^k, \tag{3.5}$$

$$g(-Z) F_K(K,E) = r + T^K. \tag{3.5'}$$

If capital employed in a country is taxed, an investment will be undertaken there only if the marginal productivity of capital exceeds the international interest rate plus the tax rate.[6]

Finally, welfare is a function of consumption and environmental quality:

$$w = u(c,-z), \tag{3.6}$$

$$W = U(C,-Z). \tag{3.6'}$$

where $u(.\,,.)$ and $U(.\,,.)$ are assumed to be additively separable and to have the usual properties of utility functions, i.e.

$$u_1 > 0, u_2 > 0, u_{11} < 0, u_{22} < 0.$$

The major difference between this and other models of international factor mobility is the occurrence of external effects on production. This will cause a number of ambiguities in the results. The results for the simplified version of the model in which there are no such externalities will also be presented.

3.3 Explaining Patterns of Factor Mobility

Capital will move from the country with a low marginal productivity of capital to the country with a higher productivity. It moves from the foreign to the home

[5] If the tax turns out to be negative, i.e. if a subsidy is given, the tax revenue necessary to finance subsidies is assumed to be generated by lump-sum taxes.

[6] Such a capital income tax is equivalent to a tax on repatriated profits if the taxing country is a capital importer and to a subsidy on repatriated profits if it is an exporter.

country if the rate of return on capital in autarky is larger at home than abroad. Taking account of capital taxes, we have

$$g(-z)f_k(k_0,e) - t^k > r > g(-Z) F_K(K_0,E) - T^K. \tag{3.7}$$

The first explanation of international capital mobility is differences in technology. If this trivial explanation is excluded by the assumption of identical technologies across countries, there remain a number of other variables that affect the allocation of capital.

Let us consider the case of a small economy, i.e. its impact on the rest of the world is negligible.[7] We consider the home country and assume that emissions are given by the environmental policy of the government. This corresponds to the concept of *de facto* endowment with environmental resources that was introduced in Chapter 2. The marginal productivity of capital in a closed economy is a function of the input of the other factor of production, i.e. emissions, and of environmental quality, which itself is a function of the environmental-impact parameters, emissions and consumption:

$$d(gf_k) = gf_{ke} \, de - g'f_k \, dz. \tag{3.8}$$

An increase in emissions raises the productivity of capital and an increase in pollution reduces it. dz can be determined via equation (3.2) and the budget constraint $c = g(-z)f(k_0,e)$. Total differentiation of these equations yields

$$\begin{pmatrix} 1 & -sb \\ g'f & 1 \end{pmatrix} \begin{pmatrix} dz \\ dc \end{pmatrix} = \begin{pmatrix} sa \, de \\ gf_e \, de \end{pmatrix} + \begin{pmatrix} se \, da + sc \, db + (ae + bc)ds - (AE + BC)dS \\ 0 \end{pmatrix}. \tag{3.9}$$

Applying Cramer's rule yields the following results:

$$\frac{dz}{de} = \frac{sa + sbgf_e}{1 + sbg'f} > 0. \tag{3.10a}$$

$$\frac{dz}{da} = \frac{se}{1 + sbg'f} > 0. \tag{3.10b}$$

$$\frac{dz}{db} = \frac{sc}{1 + sbg'f} > 0. \tag{3.10c}$$

$$\frac{dz}{ds} = \frac{ae + bc}{1 + sbg'f} > 0. \tag{3.10d}$$

$$\frac{dz}{dS} = -\frac{AE + BC}{1 + sbg'f} < 0. \tag{3.10e}$$

The effects have the expected signs. Together with equation (3.8), they imply the following proposition:

Proposition 3.1: Let the level of emissions be fixed by environmental policies. A country is capital-poor, i.e. it attracts foreign direct investments, if its

---

[7] If the economy were large, then a change in its environmental policy would have an impact on the state of the environment in the other country. This would affect the allocation of factors there and, due to the transfrontier pollution spillover, there could be a feedback on the economy under consideration.

environmental-impact coefficients are small and if the pollution spillover from the other country is not too large. The impact of emissions is ambiguous.

The interpretation of this theorem is straightforward. If the environmental-impact coefficients are large, then—everything else being equal—the level of environmental disruption is relatively high and, therefore, the productivity of capital is low. Since the environmental-impact parameters reflect the capability of the country's natural resources to assimilate or withstand environmental disruption, they contribute to the country's endowment with environmental resources. This endowment is relatively large if the parameters are small. The impact of the environmental regulation of production is ambiguous since, on one hand, emissions directly increase the productivity of capital but, on the other hand, tend to reduce the productivity indirectly via the external effect. Thus, a country may be viewed as well endowed with environmental resources if the environmental regulation is lax and the direct effect dominates the external effect or if the environmental regulation is relatively restrictive and the external effect is stronger than the direct effect.

For the simplified version of the model in which $g' = 0$, we obtain unambiguous results. A country is capital-poor, i.e. it attracts foreign direct investments if its emissions are high. The other parameters have no impact. This is a very intuitive result. If environmental quality does not affect the factor productivities, it also has no impact on the allocation of capital.

Matters are bit more complicated if the environmental-policy instrument is an emission tax. An additional equation, (3.4), has to be taken into account. None the less the effects and their interpretations are the same:

Proposition 3.2: Let the environmental-policy instrument be a tax. A small country is capital-poor, i.e. it attracts foreign direct investments, if the environmental-impact coefficients are small or if the pollution spillover from the other country is not too large. The impact of the emission tax rate is ambiguous.

For a proof see the appendix to this chapter. The following intuition can be given for this result:

- An increase in the environmental-impact parameters of course reinforces the problem of environmental degradation. Additionally, it leads to a reduction of emissions. This secondary effect is due to the production externality. Since environmental degradation is increased, the marginal productivity of emissions is diminished and, with a given emission tax rate, the producers will reduce the input of environmental resources. This enhances the decline of capital productivity caused by the deterioration of environmental quality.
- An increase in the emission tax rate reduces emissions and raises environmental quality. The first effect is negative for the remuneration of capital, the second effect is positive. This is depicted in Figure 3.1. For the graphical representation, it is assumed that $b = 0$, i.e. that consumption externalities are negligible. Moreover, assume for a moment that $f(\ldots)$

exhibits constant returns to scale. Then the interest rate, r, is a declining convex function of the emission tax rate, t, for a given level of environmental quality. This is the factor-price frontier, denoted by FPF and depicted in the left-hand part of the figure. The right-hand side depicts the marginal productivity of emissions (which equals the emission tax rate under perfect competition) as a declining function of emissions. A shift in the tax rate from t' to t'' leads to a reduction of emissions from e' to e''. This implies that environmental quality is improved and the factor-price frontier is shifted upwards since total factor productivity is enhanced. The direction of change of the interest rate is ambiguous. In the example considered in this figure, the remuneration of capital is reduced. The direct effect of reducing emissions (corresponding to the movement along the factor-price frontier) dominates the external effect (represented by the shift of the factor-price frontier itself).

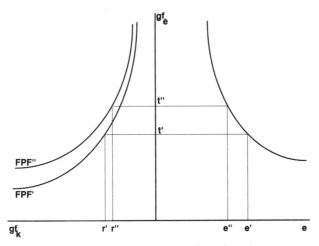

FIG. 3.1 Changes in Emissions and the Remuneration of Capital

For the simplified model, in which $g' = 0$, a number of effects vanish and the result turns out to be that a country is capital-poor, i.e. it attracts foreign direct investments if the emission tax rate is low. The impact of the other parameters is zero. In Figure 3.1, there would be no shift in the factor-price frontier and r would be reduced unambiguously.

Up to here, we have dealt with the *de facto* endowment of a country with factors of production. The endowment with capital and environmental resources depends on the government's policy, which is not necessarily in accordance with the preferences of the people. If these preferences were properly considered, the environmental policy would reflect the 'true' endowment of the country with factors of production. Thus, if the 'true' endowment is sought, the optimal environmental policy has to be determined.

The first-order condition for an optimal environmental policy is:[8]

$$\frac{dw}{de} = u_1 \frac{dc}{de} - u_2 \frac{dz}{de} = 0,$$

where u_i is the partial derivative of $u(.\,,.)$ with respect to its ith argument and the partial derivatives of consumption and pollution follow from equation (3.9). Using these results, one obtains

$$u_1 (gf_e - sag'f) - u_2(sa + sbgf_e) = 0. \tag{3.11}$$

Rearranging terms yields the optimal emission tax, t^{e*}, which, under perfect competition, turns out to be

$$t^{e*} = gf_e = \frac{sag' fu_1 + sau_2}{u_1 - sbu_2}. \tag{3.12}$$

The following effects that have to be taken account of by the optimal emission tax. Emissions raise output and, therefore, consumption possibilities. This increase in consumption possibilities causes environmental disruption. None the less, the net welfare effect of the increase in consumption possibilities, represented by the denominator on the right-hand side of equation (3.12), must be positive.[9] There are two negative external effects of an increase in emissions, which are to be found in the numerator. First, there is the external effect on production and, secondly, there is the direct effect of increased emissions on environmental quality as a consumption good. As one expects, the optimal tax rate is an increasing function of the pollution-impact parameters, a and b, the share of pollutants that remain in the country, s, and of the production externality, g'.

To derive the impact of the parameters on the direction of the foreign direct investment, we will proceed in two steps. In the first step, the impact of the parameters on the optimal emission level is determined. Then, we will look at the impact of this change in emissions on the incentive to invest abroad, i.e. on the remuneration of capital. Comparative-static results will be derived for two parameters. The first one is the evaluation of environmental quality, which can be measured by the marginal utility, u_2. The underlying idea is that we compare two countries that attach different weights to environmental quality. The environmentally more concerned country will—everything else being equal—be characterized by a larger value of u_2. The second parameter used for the comparative-static analysis is a. The effects of changes in the other impact parameters can be obtained by analogy.

Total differentiation of equation (3.11) yields:

[8] The second-order condition is satisfied due to the properties of the welfare and production functions.

[9] Algebraically, this condition is satisfied if the marginal utility of consumption, u_1, goes to infinity if consumption goes to zero.

$$w_{ee} \, de = \frac{sa + sbgf_e}{1 + sbg'f} \, du_2 + \frac{1}{1 + sbg'f} \left[su_1 g'f + su_2 - (gf_e - sag'f)u_{11} \frac{dc}{da} \right. \quad (3.13)$$

$$\left. - [u_1(sag''f - g'f_e) + sbg'f_e u_2 + (sa + sbgf_e)u_{22}] \frac{dz}{da} \right] da.$$

Note that w_{ee} is negative since it has been assumed that the second-order condition of optimality is satisfied. dc/da and dz/da can be derived from equation (3.9). dc/da is negative, dz/da is positive. Since $(gf_e - sag'f)$ and $(u_1 - sbu_2)$ are positive, it follows that a has a negative impact on emissions. The higher the environmental-impact parameter the stricter is the environmental policy. Similar results can be obtained for the other parameters that measure the impact of emissions on environmental quality. The other parameter also produces the expected result. An increase in the evaluation of environmental quality, modelled by an increase in marginal utility, u_2, leads to reduction of emissions since there are incentives to implement a more restrictive environmental policy.

Unfortunately, the impact of a change in emissions on the marginal productivity of capital is ambiguous. See equation (3.8). It depends on the cross-derivative of the production function, f_{ke}, and on the external effect of pollution on production. This implies that the impact of environmental concern (measured by the marginal utility of environmental quality) on the marginal productivity of capital is also ambiguous.

Proposition 3.3: Let the environmental policy be welfare-maximizing. In the case of a small effect of environmental quality on production, a country will attract capital if its environmental-impact parameters are low and its population is not much concerned about environmental quality. If the external effect on production is substantial, it will be a capital importer if the environmental-impact parameters are large or if the population is relatively concerned about environmental quality.

Thus, the impacts of the parameters of the model on the 'true' endowment of a country with environmental resources are indeterminate for the general version of the model. For the simplified version of the model without the effect of environmental quality on production, one obtains the following result: If $g' = 0$, a country attracts foreign direct investment if its citizens care less about environmental quality and/or if the environmental-impact coefficients are small. In both cases, a benevolent government will implement a relatively lax environmental policy and this raises the marginal productivity of capital.

3.4 Access to the World Capital Market: The Small Country

Environmentalists often argue that trade and international capital mobility cause welfare losses due to their impact on the allocation of factors of production. These welfare effects are the subject of the following investigation. In a first step, we consider a single small country, unable to influence the rate of return in the international capital market. Let us look at a marginal opening of the country, e.g. caused by a marginal reduction of a quantitative restriction on foreign direct investments. If the level of emissions remains constant, matters are relatively simple. Environmental quality, consumption, and foreign direct investment are an implicit function of the foreign direct investment and this function is determined by equations (3.2) and (3.3). Total differentiation yields

$$\begin{pmatrix} 1 & -sb \\ g'f & 1 \end{pmatrix} \begin{pmatrix} dz \\ dc \end{pmatrix} = \begin{pmatrix} 0 \\ (gf_k - r)\, dI \end{pmatrix}. \tag{3.14}$$

Since the home country is capital-poor, a restriction on international factor mobility implies that $gf_k - r > 0$. The comparative-static results turn out to be

$$\frac{dz}{dI} = \frac{sb(gf_k - r)}{1 + sbg'f} > 0. \tag{3.15a}$$

$$\frac{dc}{dI} = \frac{gf_k - r}{1 + sbg'f} > 0. \tag{3.15b}$$

Increased openness raises foreign direct investment, consumption, and environmental degradation. The increase in pollution is a result of increased consumption.[10] The welfare effect of a change in international capital mobility is

$$\frac{dw}{dI} = (gf_k - r)\frac{u_1 - sbu_2}{1 + sbg'f}. \tag{3.16}$$

The sign of this expression is indeterminate.[11] It depends on the pollution coefficients and on the relative appreciation of consumption and environmental quality. If the environmental policy chosen by the government is an optimal one, then dw/dI is unambiguously positive. This follows from inserting equation (3.12) into (3.16). The economic intuition behind this result is the following one. An optimal environmental policy equalizes the marginal benefits and marginal costs of the use of environmental resources. The marginal benefit in this model is an increase in consumption, the marginal cost consists of two components, pollution by production and pollution by consumption. Since emissions from production are constant by assumption (e is fixed), only consumption is affected by increased openness and the net welfare effect of the marginal increase in consumption must be positive.

Proposition 3.4: In the case of given emissions, increased factor mobility raises consumption and pollution. The welfare effect is ambiguous. If the environmental policy is close to the optimal one, the welfare effect is positive.

This proposition has been derived for the case of the capital-poor home country, but the same result can be established for the capital-rich foreign country.

---

[10] The impact of increased openness on emissions is sb times the impact on consumption.

[11] If t^k is zero, i.e. if $f_k = r$, the welfare change is also zero. This implies that a zero tax rate on the mobile factor is optimal. We will turn to this later.

Proposition 3.4 can be represented graphically as follows. Since emissions are fixed, pollution depends only on the level of consumption and, therefore, environmental quality is a linear declining function of consumption. This is depicted in the left-hand part of Figure 3.2. Additionally, there is a system of indifference curves measuring the trade-off between consumption and environmental quality. Moreover, one can conclude from equation (3.15b) that consumption is a hill-shaped function of I.[12] This is the right-hand part of Figure 3.2. Initially, there is a barrier to factor mobility and the domestic marginal productivity of capital is higher than the world-market interest rate, i.e. the slope of the hill-shaped curve in the right-hand part of the diagram is positive. The foreign direct investment is I' and the corresponding levels of consumption and environmental quality can be derived in the left-hand part of the figure. If the impediment to capital mobility is removed, the direct investment rises to I''. Consumption is increased and environmental quality is reduced. The welfare effect is represented by the shift from the initial indifference curve, u', to the new indifference curve, u''. In this example, there is a welfare loss, meaning that the initial environmental policy was not optimal. An optimal environmental policy would have been characterized by a lower hill-shaped curve in the right-hand side of the diagram.

Matters are more complicated if the environmental policy instrument is an emission tax. Then, equation (3.4) has to be taken into account in addition to equations (3.2), (3.3), and (3.5). The following conclusion can be drawn.

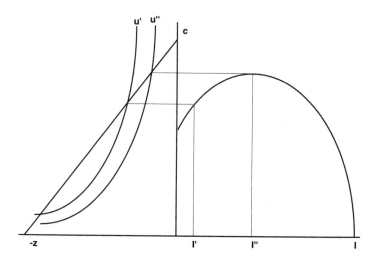

FIG. 3.2 Welfare Effects of International Capital Mobility

---

[12] For I being small, productivity gains exceed the rate of interest. If I is large, the productivity gains are relatively small compared to the interest rate that has to be paid, and consumption is a declining function of I.

Proposition 3.5: Let the environmental-policy instrument be an emission tax. Increased openness will lead to an increase in pollution if the country is capital-poor and to a reduction in emissions if the country is capital-rich. The impacts on the other variables and the welfare effects are ambiguous. If the environmental policy is optimal, the welfare effects are always positive.

The proof is in the appendix to this chapter. Due to the complexity of the model, an intuitive explanation is hard to give. In the simplified model in which environmental quality does not affect output, the ambiguities vanish. So let $g' = 0$. In a capital-poor country, increased openness leads to an increase in emissions, pollution, and consumption. In a capital-rich country, emissions are reduced but the impact of increased openness on environmental quality and consumption is ambiguous. The welfare effects are ambiguous unless the optimal environmental policy has been chosen. In this case, openness raises social welfare.

This result can be interpreted rather easily. Increased capital mobility induces foreign direct investments of capital-rich in capital-poor countries. Additional capital is employed in the capital-poor economy and this raises the marginal productivity of the environmental factor of production. At a given emission tax rate, more of this factor will be employed. Emissions are increased. Correspondingly emissions are reduced in the capital-rich economy. This is one of the results of international factor movements that environmentalists worry about: the capital-rich country pollutes the capital-poor country via foreign direct investments.[13] However, in spite of the increased emissions, the capital-poor country may still experience welfare gains. This is due to the increase in consumption possibilities which is the result of an improved allocation of capital and of increased emissions. In the capital-rich country, consumption may be reduced since the reduction in output due to lower emission levels may offset the gain from the better allocation of capital. The effects of increased openness on environmental quality can be obtained by adding up the impacts of the changes in emissions and in consumption. The welfare effect is indeterminate since consumption and environmental quality may be changed into opposite directions. Negative welfare effects of increased openness are possible if the environmental policy is chosen in a suboptimal fashion, i.e. if emission tax rates are lower or higher than the Pigouvian tax rates. If, however, the environmental policy is optimal, the negative effect and some of the positive effects cancel out. The remainder is the efficiency gain that is due to the improved allocation of capital.

Unfortunately, the optimistic view of the welfare effects of international economic integration is limited to the case of a small country. In the large-country case, negative pollution spillovers may be induced which offset the efficiency gains due to the relocation of capital. Moreover, there can be negative

---

[13] The same effect is possible in models of international trade, where capital is mobile across sectors rather than across national borders and Siebert (1995: 176) has coined the phrase 'pollute thy neighbour via trade' for this phenomenon. This issue will be discussed in ch. 5.

effects arising from the change of the world market interest rate. These effects have been discussed in more detail by Rauscher (1991*b*) for a simplified version of the model.

Finally, I shall address the question of how a country opening its borders to international capital movements should adjust its environmental policy. The optimality condition has to be differentiated totally with respect to *e* and *I*. This yields

$$(1 + sbg'f)w_{ee}\, de = \left[(sag'f_k - gf_{ke})u_1 + sbgf_{ke}u_2 - (gf_e - sag'f)u_{11}\frac{dc}{dI} \right. \quad (3.17)$$

$$\left. + (g'f_e - sag''f) - sbg'f_e u_2 - (sa + (sa + sbgf_e)u_{22}\frac{dz}{dI} \right] dI,$$

where dc/dI and dz/dI are given by equations (3.15*a*) and (3.15*b*). The impact of openness on the optimal level of emissions is ambiguous and the various effects are difficult to interpret. Let us therefore assume that external effect on production is negligible, i.e. $g' = g'' = 0$. Then we have

$$w_{ee}\, de = (-gf_{ke}(u_1 - sbu_2) - gf_e u_{11} t^k - s^2 b(a + bgf_e)\, u_{22} t^k)\, dI$$

for the home country and, correspondingly,

$$W_{EE}\, dE = (GF_{KE}(U_1 - SBU_2) - GF_E U_{11} T^K - S^2 B(A + BGF_E)U_{22} T^K)\, dI$$

for the capital-rich foreign country. It follows that:

Proposition 3.6: Let $g' = G' = 0$. A capital-rich country should reduce its socially optimal emissions as a response to increased openness. The impact on the optimal policy in the capital-poor economy is ambiguous.

There are three effects determining this result. First, there are efficiency gains leading to increased consumption. The marginal utility of consumption is reduced, which means that the evaluation of consumption goods declines. Secondly, an increase in consumption causes increased pollution and the marginal damage due to environmental disruption rises. These two effects are in favour of an emission reduction. The third effect has a country-specific sign. The marginal productivity of emissions is increased in the capital-poor and reduced in the capital-rich country. This effect demands higher emissions in the capital-poor country and lower emissions in the capital-rich country. Thus loosely speaking, openness is good for the environment in capital-rich countries and may be bad in capital-poor countries.

As a caveat, one should note that these effects of increased openness on environmental policies are at least partly an artefact of the specification of the welfare function. The additive separability implies that the goods under consideration are normal goods, i.e. the income effect is positive. Obviously, this also concerns the demand for environmental quality. Therefore, an income gain, e.g. due to an improvement in the factor allocation, makes the benevolent policy-maker implement stricter environmental standards.

3.5 Effects of Changes in Environmental Policy

In the preceding sections, the questions have been addressed as to how international factor movements can be explained by cross-country differences in environmental regulation and of what the welfare effects of a move from autarky towards international factor movements are. For the remainder of this chapter it is assumed that there are foreign direct investments and that the flow of capital can be affected by governments, e.g. via their environmental policies. As a first step, we will look at a small country which takes the international rate of interest as given. In a simplified version of the model analysed here, Rauscher (1995a) shows that a country attracts internationally mobile capital by increasing its emissions, i.e. by relaxing environmental regulation. This is intuitive in a world where there are no consumption externalities and where production is not affected by environmental quality. The question arises whether this is also true for the more general model under consideration here.

In a world without impediments to international factor mobility, the small open economy is represented by equations (3.2), (3.3), and (3.5). The impact of foreign polluters on domestic environmental quality can be neglected due to the small-country assumption. Total differentiation of these equations yields equation (3.18) which is almost the same as (3.14). Here we assume that there is free factor mobility ($t^k = 0$), and the comparative statics are determined with respect to changes in emissions, e, that were constant in equation (3.14).

$$\begin{pmatrix} 1 & -sb & 0 \\ g'f & 1 & 0 \\ -g'f_k & 0 & gf_{kk} \end{pmatrix} \begin{pmatrix} dz \\ dc \\ dI \end{pmatrix} = \begin{pmatrix} sa \\ gf_e \\ -gf_{ke} \end{pmatrix} de. \tag{3.18}$$

The comparative static results are

$$\frac{dz}{de} = \frac{sa + sbgf_e}{1 + sbg'f} > 0. \tag{3.19a}$$

$$\frac{dc}{de} = \frac{gf_e - sag'f}{1 + sbg'f}. \tag{3.19b}$$

$$\frac{dI}{de} = \frac{-gf_{ke}}{gf_{kk}} + \frac{g'f_k(sa + sbgf_e)}{gf_{kk}(1 + sbg'f)} \tag{3.19c}$$

The effects on z and c are the same as in the closed economy (see equations (3.10a) and (3.10b)). The effect on the foreign direct investment is ambiguous. This equation can be rewritten:

$$\frac{dI}{de} = \frac{1}{1 + sbg'f} \frac{f_k}{ef_{kk}} \left[\left(\frac{sag'e}{g} - \frac{f_{ke}e}{f_k} \right) + sbg'f\frac{f_{ke}e}{f_k}(1 - \zeta) \right], \tag{3.19c'}$$

where ζ is the elasticity of substitution between capital and the environmental resource (see equation (2.9) in the previous chapter). dI/de consists of two components. The first one is the productivity effect of increased emissions, which itself contains two elasticities: the elasticity of the efficiency parameter, g, with respect to e and the elasticity of the capital productivity, f_k, with respect to e. If the former is smaller than the latter, then emissions enhance capital productivity and capital tends to be attracted. But there is also a second effect. It turns up only if consumption externalities matter ($b > 0$). For a large elasticity of substitution, this effect is positive, i.e. foreign capital tends to be attracted. Thus, one may conclude

Proposition 3.7: By relaxing its environmental policy, a country attracts internationally mobile capital if the negative external effect of increased pollution on production is small and if the elasticity of substitution between capital and emissions is large. Otherwise, it may repel foreign direct investments. It drives capital out of the country if this effect dominates the direct effect of emissions on capital productivity.[14]

This result, albeit not particularly surprising or counter-intuitive, is quite remarkable. In contrast to commonplace thinking, it states that capital does not always move to pollution havens. In certain circumstances foreign investors may be allured by green environmental policies instead of lax pollution-abatement requirements. In reality, this may in particular apply to human-capital-intensive sectors where highly qualified employees are not willing to move to environmentally hot spots.[15]

Matters are a bit more complicated if the country under consideration is large. National environmental policies influence the world market rate of return on internationally mobile capital. r is no longer given exogenously but equals the foreign country's marginal-capital productivity on which the domestic environmental regulation has an impact. Two cases may be distinguished. In the first scenario, the emissions of the other country are given. It the second scenario, they are variable and we assume that there is a constant emission tax rate.

In the case of constant foreign emissions, five equations have to be considered:

$$z = s(ae + bc) + (1 - S)(AE + BC), \tag{3.2}$$

$$Z = (1 - s)(ae + bc) + S(AE + BC). \tag{3.2'}$$

$$c = g(-z)f(k_0 + I,e) - g(-z)f_k(k_0 + I,e)I + t^k I, \tag{3.20}$$

$$C = G(-Z)F(K_0 - I,E) + G(-Z)F_K(K_0 - I,E)I - T^K I. \tag{3.20'}$$

$$g(-z)f_k(k_0 + I,e) - t^k = G(-Z)F_K(K_0 - I,E) - T^K. \tag{3.21}$$

Equations (3.20), (3.20'), and (3.21) follow from (3.3), (3.3'), (3.5), and (3.5'). Total differentiation yields

---

[14] This result also holds for the capital-rich foreign country, although the changes in I are in the opposite direction. If I is reduced, this means that internationally mobile capital moves back to the foreign country.

[15] This does not mean that less qualified people have different preferences, but often they have not as much choice.

$$\begin{vmatrix} 1 & 0 & -sb & (S-1)B & 0 \\ 0 & 1 & (s-1)b & -SB & 0 \\ g'f-g'f_kI & 0 & 1 & 0 & gf_{kk}I-t^k \\ 0 & G'F+G'F_KI & 0 & 1 & GF_{KK}I+T^K \\ -g'f_k & G'F_K & 0 & 0 & gf_{kk}+GF_{KK} \end{vmatrix} \begin{pmatrix} dz \\ dZ \\ dc \\ dC \\ dI \end{pmatrix} = \begin{pmatrix} sade \\ (1-s)a\,de \\ (gf_e-gf_{ke}I)\,de \\ 0 \\ -gf_{ke}\,de \end{pmatrix}.$$

Since the comparative-static results turn out to be rather complex, we will address only the case of unrestricted factor mobility ($t^k = T^K = 0$.[16] Moreover, two simplified versions of the model will be considered. In scenario 1, there is no pollution due to consumption, i.e. $b = B = 0$. In scenario 2, output is independent of environmental quality, i.e. $g' = G' = 0$.

Scenario 1 ($b = B = 0$)

Using Cramer's rule, the following comparative-static results can be established:

$$\frac{dz}{de} = sa > 0, \tag{3.23a}$$

$$\frac{dZ}{de} = (1-s)\,a > 0, \tag{3.23b}$$

$$\frac{dI}{de} = \frac{-gf_{ke} + sag'f_k - (1-s)aG'F_K}{gf_{kk} + GF_{KK}}. \tag{3.23c}$$

$$\frac{dc}{de} = gf_e - gf_{ke}I - sa(g'f - g'f_kI) - gf_{kk}I\frac{dI}{de} \tag{3.23d}$$

$$= gf_e - sag'f - \frac{I[gf_{ke}GF_{KK} - sag'f_k - (1-s)aG'F_Kgf_{kk}]}{gf_{kk} + GF_{KK}},$$

$$\frac{dC}{de} = -(1-s)a(G'F + G'F_K) - GF_{KK}I\frac{dI}{de} \tag{3.23e}$$

$$= -(1-s)aG'F + \frac{I[gf_{ke}GF_{KK} - sag'f_kGF_{KK} - (1-s)aG'F_Kgf_{kk}]}{gf_{kk} + GF_{KK}}.$$

There is the following intuition for these results:

- It is obvious that environmental pollution in both countries is an increasing function of domestic emissions (equations (3.23a, b).
- There are three effects determining foreign direct investments (equation (3.23c)). (i), the direct effect of emissions on the marginal productivity is positive and, if this effect is the dominant one, the country attracts foreign capital. But the environmental disruption caused by these emissions has detrimental effects on (ii) the domestic and (iii) the foreign capital productivity. If effect (ii) dominates, then the foreign direct investment tends to be reduced.
- Domestic consumption is affected by a change of environmental policy in various ways. Consider the first line of equation (3.23d). The productivity

[16] The reason why these tax rates have been introduced here is that they will be used later on, in Sect. 3.9.

effect of increased emission raises consumption possibilities. But it also has a detrimental effect on consumption since it raises the remuneration of capital and, therefore, the share of domestic output going to foreign capital owners. Environmental disruption also has two effects. On the one hand, consumption possibilities tend to be reduced due to the external effect. On the other hand, income is raised since the marginal productivity of capital is reduced, and this means that the payments going to foreign capital owners are reduced. Finally, there is the impact of the change in foreign direct investment on the rate of return, which itself consists of three components. Inserting for dI/de and rearranging terms yields the second row of this equation, and it is seen that the direct effects of the change in emissions and in environmental quality dominate the indirect effects that are due to the induced change in foreign direct investment. Thus there remain five effects on domestic consumption: (i) the positive direct productivity effect gf_e, (ii) the negative externality $sag'f$, (iii) a negative effect of an increase in emissions via the rate of return, and the positive effects of (iv) domestic and (v) foreign environmental quality via the rate of return. The signs of the last three effects are changed if the country is capital-rich rather than capital-poor.

- Similar arguments can be used to derive the effects on foreign consumption. It is seen that the rate-of-return effects in equations (3.23d) and (3.23e) are of the same magnitude but of opposite signs. This means that the rate-of-return effect is purely redistributive.

Scenario 2 ($g' = G' = 0$)
The comparative-static results are

$$\frac{dI}{de} = \frac{-gf_{ke}}{gf_{kk} + GF_{KK}} > 0, \tag{3.24a}$$

$$\frac{dc}{de} = gf_e - \frac{gf_{ke}GF_{KK}I}{gf_{kk} + GF_{KK}}, \tag{3.24b}$$

$$\frac{dC}{de} = \frac{gf_{ke}GF_{KK}I}{gf_{kk} + GF_{KK}} > 0, \tag{3.24c}$$

$$\frac{dz}{de} = sa + sbgf_e + \frac{gf_{ke}GF_{KK}I[(1-S)B - sb]}{gf_{kk} + GF_{KK}} \tag{3.24d}$$

$$= sa + sb\frac{dc}{de} + (1-S)B\frac{dC}{de},$$

$$\frac{dZ}{de} = (1-s)a + (1-s)bgf_e + \frac{gf_{ke}GF_{KK}I[SB - (1-s)b]}{gf_{kk} + GF_{KK}} \tag{3.24e}$$

$$= (1-s)a + (1-s)b\frac{dc}{de} + SB\frac{dC}{de}$$

The foreign direct investment is an increasing function of emissions because of the increase in capital productivity. The foreign consumption is increasing. This is due to the fact that the international rate of return on mobile capital is raised by relaxed environmental standards.[17] Therefore, the remuneration of the capital invested in the home country is increased, and this raises foreign income. The home country suffers from this rise in the remuneration of foreign capital but it benefits from increased production. The overall effect is ambiguous.[18] The effects of increased emissions on environmental quality are also ambiguous. They are composed of the direct effects of increased emissions that are negative, and of the indirect effects via the changes in domestic and foreign consumption. The increase in foreign consumption will add to the negative effect of increased emissions whereas the direction of change of domestic consumption is ambiguous.

The rate-of-return effect of a change in emissions can be represented graphically as follows. The horizontal axis in Figure 3.3 measures the world capital stock where the domestic endowment is OA and the foreign endowment is O^*A. The vertical axis measures the marginal productivity of capital in the home country, gf_k, and in the foreign country, GF_K. The marginal productivities are declining functions of the capital stocks. The point of intersection determines the perfect-mobility equilibrium. The foreign country moves a part of its capital stock, AE, to the home country and receives interest payments at the rate r. Now the home country increases its emissions. The

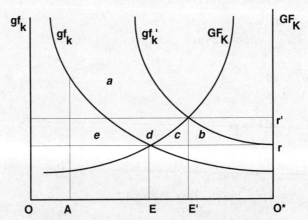

FIG. 3.3 The Rate of Return Effect of Environmental Policy

[17] As in the other scenario, this effect has two components. The direct impact of emissions raises the rate of return on mobile capital. But there is also an indirect effect since the change in environmental policy induces a change in foreign direct investment. The additional investment yields a reduction in marginal capital productivity. Nevertheless, one can show that the direct effect always dominates the indirect effect.

[18] Again, the rate-of-return effects are of the same magnitude but show opposite signs for the two countries. Thus, changes in environmental regulation lead to an international redistribution of income.

marginal-productivity curve of the home country is shifted upwards and the foreign direct investment is increased by EE'. If the interest rate did not change, the domestic income increase would be $a + b + c + d$. This corresponds to the first term on the right-hand side of equation (3.24b). If the country is large, the interest rate is changed and this leads to an income reduction, $- b - c - d - e$. This is the rate-of-return effect, which is captured by the second term on the right-hand side of equation (3.24b). The net income effect is $a - e$, and it may be negative for some particular parameter constellations. The foreign country profits from the increase in the rate of return on the mobile factor. Its income is increased by $d + e$ (see equation (3.24c)). In the graphical representation, the rate-of-return effects for the two countries are of different magnitudes. If, however, the change in emissions goes to zero, then the areas b and c become infinitesimally small compared to the other areas. This implies that the rate-of-return effects on the home and the foreign country cancel out at the margin (as equations (3.24b) and (3.24c) suggest).

All these results have been derived for the capital-poor home country. The corresponding results for a capital-rich country can be obtained by simply reversing the sign of the foreign direct investment, I. The rate-of-return effects change their signs and everything else remains the same. The results derived up to here can be summarized as follows

Proposition 3.8: Let there be no consumption externalities. Then an increase in domestic emissions leads to increased pollution in both countries. The impact on foreign direct investment depends on the size of the direct increase in capital productivity and the negative externality on production. The impact on consumption depends on the direction of change of the foreign direct investment. Let there be no external effect on production. Then an increase in emissions attracts foreign direct investment. Consumption is affected by the induced change in the rate of return. The impact on the environment is ambiguous since the (indeterminate) consumption externalities add to the direct effect of increased emissions.

In the preceding analysis it has been assumed that emissions in the foreign country are fixed by government policy. This is not always a realistic assumption. In the case of emission taxes, for instance, the quantity of emissions is changed by the producers if some of the economic fundamentals are changed. This case is considered explicitly in the appendix to this chapter and the following results are derived:

Proposition 3.9: Let there be an emission tax in the foreign country. If there are no externalities affecting production, an increase in domestic emissions attracts capital and leads to a reduction of emissions in the foreign country. All other effects are ambiguous.

The second part of this proposition is not surprising. Since the introduction of emission taxes requires the consideration of an additional equation, it is quite natural that some of the results become ambiguous. The different components of these indeterminate effects and their interpretation can be deduced from the equations of the appendix. The first part of the proposition has an intuitive explanation. The direct effect of an increase in domestic emissions is an increase in foreign direct investment. If productivity is not affected by the state of the environment, there tends to be a reduction in marginal productivity of emissions in the foreign country since it now employs a smaller capital stock. With a lower productivity of the environmental resource and a given emission tax, the foreign producers will reduce their emissions.

Turning propositions 3.8 and 3.9 around, we obtain:

Proposition 3.10: Tighter environmental regulation of production in one country may induce increased pollution from consumption in this country and/or additional emissions in the other country.

In theory, these indirect effects may offset the direct effects of tight environmental policies. But, given the weak empirical evidence on the link between environmental regulation and international capital allocation, this is rather unlikely to happen in reality, at least on the aggregate level.

The channels through which a tighter regulation of one activity may generate additional pollution from other activities are the following ones:

- First look at the case of given emissions in the foreign country. Let us assume that the home country is capital-poor, i.e. it has attracted foreign capital. The reduction in domestic emissions, on one hand, reduces output but, on the other hand, also reduces the rate of return on capital and this raises income (since payments to foreign capital owners are reduced). If the second effect dominates the first one, pollution through consumption is increased and, at least in theory, this may offset the effect of reduced emissions in the production process. This effect is contained in equation (3.24d). The term $sbgf_{ke}$ must be large compared to the other terms.[19]
- In the case of the capital-rich country, its own consumption is unambiguously reduced by a restrictive environmental policy but, due to the rate-of-return effect, consumption is raised in the capital-poor country and a part of the additional pollutants generated in the process of consumption spill over to the capital-rich country. This effect can also be derived from equation (3.24d) for $I < 0$. If the term $(1-S)bgf_{ke}$ is large, the counter-intuitive scenario becomes feasible.
- A third mechanism is possible if there is a given emission tax in the other country. In this case it is possible (and plausible) that the country adopting stringent environmental policy measures repels capital which is internationally mobile. This capital is invested abroad and this raises the marginal productivity of emissions. Since the emission tax rate is given and constant, there is an incentive to increase emissions and a part of the pollutants spill over to the home country.[20]

[19] This can also be seen from Fig. 3.3, where it has been shown that the net effect of increased emissions on consumption may be negative (the area a–e). A reduction of emissions from production may raise consumption and, thus, emissions from consumption.

[20] See also Merrifield (1988) and Rauscher (1995a). Of course, an emission tax is still a rare animal in the real world. But similar results would be obtained if the foreign country chose other

In particular, this third mechanism has some important economic-policy consequences. If producers are driven to pollution havens by restrictive environmental policies, there are no problems as long as transfrontier pollution is insignificant. But if there are spillovers, as in the case of global pollutants, then a part of the positive effects of tighter regulation in the home country may be offset by capital relocation effects. In the literature on the economics of the greenhouse effect, this problem has been addressed under the heading 'carbon leakage'. Taxes on CO_2, imposed unilaterally by single countries, may lead to an international relocation of energy-intensive production processes such that the effect of the tax is reduced or even reversed. Burniaux and Oliveira-Martins et al. (1993), Felder and Rutherford (1993), and Alistair A. Ulph (1994a) provide estimates that range from three to more than 60 per cent of the original effect of the tax.[21] There are two important conclusions to be drawn here. First, the weak incentive to take unilateral actions against global environmental problems is weakened further if international capital movements offset a part of the benefits of such a policy. Second, since this phenomenon occurs only if economies are open, one may be tempted to argue in favour of environmentally motivated barriers to factor mobility. These issues will be taken up in the following sections.

The analysis in this section has been based on two simplified versions of the original model. It should be noted that the original model, in which none of the parameters b, B, g', and G' vanishes, produces an even greater variety of results since there are interaction effects of the consumption externalities and the external effects on production that we have not been able to consider above.

3.6 Optimal Environmental Policies

Having analysed the effects of changes in environmental policies on consumption and environmental quality, we may now ask how the various effects of changes in environmental policy on income and environmental quality are translated into welfare gains and losses. In which circumstances will a society benefit from relaxing or tightening its environmental standards? The most important aspect of this question is that of optimal environmental regulation. What is the environmental policy that maximizes social welfare? In a first step, it is assumed that international factor movements are free and that emission control is the only policy instrument available. It will be seen that in these

policy instruments that leave emissions flexible. For instance, if environmental policy related emissions to installed capacity or output, the capital movement from the home country to the foreign country would induce additional emissions there as well.

[21] It should be noted that the models used by the authors of these studies are not fully compatible with the model discussed here. Oliveira-Martins et al. (1993) and Felder and Rutherford (1993) use trade models where capital is mobile across the sectors of an economy but not internationally. Ulph (1994a) considers a model in which capital moves across national borders but he uses the assumption of non-competitive markets.

circumstances environmental policy becomes a multipurpose instrument and it is not only used to internalize the social costs of environmental disruption. Later on, a capital income tax will be introduced into the model.

Scenario 1 ($b = B = 0$)

The home country's welfare function is differentiated with respect to emissions. Rearranging of terms then yields the following condition for the optimal level of emissions:[22]

$$gf_e = sa\frac{u_2}{u_1} + sag'f + \frac{I[gf_{ke}GF_{KK} + sag'f_kGF_{KK} - (1-s)aG'F_Kgf_{kk}]}{gf_{kk} + GF_{KK}}. \qquad (3.25)$$

gf_e is the optimal emission tax rate.[23] This tax rate consists of three components. The first term is the marginal cost of reduced environmental quality as a consumption good. The second term is the cost of reducing environmental quality as a factor of production. These two terms take account of the pure environmental externalities. The third term is the rate-of-return effect that has to be considered in a large open economy. It itself consists of the three components that have been discussed above. If the direct rate-of-return effect (the first term in the numerator) dominates the other two terms and if the country is capital-poor ($I > 0$), the optimal tax rate is higher than that internalizing the pure social cost of environmental disruption.[24] What is the explanation for this result? A capital-poor country has a partial monopoly for environmental resources on a global scale. Producers act competitively and, therefore, are unable to appropriate the corresponding rent. The state can now intervene and increase the relative scarcity of environmental resources by tightening environmental standards. The relative abundance of the other factor, capital, is increased and its price is reduced.

Scenario 2 ($g' = G' = 0$)

The optimal emission tax rate is

$$gf_e = sa\frac{u_2}{u_1} + sbgf_e\frac{u_2}{u_1} + \frac{gf_{ke}GF_{KK}I[(1-S)B - sb]u_2}{(gf_{kk} + GF_{KK})u_1} + \frac{gf_{ke}GF_{KK}I}{gf_{kk} + GF_{KK}}. \qquad (3.26)$$

There are four components. The first three effects are the social costs of reducing environmental quality as a consumption good. The first one is due to

[22] The first-order condition is sufficient for an optimum if the welfare functions are concave in emissions. The problem here is that the objective function itself contains terms which are derivatives of a function, i.e. the marginal productivities of capital. This implies that second derivatives of the production function occur in the first-order condition and that the second-order condition contains third derivatives. The same applies to comparative-static effects. The results would be ambiguous and hardly interpretable. Thus, we will simply assume that the second-order condition of optimality is satisfied. To make matters simple, it is assumed that there is an interior solution to the maximization problem.

[23] In the case of perfect competition, the tax rate equals the marginal productivity of emissions (see equation (3.4)).

[24] The capital-rich country will choose a tax rate lower than the marginal social cost of pollution. According to our definition, this may be called environmental dumping since not even the domestic share of environmental externalities is internalized by the environmental policy. None the less, many would hesitate to use this term for the framework of this model where there is no international goods trade at all.

emissions directly, the second to increased consumption possibilities as a consequence of increased emissions, and the third to the change in the consumption possibilities of the two countries caused by the rate-of-return effect. Finally, the fourth term is the impact of the change in the rate of return on domestic consumption. This term is unambiguously positive for the capital-poor country and negative for the capital-rich country. A social planner in the capital-rich country would adopt a policy that does not fully internalize the cost of environmental disruption. The intuitive explanation for this result has already been give above when the results for scenario 1 were discussed.

Until now it has been assumed that the home country chooses its optimal environmental policy for given emissions in the other country. It can, however, be shown that the results are changed substantially if the other country uses an emission tax as its policy instrument. Then, a change in domestic environmental policy has an impact on foreign emissions and, since there are spillover effects, this has to be taken into account by the domestic policy-maker. Define as scenario 3 a situation in which the foreign government uses a tax as its environmental policy instrument and in which neither consumption affects environmental quality nor environmental quality has an impact on output. The following result is obtained.[25]

Scenario 3 ($b = B = g' = G' = 0$, T^e given)
The optimal tax rate is

$$gf_e = sa\frac{u_2}{u_1} + \frac{G^2(F_{KK}F_{EE} - F_{KE}^2)g f_{ke}I}{G^2(F_{KK}F_{EE} - F_{KE}^2) + GF_{EE}g f_{kk}} \tag{3.27}$$

$$- \frac{(1-S)Ag f_{ke}GF_{KE}}{G^2(F_{KK}F_{EE} - F_{KE}^2) + GF_{EE}g f_{kk}}\frac{u_2}{u_1}.$$

The first term is the domestic externality of increased emissions. The second term is the rate-of-return effect. If the country is capital-poor, the relative scarcity of environmental resources can be increased by a more restrictive environmental policy. The price of capital falls and this is beneficial to the capital-poor country. The foreign country, which is capital-rich, should choose a less restrictive environmental policy since it benefits from high interest rates. The third term is due to the increase in foreign emissions. If the government knows capital will be driven out of the country by strict environmental policies and that this will induce additional emissions in the foreign country, then it should refrain from using too restrictive environmental regulations in the case of substantial transboundary pollution spillovers. According to the definition given in Chapter 2, this may be called ecological dumping since there is a tendency towards underinternalization of the domestic external effects. The idea behind this policy is to keep a larger stock of capital in the home country to subject it to one's own environmental regulation instead of letting it move abroad where

---

[25] It follows directly from the appendix by inserting equations (3.A9c) and (3.A9e) into the first-order condition.

the government has no incentive to take domestic environmental concerns into consideration. If all countries sharing a common environmental system follow this rationality, the problem of insufficient internalization of transnational environmental problems is aggravated. The underinternalization of even the domestic parts of the environmental damage would not occur if capital were internationally immobile. Therefore, one may conclude:

Proposition 3.11: International capital mobility may aggravate international environmental problems by reducing domestic environmental benefits of tight environmental taxes and standards.

Figure 3.4 depicts the impact of capital movements on the emissions of the two countries. Let the solid lines, *r* and *R*, be the reaction curves of domestic and foreign environmental policy in autarky. In autarky, the choice of the policy instrument does not matter and, thus, a representation in an (e, E) diagram can be used. As in Figure 2.2, the reaction curves are negatively sloped because additional emissions in one country raise the marginal environmental damage in the other country. Now capital movements are introduced and potential carbon-leakage problems make the governments choose laxer environmental taxes. Both reaction curves are shifted to the right. The figure shows a scenario where both countries raise their emissions but one may conceive of other cases where only one country raises its emissions whereas the other country reduces its emissions. This may have the counter-intuitive consequence that global environmental quality is increased although both countries have incentives to relax their environmental regulation (for given environmental regulation of the other country).

A precondition for proposition 3.11 is that environmental policy uses instruments that do not keep the emissions of a country constant but allow them to rise with an increasing capital stock. This condition is likely to be met in most

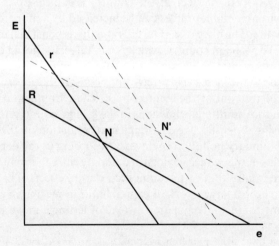

FIG. 3.4 The Impact of Capital Movements on Emissions

countries. None the less, the optimality conditions derived in this section contain also terms that point towards an overinternalization of pollution costs and it is unclear which of these effects will dominate in the real world.

The results on optimal environmental policies derived in this section can be summarized as follows:

Proposition 3.12: The optimal emission tax serves three purposes. It deals with the external effects of domestic production and consumption. It is used to affect the rate of return on the internationally mobile factor of production. It is used to deal with the transfrontier pollution that is induced by international factor mobility.

Of course this cannot be a first-best economy policy because the number of policy objectives exceeds the number of instruments. The consideration of additional policy instruments, therefore, is one of the directions into which the investigation may now proceed. However, before this step is undertaken, two other issues will be addressed. In the next section, we will be concerned with the problem of conjectural variation. It will be seen that environmental policy in one country depends on the choice of the policy instrument in the other country. Afterwards, in Section 3.8, we look at the interaction of environmental policies in different countries, i.e. at Nash equilibria of environmental policies. Then, in Section 3.9, a tax on capital will be introduced as an additional policy instrument.

3.7   The Impact of the Policy Measure Chosen in the other Country

Since the some of the effects determining optimal environmental policies occur only if emissions in the other country are variable, e.g. if there is a given emission tax, the question arises to what extent environmental policies in one country depend on the kind of the policy instruments chosen in the rest of the world. In oligopoly theory, an equivalent question has been discussed within the context of conjectural variation. Does the other firm keep its price or its quantity constant or has it chosen still another response function? The concept of conjectural variation has been subject to severe criticism in the industrial organization literature and the accepted view now seems to be that it is logically flawed since it uses pseudo-dynamic arguments in an inherently static model framework (see Tirole (1988: 244–45) and Shapiro (1989: 353–356)). In the context of international environmental problems, it appears to make more sense to look at conjectural variations. The instruments decided on by politicians are to some extent inflexible. If there is an emission tax today, it is likely that there will be an emission tax in the future. Thus, we are talking about observations rather than conjectures.

It is not difficult to determine the impact of a country's choice of its environmental policy instrument on the optimal policy of the other country at least for the most simple version of the model, scenario 3 in which $b = B = g' = G' = 0$. Equation (3.27) can be rewritten such that

$$gf_e = sa\frac{u_2}{u_1} + \frac{GF_{KK}gf_{ke}I}{GF_{KK} + gf_{kk}} + \frac{GF_{KE}gf_{kk}I}{GF_{KK} + gf_{kk}}\frac{dE}{de} + (1-S)A\frac{u_2}{u_1}\frac{dE}{de} \tag{3.28}$$

and

$$GF_E = SA\frac{U_2}{U_1} - \frac{gf_{kk}GF_{KE}I}{GF_{KK} + gf_{kk}} - \frac{gf_{ke}GF_{KK}I}{GF_{KK} + gf_{kk}}\frac{de}{dE} + (1-s)a\frac{U_2}{U_1}\frac{de}{dE} \tag{3.28'}$$

for the home and the foreign country, respectively. For the case of a foreign emission tax, dE/de is given by equation (3.A9b) in the appendix to this chapter. The equation for the foreign country follows from interchanging upper-case and lower-case letters and by noting that an increase of the capital stock in the home country implies that the capital stock in the foreign country is reduced. Thus, all terms containing I change their signs.

The partial derivatives dE/de and de/dE are the conjectural-variation parameters. If they are zero, we obtain the optimal tax formula for the case of given emissions in the other country. Compare equation (3.26).[26] If we now move from a scenario with given emission levels to a scenario with given emission taxes, the following effects can be observed. The conjectural-variation parameters that have been zero initially now become negative. This has two effects. First, the rate-of-return effect is diminished. If additional emissions at home reduce the emissions abroad, then the pressure on capital to move to the home country is increased. Therefore, the necessity to adjust the emission tax in order to influence the rate of return is reduced. If this were the only effect, the value of the right-hand side of equation (3.28) would be reduced and that of the right-hand side of equation (3.28') would be increased. This implies that the first-order condition is not satisfied any more and emissions should be raised in the home country and reduced in the foreign country.[27] The second effect has a negative impact on the right-hand side of the optimal tax equation in both countries. Thus, the effect on emissions is also negative and this is quite obvious since a reduction of emissions at home leads to an increase of pollution coming from abroad. Thus, the environmental policy must not be too strict.

Proposition 3.13: Assume that consumption externalities and the productivity effect of environmental disruption are negligible. For any level of emissions in the other country, the capital-poor country's emissions are larger if the other country chooses a tax than if it chooses a constant emission level. The same is true for the capital-rich country if the transfrontier externality is large compared to the rate-of-return effect. If the latter effect dominates, the optimal emissions are higher in the tax scenario.

[26] Equation (3.26) differs from (3.28) even in the case of given emissions ($dE/de = 0$) since it still contains the consumption externality parameters b and B that have been assumed to be zero for the derivation of equation (3.28).

[27] This follows from the concavity of the welfare function that has been assumed above. If the right-hand side of equations (3.28) and (3.28') is positive, then the marginal welfare is negative, implying that too much is discharged

A related result has been established by Wildasin (1988) in a model in which the mobile factor of production is taxed. He has shown that the results depend decisively on the policy instruments chosen by the other country in his model as well.

One could proceed from here by identifying the impact of the conjectural variation not only on the decision of a single country but also on the resulting Nash equilibrium of environmental policies. One could even endogenize the choice of the policy instruments.[28] However, these ideas will not be pursued here. One the one hand, such a model extension would be a rather academic exercise of limited practical relevance. On the other hand, the results would be ambiguous anyway. For instance, the slopes of the reaction functions are ambiguous since the formulae contain several third derivatives that lack an economic interpretation.[29] And even in the case of quadratic production functions (with zero third derivatives), the slope of one of the reaction functions is ambiguous such that a large variety of results would become possible.

3.8 Co-operative versus Non-co-operative Equilibria

If each country chooses its environmental policy unilaterally, it does not take account of the external effect it imposes on the other country. Thus, there will be gains from co-operation. The question arises as to how these gains can be realized. Would both countries be better off if they both agreed to reduce their emissions or would another kind of co-operation be preferable? In order to be able to give an answer, one has to look at the type of externalities that occur in the non-co-operative policy game. Algebraically, they are determined by

$$\frac{dW}{de} = U_1 \frac{dC}{de} - U_2 \frac{dZ}{de}, \tag{3.29}$$

$$\frac{dw}{dE} = u_1 \frac{dc}{dE} - u_2 \frac{dz}{dE} \tag{3.29'}$$

where the derivatives with respect to e and E correspond to those derived in Section 3.4. Assuming that the foreign country has chosen the emission level as its environmental policy instrument, equations (3.23b) and (3.23e) or (3.24c) and (3.24e) can be inserted and we obtain for scenario 1 ($b = B = 0$):

[28] The appropriate framework would a two-stage game where the strategic variable would be chosen in the first stage and its value (the tax rate or the number of pollution permits) would be determined in the second stage. For a paper dealing with the issue in a simpler model framework, see Wildasin (1991).

[29] The first-order conditions of the producers (profit maximization) are constraints of governmental policy. Thus, the government's first-order condition contains second-order derivatives (see equations (3.25) to (3.28)). The determination of the reaction curves and of comparative-static results would then involve third derivatives.

$$\frac{dW}{de} = -(1-s)a(U_1 G' F + U_2) \tag{3.30}$$

$$+ \frac{I[gf_{ke}GF_{KK} - sag' f_k GF_{KK} - (1-s)aG' F_K gf_{kk}]U_1}{gf_{kk} + GF_{KK}},$$

$$\frac{dw}{dE} = -(1-S)A(u_1 g' f + u_2) \tag{3.30'}$$

$$- \frac{I[GF_{KE}gf_{kk} - SAG' F_K gf_{kk} - (1-S)Ag' f_k GF_{KK}]u_1}{gf_{kk} + GF_{KK}},$$

and for scenario 2 ($g' = G' = 0$)

$$\frac{dw}{dE} = -U_2[(1-s)a + (1-s)bgf_e] + \frac{gf_{ke}GF_{KK}I[U_1 - U_2(SB - (1-s)b)]}{gf_{kk} + GF_{KK}}, \tag{3.31}$$

$$\frac{dW}{de} = u_2[(1-S)A + (1-S)BGF_E] - \frac{GF_{KE}gf_{kk}I[u_1 - u_2(sb - (1-S)B)]}{gf_{kk} + GF_{KK}}. \tag{3.31'}$$

The components of the external effects have already been discussed in Section 3.4, where the effects of changes in environmental policy on environmental quality and income have been investigated.

It would be desirable to look at the interaction of domestic and foreign policies in a Nash-equilibrium framework. However, the derivation of reaction functions turns out be very tedious. Thus, it is simply assumed that a unique Nash equilibrium exists. The iso-welfare curves for the home country and the foreign country can be inferred from the external effects. The Nash equilibrium, N, and the iso-welfare contours, w and W, are depicted in Figure 3.5. Four cases are imaginable:

1. The first diagram depicts a situation in which both countries would benefit from a mutual reduction in emissions. This case occurs if (but not if and only if) the rate-of-return effects are relatively unimportant. The transfrontier pollution spillover dominates. Since each country does not take into account the damage it causes in the other country, it discharges too much. A co-operative solution without side-payments would yield a new equilibrium inside the shaded area which is Pareto-superior to the Nash equilibrium.

2. In the second diagram, the home country imposes a positive externality on the foreign country, but itself is negatively affected by foreign emissions. There are various possibilities of obtaining this scenario. The most simple one is a situation in which the external effects on production are negligible (scenario 2 with $g' = G' = 0$) and the problem of transfrontier pollution is of minor relevance. The home country chooses a too strict environmental policy since this reduces the interest rate. The foreign country, in contrast, chooses a policy that is too lax since it prefers a high interest rate. A co-operative equilibrium could be located in the shaded area, where both countries would be better off if the home country increased its emissions and the foreign country used stricter environmental standards.

3. The third diagram shows the opposite external effects. They are possible if, for instance, the external effect on production is substantial and the transfrontier pollution spillovers are negligible. In this case, the rate of return on capital is reduced by lax environmental policies and increased by strict standards. Thus, the capital-poor home country chooses a high level of emissions and this negatively affects the income and the welfare of the foreign country. The foreign country imposes a negative externality on the home country by choosing a restrictive environmental policy. Both countries would be better off if the home country reduced its emissions and the foreign country increased its emissions.

4. The final diagram depicts a situation in which both counties discharge too few pollutants and would benefit from discharging more. This is possible if the external effect on production is small in the home country and large in the foreign country. Now both countries try to influence the rate of return in their own favour by restricting emissions. Less restrictive policies yield welfare gains for both countries.

All these interpretations are based on scenario 1, where there are no consumption externalities. The same anything-can-happen result can be obtained for scenario 2, in which there are no external diseconomies in the production processes. Thus we have:

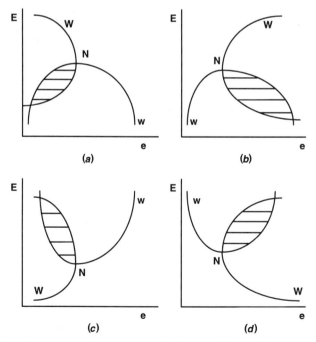

FIG. 3.5 Non-Co-operative Environmental Policies and Pareto Improvements

Proposition 3.14: Non-co-operative equilibria are not Pareto-optimal. Whether the countries should increase or reduce their emissions depends on the values of the parameters of the model.

A question that remains to be answered is whether it is possible that the competition among environmental regulations may lead to undesirably low levels of environmental regulation even in situations without transfrontier pollution. If there is transboundary pollution, it is not particularly amazing that emissions are too high. This has nothing to do with international capital mobility but just with simple free-riding behaviour.[30] To give an example that case 1 of Figure 3.5 is possible even in the absence of international environmental externalities, consider scenario 1 and set $s=S=1$ in equations (3.30) and (3.30′):

$$\frac{dW}{de} = \frac{gf_{ke} - ag'f_k}{gf_{kk} + GF_{KK}} IGF_{KK}U_1,$$

$$\frac{dw}{dE} = -\frac{GF_{KE} - SAG'F_K}{gf_{kk} + GF_{KK}} Igf_{kk}u_1.$$

It is seen that it is indeed possible that both countries impose negative external effects on each other even in the absence of transboundary pollution. This is possible if g' is large and G' is small. In this case both countries try to influence the rate of return on capital in their own favour by using lax environmental policies and thereby negatively affect the other country's national income.

Proposition 3.15 Even without international pollution spillovers, it is possible that the objective to influence international capital movements leads to undesirably low levels of environmental regulation in both countries.

Mutual gains from co-operation can be increased if side-payments are introduced. In the graphical representation, this leads to shifts in the systems of iso-welfare curves and, therefore, welfare comparisons cannot sensibly be made. None the less, it is possible to determine side payments algebraically for the jointly optimal solution. The objective is to maximize

$$u(c,-z) + U(C,-Z)$$

subject to the constraints

$$z = s(ae + bc) + (1 - S)(AE + BC), \tag{3.2}$$

$$Z = (1-s)(ae + bc) + S(AE + BC). \tag{3.2′}$$

$$c = g(-z)f(k_0 + I,e) - g(-z)f_k(k_0 + I,e) I + t^k I - \sigma, \tag{3.32}$$

$$C = G(-Z) F(K_0 - I,E) + G(-Z) F_K(K_0 - I,E) I - T^K I + \sigma, \tag{3.32′}$$

$$g(-z)f_k(k_0 + I,e) - - t^k = G(-Z) F_K(K_0 - I,E) - T^K. \tag{3.21}$$

σ is the side-payment from the home to the foreign country which, of course, may be negative. Total differentiation yields equation (3.22) with a vector

---

[30] However, as has been argued before, the degree of underinternalization of environmental damage may be increased by capital mobility.

added on the right-hand side that accounts for variations in the level of side-payment. The results will again be derived for the special scenarios that have been discussed before.

Scenario 1 ($b = B = 0$)

Since consumption does not affect the environment, the side-payment has an impact merely on the consumption possibilities of the two economies. The optimality condition is

$$u_1 = U_1.$$

Using this and the comparative static results with respect to e (equations (3.23a–e)), the optimal emission tax rates can easily be determined. They are

$$gf_e = sag'f + sa\frac{u_2}{u_1} + (1-s)aG'F + (1-s)a\frac{U_2}{u_1}, \tag{3.34}$$

$$GF_E = SAG'F + SA\frac{U_2}{u_1} + (1-S)Ag'f + (1-S)A\frac{u_2}{u_1}. \tag{3.34'}$$

The four effects on the right-hand sides of these equations are the damages due to the reduction in domestic consumption possibilities, to the reduction of domestic environmental quality, to the reduction of foreign consumption, and to the reduction of foreign environmental quality. All rate-of-return effects cancel out.

Scenario 2 ($g' = G' = 0$)

Since consumption now affects the environment, the side-payment also has an impact on environmental quality. The optimality condition is

$$u_1 - sb\,u_2 - (1-s)b\,U_2 = U_1 - SB\,U_2 - (1-S)B\,u_2. \tag{3.35}$$

A transfer of income from the home to the foreign country has the following effects on the environment: the reduction of domestic consumption is beneficial to environmental quality in both countries but environmental quality suffers from increased foreign consumption. Condition (3.35) assures that the marginal welfare gains and losses ad up to zero. Using this and the comparative-static results with respect to e (equations (3.24a–e)), the optimal emission tax rates can easily be determined. They are

$$gf_e = \frac{sau_2 + (1-s)aU_2}{u_1 - sbg f_e u_2 - (1-s)bg f_e U_2} \tag{3.36}$$

$$GF_E = \frac{SAU_2 + (1-S)Au_2}{u_1 - sbg f_e u_2 - (1-s)bg f_e U_2}. \tag{3.36'}$$

The denominators on the right-hand sides of these equations are positive if some Inada-type conditions (in particular infinite marginal utility at zero consumption or environmental quality) are satisfied. The numerators contain the marginal damage of environmental quality in the two countries. Again, all rate-of-return effects cancel out.

Proposition 3.16 Co-operative solutions are characterized by emission taxes that internalize foreign and domestic external effects. There are no rate-of-return effects.

This result also holds for the case in which the other government has chosen an emission tax rate instead of an emission level. The reason for the absence of a rate-of-return term in the optimal tax rates lies in the nature of the rate-of-return effects. It has been shown that, at the margin, these effects are redistributive. The income gains and losses add up to zero. However, if environmental legislation were used to affect the rate of return, a distortion would be induced on a supramarginal scale and the global allocation of factors would become suboptimal.[31] Thus, in a co-operative world, an efficient factor allocation is chosen in the first step and then the pie is shared among the co-operating parties.

The improved factor allocation is one of the sources of the gains from co-operation. The other one is the perfect internalization of environmental damage even if this occurs across the border.

3.9 Capital Taxation as an Instrument of Environmental Policy

In Section 3.7, it has been shown that a government may be tempted to use its environmental policy to achieve non-environmental objectives, like increasing national income by influencing the remuneration of internationally mobile factors. In such a situation, the emission tax serves up to three purposes. It internalizes the domestic social cost, it internalizes a part of the transboundary externality, and it improves the country's position in the world capital market. This is usually not a first-best policy. Welfare improvements become possible if an additional policy instrument is introduced. The appropriate policy measure here is a capital income tax. The optimal policy can be determined by differentiating the welfare function with respect to e and t^k. The optimality conditions

$$\frac{dw}{de} = u_1 \frac{dc}{de} - u_2 \frac{dz}{de}$$

and

$$\frac{dw}{dt^k} = u_1 \frac{dc}{dt^k} - u_2 \frac{dz}{dt^k}$$

yield explicit solutions for the optimal tax rates if dz/dt^k, dc/dt^k, dz/de, and dc/de are determined by applying Cramer's rule to equation (3.22). The effect of a change in the profit tax rate is introduced by adding the transpose of

---

[31] This can be seen in Fig. 3.3. Assume that the initial policy is optimal if the rate-of-return effect is not taken into account. Then, the income increase measured by area $a+b+c+d$ is offset by a corresponding reduction in environmental quality. The remaining income loss due to the change in the rate of return is smaller than the income gain accruing to the foreign country. The difference is $b+c$.

$(0, 0, I \, dt^k, 0, dt^k)$

to the right-hand side of equation (3.22). Assume that emissions in the foreign country are taken as given. Then, the following results are obtained.

Scenario 1 $(b = B = 0)$

$$\frac{dz}{dt^k} = 0. \tag{3.37a}$$

$$\frac{dc}{dt^k} = \frac{GF_{KK}I + t^k}{gf_{kk} + GF_{KK}}. \tag{3.37b}$$

$$\frac{dz}{de} = sa. \tag{3.37c}$$

$$\frac{dc}{de} = gf_e - sag' f + \frac{sag' f_k(GF_{KK}I + t^k) + (1-s)aG \, F_K(gf_{kk}I - t^k)}{gf_{kk} + GF_{KK}} - gf_{ke}\frac{dc}{dt^k}. \tag{3.37d}$$

The optimal tax rates are

$$t^{k*} = -GF_{KK}I \tag{3.38a}$$

and

$$t^{e*} = sa\frac{u_2}{u_1} + sag'f - (1-s)aG'F_KI. \tag{3.38b}$$

The condition for the optimal tax rate on capital is well known from the literature on capital taxation (see *Sinn* (1987, ch. 7) for this result and a graphical illustration). A capital-poor country should tax capital. This drives capital out of the country and increases the capital stock in the rest of the world. Due to the declining marginal productivity of capital, the international interest rate and the interest payments to the other country are reduced. Of course, if the country is capital-rich, it should take the opposite action and subsidize the use of capital. The optimal emission tax rate consists of three components. The first one is the marginal cost of loss of environmental quality as a consumption good. The second one is the marginal cost of loss of environmental quality as a factor of production. The third component is a rate-of-return effect. The emissions spill over to the foreign country and cause a decline of capital productivity there. The international interest rate is reduced. If the country under consideration is capital-poor, it benefits from this effect. Therefore, this component of the tax rate is negative in this case.

Scenario 2 $(g' = G' = 0)$

The comparative statics are:

$$\frac{dz}{dt^k} = \frac{sb(GF_{KK}I + t^k) - (1-s)B(GF_{KK}I + T^K)}{gf_{kk} + GF_{KK}} \tag{3.39a}$$

$$\frac{dc}{dt^k} = \frac{GF_{KK}I + t^k}{gf_{kk} + GF_{KK}}. \tag{3.39b}$$

$$\frac{dz}{de} = sa + sbgf_e - gk_{ke}\frac{dz}{dt^k} .$$

(3.39c)

$$\frac{dc}{de} = gf_e - gk_{ke}\frac{dc}{dt^k} .$$

(3.39d)

The optimal tax rates are

$$t^{k*} = -GF_{KK}I - \frac{(1 - S)B(GF_{KK}I + T^K)u_2}{u_1 - sbu_2}$$

(3.40a)

and

$$t^{e*} = \frac{sau_2}{u_1 - sbu_2}$$

(3.40b)

The same emission tax rate has been derived in the case of the small economy (see equation (3.12)). It just serves the purpose of internalizing the domestic externalities. The transborder pollution spillovers as well as the country's market power on the international capital market is taken into account by the capital tax. If the foreign country's tax rate is not too large, then the domestic tax rate is not only positive; it is even larger than the tax rate that would be optimal in a scenario without transfrontier pollution. This has the following intuitive explanation. If foreign consumption has a negative impact on domestic environmental quality, then the domestic government should use its policy instruments to reduce foreign consumption. Since a tax on internationally mobile capital has just this effect, it is the appropriate policy instrument to deal with this transfrontier pollution issue. The tax rate is an increasing function of the transfrontier pollution spillover parameter, $(1-S)$.[32] Hence, one may call this instrument a 'green' barrier to international factor movements.

In the same fashion, one can derive emission and capital tax rates for the scenario in which not the level of foreign emissions but the emission tax rate is given. The optimal tax rates for scenario 3, in which there are neither consumption externalities nor external diseconomies of scale, then are:

Scenario 3 ($b = B = g' = G' = 0$, T^e given)

Using the results from the appendix to this chapter, the following optimal tax rates can be derived:

$$t^{k*} = -\frac{G(F_{EE}F_{KK} - F_{KE}^2)I}{F_{EE}} + (1 - S)A\frac{F_{KE}u_2}{F_{EE}u_1}$$

(3.41a)

and

---

[32] A formal proof involves the total differentiation of the first-order condition with respect to t^k and $(1-S)$. This yields

$$\frac{d^2w}{(dt^k)^2}dt^k = -\frac{B(GF_{KK}I + T^K)}{gf_{kk} + GF_{KK}}d(1 - S) .$$

If the second-order condition is satisfied, the tax rate is an increasing function of the spillover.

$$t^{e*} = sa \frac{u_2}{u_1}. \tag{3.41b}$$

The optimal emission tax simply internalizes the domestic external effects. The capital income tax consists of two components. The first one is the rate-of-return effect. A tax on foreign capital leads to a relocation of this factor of production. The capital stock employed in the foreign country is now larger. If there are decreasing returns to scale in the foreign industry (i.e. $F_{KK}F_{EE} - F_{KE}^2 > 0$), then the world interest rate is reduced and the home country benefits. In the case of constant returns to scale, the rate-of-return effect vanishes.[33] The other component of the tax on capital is due to transfrontier pollution. It is negative; foreign investors are subsidized by the domestic government. If there is transboundary pollution from the foreign to the home country, the domestic government is willing to reduce this pollution spillover. The appropriate instrument is a subsidy on foreign direct investment. Capital is moved from abroad to the home country. This reduces the marginal productivity of emissions in the foreign country and, at a given emission tax rate, foreign producers will discharge less. The foreign government, in contrast, is interested in keeping the capital inside the country. The appropriate instrument is a subsidy to capital owners, as well. This is the 'green' component of the optimal capital market intervention.

The results derived from the three scenarios are:

Proposition 3.17: The optimal capital tax is used to take account of changes in the world interest rate and of the effects of transfrontier pollution coming from abroad. The optimal emission tax then merely internalizes the domestic social cost of environmental disruption.

Thus, it has indeed been established that the subsidization of the mobile factor of production is an appropriate means to solve some transfrontier pollution problems. Nevertheless, this instrument is not the efficient one. Capital market interventions cause real efficiency losses that could be avoided by transfer payments. This can be shown graphically for the case of scenario 3, where there are neither consumption externalities nor external diseconomies in production. Figure 3.6 consists of two parts. The left-hand side depicts the marginal productivities of the capital stocks employed in the home and the foreign country. The right-hand part of the diagram depicts the foreign country's factor-price frontier, which is fixed if we assume constant returns to scale. The foreign emission tax rate, T^e determines the foreign country's marginal productivity of capital. This equals the world interest rate, r. We start from a situation with unrestricted factor movements. OE and O^*E represent the capital stocks employed in the home and the foreign country initially. Now the home country becomes aware of transfrontier pollution and wishes to reduce foreign emissions by attracting additional foreign capital. Subsidization of foreign

---

[33] Constant returns to scale imply a factor-price frontier that does not change its location. Thus, if the foreign emission tax rate is fixed, the remuneration of capital is fixed as well.

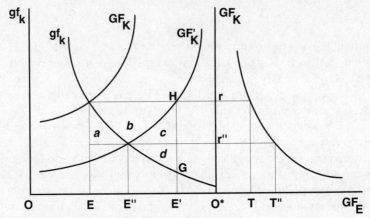

FIG. 3.6 Effects of Factor Market Interventions

capital results in a downward shift of the foreign marginal-productivity curve.[34] If the domestic emission level does not change, the new equilibrium allocation of capital is given by point E'. The size of the subsidy is GH. Compared to a situation without subsidies, the home country has lost a part of its income, $b + c + d$. This loss of income is accompanied by an improvement of environmental quality not shown in this diagram. Now consider a situation in which the domestic government is able to persuade the foreign government to change its environmental policy such that the foreign emissions remain unchanged but the subsidy can be removed. This corresponds to a shift along the GF'_K curve until the point of intersection with the gf_k curve is reached. The allocation of the capital stock is now determined by E'', where the foreign country has reduced its direct investment by $E'E''$. The interest rate is reduced from r to r'' and the foreign country's emission tax rate rises from T to T''. What are the impacts on income and the welfare effects? The home country gains $a + b + c + d$ since it does not subsidize any more. The foreign country, however, loses $a + b$. The net income gain is $c + d$. Thus, a transfer scheme is possible which makes both countries better off in terms of consumption possibilities while, at the same time, leaving emissions and environmental quality constant. Intervening in international factor markets is, therefore, only a second-best approach for dealing with transfrontier pollution problems.

Proposition 3.18: An efficient solution to transfrontier environmental problems involves an international environmental agreement with side-payments and undistorted factor movements. If co-operation does not work, an optimal policy mix of emission taxation and capital market interventions is the second-best solution from the point of view of a single country.

---

[34] This shift is explained by the fact that foreign emissions are reduced if the home country attracts foreign capital.

3.10 Political Factors Determining Environmental Policies in Open Economies

The validity of the implications concerning optimal environmental quality and welfare gains and losses that have been derived above depends on the choice of the welfare function. One may argue that the concept employed here to measure welfare is appropriate from an economic-theory point of view, but that real-world environmental policies are based on different considerations. In theory, it is argued that capital mobility is good since it helps to exploit interest rate differentials and, therefore, raises income. In the public opinion, however, investments abroad are often suspected to be responsible for a decline in domestic employment: domestic entrepreneurs who invest abroad instead of at home create labour demand in the wrong country. Whether or not this argument is true, it has a major impact on real-world trade policies and it will, therefore, be taken up here.

For simplicity, assume that there is a Leontief technology characterized by a fixed capital-employment ratio. Choose the units of employment such that one unit of labour, l, is needed to operate one unit of capital. This implies

$$l = k_0 + I. \tag{3.42}$$

$$L = K_0 - I. \tag{3.42'}$$

If employment is low, the chance for the government to be re-elected is low. Thus, the government derives some utility from a high level of employment. Let this utility be represented by an increasing and strictly concave function, $\omega(l)$. The objective function of the domestic government is

$$u(c,-z) + \omega(k_0 + I)$$

and the foreign government has a similar policy objective.[35]

If there are no interventions in the capital market, the following emission tax rates can be determined.

Scenario 1 $(b = B = 0)$

$$gfe = sa\,\frac{u_2}{u_1} + sag'f + \frac{I\,[gf_{ke}GF_{KK} + sag'\,f_k GF_{KK} - (1-s)aG'\,F_{kg}f_{kk}]}{gf_{kk} + GF_{KK}}$$

$$-\,\frac{-gf_{ke} + sag'\,f_k - (1-s)aG'\,F_K}{gf_{kk} + GF_{KK}}\,\frac{\omega'}{u_1}, \tag{3.43}$$

The additional term, which is due to the employment target, is ambiguous. If the external effect on production is relatively unimportant, the optimal emission tax rate is negatively influenced by the consideration of the additional policy objective.

---

[35] A behavioural foundation of such an objective function based on lobbying activities has been given by Grossman and Helpman (1994). See also Ch. 7 for a motivation of this approach.

Scenario 2 ($g' = G' = 0$)

$$gf_e = sa\frac{u_2}{u_1} + sbgf_e\frac{u_2}{u_1} + \frac{gf_{ke}GF_{KK}I[(1-S)B-sb]u_2}{(gf_{kk}+GF_{KK})u_1} + \frac{gf_{ke}(GF_{KK}I+\frac{\omega'}{u_1})}{gf_{kk}+GF_{KK}}. \quad (3.44)$$

The additional term, which reflects the consideration of the employment target, is negative. The optimal emission tax rate is negatively influenced by the consideration of the employment motive.

Scenario 3 ($b = B = g = G = 0$, Te given)

$$gf_e = sa\frac{u_2}{u_1} + \frac{-(1-S)Agf_{ke}GF_{KE}\frac{u_2}{u_1}+gf_{ke}(G^2(F_{KK}F_{EE}-F_{KE}^2)I-G^2F_{EE}\frac{\omega'}{u_1})}{G^2(F_{KK}F_{EE}-F_{KE}^2)+GF_{EE}gf_{kk}}. \quad (3.45)$$

Again, the impact of the additional policy objective is negative.

The same results are obtained for the other country. Summarizing, the main result is:

Proposition 3.19: Let employment be an increasing function of the capital stock and let the government explicitly consider the employment effects of capital movements. Provided that the negative external effect on production is sufficiently small, the government will choose a higher emission level for any given emission level of the foreign country than in a situation in which employment objectives are not considered. The effect on the Nash equilibrium is ambiguous.

The first part of this proposition follows from the fact that a restrictive environmental policy normally repels foreign capital and, therefore, reduces employment. Thus, it is optimal to subsidize domestic firms through too low emission taxes. This may be called ecological dumping according to the definition given in Chapter 2. The consequences for the Nash equilibrium of environmental policies are, none the less, unclear. The change in the location of the equilibrium is ambiguous since the slopes of the reaction curves are indeterminate. None the less, there tends to be a strong tendency towards higher emissions, more environmental disruption, and lower welfare. This is due to the fact that the international competition for mobile capital is a zero-sum game since the total capital stock is fixed. Since the gains from increased employment sum up to zero, the remaining effects are the distortions of environmental policy that have been created to attract foreign capital.

Again the policy derived here as the optimal one is not first best. It would be better to use a capital market intervention than an adjustment in environmental policy to attract foreign capital. If this were done, the optimal emission tax rate would just internalize the social costs of environmental disruption.

3.11 Non-Competitive Market Structures and Optimal Environmental Policies

The preceding investigation has been based on the assumption of perfect competition in all relevant markets. However, this assumption is not always realistic. Often, investment decisions are made by large multinational enterprises that enjoy some market power. On the other side of the market, there is a competition for internationally mobile capital between smaller entities, like small countries, regions, or even local communities. One may suspect that in such a situation there is a large pressure on environmental standards. Governments compete with each other down to undesirably low levels of environmental regulation. This section addresses the question whether or not this conjecture is correct.

Consider the following situation. There is a large number of capital-poor countries on the demand side of the capital market and one firm on the supply side which is willing to undertake an investment.[36] The cost of investment is r^c per unit of investment. On a competitive market, this would be the rate of interest. Here, however, the firm can exploit its market power and appropriate a rent. Therefore, one may expect that the interest rate charged by the monopolist exceeds the cost of investment. This interest rate is denoted by r^m.

In a first step, the demand function of the potential host countries for foreign capital is derived. Let us assume that these countries are identical. Thus, they can be aggregated and a model of a single economy, the home country, can be used to represent the demand side of the capital market. It is assumed to use an optimal environmental policy, determined by equations (3.11) or (3.12). The demand for capital can now be derived by maximizing the social-welfare function with respect to I at a given interest rate. The comparative statics are given by equations (3.15a,b) and (3.16) and the demand for foreign capital is, not surprisingly, characterized by

$$gf_k = r. \tag{3.46}$$

It is now possible to determine the effects of changes in the interest rate on emissions and the size of the foreign investment by totally differentiating equations (3.11) and (3.46), noting that $dw/dI = 0$. The comparative static results are obtained by applying Cramer's rule to

$$\begin{pmatrix} (1 + sbg'f)w_{ee} & (u_1 - sbu_2)gf_{ke} - sag'f_ku_1 \\ (u_1 - sbu_2)gf_{ke} - sag'f_ku_1 & (u_1 - sbu_2)gf_{kk} \end{pmatrix} \begin{pmatrix} de \\ dI \end{pmatrix} = \begin{pmatrix} 0 \\ dr \end{pmatrix},$$

where the matrix on the left-hand side is a Hessian with negative diagonal elements and a positive determinant, Δ.[37] They are

---

[36] The assumption of a supply-side monopoly is not essential. The qualitative result would be the same if there were a finite number of oligopolistic firms. However, the algebra would be much more cumbersome whereas no additional insights are to be gained.

[37] One can establish that the determinant is positive by computing w_{ee}. Note that both equations (3.11) and (3.46) are optimality conditions and the Hessian should have a positive determinant if the second-order conditions are satisfied.

$$\frac{de}{dr} = -\frac{1}{\Delta}\left((u_1 - sbu_2)gf_{ke} - sag'f_k u_1\right),$$ (3.47a)

$$\frac{dl}{dr} = \frac{1}{\Delta}(1 + sbg'f)w_{ee} < 0.$$ (3.47b)

The demand for foreign capital is a declining function of its remuneration. This implies that the usual textbook approach to monopolistic behaviour can be used and that the rate of return on foreign capital can be derived by equalizing the marginal interest revenue and the marginal cost of investment, i.e. the competitive interest rate. This will be done later on in a diagram, but even without this graphical representation it is obvious that the monopolistic rate of return exceeds the competitive interest rate. The impact of the interest rate on emissions is determined by equation (3.47a). It is ambiguous. If the external effect of environmental quality on production is small, then there is a negative relationship. The reduced availability of capital leads to a reduction in the marginal productivity of emissions. Therefore, it is optimal to reduce emissions until the marginal benefits equal the marginal cost of emissions. The opposite result is derived if the external diseconomies are substantial.

If emissions are a declining function of the interest rate, then the environment benefits from monopoly power in the world capital market.[38] This effect is amplified by the reduction of consumption activities induced by the decline of consumers' surplus. However, the hypothesis has not been that imperfect competition is bad for the environment. Rather has the argument been that monopolistic supply of capital leads to lower environmental standards. Therefore, a measure for the strictness of environmental regulation has to be considered. The appropriate measure is the emission tax rate, which equals the marginal productivity of emissions if the firms inside the small country behave in a competitive fashion. Thus, we have to investigate

$$\frac{d(gf_e)}{dr} = \left(gf_{ke} - g'f_e\frac{dz}{dI}\right)\frac{dI}{dr} + \left(gf_{ee} - g'f_e\frac{dz}{de}\right)\frac{de}{dr}.$$

Using equations (3.10a), (3.15a), (3.46), and (3.47a, b), one can rewrite this:

$$\frac{d(gf_e)}{dr} = \frac{1}{\Delta}\left[gf_{ke}(1 + sbg'f)w_{ee} - \left(gf_{ee} - g'f_e\frac{sa + sbg'f_e}{1 + sbg'f}\right)\right.$$
$$\left.\left((u_1 - sbu_2)gf_{ke} - sag'f_k u_1\right)\right].$$

By computing the second derivative of the welfare function, w_{ee}, it can be shown that some terms cancel out and that the sign of $d(gf_e)/dr$ is unambiguously positive:

---

[38] This reminds us of a rather general result in environmental and resource economics for which Solow (1974: 8) has coined the phrase that "the monopolist is the conservationist's friend". For the derivation of the same result in the framework of a static model of environmental disruption, see Ebert (1991). These models are based on the assumption of non-competitive ownership of property rights to a resource. In contrast, the model presented here considers the non-competitive supply of a factor of production for which the resource is a substitute.

$$\frac{d(gf_e)}{dr} = \frac{1}{\Delta}\left[gk_{ke}\left(-sag'f_eu_1 + sag''fu_1 + u_{11}\frac{(gf_e - sag'f)^2}{1 + sbg'f} + u_{22}\frac{(sa + sbgf_e)^2}{1 + sbg'f}\right)\right.$$

$$\left. + sag'f_ku_1\left(gf_{ee} - g'f_e\frac{sa + sbgf_e}{1 + sbg'f}\right)\right] < 0. \tag{3.48}$$

Proposition 3.20: Monopolistic supply of foreign capital leads to lower emission taxes.

Thus, the algebra has shown that the intuition has been correct. Monopoly in the world capital market leads to relaxed environmental standards. An interpretation of this result is given in Figure 3.7. It consists of two parts. The left-hand side shows the factor-price frontier (*FPF*). At a given level of environmental quality, the factor-price frontier does not depend on output if the production function $f(k,e)$ exhibits constant returns to scale. Improvements in environmental quality shift the curve upwards, environmental deterioration implies a downward shift. The right-hand side of the diagram depicts the country's demand function for foreign capital, $d(r)$, with a negative slope determined by equation (3.47b). It is important to note that this curve is not a normal marginal-productivity curve along which the utilization of the other factors of production is fixed. Along the $d(r)$ line, the emissions change. The willingness to pay for foreign capital does not only depend on the technical parameters but also on environmental considerations. We can now apply the conventional method of partial-equilibrium analysis of monopolistic markets to this figure. k_0 is the country's capital endowment and defines the starting point of the demand function. The monopolist's marginal revenue curve, MR, is steeper than the demand curve. r^c is the cost the monopolist has to bear to finance the investment. Equating marginal cost and marginal revenue yields the monopolistic supply of capital, I^m, which is smaller than the competitive

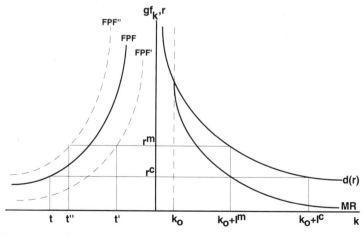

FIG. 3.7 Monopolistic Supply of Foreign Capital

supply, I^c. Correspondingly, the rate of return to capital, r^m, is higher than the one that would prevail under perfect competition. Moving to the other part of the diagram, the emission tax rate, t, can be derived from the factor-price frontier. It has to be taken into account, however, that the factor-price frontier may be shifted by the change in emissions (see equation (3.47a)). Increasing emissions imply a downward shift; if emissions are reduced, the curve is shifted upwards. Both cases are depicted in the diagram. The algebra has shown that if there is an upward shift, the resulting emission tax rate will still be lower than the one obtained for the lower interest rate. t' and t'' are smaller than t.

Since in the case of externalities that affect production, the comparative-static effects of the model are rather complex, an economic intuition for this result is hard to give. Matters are simpler if this externality is negligible. In this case, the location of the factor-price frontier is fixed. A monopoly on the supply side of the capital market implies that the interest rate is raised. In the case of constant returns to scale, this implies that the remuneration of the other factor, i.e. the environmental resource, has to go down. Thus, the emission tax rate is smaller under monopoly than under perfect competition.

It is obvious that countries subject to monopolistic supply of foreign capital are worse off than countries which have access to a competitive capital market. Since the remuneration of foreign capital is an element in the country's budget constraint, a higher interest rate reduces the set of choices available to the inhabitants of the country. As has been shown above, the government is induced to relax environmental standards.

Other models of non-competitive market structure and foreign direct investment have been developed by Markusen *et al.* (1993, 1995), Motta and Thisse (1993), Hoel (1994), D. Ulph (1994), and Rauscher (1995c). They differ from the model discussed here in several respects. The major differences are (i) that they use a partial-equilibrium framework instead of looking at the economy as a whole and (ii) that international trade is considered explicitly in these models. They will be presented in Chapter 6 when environmental policies in non-competitive foreign-trade models are discussed.

3.12 The Choice of the Wrong Environmental Policy Instrument

In the preceding sections, we have assumed implicitly that all firms are owned by residents of a country but not by foreigners. Foreign capital is merely rented on the world capital market. This assumption implies that the results derived up to here are not affected by the choice of the environmental policy instrument. Independently of the instrument chosen, the rent which is due to the scarcity of environmental resources remains inside the regulating country. If emissions are taxed, the government appropriates a tax revenue. If pollution permits are auctioned, the revenue goes to the state as well. And if a command-and-control approach is chosen, a rent accrues to the owners of regulated domestic enterprises. In any case, this revenue or rent constitutes a part of the domestic consumable income and, therefore, the variables of the objective function of the government are not affected by the choice of the environmental policy instrument. Matters are different, however, if a part of the scarcity rent goes to foreigners. This may happen if they do not merely let a part of their capital to domestic entrepreneurs but really undertake foreign direct investments. Then, policy instruments matter. Consider a situation where the government does not skim off the scarcity rent by using emission taxes or tradable pollution permits. Then a part of this income goes to foreigners and the domestic GNP is smaller than in a scenario with the appropriate policy instruments. The change in GNP affects the objective function of the government and, therefore, the costs and benefits of environmental policy (see Sinn (1994: 104–5) and Wellisch (1995) for this argument). We will elaborate it for the model under consideration here.

Assume that both governments choose the command-and-control approach and that all scarcity rents accrue to the owners of capital. Foreign investors can appropriate a share of the rent corresponding to their share of the capital stock which is subject to domestic environmental regulation. This implies:

$$GF_K \frac{EGF_E}{K_0 - I} = r = gf_k + \frac{egf_e}{k_0 + I}, \tag{3.49}$$

where egf_e and EGF_E are the domestic and foreign scarcity rents. This change in the determination of the world interest rate has important consequences for the gains from free factor movements and for the determination of environmental policy.

Let us first look at the effect of a liberalization of international factor movements on an initially autarkic economy. Assume that the country is small, i.e. the world market interest rate is not affected by this change. Then the welfare effect is

$$\frac{dw}{dl} = (gf_k - r) \frac{u_1 - sbu_2}{1 + sbg'f}. \tag{3.16}$$

In a situation with an optimal environmental policy in the autarky state, again determined by equation (3.12), the fraction on the right-hand side is positive. However, gf_k may now be smaller than r. How can this be explained? Under the assumption that domestic scarcity rents can be appropriated by foreigners, capital moves from the foreign to the home country if its rate of return exceeds the world interest rate. Here, however, the rate of return to foreign direct investment in the home country is its marginal productivity plus the share of the scarcity rent. Thus, capital movements from the foreign to the domestic economy may occur even if initially $gf_k < r$. Therefore, dw/dl may be negative.

The reason underlying this result is that the owners of foreign capital are paid too much and, therefore, invest too much. From the point of view of the host country, foreign investment should come to a halt when the marginal productivity of foreign capital equals the world interest rate. The return on investment, as viewed by the investor, however, is the marginal productivity plus a share of the scarcity rent. The foreign investor receives a subsidy. This is an incentive to invest additional capital. Welfare losses in the host country occur because it spends more than it should on foreign capital. On top of all other arguments against the command-and-control approach to environmental policy, this is an additional reason to introduce environmental taxes or tradable pollution permits as instruments of environmental policy.

The capital-rich country, in contrast, will always be better off if its level of emissions is not too far away from the optimal one. If a binding restriction on capital mobility is removed, direct investments will be undertaken and the allocation of foreign capital is moved closer to the optimal one. However, an optimum capital allocation will never be attained. The capital stock is too large because, as in the capital-poor country, capital owners are paid more than the marginal product of their factor. Due to this subsidy, capital owners do not take account of profitable investment opportunities in the rest of the world.

It is not surprising that, given these distortions, the net effect on the allocation of the world capital stock is not necessarily positive any more. The capital-poor country may lose more than the capital-rich country gains. Due to the indirect subsidy, the allocation of the world capital stock may be more inefficient in the presence of capital movements than in autarky. This is depicted by Figure 3.8. The capital stock employed in the home country is measured from O, the capital stock employed in the foreign country from O^*. The autarky capital allocation is A and gf_k and GF_K are the marginal productivities of capital. sr denotes the scarcity rent per unit of capital in the home country for a given environmental policy. The foreign country is assumed to use an environmental policy instrument which skims off the scarcity rent. The optimum allocation of capital in this figure would be attained at point E, where the gf_k

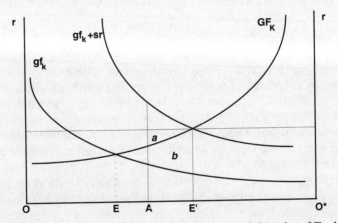

Fig. 3.8 Inefficient Environmental Policy Instruments and the gains of Trade

and GF_K curves intersect. Due to the subsidy, however, capital moves in the opposite direction, to E'. The welfare gain of the foreign country, a, is smaller than the welfare loss of the home country, $a+b$.

Proposition 3.21: If environmental regulation allows foreigners to appropriate domestic scarcity rents, the welfare effect of capital mobility in the capital-poor country can be negative even in the case of an optimal initial emissions level. It is positive in the capital-rich country if its emissions are not too suboptimal. The efficiency of the allocation of the world capital stock may be deteriorated.

The preceding analysis rests on the assumption of a given and constant environmental policy. However, when costs and benefits change, policies tend to be adjusted. What does an optimal policy look like when the scarcity rent of environmental resources goes to the owners of the mobile factor? In order not to confuse the effects of the change in the policy instrument with the rate-of-return effects of environmental policy that have been discussed earlier, we look at the small-country case. Three equations are relevant in this context: equation (3.2), which defines environmental quality, equation (3.3), which determines consumption, and equation (3.49), which determines the foreign investment at a given interest rate. For the sake of a more straightforward interpretation of the results, we will not consider the last of these equations explicitly. Thus, we have

$$z = s(ae+bc) + (1 - S)(AE + BC),$$ (3.2)

$$c = g(-z)f(k_0 + I,e) - rI,$$ (3.3)

and the comparative statics are given by

$$\begin{pmatrix} 1 & -sb \\ g'f + (r - gf_k)\dfrac{dI}{dz} & 1 \end{pmatrix} \begin{pmatrix} dz \\ dc \end{pmatrix} = \begin{pmatrix} 1 \\ g'f - (r - gf_k)\dfrac{dI}{de} \end{pmatrix} de.$$ (3.50)

Maximization of the welfare function yields as a condition for an optimal environmental policy

$$t^{e*} = gf_e = sa\frac{g'fu_1 + (r - gf_k)u_1\dfrac{dI}{dz} + u_2}{u_1 - sbu_2} + (r - gf_k)\frac{dI}{de}.$$ (3.51)

Compared to equation (3.12), which determines the optimal environmental policy in the case where the government skims off the scarcity rent, the tax rate is augmented by the two terms containing dI/dz and dI/de. These terms did not turn up in equation (3.12) due to $r = gf_k$. However, if the scarcity rent goes to the owners of capital, the rate of return exceeds the marginal productivity of capital. The implication of equation (3.51) then is:

Proposition 3.22: If lax environmental policies and high levels of environmental pollution attract foreign direct investment, then a country which leaves the scarcity rent of environmental resources to capital owners, uses a higher emission tax rate than a country in which the government collects this rent.

This is a generalization of the result obtained by Wellisch (1995), who did not discuss external effects on production. The explanation is that environmental taxes are used not only to internalize environmental damage but also to correct for the distortion which is generated by the subsidization of capital. Since it is known that a part of the scarcity rent leaves the country if foreign direct investment is undertaken, environmental policy is used to restrict this outflow of income by reducing the attractiveness of the country to foreign investors. If foreign direct investments react to changes in environmental policy in the expected way, this can be achieved by a restrictive environmental policy. Tight environmental policies drive capital out of the country and reduce the outflow of income. Therefore, the emission tax rate tends to be higher than the marginal environmental damage. This is the opposite of what has been called environmental dumping.

It should be noted, however, that environmental policy does not always have the expected impact on foreign direct investment. This is so far several reasons two of which will be mentioned here. The first one is evident from equation (3.51). A polluted environment may have a negative impact on capital productivity and, therefore, may make a country less attractive for foreign investors. If this effect dominates, then a lax environmental policy is advisable to reduce the appropriation of rent income by foreigners. The second reason is that it is by no means clear that a lax environmental policy attracts foreign capital even if production is independent of the state of the environment, i.e. if $g' = g'' = 0$. Total differentiation of the home-country part of equation (3.49) yields

$$\frac{dI}{de} = \frac{gf_e + egf_{ee} + (k_0 + I)gf_{ke}}{r - gf_k - (k_0 + I)gf_{kk} - egf_{ke}} \tag{3.52}$$

The first two terms in the numerator denote the effect of a change in emissions on the scarcity rent. This may be positive or negative, e.g. if the (hypothetical) emission tax revenue has the properties of a Laffer curve. Remember that foreign capital owners benefit from a large scarcity rent. The third term is the effect of emissions on the marginal productivity of capital and it is positive. The first three terms in the denominator together are positive, the last one is negative. It denotes the negative impact of foreign direct investment on the scarcity rent. If the absolute value of this term is large, the sign of dI/de may be reversed.[39]

---

[39] An alternative explanation is given by Sinn (1994). Equation (3.49) can be rewritten: $(k_0+I)gf_k+egf_e = (k_0+I)r$. On the left-hand side we have capital income plus the scarcity rent of the environmental resource. In the case of constant returns to scale, this income exhausts the GDP and the rate of return equals the average productivity of capital. In the case of diminishing returns to scale, there remains a residual: the income of an additional, immobile factor which we call labour, l. If we take account of this factor and augment $f(k,e)$ by a third argument, we can rewrite (3.52) such that $gf - lgf_l = (k_0+I)r$. Total differentiation then yields.

$$\frac{dI}{de} = \frac{gf_e - lgf_e}{r - gf_k + lgf_{kl}}$$

If labour and emissions and labour and capital are substitutes (i.e. $gf_{le}>0$ and $gf_{kl}>0$), dI/de is positive. Otherwise, it may be negative.

Finally, consider the case of constant returns to scale. For this scenario, the rate of return equals the average productivity, and we have $c = rk_0$. Consumption is independent of the allocation of the capital stock since competition between capital owners makes the whole scarcity rent disappear. This implies that the opportunity cost of reducing emissions is zero and that, therefore, prohibitive environmental standards are chosen. Such a country would transfer its whole capital stock abroad and domestic production would be zero. This is rather unrealistic—as are constant returns to scale in this model. Constant returns to scale with respect to capital and emissions would be reasonable if there were no private immobile factors of production.

The conclusion that a command-and-control approach to environmental policy tends to lead to too stringent environmental policies may be viewed as a variation of well-known results in the tax-competition literature. There, it has been shown that taxation of the mobile factor of production leads to an underprovision of public goods (including environmental quality) (see Wilson (1986, 1987) and Zodrow and Mieszkowski (1986)). A fiscal externality is generated since jurisdictions compete against each other for a part of the tax base. They do this either by means of low taxes on capital or by subsidizing the use of public goods (like environmental resources) by private enterprises. In this section, we have obtained the opposite result since capital is not taxed but subsidized. The ambiguities in the results arise from the fact that the subsidy is not related to the use of the public input itself but to the revenue that could be derived from taxing this input.

3.13 Summary of Results

1. A small economy benefits from increased openness if it has chosen an efficient environmental policy instrument and if its environmental policy is optimal.
2. In the large-country case, the efficiency gains from increased openness may be offset by the negative effects of transfrontier pollution spillovers even if the environmental policy is optimal.
3. The international capital movements induced by a tight environmental policy of a large country may cause increased pollution from abroad and/or increased pollution from domestic consumption. The latter effect, however, requires a substantial change in the rate of return on the mobile factor which is unlikely to be observed in reality.
4. International capital mobility may aggravate international environmental problems. Tight environmental policies induce capital flight and increased emissions in the host country. This reduces the benefits of such a policy in terms of environmental quality improvements. Therefore, too lax policies tend to be chosen.

5. Large countries can use environmental policies to affect the remuneration of the mobile factor in their favour. In reality, however, this effect is probably very small.

6. The optimal environmental policy chosen in one country is affected by the policy instrument chosen in the other country.

7. The utilization of environmental policy to affect the remuneration of the internationally mobile factor leads to a suboptimal factor allocation. Too lax environmental standards in all countries are possible even in the case of purely domestic pollution.

8. Interventions in capital markets that take the shape of subsidies or taxes can help a large country to reduce negative pollution spillovers from abroad. The underlying mechanism is the reduction of environmental capital flight.

9. In the case of transfrontier pollution problems, the first-best policy is a combination of free international capital movements and an international environmental agreement that involves side-payments.

10. Monopolistic supply of foreign capital leads to relaxed environmental standards.

11. If the scarcity rent of the environmental resource is appropriated by capital owners, a move from autarky to capital imports leads to welfare losses even if the initial environmental policy has been optimal.

12. If the scarcity rent of the environmental resource is appropriated by capital owners, optimal environmental policies may either under or over-internalize environmental damage. The case of too strict environmental standards appears to be the more realistic one.

13. If the mobile factor of production is taxed, small countries tend to choose too lax environmental policies.

Appendix: Results for the Case of Emission Taxes

3.A1 Parameter Changes in the Small Country

There are three equations determining consumption, emissions and environmental quality. Total differentiation yields:

$$\begin{pmatrix} gf_{ee} & -g'f_e & 0 \\ -sa & 1 & -sb \\ -gf_e & g'f & 1 \end{pmatrix} \begin{pmatrix} de \\ dz \\ dc \end{pmatrix} = \begin{pmatrix} dt^e \\ se\,da + sc\,db + \dots \\ 0 \end{pmatrix} \tag{3.A1}$$

and by applying Cramer's rule, we obtain

$$\frac{de}{dt^e} = \frac{1 + sbgf'}{gf_{ee}(1 + sbg'f) - g'f_e s(a + bgf_e)} < 0, \tag{3.A2a}$$

$$\frac{dz}{dt^e} = \frac{s(a + bgf_e)}{gf_{ee}(1 + sbg'f) - g'f_e s(a + bgf_e)} < 0, \tag{3.A2b}$$

$$\frac{de}{da} = \frac{sag'f_e}{gf_{ee}(1 + sbg'f) - g'f_e s(a + bgf_e)} < 0, \tag{3.A2c}$$

$$\frac{dz}{da} = \frac{segf_{ee}}{gf_{ee}(1 + sbg'f) - g'f_e s(a + bgf_e)} > 0, \tag{3.A2d}$$

The numerator of the fractions on the right-hand side, i.e. the determinant of the matrix in equation (3.A1) is negative. Among the environmental-impact parameters, a has been taken as an example. The impact of the other parameters follows by analogy. It follows that the effects on the autarky rate of return on capital are

$$\frac{d(gf_k)}{dt^e} = \frac{gf_{ke}(1 + sbg'f) - g'f_k s(a + bgf_e)}{gf_{ee}(1 + sbg'f) - g'f_e s(a + bgf_e)}, \tag{3.A3a}$$

$$\frac{d(gf_k)}{da} = \frac{segg'(f_e f_{ke} - f_k f_{ee})}{gf_{ee}(1 + sbg'f) - g'f_e s(a + bgf_e)} < 0. \tag{3.A3b}$$

The marginal productivity of capital is increased if the impact parameter is raised. The effect of the emission tax rate is ambiguous.

3.A2 Effects of Increased Openness in the Small Country

Totally differentiating equations (3.2), (3.3), and (3.4) yields

$$\begin{pmatrix} gf_{ee} & -g'f_e & 0 \\ -sa & 1 & -sb \\ -gf_e & g'f & 1 \end{pmatrix} \begin{pmatrix} de \\ dz \\ dc \end{pmatrix} = \begin{pmatrix} -gf_{ke}\,dI \\ 0 \\ (gf_k - r)\,dI \end{pmatrix}. \tag{3.A4}$$

It follows that

$$\frac{de}{dI} = \frac{t^k sbg' f_e - gf_{ke}(1 + sbg' f)}{gf_{ee}(1 + sbg' f) - g' f_e s(a + bgf_e)},$$ (3.A5a)

$$\frac{dz}{dI} = \frac{sbt^k gf_{ee} - s(a + bgf_e)gf_{ke}}{gf_{ee}(1 + sbg' f) - g' f_e s(a + bgf_e)} > 0,$$ (3.A5b)

$$\frac{dc}{dI} = \frac{t^k(gf_{ee} - sag' f_e) + (sag' f - gf_e)gf_{ke}}{gf_{ee}(1 + sbg' f) - g' f_e s(a + bgf_e)}.$$ (3.A5c)

The impact of increased openness on consumption and emissions is ambiguous. Environmental quality is reduced. The ambiguities are due to the externality affecting production. Without this external effect, the comparative-static results would be unambiguous: dc/dI and de/dI would both be positive.

The effect of increased openness on welfare is

$$\frac{dw}{dI} = \frac{t^k gf_{ee}(u_1 - sbu_2) - t^k sag' f_e - u_1 gf_{ke}(gf_e - sag' f - s(a + sbg_e)\frac{u_2}{u_1})}{gf_{ee}(1 + sbg' f) - g' f_e s(a + bgf_e)}.$$ (3.A6)

In the case of an optimal environmental policy, equation (3.11) can be used and

$$\frac{dw}{dI} = \frac{t^k gf_{ee}(u_1 - sbu_2) - t^k sag' f_e}{gf_{ee}(1 + sbg' f) - g' f_e s(a + bgf_e)} > 0.$$

The results for the capital-rich country differ from those of the capital-poor country. This is due to the fact that, with increased openness, the foreign country employs less capital than before whereas the capital stock employed in the home country is increased. The formulae of the comparative statics for the foreign country are very similar to those derived above. All lower-case letters are replaced by upper-case letters and, most importantly, we have $-GF_{KE}$ instead of gf_{ke} everywhere. This implies that in the foreign country emissions are an increasing function of openness whereas the impacts on consumption and environmental quality are ambiguous.

3.A3 Changes in Environmental Policies

In addition to equations (3.2), (3.2'), (3.20), (3.20'), and (3.21), a sixth equation has to be considered: the marginal productivity of emissions should equal the emission tax (equation (3.4')). Total differentiation yields

$$\begin{vmatrix} 1 & 0 & -sb & (S-1)B & 0 & (S-1)A \\ 0 & 1 & (s-1)b & -SB & 0 & -SA \\ -g'f - g'f_k I & 0 & 1 & 0 & gf_{kk}I - t^k & 0 \\ 0 & G'F + G'F_K I & 0 & 1 & GF_{KK}I + T^K & -GF_E - GF_{KE}I \\ -g'f_k & G'F_K & 0 & 0 & gf_{kk} + GF_{KK} & -GF_{KE} \\ 0 & -G'F_K & 0 & 0 & -GF_{KE} & GF_{EE} \end{vmatrix} \begin{pmatrix} dz \\ dZ \\ dc \\ dC \\ dI \\ dE \end{pmatrix} = \begin{pmatrix} sa\,de \\ (1-s)a\,de \\ (gf_e - gf_{ke}I)\,de \\ 0 \\ -gf_{kk}de \\ 0 \end{pmatrix}.$$ (3.A7)

The two scenarios will be discussed in which either there are no external effects on production or no consumption externalities.

Scenario 1 $b = B = 0$

The determinant, Δ, is positive:

$$\Delta = G^2 \left(F_{KK} F_{EE} - F_{KE}^2 \right) + g f_{kk} GF_{EE} + (1 - S) AGF_{KE} g' f_k$$
$$+ SAG'(F_K GF_{KE} - F_E(GF_{KK} + gf_{kk}))$$

and the effects of a change in domestic emissions on domestic environmental quality and on foreign emissions are:

$$\frac{dE}{de} = \frac{1}{\Delta}(-GF_{KE}(gf_{ke} - sag' f_k) - (1-s)aG' (F_K GF_{KE} - F_E(GF_{KK} + gf_{kk}))), \qquad (3.A8a)$$

$$\frac{dz}{de} = \frac{1}{\Delta}(sa(G^2(F_{EE}F_{KK} - F_{KE}^2) + GF_{EE}gf_{kk}) - (1 - S)AGF_{KE}gf_{ke}$$

$$+ ((1-s)a(1-S)A - saSA)(G' F_E(GF_{KK} + gf_{kk}) - G' F_K GF_{KE})). \qquad (3.A8b)$$

Both effects are ambiguous. Since there is an external effect on production, the direction of the induced capital flow becomes indeterminate and thus the effect on the marginal productivity of emissions in the foreign country is ambiguous. The effect of emissions on environmental quality becomes ambiguous since foreign emissions may be a declining function of domestic emissions. The impacts on consumption and foreign direct investments remain ambiguous.

Scenario 2 ($g' = G' = 0$)

Matters are a bit simpler in this case and the comparative-static results are

$$\frac{dz}{de} = \frac{-GF_{EE}gf_{ke}}{G^2(F_{EE}F_{KK} - F_{KE}^2) + GF_{EE}gf_{kk}} > 0, \qquad (3.A9a)$$

$$\frac{dE}{de} = \frac{-GF_{KE}gf_{ke}}{G^2(F_{EE}F_{KK} - F_{KE}^2) + GF_{EE}gf_{kk}} < 0, \qquad (3.A9b)$$

$$\frac{dc}{de} = gf_e - gf_{ke} \frac{GF_{EE}t^k + G^2 (F_{EE}F_{KK} - F_{KE}^2)I}{G^2(F_{EE}F_{KK} - F_{KE}^2) + GF_{EE}gf_{kk}}, \qquad (3.A9c)$$

$$\frac{dC}{de} = gf_{ke} \frac{G^2(F_{FF} - F_{KE}^2)I - GF_{EE}T^K - GF_E GF_{KE}}{G^2(F_{EE}F_{KK} - F_{KE}^2) + GF_{EE}gf_{kk}}, \qquad (3.A9d)$$

$$\frac{dz}{de} = sa + (1 - S)A\frac{dE}{de} + sb\frac{dc}{de} + (1 - S)B\frac{dC}{de}, \qquad (3.A9e)$$

$$\frac{dZ}{de} = (1 - s)a + SA\frac{dE}{de} + (1 - s)b\frac{dc}{de} + SB\frac{dC}{de}. \qquad (3.A9f)$$

3.A4 Barriers to Factor Mobility and Environmental Policies

If the impact of a barrier to factor mobility is to be considered, a column vector equalling the transpose of $(0, 0, I\, dt^k, 0, dt^k, 0)$ has to be added to the right-hand side of equation (3.A7). For scenario 2 ($g' = G' = 0$), the following results are obtained:

$$\frac{dI}{dt^k} = \frac{GF_{EE}}{G^2(F_{EE}F_{KK} - F_{KE}^2) + GF_{EE}gf_{kk}} < 0, \qquad (3.A10a)$$

$$\frac{dE}{dt^k} = \frac{GF_{KE}}{G^2(F_{EE}F_{KK} - F^2_{KE}) + GF_{EE}gf_{kk}} > 0, \tag{3.A10b}$$

$$\frac{dc}{dt^k} = \frac{GF_{EE}t^k + G^2(F_{EE}F_{KK} - F^2_{KE})I}{G^2(F_{EE}F_{KK} - F^2_{KE}) + GF_{EE}gf_{kk}}, \tag{3.A10c}$$

$$\frac{dC}{dt^k} = \frac{G^2(F_{EE}F_{KK} - F^2_{KE})\,I - GF_{EE}T^k - GF_EGF_{KE}}{G^2(F_{EE}F_{KK} - F^2_{KE}) + GF_{EE}gf_{kk}}, \tag{3.A10d}$$

$$\frac{dz}{dt^k} = (1-S)A\frac{de}{dt^k} + sb\frac{dc}{dt^k} + (1-S)B\frac{dC}{dt^k}, \tag{3.A10e}$$

$$\frac{dZ}{dt^k} = SA\frac{dE}{dt^k} + (1-s)b\frac{dc}{dt^k} + SB\frac{dC}{dt^k}. \tag{3.A10f}$$

4

International Trade in Hazardous Waste

4.1 Introduction

International trade in toxic waste is a controversial issue. The extreme positions are those of the free-trade advocate and of the environmentalist.[1] The liberal position is that the acceptance of toxic waste in exchange for goods must be mutually beneficial. Otherwise the exchange would not take place. The exporters benefit since they get rid of the problem of storing the waste; the importers gain because they are compensated in terms of better-consumption possibilities.[2] Environmentalists argue that the recipients of the waste are not free to choose. Usually these countries are relatively poor and, therefore, have a weaker position than the waste exporters. Moreover, it is often argued that the storing facilities in poor countries are unsafe compared to those existing in the exporting countries and the worldwide pollution problems may be aggravated for that reason. On top of that, there may be information asymmetries in that the exporter has better information about the composition of the toxic waste and about its least damaging treatment. Thus, trade in toxic waste tends to be inefficient–at least in the technical meaning of the term. Another green argument is that the possibility to export environmental problems reduces the incentives to solve them. If trade in hazardous waste were banned, the main exporters would have to find ways to avoid the creation of waste, and this would be beneficial to the environment.[3]

This chapter is devoted to the examination of these views on the advantages and disadvantages of free trade in hazardous substances. Moreover, a number of other problems will be addressed. One of them is the choice of the environmental policy. How does the possibility to dump one's own waste into one's neighbour's backyard affect the design of environmental policy? In a next step, strategic considerations have to be taken into account. There may be incentives to capture rents by designing environmental policies appropriately. This results

[1] See Wynne (1989) and Hilz and Ehrenfeld (1991) for arguments in favour of and against toxic-waste trade.

[2] This line of argument has been carried to extremes by Lawrence Summers in an internal World Bank memo parts of which have been published in *The Economist* 1992 and led to major controversies (see Anonymous (1992)). He argued that it would be optimal to export toxic waste to the countries with the lowest incomes since toxic waste would cause the least damage there in terms of forgone income. For a critique, see Swaney (1994).

[3] These and other green positions are presented by Moyers (1990) and Daly and Goodland (1994).

in non-co-operative policy equilibria that are usually suboptimal. Another question is that of regulating trade in toxic waste. Can barriers to trade solve environmental problems? Finally, there is the issue of power. A large country wishing to dump its waste on another country's territory may profit from its economic power if the recipient country is small. This is one of the problem areas of the North–South debate. The question is whether the recipient country will experience welfare losses and how they can be avoided.

These questions will be addressed in the framework of a simple two-country model. Two goods are considered. They are a consumption good and hazardous waste. Strictly speaking, toxic waste is not a good but a bad. Its price is negative. Trade is characterized by a materials flow into only one direction. The waste-exporting country also exports consumption goods which compensate the recipient for the effort to store the waste. Thus, what is really traded is not waste but the service of storing it. The model will be simpler than normal trade models since the storage of waste is assumed not to require any resources. It simply aggravates the recipient country's environmental problems. The model is closely related to the factor-movements model in the respect that only one good, the consumption good, is produced. In the autarky case the two models are indeed identical. A similar model has been investigated by Copeland (1991), albeit only for the small-country case and without consideration of transfrontier pollution.

Although the model is rather general, it will not encompass all relevant problems. One important simplification is the neglect of intertemporal issues. The accumulation of waste will not be considered. If waste decays very slowly, this generates an irreversibility problem which is similar to the exhaustion problem that a resource-exporting country faces.[4] Another major issue in the public policy debate which will not be addressed here is that of illegal waste exports.[5] Notwithstanding that this is an enormous problem in reality, the following analysis will deal with normative issues rather than issues of enforcement and control. None the less, enforcement problems can be introduced into the model by reinterpreting some variables, e.g. an emission tax may be interpreted as the expected penalty for discharging pollutants, i.e. the penalty times the probability of being detected.

This chapter is organized as follows. The next section presents the model. Section 3 is devoted to the explanation of patterns of trade. In Section 4, gains and losses from trade will be analysed. The impact of environmental policies on international trade and the design of optimal environmental policies will be addressed in Section 5. Section 6 deals with the effects of conjectural variation and Section 7 looks at the interaction of national environmental policies in a Nash-equilibrium framework. In Section 8, we will address the question of barriers to trade and the issue of market power will be dealt with. Section 9 summarizes the results.

[4] See Siebert (1985b) and Withagen (1985) for overviews.
[5] Copeland's (1991) paper deals with illegal waste exports explicitly.

4.2 The Model

There are two countries, the home country (represented by lower-case letters) and the foreign country (represented by upper-case letters). The notation has been introduced in Section 2.6. It is assumed that all toxic waste is generated during the production process.[6] The quantities of toxic waste generated by the home country and by the foreign country are e and E, respectively. x is the quantity exported from the home to the foreign country. Of course, x would be negative if the direction of trade were reversed. e^0 and E^0 denote the quantities of waste finally deposited in the home and the foreign countries. Thus

$$e = e^0 + x, \tag{4.1}$$

$$E = E^0 - x. \tag{4.1'}$$

In order to simplify notation, we assume that the countries are named such that the home country is always the exporter of toxic waste and the foreign country is always the importer of toxic waste:

$$x > 0.$$

As in the previous chapter, the pollutants are modelled as inputs into the production process. Thus, the factors of production are capital and waste and there is a negative external effect of pollution on output. The functions are specified as in Chapter 3.

$$q = g(-z)f(k, e^0 + x), \tag{4.2}$$

$$Q = G(-Z)F(K, E^0 - x). \tag{4.2'}$$

In contrast to the previous section, it is assumed that consumption does not pollute the environment. This assumption will simplify the analysis considerably. Moreover, we wish to concentrate on the supply-side effects of toxic-waste generation and trade. A change in the hazardous-waste trade, for instance, may affect consumption but the environmental impact of these changes in consumption will be small compared to that of toxic-waste trade. Thus, we assume that the environmental-impact parameters of consumption are zero: $b = B = 0$. Let a and A be the environmental-impact parameters of toxic waste. One may argue that $a = A$ since, due to equations (4.1) and (4.1'), domestic and foreign toxic waste can be added up and are, therefore, the same substances. Nevertheless, there may still be some differences, e.g. in the technologies of storage such that this restricting assumption needs not to be made. (It does not change the results anyway.) γ denotes the environmental damage due to the international transport of hazardous waste. For simplicity, it is assumed that

---

[6] Of course, this is a restrictive assumption. None the less, anecdotal evidence suggests that toxic waste generated by households is much less important then toxic industrial waste. A generalized version of the model, which includes trade in toxic waste generated by consumption activities, would be even more difficult to handle than the present version.

the transport risk is equally shared between the two countries. If x is negative, γ should be negative as well.

$$z = sae^0 + (1 - S)AE^0 + \gamma\, x, \tag{4.3}$$

$$Z = (1 - s)ae^0 + SAE^0 + \gamma\, x \tag{4.3'}$$

Let the consumption good be the numéraire and let p be the world market price of the service of storing toxic waste in terms of the consumption good. Assume that trade is balanced. Then the consumption possibilities in the two countries are given by the output of the economy plus or minus the payment made to the country receiving the toxic waste.

$$c = g(-z)f(k, e^0 + x) - p\, x, \tag{4.4}$$

$$C = G(-Z)F(K, E^0 - x) + p\, x \tag{4.4'}$$

Given these basic equations that characterize the two economies, it is obvious that the storage of hazardous waste is modelled in a rather simplistic way. Storing waste merely affects current environmental quality. It does not require factors of production, there are no pollution-abatement activities that are associated with the storage process, and intertemporal issues are neglected as well. This is a simplification compared to Copeland's (1991) model.

Two policy instruments are considered. The government may regulate the use of environmental resources and the trade in toxic substances. The environmental policy instrument may be an emission tax or an upper limit to emissions accompanied by a tradable-permits scheme. In a competitive economy, these instruments are equivalent. The emission tax is denoted by a superscript e and a trade tax by a superscript t. The emission tax rate, t^e or T^e, is to be paid for hazardous waste stored in the home and the foreign countries, respectively: the tax bases are e^0 and E^0, respectively. Under perfect competition, the following conditions will hold:

$$g(-z)f_e(k, e^0 + x) = t^e = p + t^t, \tag{4.5}$$

$$G(-Z)F_E(K, E^0 - x) = T^e = p - T^t. \tag{4.5'}$$

The domestic exporters of toxic waste pay the world market price plus the home country's export tax. In the optimum, they are indifferent between exporting and paying domestic taxes. Foreign importers are paid the world market price minus the import tax and an analogous indifference condition holds. Tax revenues are assumed to be redistributed in a lump-sum fashion.

Finally, welfare is a function of consumption and environmental quality:

$$w = u(c, -z), \tag{4.6}$$

$$W = U(C, -Z), \tag{4.6'}$$

where $u(.\,,.)$ and $U(.\,,.)$ are assumed to be additively separable and to have the usual properties of utility functions. This completes the exposition of the model.

4.3 Explaining the Patterns of Trade

The home country will export toxic waste if its autarky price is higher than that of the foreign country. The domestic producers are willing to pay a price which is below the domestic emission tax rate. Foreigners are willing to accept waste at a price that exceeds the emission tax rate that they have to pay to their government. Thus, the condition for trade in toxic waste turns out to be

$$g(-z)f_e(k,e) = t^e > T^e = G(-Z)F_E(K,E) \qquad (4.7)$$

Proposition 4.1. The country with the lower emission tax rate will be the exporter of toxic waste.

This is a rather simple condition and it reflects the simplistic assumption of the model that no resources are required for storing toxic waste. In a more general model the cost of storage should be taken into account additionally.

If the government has chosen environmental taxes as the policy instrument, then condition (4.7) determines the direction of trade and other parameters have no influence. If, however, the government employs a quantitative instrument, e.g. if it fixes the economy-wide level of emissions (quantity of toxic waste) and employs a tradable-permits scheme to allocate emission rights to individual producers, the implicit tax rate may be affected by the parameters of the model. Totally differentiating equation (4.3) yields $dz/de^0 > 0$, $dz/dE^0 > 0$, $dz/da > 0$, $dz/dA > 0$, $dz/ds > 0$, $dz/d(1 - S) > 0$. The impacts of changes in e^0 and the other parameters on the implicit tax rate can now easily be determined:

$$d(gf_e)/de^0 = gf_{ee} - sag'f_e < 0, \qquad (4.8a)$$

$$d(gf_e)/dE^0 = -(1 - S)Ag'f_e < 0, \qquad (4.8b)$$

$$d(gf_e)/d(sa) = -e^0g'f_e < 0, \qquad (4.8c)$$

$$d(gf_e)/d((1 - S)A) = -e^0g'f_e < 0. \qquad (4.8d)$$

Moreover, it has been assumed that the cross-derivative of the production function is negative. This allows us to derive the impact of the capital endowment on the implicit tax rate on toxic waste:

$$gf_{ke} > 0. \qquad (4.8e)$$

Thus:

Proposition 4.2. Let the government determine the quantity of the waste deposited in a country. Then a country exports toxic waste if the environmental regulation is restrictive (i.e. if domestic deposition is small) or if its environmental-impact parameters are small. Everything else being equal, the (capital-) rich country will export toxic waste.

It is obvious that low emissions imply a high implicit emission tax rate and therefore lead to waste exports. But why are low environmental-impact parameters responsible for waste exports? If these parameters are small, environmental quality is good and the producers face a high productivity of the environmental resource. Thus, they wish to increase the quantity of this input. However, the domestic stock of waste, e^0, is fixed and the input of the environmental resource can be increased only if toxic waste is exported. The impact of the capital stock can be explained as follows. If the external effect on production is small, the marginal productivity of emissions is an increasing function of the capital stock for a given level of emissions. A capital-rich country having set the same level of emissions as a capital-poor country uses relatively strict environmental standards and will export toxic waste. This result may be reversed if the external effect on production is substantial.

What determines environmental policy? If politicians are benevolent, they take into account not only the technological parameters but also preferences. The welfare-maximizing policy is characterized by

$$t^{e*} = gf_e = sag'f + sa\frac{u_2}{u_1}, \tag{4.9}$$

where t^{e*} is the optimal emission tax rate.[7] The optimal emission tax rate equals the social cost of environmental disruption, which negatively affects environmental quality as a factor of production as well as a consumption good. The impact of the various parameters on the optimal emission level can now be obtained by total differentiation of this equation. Three parameters are considered: the degree of environmental concern, measured by the marginal utility of environmental quality, u_2, the wealth of the economy, measured by its capital stock, k, and one of the pollution-impact parameters. Comparative-static results for the other parameters can be obtained by analogous reasoning. Application of implicit-function theorem yields:

$$w_{ee}de^0 = sa\,du_2 + [(sag'f_k - gf_{ke})u_1 - (gf_e - sag'f)u_{11}gf_k]\,dk + [u_1g'f + u_2$$
$$- (gf_e - sag'f)u_{11}e^0g'f - (u_1(sag''f - g'f_e) + sau_{22})e^0]\,d(sa). \tag{4.10}$$

One should note that the term $(gf_e - sag'f)$, which occurs in the squared brackets on the right-hand side, is positive. This can be seen by rearranging the first-order condition, equation (4.9). Thus, the following results are obtained:

- The impact of du_2 on the optimal level of waste deposition is unambiguously negative. An increase in environmental concern leads to a reduction in domestic deposition and, therefore, to an increase in the emission tax rate.[8] The willingness to export toxic waste is increased.
- The capital stock has an ambiguous effect on the optimal level of deposition of toxic waste. This would be the case even in a simple model without external effects on production. On the one hand, an additional unit of capital raises the productivity of emissions and therefore the consumption possibility set; on the other hand, the increase in consumption leads to a

[7] A similar result was derived in Ch. 3. Compare equation (3.12). The difference is that we have assumed now that consumption does not pollute the environment.

[8] That lower emissions require higher emission taxes is economically intuitive. Algebraically, it follows from $d(gf_e)/de = gf_{ee} - g'f_e\,(dz/de)$.

reduction of the marginal utility of consumption. It is not clear which effect will dominate. The external effect on production has an additional impact. An increase in the capital stock increases the importance of change in the efficiency parameter, g', for the productivity of emissions. Thus, the larger k, the smaller e^0, if this effect is the dominant one. The impact of the capital endowment on the emission tax rate is ambiguous as well.

- The effect of a change in sa on waste deposition is negative. This is plausible since any increase in sa will raise the marginal cost of environmental disruption. An ambiguity arises if the effect on the marginal productivity of emissions is concerned. Although an increase in a leads to a reduction of the optimal emission level, this does not necessarily imply a higher emission tax rate. Since $dz/d(sa) > 0$ (from equation 4.8c)), the marginal productivity, gf_e, may be reduced by an increase in a. Of course, this effect is relatively unimportant if g'' is small.

Proposition 4.3. Let the environmental policy be welfare-maximizing. Everything else being equal, the country with a higher degree of environmental concern will be the exporter of toxic waste. The impact of the pollution-impact parameters is generally indeterminate. If the external effect on production is small, the country in which one of these parameters is higher will be an exporter of toxic waste. The effect of the capital endowment is ambiguous.

Summarizing the results of this section, we end up with the conclusion that tight environmental standards or preferences and technological parameters that lead to tight standards are likely to make a country export toxic waste. This does not mean that tight standards are a bad thing. It just reflects the fact that tight standards lead to a reduction of domestic deposition and one way of achieving this is to export toxic waste. It is often argued by environmentalists that domestic generation of hazardous waste should be reduced instead and that, therefore, these exports are undesirable. The desirability of toxic-waste trade will be the subject of the next section.

4.4 Benefits and Losses from Trade in Toxic Waste

Liberals argue that trade in toxic waste is beneficial to all parties involved. If there are losers due to differences in endowments, the losers may be compensated by those who gain and the net effect is positive. The green position, in contrast, is that trade in toxic waste is harmful, in particular to the importers of toxic waste, and that each country should take care of its own waste. It will be shown that both views can be correct in certain circumstances. The method of addressing this issue will be the following one. We will start from a situation with a trade restriction that prevents trade completely. Then the border is opened marginally and the effects of toxic-waste exports on consumption and environmental quality are analysed. These effects then determine the welfare effect. The analysis is restricted to the small-country case, i.e. it is assumed that trade in toxic waste does not induce changes of environmental policies in the other country (the rest of the world). Thus, p is constant.

In a first step, it is assumed that environmental policies determine e^0. The government defines the maximum quantity of toxic waste that may be deposited in the country. Total differentiation of equations (4.3) and (4.4) yields

$$\begin{pmatrix} 1 & 0 \\ g'f & 1 \end{pmatrix} \begin{pmatrix} dz \\ dc \end{pmatrix} = \begin{pmatrix} \gamma\,dx \\ (gf_e - p)\,dx \end{pmatrix}. \tag{4.11}$$

It follows that

$$\frac{dz}{dx} = \gamma > 0, \tag{4.12a}$$

$$\frac{dc}{dx} = (gf_e - p) - \gamma g' f. \tag{4.12b}$$

The same kind of reasoning applied to the waste-importing foreign country yields

$$\frac{dZ}{dx} = \gamma > 0, \tag{4.12'a}$$

$$\frac{dC}{dx} = (p - GF_E) - \gamma G' F. \tag{4.12'b}$$

It should be noted that, according to (4.7),

$$gf_e > p > GF_E.$$

This results in an efficiency gain since the willingness of the waste-exporting country to pay for the storage of toxic waste exceeds the price and the price exceeds the willingness of the importing country to accept compensation.

Equations (4.12a) and (4.12'a) state that the impact of toxic-waste trade on pollution is positive due to the transportation problem. Note that the total quantities of toxic substances prevailing in the two countries have been assumed to be constant. The effect of trade on consumption is ambiguous since the efficiency gain may be offset by a negative environmental externality due to the transport cost.

The welfare effects are

$$\frac{dw}{dx} = (gf_e - p)u_1 - \gamma(g' f u_1 + u_2), \tag{4.13}$$

$$\frac{dW}{dx} = (p - GF_E)U_1 - \gamma(G' F U_1 + U_2). \tag{4.13'}$$

This implies:

Proposition 4.4. If the transport problem is small and if environmental policies fix the total quantity of toxic substances in each country, then trade is mutually beneficial.

This optimistic result is an artefact of the assumptions underlying this analysis. Since it has been assumed that e^0 and E^0 are given, the quantities of hazardous waste deposited in the countries will remain unchanged. The waste-importing country reduces its own emissions of toxic waste by one unit for each unit of waste it imports. This is not particularly realistic and one may, therefore, wish to look at other cases.

An alternative assumption is the existence of an emission tax. The algebraic results are derived in the appendix. It can be seen that almost anything can happen in the general case and an economic intuition is often hard to give. Therefore, the following considerations will refer to the case without external effects on production ($g' = G' = 0$). Additionally, we will assume for a moment that transfrontier pollution is not a problem. If there is a given tax rate on the environmental factor of production, this factor is allocated such that its marginal productivity equals the tax rate. In the case of a marginal opening of the country to trade in toxic waste, this emission tax remains relevant for the producers.[9] Thus, the quantities of toxic waste generated by each country, $e^0 + x$ and $E^0 - x$, remain unchanged since the last unit of toxic substances is still subject to the regulation of the country under consideration. It follows that if trade is increased by one unit, the quantity of toxic substances deposited inside the country is reduced by one unit in the home country and increased by one unit in the foreign country. The domestic environment benefits and the foreign environment is harmed. Since the output is fixed if the input of the environmental resource is fixed, consumption possibilities are affected only by the compensation payments for the storage of hazardous waste. Thus, consumption is diminished in the waste-exporting home country and raised in the waste-importing foreign country. Moreover, the negative external effect of transportation has to be taken into account. If transportation costs are zero and if the environmental policy is optimal initially, there will be positive gains from trade.

In the case of non-optimal policies, there may be welfare losses. Consider the home country for a moment. It follows from the appendix, that in a situation where foreign waste generation and the world market price are given, where $g' = g'' = 0$, and where transfrontier pollution is negligible, the welfare effect of an increase in waste exports is

$$\frac{dw}{dx} = -u_1 p + u_2(sa - \gamma).^{10}$$

Using the marginal productivity condition, $t^e = gf_e$ yields

$$\frac{dw}{dx} = u_1(gf_e - p) - u_2\gamma - u_1\left(t^e - sa\frac{u_2}{u_1}\right).$$

[9] If there were a change from no trade to free trade, the tax rate would no longer be relevant and the world market price of toxic waste would determine the allocation of environmental resources. Thus, there would be a discrete change in emissions.

[10] The term in brackets on the right-hand side is the impact of hazardous-waste exports on domestic environmental quality. It is constant. The reason is that foreign generation of waste has been assumed to be constant and that due to the given world market price, domestic producers will not change their output of toxic waste as well.

The corresponding equation for the waste-importing foreign country is

$$\frac{dW}{dx} = U_1(p - GF_E) + U_2\gamma + U_1(T^e - SA\frac{U_2}{U_1}).$$

There are three effects. The first one is the efficiency gain. It is positive. The second effect measures the change in transfrontier pollution plus the transport costs. The impact of transportation is negative in both countries. The transfrontier-pollution effects differ across countries. The waste-exporting country will suffer from increased transfrontier pollution, the foreign country will profit from lower emissions in the home country. The third effect is a distortion due to non-optimal environmental policies. If environmental policies are optimal, the terms in brackets are zero. In the case of a regulatory deficit, they are negative since the emission tax is too low. In the case of too high taxes, they are positive. Let us take the scenario of the regulatory deficit to illustrate the point. In the home country, the export of hazardous waste leads to a reduction of the quantity of toxic substances. The level of pollution is reduced and is now closer to the optimal one. In the foreign country, in contrast, the level of pollution, which has already been too high initially, is further increased.

The situation can be depicted in a $(-z, c)$ space (see Figure 4.1). Part (a) refers to the home country, part (b) to the foreign country. The concave curve, T, is the transformation locus depicting the feasible combinations of consumption and environmental quality. Its shape follows from the assumptions on the production function and the specification of the pollution impacts.[11] For each country, two initial situations, A and B, are considered. Both yield the same

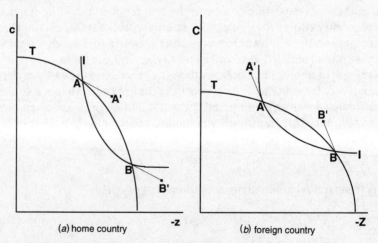

FIG. 4.1 Welfare Effects of Trade in Toxic Waste

[11] In the autarky situation, consumption is $c = g(-sae^0)f(k, e^0)$. Since $d^2c/(de^0)^2 = gf_{ee} - 2sag'f_e + (sa)^2g''f < 0$ and $z = sae^0$, it follows that c is a concave function of $-z$. The function may have an increasing segment for small values of $-z$ if the external effect on production is so strong that it dominates the direct productivity effect. This is, however, not shown in the diagram.

welfare level shown by the indifference curve I. In A, the environmental law is too strict, in situation B it is too lax. Due to the given environmental tax rate, the point of production will not be changed when trade becomes feasible. Exports and imports of toxic waste yield new consumption possibilities. The home country will profit from increased environmental quality but loses a part of its consumption bundle. The foreign country benefits in terms of goods consumption but suffers from additional environmental disruption. It is seen that the welfare effects are those derived above. First consider the foreign country. If its environmental policy is suboptimal, its emissions are too high and the marginal environmental damage is large. Toxic-waste imports cause additional damage and these welfare losses may exceed the increase in consumption possibilities due to the trade revenue. This is depicted as case A in Figure 4.1. Point A represents a lax environmental policy (with low environmental quality and a lot of consumption). B depicts a strict environmental policy. Neither of them is optimal. This example is constructed such that A and B yield the same utility level, represented by the indifference curve, I. The country now starts to import waste. It receives a compensation payment but the environmental quality is reduced. The transformation locus is shifted in a north-western direction. In case A, the lax policy, the new situation is depicted by A'. Since this point is on a lower indifference curve (which is not depicted here), there will be a welfare loss. The additional damage dominates the increase in consumption possibilities.[12] In case B, the strict policy, there will be a welfare gain. The direction of the shift is reversed for the waste-exporting country and so are the welfare effects. The waste-exporting country will experience additional welfare gains if its environmental policy is suboptimal. Exporting hazardous waste leads to large reductions in environmental damage whereas the payments to the foreign country are relatively small. Loosely speaking, the possibility to export hazardous waste is a substitute for a good domestic environmental policy.

If we now reintroduce transfrontier pollution, we may arrive at the following scenario.

Proposition 4.5. If the environmental regulation in the waste-importing country is too lax and if there are transfrontier-pollution spillovers, both countries may experience welfare losses after the opening to trade even in the case of negligible transport costs.

A real-world case may illustrate this problem. In the 1970s and 1980s, large quantities of West German toxic waste were exported to the GDR, where compensation payments were relatively low due to lax environmental standards. Arguably, these standards did not represent the true scarcity of environmental resources, then the environmental damage due to toxic-waste imports may have exceeded the compensation payments and the net welfare effect may have

---

[12] This result has also been established by Copeland (1991) in a different model framework. Illegal activities, which have been considered by Copeland (1991) explicitly, may be introduced into this model by assuming that emission taxes are paid only by a subgroup of those who store or process hazardous substances.

been negative for the GDR. Moreover, there was a serious spillover problem since the GDR stored most of these toxic substances in a place named Schönberg, which is in close vicinity to the West German city of Lübeck with more than 200,000 inhabitants. Schönberg and Lübeck share the same ground-water system and in the case of leakage, the damage to the West German economy may have turned out to be larger than the benefits from getting rid of the rubbish at a cheap price.

This confirms fears expressed by environmentalists. It would be optimal to ban toxic-waste trade. This issue will be addressed in Section 7 of this chapter.[13]

Finally, the question arises of how the possibility to import or export toxic waste affects the design of environmental policies. It is obvious that a trade tax should be introduced since the transport of toxic waste may cause environmental disruption. If there is no policy co-ordination, taxes will be set such that national damages are internalized. The optimal tax rates equal the marginal damages due to transportation. If the external effect on production is taken into account, then:[14]

$$t^{t*} = gf_e - p = \gamma\left(\frac{u_2}{u_1} + g'f\right) = \frac{\gamma}{sa} t^{e*}. \tag{4.14}$$

$$T^{T*} = p - GF_E = \gamma\left(\frac{U_2}{U_1} + G'F\right) = \frac{\gamma}{SA} T^{e*}. \tag{4.14'}$$

It is intuitive that the two tax rates are proportional. The marginal damage due to trade is γ/sa times the marginal damage due to toxic waste remaining in the domestic economy. If the transport risk is small, i.e. if $\gamma < sa$, trade in toxic waste is desirable for the home country. Otherwise, the environmental problems due to transport exceed the positive effect of waste reduction.

Using $t^e = gf_e$ and $T^e = GF_E$, one obtains

$$t^{e*} = gf_e = \frac{sa}{sa - \gamma} p,^{15} \tag{4.15}$$

$$T^{e*} = GF_E = \frac{SA}{SA - \gamma} p. \tag{4.15'}$$

It follows that the optimal emission tax in a small open economy is proportional to the price emerging in the international toxic-waste market. The higher

[13] From an economic-theory point of view, one is led to ask why the countries trade if this reduces national welfare. The answer is that the trading activities are performed by private firms or households who do not take account of the social costs of environmental disruption. A domestic exporter of toxic waste is only interested in the difference between domestic and foreign environmental taxes but neither in correcting environmental-policy failure nor in taking into account the effects of transfrontier pollution. Thus an activity which is rational from an individual point of view may be harmful from the point of view of society as a whole.

[14] Algebraically, these results are obtained by differentiating the welfare functions (4.6) and (4.6') with respect to x and taking account of the impact of waste exports on consumption and pollution, equations (4.12a, b) and (4.12'a, b). t^{e*} and T^{e*} are introduced via the first-order condition (4.9) and its equivalent for the foreign country.

[15] Of course, it is possible that $sa < \gamma$. Then the optimal policy would be to use a prohibitive tax on waste exports and determine the domestic tax rate according to equation (4.9).

the world market price, the higher the tax rate. The same relationship holds between the trade tax and the world market price. Now the impact of trade liberalization on emission taxes can be derived easily. If trade barriers are removed, the world market price is reduced from the point of view of the waste-exporting country and increased from the point of view of the waste-importing country. This implies

Proposition 4.6. Foreign trade requires the introduction of trade taxes. The removal of trade barriers leads to lower environmental taxes in the waste-exporting country and to higher taxes in the waste-importing country.

This is quite intuitive. The opportunity to 'solve' environmental problems by exporting them makes a laxer policy desirable. A country which imports toxic waste raises the marginal damage of environmental disruption and the consequence is to tighten environmental process standards.

4.5 Effects of Changes in Environmental Policy and the Design of Optimal Policies

After having analysed the effects of trade in toxic waste on welfare and on the optimal emissions, we will now turn to the question of how changes in environmental policy affect international trade. In a first step, one may wish to look at the small-country case, where the price, p, is taken as given and constant.[16] This implies that, according to equations (4.5) and (4.5'), the emission tax rates are given and constant. Since not only the price and the emission taxes are fixed but also the capital stock, not much will happen. Total differentiation of (4.5) and (4.5') yields

$$(gf_{ee} - sag'f)de^0 = -(gf_{ee} - \gamma g'f)dx, \tag{4.16}$$

$$(GF_{EE} - SAG'F)dE^0 = (GF_{EE} + \gamma G'F)dx \tag{4.16'}$$

Since an increase in e^0 denotes a relaxation of environmental regulation, equations (4.16) and (4.16') imply:

Proposition 4.7. By relaxing its environmental policy, a small country tends to reduce its waste exports. The waste-importing country will increase its waste imports if the external effect on production is small or if the transportation costs are low. Otherwise, waste imports may be reduced.

The first part of this proposition is intuitive. If a waste-exporting country relaxes its environmental regulations, there will be less pressure on domestic producers to 'solve' environmental problems by exporting toxic waste. The waste-importing country tends to raise its imports of toxic waste. With a relaxed environmental regulation, the willingness to accept foreign toxic materials is

[16] Moreover, it is assumed that the environmental policy in the other country, defined by E^0 and e^0, respectively, is not affected.

increased. This effect may be reversed, however, if the external effect on production or the transportation risk is substantial. This is for the following reason. An increase in E^0 at a given level of exports reduces the marginal productivity of emissions towards a level below the emission tax rate (which is determined by the world market price, p). If the negative environmental impact of waste imports is substantial, it may be possible that only a reduction of waste imports can establish the old equilibrium in which the marginal productivity of emissions equalled the emission tax rate. This scenario requires extreme parameter combinations (high values of γ and of G') and is, therefore, not particularly realistic. The normal case is the other one in which producers initially have no incentive to increase the emissions (due to the given tax rate) and the new emission level, E^0, can only be attained by increased waste imports.

Matters are a bit more complicated if the country under consideration is large. The price for storing toxic waste is no longer exogenous and fixed. Moreover, transfrontier pollution has to be taken into account. The relevant equations are (4.3) to (4.5) and (4.3') to (4.5'). Since consumption does not affect environmental quality, it does not have to be considered when deriving comparative-static results for the other variables. Moreover, we assume that trade is not restricted, i.e. $t^t = T^t = 0$. Total differentiation of equations (4.3), (4.3'), (4.5), and (4.5') yields

$$\begin{pmatrix} 1 & 0 & -\gamma & 0 \\ 0 & 1 & -\gamma & 0 \\ g'f_e & 0 & -gf_{ee} & 1 \\ 0 & G'F_E & GF_{EE} & 1 \end{pmatrix} \begin{pmatrix} dz \\ dZ \\ dx \\ dp \end{pmatrix} = \begin{pmatrix} sa\,de^0 \\ (1-s)a\,de^0 \\ gf_{ee}\,de^0 \\ 0 \end{pmatrix}. \tag{4.17}$$

For the most of the remainder of this chapter, it will be assumed that transport externalities are negligible or that they are not taken into account by the government's environmental policy, i.e.

$$\gamma = 0.$$

Transport externalities will be reintroduced when the optimal tariff policy is sought.

With Cramer's rule, the comparative-static results turn out to be:

$$\frac{dz}{de^0} = sa, \tag{4.18a}$$

$$\frac{dZ}{de^0} = (1-s)a, \tag{4.18b}$$

$$\frac{dx}{de^0} = \frac{-gf_{ee} + sag'f_e - (1-s)aG'F_E}{gf_{ee} + GF_{EE}} \tag{4.18c}$$

$$\frac{dp}{de^0} = \frac{gf_{ee}GF_{EE} - sag'f_eGF_{EE} - (1-s)aG'F_Egf_{ee}}{gf_{ee} + GF_{EE}} < 0. \tag{4.18d}$$

Inserting this into the equations defining the level of consumption, one obtains

$$\frac{dc}{de^0} = gf_e - sag'f - x\frac{dp}{de^0} + (gf_e - p)\frac{dx}{de^0}, \qquad (4.18e)$$

$$\frac{dC}{de^0} = -(1-s)aG'F + x\frac{dp}{de^0} - (GF_E - p)\frac{dx}{de^0}. \qquad (4.18f)$$

The results can be interpreted as follows:

- Environmental pollution in both countries is an increasing function of domestic emissions, equations (4.18a, b). This is intuitive.
- Three effects determine the exports of toxic waste. The first two of them exhibit the expected signs. With laxer environmental policies in the home country, waste exports tend to be reduced. The other impact is via transfrontier pollution. Any increase in domestic emissions leads to a reduction of the foreign productivity of emissions. This implies a reduction in the foreign emission tax rate and waste exports tend to be increased. If the foreign country is considered, these effects change their signs and the underlying intuition is similar.
- The price paid to the foreign country for storing toxic waste is negatively affected by relaxed environmental standards. A relaxed environmental policy reduces the necessity to export toxic waste.
- Domestic consumption is affected by a change of environmental policy in various ways. First, there is the direct effect of increased emissions on output and consumption. The second effect measures the external effect on output. Thirdly, there is the terms-of-trade effect. It is positive, since the home country pays less to the foreign country after having relaxed its environmental standards. Finally, there is an effect on tax revenue if the country has chosen to tax waste exports.
- Similar effects determine the change in foreign consumption. There is a transfrontier pollution spillover, a terms-of-trade effect, and a tariff-revenue effect.

Figure 4.2 illustrates some of the results. It is divided into two parts. The first depicts the effects of a change in domestic environmental policy and the second one a change in foreign policy. In both cases emissions are increased. It is easily shown that the supply of toxic waste, s, is negatively sloped whereas the foreign country's import demand curve, D, exhibits a positive slope (the trade in toxic waste is originally a trade in the service of storing toxic waste with the reversed direction of trade).[17] An increase in emissions in the home country shifts the supply curve downwards.[18] In the case of no external effects on production, the foreign country's import curve, D, remains unchanged and the price and the traded quantity of toxic waste are changed from p to p' and from x to x',

[17] Application of the implicit-function theorem to equations (4.5) and (4.5'), taking e^0 and E^0 fixed, yields $dx/dp = gf_{ee}$ for the home country and $dx/dp = -GF_{EE}$ for the foreign country.
[18] See equation (4.16) for the effect of a change in e^0 on x at a given world market price.

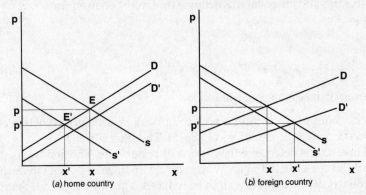

FIG. 4.2 Effects of an Increase in Emissions

respectively. If there are external effects on foreign production, however, the foreign country's import curve is moved as well. The additional emissions coming from the home country reduce the marginal productivity of the environmental factor of production abroad. The foreign producers reduce the utilization of this input. In a situation in which the environmental policy defines the total quantity of toxic waste prevailing in the foreign country, $E^0 = E + x$, waste imports will be increased until E^0 is attained. The s curve will be shifted to the right.[19] The direction of the quantity effect (the move from quantity x to x') may be reversed. By the same line of arguing, one obtains the effect of a change in foreign environmental policy in part (b) of this figure. It is seen that a reduction in domestic or foreign emissions may lead to a price reduction since the import-demand curve is shifted upwards. The quantity effect is ambiguous since in the case of substantial transfrontier pollution, the export supply curve may be shifted to the left and imports of toxic waste may be reduced.[20]

The results derived from equations (4.18a–f) and from Figure 4.2 can be summarized as follows.

Proposition 4.8. Let environmental transport costs be negligible. Then, by relaxing its environmental standards, a country reduces the price paid for the storage of toxic waste and deteriorates environmental quality at home and abroad. The effects on trade and consumption are ambiguous.

Unlike the scenario in the previous chapter, one in which a country increases its environmental problems by tightening its environmental standards is not possible here as long as transportation costs are negligible.[21] With large transportation costs this counter-intuitive result becomes feasible.

[19] Algebraically, this follows from the total differentiation of $G(-SAE^0 - (1-s)ae^0)F_E(K, E^0 - x) = p$ with respect to e^0 and x.
[20] The upward shift in the D curve follows from equation (4.16') and the shift in the s curve from total differentiation of $g(-sae^0 - (1-S)AE^0)fe(k, e^0 + x) = p$.
[21] This is due to the fact that there are no consumption externalities. A reduction of domestic emissions may result in an increase in the foreign country's revenue from trade in toxic waste. This

Proposition 4.9. If the environmental impact of transportation is large, tighter environmental standards in the exporting country can lead to additional deterioration of its environmental quality.

The intuition behind this result is that tight environmental standards at home lead to an increase in trade and, therefore, in transportation. In adverse circumstances the environmental costs of transportation may exceed those of storing the waste at home.[22]

Having identified the effects of changes in environmental policies on consumption and environmental quality, one may now pose the question of how environmental policies may be used to raise a country's welfare. The optimal environmental policy can be determined by maximization of the welfare function with respect to emissions.

The home country's welfare function is differentiated with respect to emissions. Rearranging terms then yields the following condition for the optimal level of emissions:[23]

$$g f_e = sa \frac{u_2}{u_1} + sag' f + x \frac{dp}{de^0} \tag{4.19}$$

The term on the right-hand side is the optimal emission tax rate.[24] This tax rate consists of three components. The first term is the marginal evaluation of environmental quality as a consumption good. The second term is the its marginal evaluation as a factor of production. These two terms take account of the pure environmental externalities. The third term is the terms-of-trade effect that has to be considered in a large open economy. This consists of the three components that have been discussed above. If the direct terms-of-trade effect (the first term in the numerator on the right-hand side of equation (4.18d)) dominates the other two terms and if the country is an exporter of toxic waste ($x > 0$), the optimal tax rate is lower than that internalizing the pure social cost of environmental disruption. By relaxing its environmental policy, the country

raises foreign consumption and may negatively affect environmental quality. Nevertheless, such a scenario is possible only if the parameters take values that are rather unrealistic. In particular, the transboundary pollution effects of consumption have to be substantial. The second possibility of explaining this counter-intuitive result does not rely on transfrontier pollution spillovers. If the foreign country reduces its emissions, it will benefit from the resulting increase in the world market price. Its terms of trade are improved, consumption is raised, and this has a negative effect on the environment which may dominate the positive effect of the initial emission reduction.

[22] Algebraically, this follows from applying Cramer's rule to equation (4.17) and leaving g in the expressions:

$$\frac{dz}{de^0} = \frac{sa(g f_{ee} + GF_{EE}) - \gamma g f_{ee} + \gamma(2s - 1)aG' F_E}{g f_{ee} + GF_{EE} + \gamma(G' F_E - g' f_e)}$$

[23] As in the previous chapter, there is a problem with the second-order condition since the objective function already contains a first derivative of the production function. This is due to the Stackelberg leader–follower relationship of the government and the private sector. We will again assume rather than prove that the second-order condition of optimality is satisfied and that there is an interior solution to the maximization problem.

[24] In the case of perfect competition, the tax rate equals the marginal productivity of emissions (see equation (3.4)).

reduces the price it has to pay for exporting toxic waste. This terms-of-trade improvement should be taken into account by a welfare-maximizing government. Its policy may be termed 'environmental dumping' since its environmental regulation does not take account of the social costs of environmental pollution abroad. The importing country will choose the opposite strategy and impose a tax rate higher than the marginal social cost of pollution:

$$GF_E = SA\frac{U_2}{U_1} + SAG'\,F + x\,\frac{dp}{dE^0}, \tag{4.19'}$$

where $dp/dE^0 < 0$.

Summarizing the results of this section, we arrive at

Proposition 4.10. The optimal emission tax serves two purposes. It deals with the external effects of domestic production and it is used to manipulate the terms of trade.

As in Chapter 3, this is not a first-best policy and additional policy instruments are required to improve welfare. Before we turn to this issue, however, we will look at a scenario with another foreign policy instrument.

4.6 Environmental Policies when Foreign Emission Taxes Are Taken as Given

As in the previous chapter, a conjectural variation may be considered. Until now it has been assumed that home country chooses its optimal environmental policy for given emissions in the other country. The alternative assumption is to take the foreign emission tax rate as given. In the context of this model, however, this causes a major problem. Reconsider that due to equations (4.5) and (4.5′),

$$t^e = p = T^e$$

in the absence of trade restrictions. What would happen if the emission tax rates were different across countries? The country with the lower emission tax rate would be the importer of toxic waste. The producers in the country with the more restrictive regulation would avoid paying taxes in their home country by exporting the pollutant to the foreign country which demands a lower price than the domestic tax authorities. Thus the domestic tax rate would become completely irrelevant for domestic producers. Three strategies can be chosen.

- First, the government of the home country may choose a tax rate higher than that of the foreign country. This implies that domestic producers export all the toxic waste generated in the domestic production process. This strategy is chosen if the impact of toxic waste on the domestic environment is disastrous (i.e. if *sa* is large), if domestic citizens are environmentally concerned (i.e. if u_2 is large), and if transfrontier pollution and the transport cost do not pose a major problem (i.e. if γ and $(1 - S)A$ are small). In this case, domestic environmental pollution is

$$z = (1 - S)AE^0 + \gamma x \qquad \text{with } x = e \qquad (4.20a)$$

- The second strategy is to undercut the foreign environmental taxes. Foreigners will now export all their waste to the home country. This is optimal if foreigners have a high willingness to pay if transport costs are low, if the transfrontier pollution problem is substantial, and if domestic storage is cheap in terms of environmental disruption. The environmental quality turns out to be

$$z = sae^0 + \gamma x \qquad \text{with } x = -E \qquad (4.20b)$$

If the foreign country's tax is rather low, the optimal strategy is to undercut it only by a margin. If it is large, there may be an interior optimum characterized by equation (4.19).

- The final possibility is to choose the same tax rate as the other country. In this situation, there will be no trade. The level of pollution is

$$z = sae^0 + (1 - S)AE^0. \qquad (4.20c)$$

If, at a given emission tax in the foreign country, the home country raises its own tax rate, there are two possibilities for discontinuous changes in environmental quality. If the tax rate is very low, the country imports all the toxic waste from abroad. At a particular tax level, equalling that abroad, trade will vanish and transfrontier pollution will occur. If the tax is higher than this level, the foreign country will attract all the toxic waste and transfrontier pollution is increased. Thus, there are leakage effects and in extreme cases counter-intuitive effects of environmental policies are feasible–at least theoretically.

Proposition 4.11. In the case of a given emission tax rate in the other country, tight environmental standards tend to increase the transfrontier pollution spillovers from abroad.

Finally, one may wish to ask whether situations are possible in which countries undercut each other until the level of zero regulation is attained. This is indeed possible if s and S are relatively small. If, in the extreme (and unrealistic) case, these parameters are zero, each country is negatively affected only by the waste that is stored in the other country. Thus, it is a rational strategy to avoid waste being stored in the other country. Each country has an incentive to attract all the toxic waste generated in the other country. Of course, in real-world situations, the parameters s and S are closer to one. In this case, it is likely that there is a tax level below which the environmental damage due to waste imports exceeds the compensation payment, p, which equals the emission tax rate. In this case, the process of mutual undercutting would be stopped at a positive level of the tax rate. None the less, this tax rate may be much too low compared with the one that would have been attained had environmental policies been coordinated.

What about the other extreme case? Is a not-in-my-backyard equilibrium possible? In this model, it can be excluded. Consider a situation in which the tax rates in both countries go to infinity. This implies that the compensation payment per unit of waste imported from the other country goes to infinity as well. At a low level of consumption, the marginal benefit of importing a small quantity of toxic waste will, therefore, be very large and go to infinity. The marginal environmental cost will, however, be finite. Thus, a situation with taxes going to infinity is not feasible in the framework of this model.

4.7 Co-operative versus Non-Co-operative Environmental Policies

If each country maximizes its own welfare, taking as given the environmental policy in the other country, this will result in a non-co-operative equilibrium of environmental policies. Due to the existence of externalities such as transfrontier pollution and terms-of-trade effects, non-co-operative equilibria are usually not Pareto-efficient. Both countries would benefit if they changed their environmental policies. Since each country may choose environmental policies that are either too lax or too strict, there are four possible combinations of non-optimal policies in a two-country model. Here, we are mainly interested in two of them. In which circumstances will environmental standards be too tight? This is the not-in-my-backyard case. The second case is that of too lax environmental standards. Of course, this scenario will always be the result of a policy game in which transfrontier pollution has a substantial impact. But is this scenario also possible without transfrontier pollution? If this were the case, the possibility to trade hazardous waste would be the cause of the mutual undercutting of environmental standards and one might ask whether this trade should be banned or at least restricted.

The methodological approach will be the same as in Chapter 3. We take the case of a competition in emission levels.[25] The optimal environmental policies are determined by equations (4.19) and (4.19′). These optimality conditions generate a domestic and a foreign reaction curve, and we assume that these curves intersect just once, i.e. that a unique Nash equilibrium of non-co-operative environmental policies exists. We then determine the external effects and derive iso-welfare contours. Again, it is assumed that transport costs are negligible, $\gamma = 0$.

The transboundary external effects of changes in environmental policies turn out to be

$$\frac{dZ}{de^0} = (1-s)a > 0, \tag{4.21a}$$

---

[25] The problem with the competition in emission taxes is that changes in taxes lead to discontinuities in trade and iso-welfare contours cannot be drawn.

$$\frac{dC}{de^0} = -(1-s)aG' F + x\frac{dp}{de^0} < 0, \tag{4.21b}$$

$$\frac{dz}{dE^0} = (1-S)A > 0, \tag{4.21'a}$$

$$\frac{dc}{dE^0} = -(1-S)Ag' - x\frac{dp}{dE^0}, \tag{4.21'b}$$

where dp/de^0 and dp/dE^0 are given by

$$\frac{dp}{de^0} = \frac{gf_{ee}GF_{EE} - sag' f_e GF_{EE} - (1-s)aG' F_{Eg}f_{ee}}{gf_{ee} + GF_{EE}} < 0 \tag{4.21c}$$

and

$$\frac{dp}{dE^0} = \frac{gf_{ee}GF_{EE} - (1-S)Ag' f_e GF_{EE} - SAG' F_{Eg}f_{ee}}{gf_{ee} + GF_{EE}} < 0 \tag{4.21c'}$$

The external effects of changes in environmental policy via transfrontier pollution and via the terms of trade have the expected signs. If the environmental policy in one country is relaxed, the other country will be worse off in terms of environmental quality. Moreover, the price of toxic waste will decline. The other country may be better off if it is an exporter of toxic waste; it will be worse off if it imports toxic waste. Using these results, the iso-welfare contours can be depicted in an (e^0, E^0) diagram (see Figure 4.3). Two scenarios are possible.

In case (a), the transfrontier pollution effects are substantial. Tighter environmental standards in both countries would be mutually beneficial. If the terms-of-trade effects are stronger, case (b) is possible. The waste-exporting home country would be better off if the foreign country relaxed its environmental standards since this would reduce the willingness to accept compensation for the storage of waste. The waste-importing country would benefit from tight environmental standards in the home country since this would raise the willingness to pay for the possibility to export hazardous waste.

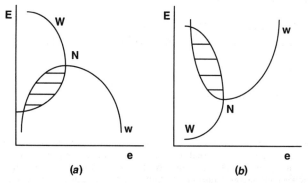

FIG. 4.3 Non-Cooperative Environmental Policies and Pareto Improvements

Proposition 4.12. Nash equilibria in environmental policies are usually not Pareto-efficient. The waste-importing country would benefit from tighter environmental standards in the other country. The waste-exporting country would benefit from tighter standards abroad in the case of substantial transfrontier pollution and from lax standards in the case of a substantial terms-of-trade effect.

A situation in which both countries chose too lax environmental policies without transfrontier pollution is not feasible here.[26] The final part of this section is devoted to the characterization of co-operative environmental policies. We will now reintroduce transportation costs:

$$\gamma \neq 0.$$

It follows that trade in toxic waste should be subject to regulation. Moreover, side-payments are introduced. They are used to compensate the country which imposes strict environmental standards for the sake of its neighbour and, moreover, as a means to redistribute tariff revenues. In a situation where transportation affects environmental policy, trade taxes make sense. It is assumed here that the foreign country raises a trade tax such that

$$g(-z)f_e(k,e^0 + x) = p = G(-Z) F_E(K,E^0 - x) + T'. \tag{4.5}$$

Let σ be the transfer payment from the home to the foreign country. Of course, this payment may be negative. Then the optimality conditions can be derived by total differentiation of the system of equations

$$z = sae^0 + (1 - S) AE^0 + \gamma x, \tag{4.3}$$

$$Z = (1 - s) ae^0 + SAE^0 + \gamma x, \tag{4.3'}$$

$$c = g(-z)f(k,e^0 + x) - g(-z)f_e(k,e^0 + x) x - \sigma, \tag{4.22}$$

$$C = G(-Z) F(K,E^0 - x) + g(-z)f_e(k,e^0 + x) x + \sigma \tag{4.22'}$$

and then using the comparative static results to determine the maximum of the joint welfare function

$$w = u(c,-z) + U(C,-Z)$$

with respect to the emission levels, e^0 and E^0, the transfer payment, σ, and exports, x. Some tedious but basic algebraic operations yield the expected results:

$$u_1 = U_1, \tag{4.23a}$$

$$t^e = gf_e = sag'f + (1 - s)aG' F + \frac{sau_2 (1 - s)aU_2}{u_1} \tag{4.23b}$$

---

[26] In the previous chapter, which dealt with capital mobility, such a scenario was possible. In the case of capital movements and external effects on production, the impact of a change in environmental policy on the remuneration of capital is ambiguous. Thus, it is possible that each country chooses too low a level of environmental regulation in order to capture a rent in the international capital market.

$$T^e = GF_E = SAG' F + (1 - S)Ag' f = \frac{(1 - S)Au_2 + SAU_2}{u_1} , \qquad (4.23c)$$

$$T^t = \gamma \left(g'f + G' F + \frac{u_2 + U_2}{u_1} \right). \qquad (4.23d)$$

The first equation is the condition for the optimal side-payment. The second and third equations define the emission taxes. All external effects are internalized. The final equation gives the optimal trade tax, which internalizes the external effects arising from international trade. Condition (4.23d) is, however, not applicable in situations where autarky is optimal, e.g. where transport costs are very large. For $x = 0$, the derivative of the welfare function with respect to x is discontinuous and an optimal tariff cannot be determined. In this situation, a complete ban on trade in hazardous waste would be desirable.[27]

Proposition 4.12. In a co-operative solution with trade in toxic waste, all externalities are internalized by the appropriate policy instruments.

It should be noted that restrictions to international trade serve the purpose of merely internalizing the environmental costs of international transport. If these are negligible, a co-operative solution does not involve any impediments to free trade. This result is in sharp contrast to the real world where multilateral negotiations have led to substantial restrictions of the hazardous-waste trade that cannot be motivated on grounds of the mere environmental costs of transportation. An example is the Basle Convention on the Control of Transboundary Movements of Hazardous Wastes and their Disposal, which will be reviewed in Chapter 9. It prohibits trade with non-signatory parties and allows waste-exporting and waste-importing countries to raise additional trade barriers against signatory states. If one believes in theoretical models, one is led to argue that agreements like the Basle Convention are based on irrational behaviour. Notwithstanding that compromises achieved in negotiations among politicians are rarely efficient from an economic point of view, this is unlikely to be the major explanation of this inconsistency between theory and reality. A better explanation lies in some insufficiencies of the model. Here we deal with a world where monitoring and enforcement are no problems and illegal activities are not considered. In the real world, many waste importers are developing countries that lack the sophistication and infrastructure necessary to monitor the storage or treatment of toxic waste and to enforce environmental rules. In such a situation, it may be efficient to shift the business of control and enforcement to the exporting country.

Figure 4.4 shows the mutual benefits of a voluntary export restraint. Let s be the toxic-waste supply. D represents the true demand function of the

---

[27] In the notation of the model, a tax on waste imports turns into a subsidy on waste exports if imports happen to be negative. Thus, if both countries are similar and if transport costs are high, then the import tax would drive imports to zero but the corresponding export subsidy induces exports that are equally undesirable.

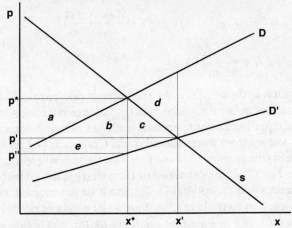

FIG. 4.4 Welfare Effects of a Voluntary Export Restraint

waste-importing country.[28],[29] Due to enforcement problems, the revealed demand is larger than the true demand. It is depicted by D'. The market equilibrium is characterized by waste exports, x', and a world market price, p'. Without an enforcement deficit, the equilibrium would be given by (x^*, p^*). How can this equilibrium be attained? Let us assume that the two countries are able to negotiate a voluntary export restraint such that exports are reduced from x' to x^*. The exporting country now pays only p'' instead of p'. Had there been an import restraint, the price would have risen to p^* and the home country would have lost $a + b + c$. In the case of a voluntary export restraint, however, the quota rent accrues to the exporting country. This is measured by $a + b + e$. The net welfare effect is $e - c$ and may be positive. The waste-importing country benefits from an improvement in environmental quality. The welfare effect of this improvement in environmental quality exceeds the change in the trade revenue, $p'(x^* - x')$, by $c + d$. But due to the fact that the rent goes to the home country, the foreign country suffers an additional loss in trade revenue, measured by e. The net welfare effect is $c + d - e$ and may be positive. Adding the welfare gains of both countries, one arrives at a global net gain of d. The voluntary export restraint provides a possibility to distribute these gains such that both countries have an incentive to participate in such an agreement.[30]

[28] Note that the demand and supply curves in Fig. 4.4 are not the same as those in Fig. 4.2. They are based on different concepts of demand. In Fig. 4.2, the curves have been derived on the basis of given environmental policies (given values of e^0 and E^0). Here, we assume that optimal environmental policies are chosen. e^0 and E^0 vary along these curves. s and D represent the willingness to pay for the storage of toxic waste or the willingness to accept compensation (from a national-welfare point of view).

[29] These curves may be backward-bending. This is shown in Sect. 4.9, where their curves are derived algebraically and some comparative static results are obtained.

[30] Of course, it may be possible in certain circumstances that the net welfare effect of an export restraint is negative for one of the countries. If this is the importing country, an incentive-compatible solution may be attained if it receives a part of the quota rent. If the exporting country turns out to be a net loser, additional side-payments have to be introduced.

Proposition 4.13. In the case of insufficient regulation in the waste-importing country, a voluntary export restraint may be better than free trade.

Of course, the voluntary export restraint is only a second-best instrument. A correct environmental policy plus some side-payments would imply even greater improvements.

4.8 Trade Barriers as an Instrument of Unilateral Environmental Policy

There are two reasons why it is in a country's own interest to restrict international trade on a unilateral basis. On the one hand, there is the transportation problem. If transportation harms the environment, it should be taxed. On the other hand, there is a second-best problem. Besides the transportation issue, there are two additional issues that the policy-maker should be concerned with—domestic environmental disruption and potential gains from terms-of-trade changes. It is obvious that two policy instruments are needed here.

Assume that the level of emissions in the other country is given and that the trade tax imposed by the other country is fixed. The home country has two variables at its disposal, its environmental policy parameter, e^0, and its exports which it can determine by choosing an appropriate tariff rate. The effects of changes in these variables on environmental quality and on the terms of trade are obtained by total differentiation of equations (4.3), (4.3'), and (4.5'):

$$\frac{dz}{de^0} = sa, \tag{4.24a}$$

$$\frac{dp}{de^0} = -(1-s)\, aG'\, F_E, \tag{4.24b}$$

$$\frac{dz}{dx} = \gamma, \tag{4.24c}$$

$$\frac{dp}{dx} = -GF_{EE} - \gamma G'\, F_E. \tag{4.24d}$$

The effects on environmental quality are intuitive, but the terms-of-trade effects deserve an additional explanation. An increase in domestic emissions will reduce the marginal productivity of emissions abroad, which equals the foreign environmental tax rate, which in turn determines the terms of trade. An increase in exports will, on the one hand, raise the demand for foreign storage facilities and, therefore, the world market price, p. On the other hand, the environmental impact of additional transport reduces foreign productivity and that makes the world market price decline. These equations can be used to determine the welfare effects of changes in domestic environmental policies and exports and to determine optimal policies. The optimal emission and trade taxes are

$$t^{e*} = gf_e = sa(g'f + \frac{u_2}{u_1}) + x\frac{dp}{de^0}, \tag{4.25}$$

$$t^{t*} = gf_e - p = \gamma(g'f + \frac{u_2}{u_1}) + x\frac{dp}{dx}. \tag{4.26}$$

The emission tax internalizes the domestic social costs and contains a term which represents the effect of domestic environmental policy on the terms of trade. This term is negative. Thus, if environmental dumping is defined as pricing environmental resources at less than domestic social cost, such an optimal tax rate falls into this category. The reason is that a lax environmental policy leads to a decline in foreign productivity. The price of storing toxic waste will decline in the other country. In the foreign country, the optimum tax rate will be higher than the one internalizing the externalities since a tight policy raises the foreign country's terms of trade.

4.9 The Issue of Market Power

It is often argued that the distribution of power in the toxic-waste market is highly asymmetric and that this leads to a proliferation of toxic waste and to enormous environmental problems. On the supply side, there are rich countries, often represented by large and powerful companies that want to get rid of hazardous waste, whereas the demand side is characterized by a large number of small countries that are keen to earn foreign exchange by almost any means to satisfy basic needs of their populations. The issue has already been touched upon in Sections 5 and 6 of this chapter, where the terms-of-trade effects of changes in environmental policies have been addressed. Now the issue of market power will be taken up explicitly.

Let us consider the following situation. Let the resource exporter be a large company which is subject to some kind of environmental regulation in its own country. It maximizes its profits

$$g(-z)f(k,e^0 + x) - p(x)x \tag{4.27}$$

with respect to x. In the optimum, marginal revenue equals marginal cost. If the firm is small on the goods market, the marginal revenue is gf_e and can be represented by a negatively sloped curve in a (p,x) diagram. The marginal cost depends on the willingness of the waste-importing countries to accept compensation payments for the pollution generated by imported waste. This inverse demand function for toxic waste can be derived from the following considerations. If the level of environmental regulation, E^0, in a representative waste-importing country is given, then matters are relatively simple and the demand function is positively sloped. This has been shown in Section 5 (see Figure 4.2, in particular). Let us, however, assume that the import demand function represents the true willingness to accept toxic waste at a price p, i.e. we consider the case of an optimal environmental policy. For the sake of simplicity, the transport risk will be assumed to be negligible. Then the import demand, x, and the optimal environmental policy, E^0, are determined by

$$GF_E = p, \tag{4.28}$$

$$ASG' FU_1 + ASU_2 = U_1 p. \tag{4.29}$$

Total differentiation yields

$$\begin{pmatrix} GF_{EE} - ASG'F_E & -GF_{EE} \\ \Xi + ASG'F_EU_1 & -ASG'F_EU_1 \end{pmatrix} \begin{pmatrix} dE^0 \\ dx \end{pmatrix} = \begin{pmatrix} 1 \\ U_1 + xU_{11}AS\dfrac{U_2}{U_1^2} \end{pmatrix} dp, \tag{4.30}$$

where

$$\Xi = -(AS)^2 \left(G'' FU_1 + U_{22} + U_{11}\frac{U_2^2}{U_1^2} \right) > 0. \tag{4.31}$$

The comparative static results are

$$\frac{dE^{\prime 0}}{dp} = \frac{GF_{EE}\left(U_1 + xU_{11}AS\dfrac{U_2^2}{U_1^2} \right) - ASG'F_EU_1}{GF_{EE}\Xi + (ASG'F_E)^2 U_1} \tag{4.32a}$$

and

$$\frac{dx}{dp} = \frac{\left(U_1 + xU_{11}AS\dfrac{U_2}{U_1} \right)(GF_{EE} - ASG'F_E) - \Xi - ASG'F_EU_1}{GF_{EE}\Xi + (ASG'F_E)^2 U_1}. \tag{4.32b}$$

If the external effect on production is small ($G' = 0$) then

$$\frac{dE^0}{dp} = \frac{U_1 + xU_{11}AS\dfrac{U_2}{U_1}}{\Xi} \tag{4.33a}$$

and

$$\frac{dx}{dp} = \frac{U_1 + xU_{11}AS\dfrac{U_2}{U_1}}{\Xi} - \frac{1}{GF_{EE}}. \tag{4.33b}$$

The toxic-waste demand curve is positively sloped for small values of x. For larger values, it may reverse its direction. It may be backward-bending. Since this is a property that the offer curves derived in international trade theory usually possess, this result is not particularly surprising.[31]

Figure 4.5 depicts the case of an increasing demand curve for toxic waste. *mp* represents the marginal productivity from the point of view of the monopolistic supplier of toxic waste. The perfect-competition equilibrium in this

---

[31] The backward-bending curve can be explained as follows. For large values of x, a small increase in the price may lead to a large increase in consumption and this reduces the marginal utility of consumption. This decrease in marginal utility means that the marginal benefits of emissions are reduced because of the value of additional consumption possibilities. In such a situation, it can be optimal to tighten environmental policies by reducing the total quantity of toxic waste, E^0. In certain circumstances, a reduction in E^0 requires a reduction in the imports of toxic waste.

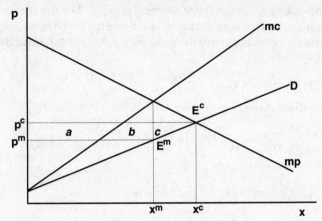

FIG. 4.5 Market Power and Trade in Hazardous Waste

market is characterized by E^c and the corresponding price and quantity are p^c and x^c, respectively. From the point of view of the monopolist on the supply side of the market, the price is not given. She knows that the price will be increased if the exports are raised. Thus the marginal cost of exporting is larger than the price. This is represented by the *mc* curve. The optimal solution for the monopolist is determined by the point of intersection of the supply curve and the marginal-cost curve. The price is reduced to p^m and the exports fall to x^m. The importers of toxic waste face a welfare loss of $a + b + c$ compared to the competitive situation.

Proposition 4.14. In the case of market power on the supply side of the hazardous-waste market, the price and the traded quantities will be below their competitive levels if the demand for toxic waste has the normal shape. The impact on environmental quality is ambiguous

The monopolist will restrict her exports to reduce the price to be paid for the storage of hazardous waste. Since waste exports are reduced, the monopolist seems to be the conservationists' friend again.[32] However, this is not necessarily true. The decline in the world market price indicates that environmental regulation in the importing countries has been relaxed. The impact of this price decline on the total quantity of pollutants in the importing country is given by equation (4.33*b*). Together with (4.33*a*), it follows that

$$\frac{dE^o}{dp} = \frac{dx}{dp} + \frac{1}{GF_{EE}}.$$ (4.34)

Thus, $dE^0/dp < dx/dp$ and may, therefore, be negative. The decline in the price for toxic waste can lead to a deterioration of environmental quality in the waste-importing country.

Finally, the question arises as to whether a not-in-my-backyard scenario is feasible. Is it possible that no one is willing to accept the toxic waste although

[32] See Sect. 10 of the previous chapter and Solow (1974: 8).

someone should? It is generally not. The reason is that trade in toxic waste involves only two parties, the importer and the exporter. The other countries remain, by and large, unaffected by the final location of storage of the toxic waste. Thus, it depends only on the willingness to pay of the exporter and the willingness to accept of the importer. Only in extreme circumstances, a not-in-my-backyard scenario becomes possible. If storage of toxic waste in the exporting country involves substantial transboundary pollution spillovers whereas storage somewhere else does not, there will be a free-rider problem on the part of the potential importers. They will accept less waste than would be desirable from a global-welfare point of view. However, such a scenario does not correspond to real-world situations and can be excluded for empirical reasons.[33]

4.10 Summary of Results

1. Countries with strict environmental policies tend to be exporters of toxic waste.
2. A small economy benefits from increased trade in hazardous waste if its environmental policy is optimal and if the transport risk is sufficiently small.
3. Waste-importing countries with insufficient environmental policies may suffer from increased trade. If there is a substantial transboundary pollution spillover, the exporting country may be worse off as well.
4. For a waste-exporting country, it is optimal to have laxer environmental standards in a situation with trade than in a situation without trade.
5. By relaxing its environmental standards, a country reduces the world price of toxic waste and deteriorates environmental quality at home and abroad.
6. A large country may increase environmental disruption by employing a strict environmental policy if there is substantial transfrontier pollution.
7. A voluntary export restraint may be beneficial to both the importer and the exporter of toxic waste.
8. If the exporter has market power and the waste-importing countries are small, waste exports and the price will be too small and the importers suffer from welfare losses.

---

[33] Matters may be different if not toxic substances but the location of a reprocessing plant is considered.

Appendix: The Gains from Trade in the Case of Emission Taxes

If the government has not set an environmental standard but a tax, emissions, e^0, may change as a response to international trade. In addition to equations (4.3) and (4.4), (4.5) has to be taken into account. Moreover, the simplifying assumption is used that the other country does not change its own emissions of toxic substances. Thus, of each unit of waste exported $(1 - S)A$ units spoil the domestic environment. This is a small-country assumption. Total differentiation yields:

$$\begin{pmatrix} 1 & 0 & -sa \\ g'f & 1 & -gf_e \\ -g'f_e & 0 & gf_{ee} \end{pmatrix} \begin{pmatrix} dz \\ dc \\ de^0 \end{pmatrix} = \begin{pmatrix} \gamma + (1-S)A \\ gf_e - p \\ -gf_{ee} \end{pmatrix} dx \qquad (4.A1)$$

and the comparative statics are

$$\frac{dz}{dx} = \frac{gf_{ee}(\gamma + (1-S)A - sa)}{gf_{ee} - sag'f_e} \begin{pmatrix} < 0 & \text{if } \gamma + (1-S)A < sa \\ = \gamma + (1-S)A - sa & \text{if } g' = 0 \end{pmatrix}, \qquad (4.A2a)$$

$$\frac{dc}{dx} = \frac{(\gamma + (1-S)A - sa)gg'((f_e)^2 - ff_{ee}) + p(sag'f_e - gf_{ee})}{gf_{ee} - sag'f_e} \quad (= -p \quad \text{if } g' = 0)) \qquad (4.A2b)$$

$$\frac{de^0}{dx} = \frac{(\gamma + (1-S)A)g'f_e - gf_{ee}}{gf_{ee} - sag'f_e} < 0 \qquad (= -1 \quad \text{if } g' = 0) \qquad (4.A2c)$$

The welfare effect is

$$\frac{dw}{dx} = \frac{u_1\big((\gamma + (1-S)A - sa)gg'((f_e)^2 - ff_e) + p(sag'f_e - gf_{ee})\big)}{gf_{ee} - sag'f_e}$$

$$- \frac{u_2 gf_{ee}(\gamma + (1-S)A - sa)}{gf_{ee} - sag'f_e} \quad (= -u_1 p + u_2(sa - (1-S)A - \gamma) \text{ if } g' = 0). \qquad (4.A3)$$

If the environmental policy is optimal, equation (4.9) can be used to substitute for $sag'fu_1 + sau_2$. Rearranging terms then yields

$$\frac{dw}{dx} = (\gamma + (1-S)A)\frac{u_1 gg'((f_e)^2 - ff_{ee}) - u_2 gf_{ee}}{gf_{ee} - sag'f_e} + (gf_e - p)u_1. \qquad (4.A4)$$

The first term is negative. It measures the impact of the transport costs and the pollution spillover. The second term is positive. It measures the efficiency gain. If the transport costs and transfrontier pollution problems are sufficiently low, there will be welfare gains.

For the foreign country, we obtain

$$\begin{pmatrix} 1 & 0 & -SA \\ G'F & 1 & -GF_E \\ -G'F_E & 0 & GF_{EE} \end{pmatrix} \begin{pmatrix} dZ \\ dC \\ dE^0 \end{pmatrix} = \begin{pmatrix} \gamma + (1-s)a \\ -(GF_E - p) \\ -gf_{EE} \end{pmatrix} dx \qquad (4.A1')$$

and

$$\frac{dZ}{dx} = \frac{GF_{EE}(\gamma - (1-s)a + SA)}{GF_{EE} - SAG'F_E} \qquad (4.A2'a)$$

$$\frac{dC}{dx} = \frac{(SA - (1-s)a + \gamma)GG'((F_E)^2 - FF_{EE}) - p(SAG'F_E - GF_{EE})}{GF_{EE} - SAG'F_E} \qquad (4.A2'b)$$
$$(= p \quad \text{if } G' = 0),$$

$$\frac{dE^0}{dx} = \frac{GF_{EE} + (\gamma - (1-s)a)G'F_E}{GF_{EE} - SAG'F_E}(= 1 \quad \text{if } g' = 0). \qquad (4.A2'c)$$

The welfare effect is

$$\frac{dW}{dx} = \frac{U_1\big((SA - (1-s)a + \gamma)GG'((F_E)^2 - FF_{EE}) - p(SAG'F_E - GF_{EE})\big)}{GF_{EE} - SAG'F_E}$$

$$- \frac{U_2 GF_{EE}(\gamma + SA - (1-s)a)}{GF_{EE} - SAG'F_E}(= -U_1 p + U^2(SA + \gamma - (1-s) \text{ if } G' = 0). \qquad (4.A3')$$

In the case of an optimal environmental policy, one can apply the same procedure as before and the welfare effect turns out to be

$$\frac{dW}{dx} = (\gamma - (1-s)a)\frac{U_1 GG'((F_E)^2 - FF_{EE}) - U_2 GF_{EE}}{GF_{EE} - SAG'F_E} + (p - GF_E)U_1. \qquad (4.A4')$$

Again, this is positive if the transportation cost is small enough.

5

International Trade in Final Goods: The Case of Perfect Competition

5.1 Introduction

As has been shown in the previous section, trade in toxic waste can be dealt with in a one-sector model. The consideration of trade in final consumable commodities requires a more general framework involving at least two goods. The present chapter uses such a model. International trade is explained by differences in the environmental resource endowments of different countries. In a first step, one may ask what determines the endowment of a country with environmental resources. This issue has already been addressed in Chapter 2, but it will be reconsidered here using a more formalized approach. Moreover, one can look at the gains from trade: in which circumstances is it possible that increased environmental disruption offsets the traditional gains from trade? Finally, the question may be addressed whether it makes sense to use environmental policy to achieve trade-related economic policy objectives and whether this will result in a race to the bottom in the field of environmental regulation. Is ecological dumping compatible with optimizing behaviour?

Basically, two kinds of trade model frameworks in which these issues can be addressed may be distinguished, the Ricardo–Viner model and the Heckscher–Ohlin model.[1]

- In a Ricardo–Viner world some factors of production are sector-specific, i.e. they cannot be moved from one sector to the other. This model has been introduced into modern trade theory by Jones (1971) and Samuelson (1971) and it represents a short-run view of the economy. Structural change, i.e. a relocation of these factors of production, takes place only in the long run.
- In the Heckscher–Ohlin model, all factors are mobile across the sectors of an economy. This model represents a long-run view since structural change usually is a matter of decades. The classic references are Heckscher (1919), Ohlin (1933), Samuelson (1948, 1949), and Stolper and Samuelson (1941).

[1] The classical one-factor Ricardian model will not be considered since its structure is too simple to capture the essential problems of the relationship between trade and the environment.

We will use a model which includes elements of both these two frameworks. Since the pollution-impact parameters of the emissions discharged by the various industries in the economy may differ, there are good reasons for using industry-specific environmental policies. In this case, pollution permits should not be fungible across industries. This is the Ricardo–Viner component of the model. However, in the process of designing its environmental policy, a government has to aggregate over the emissions of different sectors to evaluate the total environmental damage. This corresponds to adding up the factor demands of the sectors of an economy to obtain the total factor demand in the traditional Heckscher–Ohlin model. However, unlike the Heckscher–Ohlin world the total factor supply is not exogenously given but depends on the preferences of the people. One should expect that the higher the sensitivity towards environmental damage, the smaller the supply of environmental resources. In this respect the model resembles the augmented Heckscher–Ohlin model with elastic factor supply (see Walsh (1956), Kemp and Jones (1962), and Mayer (1991)). Thus, in the short run when environmental policies are given, we are in a Ricardo–Viner world, and in the longer term, when environmental policies are adjusted, we use a modified Heckscher–Ohlin approach. In a similar fashion, the capital employed by each sector can be treated as given and fixed in the short run and variable in the longer term. As in the traditional Heckscher–Ohlin model, it is assumed here that the supply of this factor is inelastic.

Some interesting aspects that are relevant in the real world will be neglected in this chapter, but they will be taken up afterwards. First, the analysis is restricted to the case of perfect competition although some of the major real-world pollution problems are generated by firms operating in non-competitive markets, e.g. the chemical industry or the electricity-generating sector. Imperfectly competitive markets will be addressed in Chapter 6. Second, the investigation is based on the assumption that all individuals are equal such that there exists no problem of aggregating over preferences and no incentives for particular subgroups with idiosyncratic interests to engage in lobbying activities. Moreover, the government is assumed to be benevolent and to maximize social welfare. The impact of lobbying activity and non-welfare-maximizing behaviour of policy-makers will be the subject of Chapter 7.

Many of the results that will be derived here are not new. Models of trade and the environment have been analysed since the mid-1970s. The references include Baumol (1971), Markusen (1975), Pethig (1976), Siebert (1977, 1979, 1985a), Asako (1979), Gronych (1980), Siebert et al. (1980), McGuire (1982), Merrifield (1988), Krutilla (1991), Rauscher (1991a, 1994a, 1995b), Anderson (1992), Lloyd (1992), Snape (1992), Copeland and Taylor (1993, 1994), Chichilniski (1994a), Copeland (1994), and Steininger (1994a, b). For a survey see Ulph (1994b). This chapter too may be viewed as a survey which reestablishes known results in a unified framework.[2] None the less, new results

---

[2] There are papers that are based on the assumption that factors are immobile across sectors, e.g. Copeland and Taylor (1993) and A. Ulph (1994b), other papers that start from the assumption

are derived as well. They concern the importance of environmental side-effects of international transport and the effects of environmental disruption on factor productivity.[3]

This chapter is organized as follows. The next section presents the model. Section 3 is devoted to the explanation of comparative advantages and the patterns of trade. The impact of environmental policy on international trade for the small-country case will be addressed in section 4. Section 5 shows that with a move from autarky to trade the relocation of the factors of production across sectors may be accompanied by a relocation of pollution across countries. In Section 6, the gains from trade will be analysed and the effects of trade liberalization on the environmental policies of a small country will be addressed. Section 7 deals with the effect of changes in the terms of trade on emissions and environmental quality. Section 8 looks at optimal environmental policies for large open economies. In Section 9, we will address the issue of environmental tariffs. Finally, in Section 10, we will introduce a non-traded good and compare emission tax rates between the export sector and the non-tradables industry.

For the sake of exposition, some analytical problems will be dealt with by making certain assumptions. For instance, it is assumed that second-order conditions for the optimization problems are all met, that factor intensity reversals do not occur, and that trade does not lead to complete specialization.[4] Moreover, we will look at a single country and model the rest of the world in a very rudimentary way by just considering its import demand or export supply function. Additionally, we restrict the analysis to the two-goods two-factors case. It is known that higher-dimensional models produce more ambiguous results and that some of the theorems derived from the traditional $2 \times 2 \times 2$ model framework hold only 'on average' in more general models.[5] Finally, as the analysis proceeds from simple to complex issues, some of the complications of the original model will be dropped. This concerns in particular the productivity effects of environmental quality but also the environmental cost of transportation.

---

that only one good (out of two) causes emissions during its production, e.g. Markusen (1975), McGuire (1982) and Rauscher (1991a), papers in which consumption externalities are neglected, Asako (1991), Krutilla (1991), Rauscher (1991a, 1994a, 1995b), papers in which general equilibrium considerations are neglected, e.g. Snape (1992), and papers in which environmental policy is not considered, Asako (1979).

[3] The latter kind have been addressed by Herberg and Kemp (1969) and Herberg et al. (1982), but not in an environmental-economics framework. In their model, external effects on production depend on the output of the different industries, but not on the input of particular factors like environmental resources.

[4] Copeland and Taylor (1995) for instance show that external effects on production can imply convex transformation curves and this leads to complete specialization and to some counter-intuitive results concerning the patterns of trade.

[5] See Bhagwati (1972) and Deardorff (1979) for the many-goods two-factors model and Dixit and Norman (1980, ch. 4), Deardorff (1982), and Ethier (1984) for the more general case where the number of factors exceeds two as well.

5.2 The Model

Consider a country producing two goods, 1 and 2, with two factors, capital, k^i, and an environmental resource, e^i. Let good 1 be the numéraire, i.e. $p^1 = 1$. The price of good 2 in terms of the numéraire is $p = p^2/p^1$ Let this be the price paid by the consumers. The producer prices are obtained by taking into account the consumption taxes. Let the indices of the goods be chosen such that the good with the lowest pollution-impact parameter of consumption is the numéraire. For simplicity assume that its consumption does not cause any pollution at all, i.e.

$b^1 = 0.$

If all goods were environmentally disruptive in their consumption, the environmental policy should involve an input tax or restriction in order to limit the consumption possibility set.[6] Since consumption of good 2 causes environmental pollution, it makes sense to introduce a consumption tax, t^{c2}. The tax rate applied to the numéraire good is zero, i.e. $t^{c1} = 0$.

The foreign country is the rest of the world and its relative price, P, is the world market price. In addition, there may be a trade tax on imports or exports of good 2, t^t, and the law of one price holds for the prices net of taxes. $\tilde{p}$ is the producer price and the consumer price, p^c, is obtained by adding the consumption tax rate. Both tax rates are expressed in terms of the numéraire. All taxes are assumed to be redistributed in a lump-sum fashion.

$$p = \tilde{p} + t^c = P + t^t + t^{c2} \tag{5.1}$$

The utility function of the representative individual is $u(c^1,c^2,-z)$ and the production functions are $g^i(-z)f^i(k^i,e^i)$. Let the utility function be additively separable such that environmental quality does not affect the structure of demand.[7] The functions $f^i(.,.)$ exhibit non-increasing returns to scale. Moreover, the utility and production functions are assumed to have the usual properties: they have positive partial derivatives, negative second derivatives, and non-negative cross-derivatives.

The general equilibrium in this country is characterized by

$$q^i = g^i(-z)f^i(k^i,e^i), \quad i-1,2, \tag{5.2}$$
$$k = k^1 + k^2, \tag{5.3}$$
$$c^1 + Pc^2 = q^1 + Pq^2, \tag{5.4}$$

[6] It would not make much sense to tax all consumption goods since this would imply a lump-sum component of consumption taxation—which then is redistributed to the consumers as a lump-sum transfer. The only possibility to reduce the consumption of all goods is a reduction in income, i.e. in the output of the economy. This can be achieved by a constraint on the use of the variable factor of production, i.e. an emission tax.

[7] This may be different in reality. Some goods are complements of environmental quality, e.g. gardening and fishing equipment, whereas others are substitutes, e.g. perhaps video games and alcoholic beverages. However, the consideration of these effects would make the model much more difficult to solve and a lot of ambiguities in the results would turn up. Some of them will be mentioned briefly later on.

$$q^2 - c^2 = M(P), \; M'(.) < 0 \tag{5.5}$$

$$pu_1(c^1) - u_2(c^2) = 0,\text{[8]} \tag{5.6}$$

$$g^1(-z)f_k^1(k^1,e^1) = \tilde{p}g^2(-z)f_k^2(k^2,e^2), \tag{5.7}$$

$$t^{e1} = g^1(-z)f_e^1(k^1,e^1), \tag{5.8a}$$

$$t^{e2} = \tilde{p}g^2(-z)f_e^2(k^2,e^2), \tag{5.8b}$$

$$z = sa^1e^1 + sa^2e^2 + sb^2c^2 + \gamma^1 \mid c^1 - q^1 \mid + \gamma^2 \mid c^2 - q^2 \mid \\ + (1 - S)(A^1E^1 + A^2E^2 + B^2C^2). \tag{5.9}$$

Equation (5.2) defines output. Equation (5.3) is the economy's resource constraint with respect to capital. As usual, capital supply is assumed to be inelastic. Equation (5.4) is the balance-of-payments equation. Equation (5.5) states that the domestic excess supply of commodity 2 equals the foreign country's import demand (which is negatively sloped). Equation (5.6) describes demand behaviour: the representative household's budget is allocated to the two goods such that the consumer price ratio equals the marginal rate of substitution. Equation (5.7) is a condition for the allocation of capital in a competitive economy. If capital is perfectly mobile across sectors, its marginal-value product has to be the same in both sectors. Equations (5.8a, b) state that in a competitive equilibrium the environmental resource is used such that its marginal-value product equals the emission tax rate. Finally, equation (5.9) defines environmental pollution as the sum of the pollution impacts of production, consumption, and transport in the home and the foreign countries. The foreign country's impact on domestic pollution cannot be modelled explicitly here since we have aggregated all the information concerning the foreign country in its import demand function. However, it will be seen that some considerations on the impact of foreign emissions on the domestic environment are nevertheless possible.

5.3 Autarky and the Patterns of Trade

As a first step, we will infer the patterns of specialization and trade from comparative price advantages. Thus, we have to determine the impacts of the environmental policy variables and the pollution-impact parameters on the autarky price ratio $\tilde{p}$. In an autarkic economy, $c^1 = q^1$ and $c^2 = q^2$. Thus, we can insert q^1 and q^2 into the utility function instead of c^1 and c^2. Moreover, equation (5.3) can be used to eliminate k^2 from the production function. If this is done, the autarky equilibrium is then determined by equations (5.6), (5.7), (5.8a, b), and (5.9). Initially, we look at the *de facto* endowment, i.e. environmental policies are not necessarily optimal. Let us assume that the government uses a tradable-permits scheme or a command-and-control approach

---

[8] Although the utility function has three arguments, its first derivative is a function of only the variable with respect to which it has been differentiated due to the linear-separability assumption.

such that emissions (but not emission taxes) are given. In this case we can neglect equations (5.8a, b). The remaining equations are

$$(\tilde{p} + t^{c2})u_1(g^1(-z)f^1(k^1,e^1)) - u_2(g^2(-z)f^2(k - k^1,e^2)) = 0. \tag{5.10a}$$

$$g^1(-z)f^1_k(k^1,e^1) - \tilde{p}g^2(-z)f^2_e(k - k^1,e^2) = 0. \tag{5.10b}$$

$$z = sa^1e^1 + sa^2e^2 + sb^2g^2(-z)f^2(k - k^1,e^2).$$

We may distinguish the short run with immobile capital and the long run with perfect intersectoral capital mobility. The comparative static results with respect to the environmental policy variables and the pollution-impact coefficients are determined by

$$\begin{pmatrix} u_1 & u_{22}g^{2'}f^2 - pu_{11}g^{1'}f^1 \\ 0 & 1 + sb^2g^2f^2 \end{pmatrix} \begin{pmatrix} d\tilde{p} \\ dz \end{pmatrix} = \begin{pmatrix} -u_1 & -pu_{11}g^1f^1_e & u_{22}g^2f^1_e & 0 \\ 0 & sa^1 & sa^2 + sbg^2f^1_ese^1 \end{pmatrix} \begin{pmatrix} dt^c \\ de^1 \\ dt^2 \\ da^1 \end{pmatrix} \tag{5.11}$$

in the case where capital is immobile (i.e. equation (5.10c) is not binding) and

$$\begin{pmatrix} u_1 & pu_{11}g^1f^1_k + u_{22}g^2f^2_k & u_{22}g^{2'}f^2 - pu_{11}g^{1'}f^1 \\ -g^2f^2_k & g^1f^1_{kk} + \tilde{p}g^2f^2_{kk} & pg^2f^2_k - g^{1'}f^1_k \\ 0 & sb^2g^2f^2_k & 1 + sb^2g^{2'}f^2 \end{pmatrix} \begin{pmatrix} d\tilde{p} \\ dk^1 \\ dz \end{pmatrix}$$

$$= \begin{pmatrix} -u_1 & -pu_{11}g^1f^1_e & u_{22}g^2f^2_k & 0 \\ 0 & -g^1f^1_{ke} & pg^2f^2_{ke} & 0 \\ 0 & sa^1 & sa^2 + sbg^2f^2_e & se^1 \end{pmatrix} \begin{pmatrix} dt^{c2} \\ de^1 \\ de^2 \\ da^1 \end{pmatrix} \tag{5.12}$$

in the case where capital is intersectorally mobile. The impacts of the pollution-impact parameters s, a^2, and b^2 have the same signs as that of a^1.

Almost all the effects on the autarky price ratio are ambiguous. Only the impact of the consumption tax in the immobile-factor scenario is positive. In this simple case, the supply side is completely inflexible and, therefore, the tax cannot be passed through to the consumers. $d\tilde{p}/dt^{c2} = -1$, i.e. the producer price is reduced by the tax rate. Thus, the higher the tax rate the larger is the comparative advantage of the 'dirty' consumption good in international markets. Or to put it another way: a country tends to export environmentally unfriendly commodities. All the other effects are ambiguous. This is due to the fact that the external effect on production introduces a Ricardian element to the process of price formation. An increase in the pollution-impact parameter a^1, for instance, leads to increased pollution and the sector least affected by the externality will have the comparative advantage.[9] An increase in the emissions of

[9] Foreign emissions that spill over to the home country have a similar effect. The sector affected most by this pollution will lose its international competitiveness. As an example consider the 'policies of the tall smoke-stack' that were adopted in the 1960s and 1970s to reduce local environmental problems in densely populated areas. The cheapest way to reduce depositions was to distribute the pollutants over a larger area by increasing the height of the smoke-stacks. Thus, local pollution problems were turned into interregional or even international problems. The transfrontier pollution coefficients were increased and downstream countries like Norway and Sweden suffered from increased acidification due to SO_2 emissions in Central Europe and the UK.

a sector raises its output and, therefore, the consumption of this good. Environmental quality is deteriorated and productivities decline. It is not clear which sector is affected most and, thus, it may happen that the sector loses competitiveness in spite of laxer environmental regulation. If capital is mobile, a change in capital allocation has to be considered as well but this does not reduce the ambiguity of the results. With capital mobility, even the impact of the consumption tax on the autarky price ratio becomes ambiguous as well. Demand is shifted from the taxed to the untaxed good. The relative producer price of the taxed good is reduced and so is the marginal-value product of capital. Capital moves to the production of the untaxed good. Since the untaxed good is environmentally friendly when consumed, environmental quality is improved. This has a cost-reducing effect on the supply side and it is not clear which sector will profit most. Therefore, the impact of the change in consumption tax rate on comparative advantage becomes ambiguous.

For the simplified version of the model in which the external effects on production are negligible, the results are straightforward:

- Consumption tax rate. The impact is negative. It is −1 if capital is immobile and greater than −1 if capital is immobile.
- Emissions. The sector in which emissions are increased becomes more competitive. If capital is mobile, it moves to this sector.
- Pollution-impact parameters. The impact is zero since environmental quality does not have any productivity effects,

Summarizing, we have

Proposition 5.1. If the effect of environmental quality on productivity is small, a high consumption tax induces a comparative advantage for the taxed commodity and laxer environmental regulation of a sector increases its competitiveness. If the externalities on production are substantial, the impact of the environmental regulation on the patterns of trade becomes ambiguous.

Moreover, we can apply the standard Heckscher–Ohlin theorem in its price version to this model. Its prerequisites are the equality of environmental tax rates in the two sectors and identical technologies (including the pollution-impact coefficients a^1 and a^2) in the two countries.[10]

Similar effects have been observed in North America where parts of Canada turned out to be the downstream victims of US pollution. Since some sectors are substantially affected by acidification (e.g. forestry) whereas others are influenced only marginally (e.g. the automobile industry), the 'policy of the high smoke-stack' may have had an impact on the comparative advantages of the downstream countries—albeit these effects are difficult to be quantify. At least, it is possible to measure some of the effects of air pollution on forestry. See Phillips and Forster (1987) and Fraser (1989), for instance, who attempt to quantify the effects of reductions in long-range air pollution on Canadian forestry.

[10] The textbook version of the theorem deals with a homogeneous factor where $a^1 = a^2 = 1$. However, if this equality does not hold, one may change the units of measurement of emissions such that $a^1 = a^2 = 1$. The production functions obtained by this modification should be equal in the two countries. If the environmental resource has been homogenized, then the assumption of equal emission tax rates in the two sectors is plausible—albeit policy-makers are free to choose other taxation schemes in reality.

Proposition 5.2. Let the technology parameters be the same in the two countries and let the scarcity of the environmental resource be measured by the ratio of the emission tax rate and the remuneration of the other factor. Then the country relatively well endowed with environmental resources exports the environmentally intensively produced good.

This is a textbook result and will, therefore, not be discussed in more detail here.[11]

We now turn to the patterns of trade in the case where the environmental regulation represents the 'true' endowment of a country with environmental resources. The optimal taxation schemes can be derived by maximizing the utility function with respect to e^1, e^2, and t^{c2}. Assume that capital is intersectorally mobile. Then the first-order conditions of optimality are

$$u_i g^i f_e^i = (u_3 + u_1 g^{1'} f^1 + u_2 g^{2'} f^2) \frac{dz}{de^i} + t^{c2} u_1 g^2 f_k^2 \frac{dk^1}{de^i}, i = 1,2,$$

$$0 = (u_3 + u_1 g^{1'} f^1 + u_2 g^{2'} f^2) \frac{dz}{dt^{c2}} + t^{c2} u_1 g^2 f_k^2 \frac{dk^1}{dt^{c2}}.$$

With the comparative-static results from equation (5.12), we get

$$t^{e1} = g^1 f_e^1 = \frac{sa^1}{1 + sb^2 g^{2'} f^2} \left(\frac{u_3}{u_1} + g^{1'} f^1 + \frac{u_2}{u_1} g^{2'} f^2 \right), \tag{5.13a}$$

$$t^{e2} = \tilde{p} g^2 f_e^2 = \frac{sa^2 (u_3 + u_1 g^{1'} f^1 + u_2 g^{2'} f^2) \tilde{p}}{\left(1 + sb^2 g^{2'} f^2\right) u_2 - sb^2 \left(u_3 + u_1 g^{1'} f^1 + u_2 g^{2'} f^2\right)}, \tag{5.13b}$$

$$t^{c2} = \frac{sb^2}{1 + sb^2 g^{2'} f^2} \left(\frac{u_3}{u_1} + g^{1'} f^1 + \frac{u_2}{u_1} g^{2'} f^2 \right). \tag{5.13c}$$

Equation (5.13b) looks a bit strange but we can use (5.13c) to eliminate the second term in brackets in the denominator. Then equation (5.6) can be inserted and this yields

$$t^{e2} = \tilde{p} g^2 f_e^2 = \frac{sa^2}{\left(1 + sb^2 g^{2'} f^2\right)} \left(\frac{u_3}{u_1} + g^{1'} f^1 + \frac{u_2}{u_1} g^{2'} f^2 \right). \tag{5.13b'}$$

Each of the tax rates equals the marginal environmental damage measured in units of the numéraire good. This damage is composed of the willingness to pay for a marginal improvement of environmental quality as a consumption good, u_3/u_1, and the additional income, $g^{1'} f^1 + (u_2/u_1) g^{2'} f^2$, that could be achieved if the production possibility set were not reduced by pollution. This marginal environmental damage has to be weighed by the pollution-impact parameter of the activity under consideration, i.e. by sa^i or sb^2. Moreover, we have to take into account that improved environmental quality increases the consumption possibility set and consumption of good 2 in turn is environmentally disruptive. This explains the term in the denominator of equations

---

[11] For an illustrative graphical derivation of the result, see Gandolfo (1986: pp. I.80–I.82).

($5.13a$, b', c). The ratios of the tax rates equal the ratios of the corresponding pollution-impact parameters: $t^{e1}/t^{e2} = a^1/a^2$ and $t^{ei}/t^{e2} = a^i/b^2$ $(i = 1,2)$.[12]

With these conditions for the optimal environmental policy, one can now determine the effects of various parameters on patterns of trade and specialization:

- Pollution impact of consumption. The direct effect of an increase in b^2 is to raise the marginal damage of consumption and, therefore, the consumption tax rate. According to what has been argued above, this tends to reduce the price of the 'dirty' good, commodity 2. However, it has to be noted that the increase in b^2 also has an impact on the supply side if the external effects on production are significant. For example, if the effect of environmental pollution on sector 2 is substantial, its supply may be reduced so much that the price change is reversed and p actually increases. Thus, the effect of an increase in b^2 on relative prices is ambiguous in the general case.
- Pollution impact of production. The direct effect of an increase in a^i is an increase in the emission tax rate in sector i, $t^{e,i}$ but it also has an impact on factor productivities via the production externalities. The total effect is ambiguous.
- Environmental concern. Environmental concern is measured by u_3. If this parameter is increased, all tax rates have to be raised and if there are substantial external effects on production, anything can happen.

Thus we have:

Proposition 5.3. If the true endowment of a country with environmental resources is reflected in its government's environmental policy, the effects of parameter changes are ambiguous due to the external effects on production.

In order to avoid these ambiguities, let us look at a simplified version of the model where external effects on production are neglected, i.e.

$$g^1 = g^2 = 1$$

Then, the environmental tax rates are

$$t^{e1} = sa^1 \frac{u_3}{u_1}, \tag{5.14a}$$

$$t^{e2} = sa^2 \frac{u_3}{u_1}, \tag{5.14b}$$

$$t^{c2} = sb^2 \frac{u_3}{u_1}. \tag{5.14c}$$

---

[12] The results would be different if there were no capital mobility. The optimal consumption tax rate would be indeterminate since this tax has no impact on the consumption bundle because of the fixed inputs. However, such an ineffectiveness of consumption taxation appears to be rather artificial and, therefore, this case will not be considered here.

Initially let us consider the case of a pure consumption externality. The equations describing the equilibrium of the economy are (5.10a–c) and (5.14c). Equation (5.14c) can be inserted into (5.10a) to eliminate t^{c2} and the comparative statics are determined by

$$\begin{pmatrix} u_1 & pu_{11}f_k^1 + u_{22}f_k^2 & -sbu_{33} \\ f_k^2 & -f_{kk}^1 - \tilde{p}f_{kk}^2 & 0 \\ 0 & sb^2 f_k^2 & 1 \end{pmatrix} \begin{pmatrix} d\tilde{p} \\ dk^1 \\ dz \end{pmatrix} = \begin{pmatrix} -sb^2 & -u_3 \\ 0 & 0 \\ 0 & f^2 \end{pmatrix} \begin{pmatrix} du_3 \\ d(sb^2) \end{pmatrix}. \tag{5.15}$$

The determinant of the matrix on the right-hand side is positive and it can be seen that both $d\tilde{p}/du_3$ and $d\tilde{p}/d(sb^2)$ are negative. This result is plausible since increased environmental concern and increased pollution intensity raise the tax rate. The producer price of the taxed good is reduced.[13] Thus:

Proposition 5.4. In the case of pure consumption externalities and optimal environmental regulation, an increase of environmental concern leads to a comparative price advantage (in the sense of a reduction of the producer price) for the pollution-intensive good.

Let us now turn to the impact of supply-side regulation on comparative advantage. The equivalent of the quantity version of the Heckscher–Ohlin theorem follows from Mayer's (1991: 112–14) results:

Proposition 5.5. In the case of a pure production externality and optimal environmental regulation, the country with the lower degree of environmental concern will export the commodity which is relatively pollution-intensive in its production.

Increased environmental concern, measured by the impact of pollution on utility, leads to a reduced supply of environmental resources for production purposes. Mayer (1991) has used a model with endogenous labour supply and his result refers to the willingness to work.[14] However, the basic structure of his model is the same as in the environmental-economics model. In the variable-labour supply model, households consider the utility of leisure which is diminished by labour supply. In our model, the government considers the utility of environmental quality which is diminished by the supply of environmental resources.

Mayer (1991) derives an additional result which is of interest here. He shows that in the case of variable labour supply a shift in preferences between the consumption goods may have counter-intuitive specialization effects. Translated into the language of our model, this implies:

Proposition 5.6. In the case of simultaneous production and consumption externalities, the effects of parameter changes on the patterns of trade are ambiguous.

Consider for instance an increase in the pollution intensity of consumption, b^2. The consumption tax will be raised, and p tends to be reduced. However, this

---

[13] As a side issue, one may note that the impact of pollution intensity, b^2, on environmental quality is ambiguous. The consumption tax increase may cause such a decline in demand that this offsets the larger emissions per unit of consumption.

[14] It should be noted that this result requires homotheticity of the demand function.

price change induces a change in the factor allocation, which in turn affects environmental quality and the level of emission taxes. With this change in emission taxes, there is another effect on factor supplies and this changes relative prices again. In a general equilibrium, all these effects work simultaneously and the overall effect on the price is unclear. Additional ambiguities arise if we drop the assumption that the demand for consumption goods is independent of environmental quality (see Pethig (1975)). A tighter environmental policy should lead to a comparative advantage for the good produced in an environmental friendly way. If, however, this commodity is a complement to environmental quality then its demand may be increased by so much that its relative price may be raised increase rather than reduced.

The obvious thing to do now would be to consider the gains from trade and look at an economy which moves from autarky to international trade. For technical reasons, however, we will defer this point to Section 5 and first look at environmental policies in the small-country case.

5.4 Environmental Policy in the Small-Country Case

Consider a small open economy. Its equilibrium is determined by equations (5.1) to (5.4) and (5.6) to (5.9). We assume that foreign pollution either does not affect the domestic environment or stays constant. Equations (5.1) to (5.3) are used to eliminate terms from the other equations. Thus, we have

$$(P + t^t + t^{c2}) u_1(g^1 f^1 + P(g^2 f^2 - c^2)) - u^2(c^2) = 0, \tag{5.16a}$$

$$g^1 f^1_k - (P + t^t)g^2 f^2_k = 0, \tag{5.16b}$$

$$t^{e1} = g^1 f^1_e, \tag{5.16c}$$

$$t^{e2} = (P + t^t)g^2 f^2_e, \tag{5.16d}$$

$$z = sa^1 e^1 + sa^2 e^2 + sb^2 c^2 \pm (\gamma^1 P + \gamma^2)(c^2 - g^2 f^2). \tag{5.16e}$$

In front of the last term of equation (5.16e), a plus (minus) occurs if good 2 (good 1) is imported. The five unknowns are c^2, k^1, z, and the emissions, e^1 and e^2 if the emission taxes are given, or the emission taxes, t^{e1} and t^{e2} if the emission levels are given. In a first step, we will neglect equations (5.16c) and (5.16d) and look at the effects of changes in environmental policies. Since there are trade-specific transport externalities, trade taxes are environmental policy instruments here as well.[15] The comparative-static results are given by

---

[15] It should be noted that the equivalence of trade taxes and environmental taxes is an artefact of the model. We have assumed here that transportation externalities are proportional to transportation services. Reality is more complex, and trade taxes would usually not be the best instruments to address transport externalities.

$$\begin{pmatrix} Ppu_{11}+u_{22} & -pu_{11}t^1 g^2 f_k^2 & pu_{11}(g^{1'}f^1 + Pg^{2'}f^2) \\ 0 & g^1 f_{kk}^1 + \tilde{p}g^2 f_{kk}^2 & \tilde{p}g^{21}f_k^2 - g^{1'}f_k^1 \\ sb^2 \pm(\gamma^2+\gamma^1 P) & \pm(\gamma^2+\gamma^1 P)g^2 f_k^2 & -1 \pm(\gamma^2+\gamma^1 P)g^{2'}f^2 \end{pmatrix} \begin{pmatrix} dc^2 \\ dk^1 \\ dz \end{pmatrix}$$

$$= \begin{pmatrix} u_1 & pu_{11}g^1 f_e^1 & pu_{11}g^2 f_e^2 & u_1 \\ 0 & -g^1 f_{ke}^1 & \tilde{p}g^2 f_{ke}^2 & g^2 f_k^2 \\ 0 & -sa^1 & -sb^2 \pm(\gamma^2+\gamma^1 P)g^2 f_e^2 & 0 \end{pmatrix} \begin{pmatrix} dt^{c2} \\ de^1 \\ de^2 \\ dt^1 \end{pmatrix}. \quad (5.17)$$

The effects of environmental regulation on international trade are in general ambiguous. This can be established algebraically by applying Cramer's rule to equation (5.17). The underlying reason is again the external effect on production that leads to changes in the factor allocation that would otherwise not occur.

Matters are simpler if we neglect the external effects on production and set $g^{1'} = g^{2'} = 0$. However, even then many of the comparative-static results of policy changes on environmental quality and on trade are indeterminate. One can derive this from equation (5.17) by application of Cramer's rule, but the issue can be illustrated better by a graphical representation. Figure 5.1(a–c) show the effects of changes in taxes on emissions from production, consumption, and trade. We use the transformation locus as a vehicle of illustration. Emissions in each sector are treated as being fixed by environmental regulation. Different allocations of capital yield the transformation locus as in the standard Ricardo–Viner model of international trade. The first figure shows the effect of a change in the regulation of production in sector 2, the second one the effect of a consumption tax on good 2, and the third one the effect of a tariff. The production and consumption points in the initial situation are denoted by P and C, and after the change in environmental policy they are moved to P' and C', respectively. It is assumed that commodity 1 is exported and commodity 2 is imported. In a first step, we look at the effects of demand and supply-side regulation on foreign trade:

- A tighter environmental regulation of sector 2 leads to a shift in the transformation locus like the one shown in part (a) of the figure. The comparative disadvantage in the production of this commodity is increased. Thus, the country specializes even more in the production of good 1 and imports are increased. This effect may be reversed if the preferences for the two consumption goods are non-homothetic and the change in available income changes the structure of demand. The homothetic case is represented by the dashed line of a constant demand ratio for given prices.
- A tax on the consumption of good 2 reduces trade because there is a substitution effect towards good 1. If good 1 were the imported good, imports would rise.

Additional ambiguities would turn up if external effects on production were taken into account.

The effects of environmental regulation on environmental quality can be shown to be ambiguous. Only if transport externalities are negligible, are the

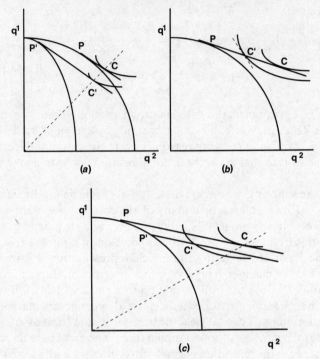

FIG. 5.1 Effects of Environmental Regulation on Trade without External Effects on Production

effects of environmental policies straightforward. High emission taxes and high consumption taxes reduce environmental harm. If international transport causes additional pollution, these effects may be reversed. Three cases may be distinguished:

- In scenario 1 of Figure 5.1, a higher emission tax leads to increased trade. In theory, the pollution impact of transportation may dominate the effect of tighter standards in production.
- In scenario 2 of Figure 5.1, a tax on consumption reduces trade. Imagine, however, a situation in which the other good, commodity 1, is imported. A tax on commodity 2 raises the demand for the (less polluting) commodity 1. This in turn raises import demand and, therefore, the volume of trade.
- In scenario 3, the trade tax causes an increase in the consumption of the good not subject to the tariff since the substitution effect happens to be stronger than the income effect. Here the commodity whose demand is raised is the environmentally friendly one. However, this need not be so. Thus, higher trade taxes—albeit reducing environmentally harmful transport—may cause additional disruption from increased consumption.[16]

---

[16] On the other hand, trade liberalization (i.e. lower trade taxes) may cause environmental improvements in spite of transportation and the income effect. Freer trade may induce substitution

Additional effects are possible if demand is non-homothetic. Then, stricter environmental regulation of production may cause additional environmental problems on the consumption side. If the 'dirty' consumption good is inferior, its demand will be increased with reduced income.

The results derived from the exercise can be summarized:

Proposition 5.7. In the small open economy, the impacts of emission taxes, consumption taxes, and trade taxes on foreign trade and environmental pollution are ambiguous even if the productivity effects of environmental disruption are negligible. If demand is homothetic, then the effects on trade have the expected signs.

The effects on environmental quality are ambiguous even if external effects on production are neglected.

The ambiguity of the effects on environmental quality is to be explained by the fact that the regulation of a polluting activity has spillover effects to other polluting activities, e.g. from production or consumption on trade. Thus, there are indirect side-effects of environmental regulation which may influence environmental policy in an unintended way.

Having discussed the effects of policy changes, we may now turn to the issue of optimal policies. The social-welfare function can be expressed as

$$w = u\big(g^1 f^1 + P(g^2 f^2 - c^2), c^2, - z\big). \tag{5.18}$$

w is differentiated with respect to t^{c2}, e^1, e^2, and t^l and the comparative-statics results from equation (5.17) are used. We now turn back to the general case where external effects on production are possible. Some basic but tedious calculations give:

$$t^{e1} = g^1 f_e^1 = \frac{sa^1}{1 + sb^2 g^{2\prime} f^2} \left(\frac{u_3}{u_1} + g^{1\prime} f^1 + \frac{u_2}{u_1} g^{2\prime} f^2 \right), \tag{5.19a}$$

$$t^{e2} = \tilde{p} g^2 f_e^2 = \frac{sa^2}{1 + sb^2 g^{2\prime} f^2} \left(\frac{u_3}{u_1} + g^{1\prime} f^1 + \frac{u_2}{u_1} g^{2\prime} f^2 \right), \tag{5.19b}$$

$$t^{c2} = \frac{sb^2}{1 + sb^2 g^{2\prime} f^2} \left(\frac{u_3}{u_1} + g^{1\prime} f^1 + \frac{u_2}{u_1} g^{2\prime} f^2 \right), \tag{5.19c}$$

$$t^l = \frac{\pm \left(\gamma^2 + P \gamma^1 \right)}{1 + sb^2 g^{2\prime} f^2} \left(\frac{u_3}{u_1} + g^{1\prime} f^1 + \frac{u_2}{u_1} g^{2\prime} f^2 \right), \tag{5.19d}$$

The emission and consumption tax rates are determined by the same formulae as in the case of the closed economy (see equations (5.13a, b', c)). They equal the marginal environmental damage due to the use of environmental resources in production and consumption, respectively. And the trade tax is a

of environmentally unfriendly by cleaner consumption goods. Similar effects can occur in the trade with intermediate goods—which is not considered here. And this may explain why many developing countries experience improvements in environmental quality when they become more open. There is a crowding out of 'dirty' domestic technology by foreign 'clean' technology. Like in the case of consumption good, this effect is not intended (see Birdsall and Wheeler (1992) for empirical evidence). Both, clean consumption goods and clean technology are purchased not because they are environmentally friendly but because they have other properties that make them desirable.

Pigouvian tax as well. Remember that trade taxes have been introduced for the non-numéraire good only. If the numéraire good is exported and the non-numéraire good is imported, the optimal trade tax is positive. Such an import tariff reduces the volume of trade and, thus, the pollution due to both exports and imports. If, however, the numéraire good is imported and the non-numéraire good is exported, then the tax rate is negative. But the tax base itself is negative since exports are negative imports. Thus, this is equivalent to a positive tax on exports, which reduces trade and environmental harm.[17] In the case of more than two traded goods, differing tax rates should be levied on the various goods according to their specific pollution impacts.

Proposition 5.8. In a small open economy, activities should be taxed according to the marginal environmental damage they cause.

It is not surprising that this Pigouvian result turns up here. Environmental disruption is the only distortion and there are as many policy instruments as sources of environmental disruption. This may change if the number of policy instruments is reduced, if some of them are subject to restrictions, or if additional distortions are added. These cases will be considered in due course.

5.5 Pollute Thy Neighbour via Trade

Before we turn to the issue of the gains (and losses) from trade another mechanism needs to be discussed through which foreign trade influences the state of the environment. Up to now, it has been assumed that emissions from production activities have been fixed by the government before the country is opened. This can happen only if the government has chosen a tradable-pollution-permits scheme with a fixed number of permits or a particular kind of command-and-control regulation. But fixed emission levels are rather unrealistic. Usually, factor relocations induced for instance by a removal of trade restrictions lead to changes in emissions from production. The easiest way to introduce this into the model is to assume that emission taxes but not emission levels are given.[18] To make matters tractable, we neglect consumption and transportation externalities and the external effect of pollution on productivities. Consumption taxes are zero as well. The general equilibrium is determined by

[17] This implies that the same effects on the environment can be achieved by an import tax and an export tax. This result is interesting in a public-choice context. Import taxes are always susceptible to being captured by regulatees lobbying for higher incomes. However, no one is particularly interested in export taxes. Thus, if these instruments have the same allocative effects, why shouldn't one choose the instrument with a smaller probability of regulatory capture? We will return to this issue in Ch. 9, when institutional implications are discussed.

[18] One may argue that emission taxes are not particularly realistic as well. However, the line of arguing and the results carry through for other regulatory approaches that allow variable emissions. An example is a regulation which specifies a constant emissions–output ratio, e.g. by imposing a limit on SO_2 emissions per megawatt-hour of electricity generated in power-plants.

$$(P + t^t) u_1(f^1 + P(f^2 - c^2)) - u_2(c^2) = 0, \tag{5.20a}$$

$$f_k^1 - (P + t^t)f_k^2 = 0. \tag{5.20b}$$

$$t^{e1} = f_e^1, \tag{5.20c}$$

$$t^{e2} = f_e^2, [19] \tag{5.20d}$$

$$z = sa^1 e^1 + sa^2 e^2. \tag{5.20e}$$

Trade liberalization will be modelled by a reduction of the trade tax, t^t. The comparative statics follow from

$$\begin{vmatrix} pPu_{11} + u_{22} & -pu_{11}t^t f_k^2 & -pu_{11}f_e^1 & -pPu_{11}f_e^2 \\ 0 & f_{kk}^1 + pf_{kk}^2 & f_{ke}^1 & -pf_{ke}^2 \\ 0 & f_{ke}^1 & f_{ee}^1 & 0 \\ 0 & -f_{ke}^2 & 0 & f_{ee}^2 \end{vmatrix} \begin{pmatrix} dc^2 \\ dk^1 \\ de^1 \\ de^2 \end{pmatrix} = \begin{pmatrix} u_1 \\ f_k^2 \\ 0 \\ 0 \end{pmatrix} dt^t \tag{5.21}$$

and the impact of the trade tax on emissions is

$$\frac{de^1}{dt^t} = \frac{-f_{ke}^1 f_k^2 f_{ee}^2}{f_{ee}^2 \left(f_{kk}^1 f_{ee}^1 - (f_{ke}^1)^2\right) + pf_{ee}^1 \left(f_{kk}^2 f_{ee}^2 - (f_{ke}^2)^2\right)} < 0 \tag{5.22a}$$

$$\frac{de^1}{dt^t} = \frac{f_{ke}^1 f_k^2 f_{ee}^2}{f_{ee}^2 \left(f_{kk}^1 f_{ee}^1 - (f_{ke}^1)^2\right) + pf_{ee}^1 \left(f_{kk}^2 f_{ee}^2 - (f_{ke}^2)^2\right)} > 0. \tag{5.22b}$$

The denominators on the right-hand sides of equations (5.22a) and (5.22b) are zero in the case of constant returns to scale.[20] Let us, therefore, assume decreasing returns to scale here. Then an increase in the tariff rate on imports of good 2 leads to an increase in the emissions of sector 2. The emissions of industry 1 are reduced. The underlying mechanism is the following one: the tariff raises the domestic price of commodity 2, and at given factor prices, this sector will attract additional capital. The availability of capital improves the productivity of the environmental resource and emissions will be increased. This again raises the productivity of capital and amplifies the capital movement and so forth. This process eventually comes to a halt because of the decreasing returns to scale. By the same line of arguing, one can explain why output and emissions in industry 1 shrink.

What are the implications of these changes in emissions on environmental quality? Using equation (5.20e), we get

$$\frac{dz}{dt^t} = \frac{f_k^2 \left(sa^2 f_{ee}^1 f_{ke}^2 - sa^1 f_{ee}^2 f_{ke}^1\right)}{f_{ee}^2 \left(f_{kk}^1 f_{ee}^1 - (f_{ke}^1)^2\right) + p^2 f_{ee}^1 \left(f_{kk}^2 f_{ee}^2 - (f_{ke}^2)^2\right)}.$$

---

[19] Here, the emission tax rate is measured in units of good itself, not in units of the numéraire. The reason for making this assumption here is that we would otherwise obtain an asymmetry in the reactions, depending on whether the trade tax is levied on the goods of sector 1 or of sector 2.

[20] This is due to the fact that in this case factor prices are functions of world market prices only and, in particular, they are independent of the emissions discharged.

In order to obtain an interpretable condition, we have to substitute some terms. Applying the implicit function theorem to equations (5.20c) and (5.20d), we get

$$\frac{de^i}{dk^i} = -\frac{f^i_{ke}}{f^i_{ee}}, \quad i = 1, 2.$$

This defines us the marginal emission intensity of production in sector i and this can be used in the equation determining dz/dt^t:

$$\frac{dz}{dt^t} = \frac{f^2_k f^1_{ee} f^2_{ee} \left(sa^1 \frac{de^1}{dk^1} - sa^2 \frac{de^2}{dk^2} \right)}{f^2_{ee} \left(f^1_{kk} f^1_{ee} - (f^1_{ke})^2 \right) + p f^1_{ee} \left(f^2_{kk} f^2_{ee} - (f^2_{ke})^2 \right)}. \tag{5.23}$$

The interpretation is now straightforward. The two components of the term in brackets in the numerator on the right-hand side are the marginal pollution intensities of the production of good 1 and good 2, respectively. It follows that if a tariff is levied on imports of good 2 and this good happens to be relatively environmentally intensive in its production, then environmental pollution will be increased. If good 1 is the environmentally intensive good, then environmental quality will be improved.

If the tariff is removed rather than implemented, we get a trade-liberalization effect. If we use proposition 5.2 to identify the relationship between endowments and trade patterns, the result can be stated as follows:

Proposition 5.9. Let there be decreasing returns to scale, let production be the only source of pollution, and let the productivities be unaffected by the state of the environment. If the environmental policy instrument is an emission tax with a given rate, then trade liberalization improves environmental quality in the capital-rich country and reduces environmental quality in the country well-endowed with environmental resources.

This is the 'pollute thy neighbour via trade' effect identified by Siebert *et al.* (1980: 120–1). A country with tight environmental policy will specialize in the production of 'clean' goods and will import commodities that are environmentally intensive in their production. In this country, environmental quality will be improved. In the other country, pollution tends to rise. Loosely speaking, the country with the sound environmental policy has 'exported' some of its environmental problems to the other country. This is something environmentalists are worried about. But is this an argument against free trade? At a first glance it may be, but there are two important issues that have been neglected here. First, environmental quality is not welfare: the country with the deteriorated environment may be compensated by an increase in material wealth. Second, environmental policies can be changed to cope with environmental disruption and a government using the same environmental policies in autarky and in a trade situation would act irrationally.[21] In a first step, we look at welfare effects, in the second step at policy adjustments.

[21] The fact that we have obtained the same formulas for environmental policies for these two cases does not mean that the environmental-policy instruments take the same values. Since the

5.6 Gains or Losses From Trade?

Welfare effects of trade liberalization are considered first in the case where emission levels are given. We differentiate the welfare function, (5.18), with respect to t^t and take into account the comparative-static results that can be derived from equation (5.17). This yields:

$$\frac{dw}{dt^t} = (t^{c2}u_1 - sb^2u_3)\frac{dc^2}{dt^t} + \left(t^tu_1 - (\pm(\gamma^2 + P\gamma^1)u_3)\right)\left(\frac{dc^2}{dt^t} + f_k^2\frac{dk^1}{dt^t}\right) \qquad (5.24)$$

with $dk^1/dt^t < 0$ and $dc^2/dt^t < 0$ from equation (5.17).[22] Let us assume that the tariff rate is reduced, i.e. that trade is liberalized. There are two effects. First, the demand for the imported good will rise. This increases material wealth but reduces environmental quality. The net effect is positive if the consumption tax rate exceeds the Pigouvian tax rate, sb^2u_3/u_1, and negative if the tax rate is lower. In the first case, the marginal increase in material well-being is larger than the marginal environmental damage. In the second case, the damage is larger. The second effect has to do with transport externalities. If the initial import tax rate is larger than the marginal environmental damage, then the reduction in distortions dominates the increase in environmental damage. If, however, the initial trade tax is already too low, then the transport externality dominates the positive effect of the removal of the distortion and there will be a welfare loss.

Moreover, we can derive a second-best result directly from equation (5.24). Assume that the trade tax equals the marginal environmental cost of transport. Then

$$\frac{dw}{dt^t} = (t^{c2}u^1 - sb^2u_3)\frac{dc^2}{dt^t} \quad \text{if } t^t = \pm(\gamma^2 + P\gamma^1)\frac{u_3}{u_1}. \qquad (5.25)$$

It follows that the country would benefit from raising barriers to trade if its regulation of environmentally harmful consumption activities is insufficient, i.e. if t^{c2} is too low. Note, however, that we have assumed here that the imported good is the environmentally unfriendly consumption good. What would happen if this good were exported? In this case, t^t would be negative, i.e. there would be an export tax. And again an increase in the tax rate would be beneficial. However, since we start from a negative initial value of t^t, this implies that the export tax is reduced. Thus, welfare would be increased by a removal of the trade barrier. The reason is that the additional demand from abroad raises the price and this reduces domestic consumption.

In a similar fashion, we can derive results for the scenario with constant emission tax rates, t^{e1} and t^{e2}. In order to keep the analysis tractable, we neglect

arguments of the functions (marginal productivities and marginal utilities) are different in the two scenarios, the values of the functions are different as well.

[22] The demand for good 2 is reduced since its price is raised and since the tariff implies a real-income loss. The demand for capital in sector 1 is reduced as well since the tariff protects industry 2, which withdraws capital from sector 1.

the environmental costs of consumption and trade: $b^2 = \gamma = 0$. Differentiation of the welfare function, equation (5.18), with respect to t^t yields

$$\frac{dw}{dt^t} = t^t u_1\left(\frac{dc^2}{dt^t} + f_k^2\frac{dk^1}{dt^t}\right) + (u_1 f_e^1 - sa^1 u_3)\frac{de^1}{dt^t} + (Pu_1 f_e^2 - sa^2 u_3)\frac{de^2}{dt^t}. \qquad (5.26)$$

dc^2/dt and dk^1/dt^t follow from equation (5.21) and it can be shown that the first term in brackets is always negative. de^1/dt^t and de^2/dt^t are given by equations (5.22a) and (5.22b), respectively. The terms in front of de^1/dt^t and de^2/dt^t are positive, negative, or zero depending on whether the environmental policy overinternalizes, underinternalizes, or correctly internalizes the environmental externality. Thus the welfare effect is composed of three components:

- The first component is the traditional gain from trade. Since the term in brackets is negative and is multiplied by the tariff rate, it follows welfare is increased if an import tax or subsidy is reduced. Free trade, $t^t = 0$, is optimal unless there are additional distortions.
- The second component is the effect of suboptimal regulation in sector 1. If the environmental regulation is too lax, the marginal environmental damage from an additional unit of emissions exceeds the marginal utility that can be derived from consuming the additional output. Since a reduction in the import tax on good 2 increases the emissions of sector 1, this leads to welfare losses.
- The third component is the effect of the regulatory deficit in sector 2. In the case of a too low tax rate, there is a positive effect of trade liberalization on welfare since the emissions of sector 2, whose marginal welfare effect is negative, are reduced.

Since the magnitudes of the impacts of the last two components depend on the degrees of regulatory failure in the two sectors of the economy, the sign and the size of the welfare effect of trade liberalization are indeterminate. In the case of a substantial underregulation of the export sector or a substantial overregulation of the import sector, the welfare effect of a removal of trade barriers can be negative.[23]

Again the question may be asked, whether there is a case for trade intervention based on second-best considerations. And again the answer is 'yes'. Assume that there are no trade barriers, i.e. $t^t = 0$. Then the first component of the welfare effect vanishes. The second and third effects are unknown in their magnitude. Each of them is the product of the degree of regulatory failure, $u_i f_e^i - sb^i u_3$, and the impact of trade interventions on emissions. The degree of regulatory failure is exogenous here. We simply assume that environmental regulation is not optimal for whatever reason. Let us normalize this by imposing the additional assumption that the degree of regulatory failure is the same in both sectors. In particular, assume that the share of non-internalized

---

[23] Similar results have been obtained by Siebert (1977) in a simpler model.

or overinternalized externalities is the same in both industries. Let ξ denote the degree of internalization, i.e.

$$\xi = \frac{u_1 f_e^1}{sa^1 u_3} = \frac{P u_2 f_e^2}{sa^2 u_3} \, .$$

If this is inserted into equation (5.26) and if we use $z = sa^1 e^1 + sa^2 e^2$, we obtain:

$$\frac{dw}{dt^t} = (\xi - 1) \frac{dz}{dt^t} \quad \text{if } t^t > = 0. \tag{5.27}$$

dz/dt^t is determined by equation (5.23). Since this depends on the pollution intensities of the two sectors, we may conclude that an import tariff is welfare-improving if the emission taxes are too low ($\xi < 1$) and if the exported good is relatively environmentally intensive in its production. Should the emission taxes be too high in both sectors ($\xi > 1$), then an import subsidy is the welfare-improving policy if the exported good is environmentally intensively produced.

We can summarize the second-best results derived in this section as follows

Proposition 5.10. Trade liberalization may have negative welfare effects if environmental policies that regulate production and consumption are not at their optimal levels. In such cases trade interventions may be used for welfare improvements and the achievement of second-best solutions. Let the environmental costs of trade and the external effect on production be negligible. Then, tariffs are welfare-improving in situations with too low environmental taxes if, ceteris paribus, *the imported good is environmentally unfriendly in its consumption or if the exported good is produced environmentally intensively.*

It should be noted that trade interventions are merely second best in this case. If pollution-intensive consumption is concerned, it would always be better to tax consumption itself instead of using an instrument that has a distorting effect on the supply side. If the emissions from production are concerned, the obvious policy would be to use appropriate emission taxes rather than going the indirect way and using a tariff which achieves the objective at the price of creating a distortion on the demand side.

Having identified the gains from trade, we may finally ask how the optimal environmental policy is affected by trade liberalization. So far, we have taken environmental regulation as given. But since trade changes relative prices and tends to increase the consumption possibilities of an economy, there may be reasons to adjust environmental taxes and standards.

Three instruments have to be considered: trade taxes, consumption taxes, and taxes on emissions from production. The following result can be derived:

- First, a trade tax should be levied to internalize the external effects arising from international transport. This tax rate may or may not be prohibitive.
- Second, the consumption tax rate has to be adjusted. A move from autarky to free trade increases the consumption possibility set. If the income elasticities of demand are positive (which we have assumed in this model), trade will increase the consumption of the imported good but the effect of

trade on the exported good remains ambiguous. This is due to the fact that the income effect is positive but the substitution effect is negative. Thus, if the imported good is environmentally intensive in its production and if the consumption tax rate has been optimal from the beginning, the disutility of increased environmental disruption dominates the utility gain from increased consumption. The optimal reaction is to raise the emission tax to shift consumption from the 'dirty' to the environmentally friendly good.

- The third instrument is emission taxation. It has been shown earlier that the optimum emission tax rates in both sectors are proportional to each other in autarky as well as under free trade. Moreover, it has been established that for given emission tax rates environmental pollution tends to be increased after trade liberalization if the environmentally intensively produced good is exported. Since the marginal environmental cost of pollution is increasing whereas the marginal productivity of environmental resources is declining, the net benefit of increased emissions is negative. It is optimal to raise the emission tax rates in order to induce a shift from of resources from environmentally intensive production to environmentally friendlier production. The opposite policy recommendation applies to the other country that has specialized on the production of the environmentally friendly good.[24]

This can be summarized:

Proposition 5.11. With a move from autarky to trade, the country well endowed with environmental resources will tighten its environmental regulation of production, the other country will relax its regulation. The country importing the good whose consumption is environmentally intensive should increase the consumption tax. The effect in the other country is unclear. Both countries should introduce measures to regulate the additional externalities of international transport.

5.7 The Terms of Trade and the Environment

How do a country's terms of trade affect its environment and its environmental policy? This question is important for the following reason. Consider a country whose consumption and/or production are environmentally disruptive. Let us additionally assume that there are transboundary spillovers of pollution and that, therefore, people in other countries care about what the country under consideration is doing in terms of environmental regulation. They may think about measures that are suitable to 'correct' the country's behaviour. What one can do (in addition to exerting political pressure on polluters or bribing them) is to use one's power in international markets to change the constraints the country under consideration is subject to. An example is a ban on the imports of the goods produced there. Such measures have been discussed

---

[24] See Rauscher (1991a: 21) for a formal proof of this result in a simpler model.

widely (not only) in environmentalist circles concerned about timber trade as a possible cause of tropical deforestation. Another example is the Montreal Protocol on Substances that Deplete the Ozone Layer. This international environmental agreement establishes time-schedules for trade bans on various goods: the substances themselves, commodities that contain these substances, and commodities that have been produced in processes involving these substances. See Chapter 9 for a more detailed discussion of the Montreal Protocol. The implementation of such measures is effective only if undertaken by a large country or a group of countries. The effect is that the trade ban reduces world-wide demand and this has an effect on the terms of trade. How will the country affected by this measure react?

Two cases will be considered: that of consumption externalities and given emissions from production and that of no consumption externalities and fixed emission taxes in production. In both cases, we will neglect environmental externalities on production and the environmental costs of transport.

In the first case, the comparative-statics follow from equations (5.16a) and (5.16b):

$$\frac{dc^2}{dP} = \frac{\left(u_1 - pu_{11}(c^2 - f^2)\right)\left(f^1_{kk} + \tilde{p}f^2_{kk}\right) + pu_{11}t'\left(f^2_k\right)^2}{\left(f^1_{kk} + \tilde{p}f^2_{kk}\right)(Ppu_{11} + u_{22})} \tag{5.28}$$

There are three effects. The first one is the substitution effect, which is negative for the good whose price has risen. The second effect is an income effect. Depending on which good is being imported, the increase in P is a terms-of-trade improvement or deterioration. If good 2 is exported, then the terms of trade are improved and demand will rise. The third effect is due to the trade tax. It is negative. The higher P the smaller the demand. It is seen that the overall effect is negative if good 2 is imported and ambiguous otherwise.

Proposition 5.12. Let the consumption tax rate be given. If a pollution-intensive consumption good is imported, an increase in its world market price reduces domestic demand and improves environmental quality. If the good is exported, the effect of the price change is ambiguous.

The ambiguity in the case of the exported good is due to the income effect of the terms-of-trade improvement.

Let us now look at the effects of the terms-of-trade changes on emissions from production. We neglect the environmental disruption from consumption and trade and we do not take into account that transportation causes environmental disruption. This makes the analysis very simple because the comparative statics are the same as in the case of trade liberalization. Thus we have formulae (5.22a) and (5.22b) again, only slightly modified by the replacement of P for t' in the denominators on the left-hand sides and P for p on the right-hand sides.

$$\frac{de^1}{dP} = \frac{-f^1_{ke}f^2_k f^2_{ee}}{f^2_{ee}\left(f^1_{kk}f^1_{ee} - \left(f^1_{ke}\right)^2\right) + Pf^1_{ee}\left(f^2_{kk}f^2_{ee} - \left(f^2_{ke}\right)^2\right)} < 0 \tag{5.29a}$$

$$\frac{de^1}{dP} = \frac{f^1_{ee} f^2_k f^2_{ke}}{f^2_{ee}\left(f^1_{kk} f^1_{ee} - \left(f^1_{ke}\right)^2\right) + Pf^1_{ee}\left(f^2_{kk} f^2_{ee} - \left(f^2_{ke}\right)^2\right)} > 0 \qquad (5.29b)$$

We can now use the same arguments as in Section 5 to derive:

Proposition 5.13. Let emission tax rates be given. A change in the world market price ratio tends to increase (reduce) the emissions of the sector whose good has become relatively dearer (cheaper). The overall effect on the environment is positive (negative) if the good whose relative price has increased is environmentally friendly (intensive) in its production.

The final question to be asked concerns the impact of terms-of-trade changes on the environmental policy. We will analyse this question for the case of mere production externalities, i.e. consumption and transport externalities will be neglected. The underlying idea is that large countries may wish to use their influence on world market prices to induce environmental policy changes in the rest of the world.[25] In contrast to the case of given environmental polices that have been discussed above, this involves an element of extraterritorialism, i.e. the attempt to influence the policy-making process in other, sovereign countries.

The impact of world market price on emissions and environmental quality can be derived from total differentiation of the system of equations that determines the equilibrium of the small open economy:

$$Pu_1 - u_2 = 0, \qquad (5.30a)$$

$$f^1_k - Pf^2_k = 0, \qquad (5.30b)$$

$$u_1 f^1_e = sa^1 u_3, \qquad (5.30c)$$

$$u_2 f^2_e = sa^2 u_3, \qquad (5.30d)$$

$$z = sa^1 e^1 + sa^2 e^2. \qquad (5.30e)$$

But we can also use Mayer's (1991: 108) result and state that

Proposition 5.14. Assume that there are constant returns to scale and that environmental regulation represents the 'true' endowment of a country with environmental resources. A price increase of the import good increases environmental disruption if this good is relatively environmentally intensive in its production.

There are two effects that are responsible for this result. On the one hand, an increase in the price of the imported good moves the country closer to its autarky position and leads to an income loss. Since we have specified the utility function such that environmental quality is a normal good, the demand for environmental quality tends to be reduced. Moreover, there is a relocation effect of factors of production on the supply side of the economy. The supply of the (dirty) import good will be increased at the expense of the (relatively clean) export good. This generates additional incentives to relax environmental

---

[25] This corresponds to a kind of a Stackelberg leader position, which is plausible if on the other side of the game there is a group of many small players acting as price-takers.

regulation. If, however, the exported good is environmentally intensive, the income and the relocation effects have opposite signs and the total effect is unknown. Figure 5.2 depicts the possible cases in terms of demand and supply functions for environmental resources. The demand curve is a normal factor demand curve expressed as a function of the environmental tax rate in terms of the numéraire good. We chose the tax rate for sector 1 but the tax rate for sector 2 is proportional to this, the factor of proportionality being a^2/a^1. The supply of environmental resources is derived from society's willingness to accept compensation for environmental damage.

The original equilibrium is E. Four scenarios are shown:

- Case A. The relative price of the environmentally intensive import good is reduced. Due to the terms-of-trade improvement, there is a positive income effect on the demand for environmental quality. The supply of environmental resources is reduced. The demand is reduced as well since the environmentally friendly sector expands and withdraws factors from the environmentally intensive sector. Environmental quality rises. The effect on the tax rate is unclear.

- Case B. The price of the environmentally intensive export good is increased. Due to the terms-of-trade improvement the resource supply curve is shifted to the left. The factor relocation effect shifts the demand curve upwards. The result is an increase in the tax rate, but the effect on environmental quality is unclear.

- Case C. The price of the environmentally intensive import good is raised. This is a terms-of-trade deterioration and the supply of environmental resources is increased. The demand rises as well since the environmentally intensive industry now attracts factors of production. There will be environmental deterioration and the effect on the tax rate is unclear.

- Case D. The price of the environmentally intensive export good is reduced. The terms-of-trade reduction shifts the supply curve to the right. The demand curve is shifted to the left. The tax rate is reduced but the effect on the environment is unclear.

Figure 5.2 depicts generalized Stolper–Samuelson effects for the case of endogenous factor supply.[26] The most relevant case for the discussion on extraterritorial use of environmental policies is D, where the country under consideration exports the pollution-intensive good. An example is a timber-exporting country. It has been established that it is by no means clear that a reduction in the price of this good will improve the environmental situation.[27]

---

[26] The Stolper–Samuelson effects of the original Heckscher–Ohlin model with inelastic factor supply would be obtained if the factor supply curve were vertical.

[27] A similar result has been obtained by Barbier and Rauscher (1994) in an intertemporal model of renewable resource use and exportation. There, the special case of complete specialization has been considered, i.e. a model where the imported good is not produced at home. If the demand for the import good is inelastic, then the environmentally disruptive activity is extended despite the reduction in the price.

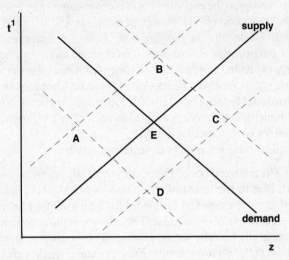

FIG. 5.2 Terms-of-Trade Changes and the Environment: The Case of Optimal Taxes

5.8 Environmental Policy in the Large-Country Case: Free Trade

A large country has an impact on world market prices and can use its environmental policy to improve its terms of trade. Perhaps more importantly, it may be able to take into account leakage effects. Strict environmental standards and taxes may induce a change in the patterns of specialization. Environmentally intensive industries will decline and this is good for environmental quality. But across the border, environmentally intensive production tends to expand. In the case of transfrontier-pollution spillovers or global environmental problems, this tends to dilute the effects of sound environmental policies. It is assumed now that trade is unrestricted. Trade interventions are not available to the country under consideration, for instance because it has signed a free-trade agreement. Moreover, we neglect the problem of transport externalities.

We consider three different scenarios for the environmental policy in the other country: (i) emissions from production are given and fixed, and there is a fixed consumption tax rate, (ii) emission taxes are given in the foreign country and foreign consumption is not a problem, and (iii) the foreign government uses its optimal environmental policy and the home government can act as a Stackelberg leader.

The equilibrium is given by the following equations

$$(P + t^{c2})u_1\left(f^1 + PM(P)\right) - u_2\left(f^2 - M(P)\right) = 0, \tag{5.31a}$$

$$f_k^1 - Pf_k^2 = 0, \tag{5.31b}$$

$$z = sa^1e^1 + sa^2e^2 + sb^2(f^2 - M(P)) + (1 - S)(A^1E^1(P) + A^2E^2(P)$$
$$+ B^2C^2(P)). \tag{5.31c}$$

The balance-of-payments constraint and the foreign import demand function have been inserted into the utility function. In the third equation, $E^1(P)$, $E^2(P)$ and $C^2(P)$ denote the impact of the terms of trade on foreign emissions from production and consumption, as they have been derived in the previous section. The comparative statics can be determined via

$$\begin{pmatrix} u_1 + pu_{11}(M + PM') + u_{22}M' & pu_{11}f_k^1 + u_{22}f_k^2 & 0 \\ -f_k^2 & f_{kk}^1 + pf_{kk}^2 & 0 \\ sb^2M' - (1-S)Zp & sb^2f_k^2 & 1 \end{pmatrix} \begin{pmatrix} dp \\ dk^1 \\ dz \end{pmatrix}$$

$$= \begin{pmatrix} -u_1 & -pu_{11}f_e^1 & u_{22}f_e^1 \\ 0 & -f_{ke}^1 & pg^2f_{ke}^2 \\ 0 & sa^1 & sa^2 + sbg^2f_e^2 \end{pmatrix} \begin{pmatrix} dt^{c2} \\ de^1 \\ de^2 \end{pmatrix} \tag{5.32}$$

with

$$Z_p = -A^1E^{1'} - A^2E^{2'} - B^2C^{2'}$$

denoting the effect of the world market price ratio on the total foreign emissions. Let

$$\Delta = (u_1 = pu_{11}(M + PM') + u_{22}M')(f_{kk}^1 + Pf_{kk}^2) + f_k^2(pu_{11}f_k^1 + u_{22}f_k^2)$$

be the determinant of the matrix on the left-hand side. Its sign is indeterminate.[28] The term causing the indeterminacy is $pu_{11}(M + PM')$. If foreign import demand is very inelastic, then this term is negative and Δ may become positive. Otherwise, it is always negative. I wish to exclude the case that $\Delta > 0$. If Δ were positive, this would cause some counter-intuitive, and probably also unrealistic, effects. Consider for instance a situation in which some additional quantity of one of the goods becomes available as a transfer (e.g. some manna from heaven). Then $\Delta > 0$ would imply that the price of this good, which has become more abundant, is increased.[29] Thus, let us assume that

$$\Delta < 0.$$

The comparative-static results are then[30]

---

[28] This corrects an error in my own Rauscher (1991a) paper, where I argued that a similar matrix had always the 'correct' sign. The indeterminacy, however, is a general property of general-equilibrium trade models that are otherwise well behaved. See Dixit and Norman (1980: 129–33) for instance.

[29] To show this, let us assume that the manna falling from heaven is $\bar{q}^2$. We can neglect the third equation and obtain

$$\begin{pmatrix} u_1 + pu_{11}(M + PM') + u_{22}M' & pu_{11}f_k^1 + u_{22}f_k^2 \\ -f_k^2 & f_{kk}^1 + Pf_{kk}^2 \end{pmatrix} \begin{pmatrix} dP \\ dk^1 \end{pmatrix} = \begin{pmatrix} u_{22}d\bar{q}^2 \\ 0 \end{pmatrix}.$$

If the determinant had a positive sign, then the impact of a transfer which increases the availability of good 2 on the price of this good would be positive. Dixit and Norman (1980. 131–2) show that a Δ with the 'correct' sign is also a condition for the stability of the market equilibrium.

[30] Results concerning the capital allocation are not stated explicitly here. A higher consumption tax always causes the decline in the sector producing the taxed good. The effect of emissions is ambiguous. They raise the marginal physical productivity, but the negative price effect may reduce the marginal value product of capital.

$$\frac{dP}{dt^{c2}} = -\frac{1}{\Delta}u_1\left(f_{kk}^1 + Pf_{kk}^2\right) < 0, \tag{5.33a}$$

$$\frac{dP}{de^1} = -\frac{1}{\Delta}\left(pu_{11}f_e^1\left(f_{kk}^1 + Pf_{kk}^2\right) + f_{ke}^1\left(pu_{11}f_k^1 + u_{22}f_k^2\right)\right) > 0, \tag{5.33b}$$

$$\frac{dP}{de^2} = \frac{1}{\Delta}\left(u_{22}f_e^1\left(f_{kk}^1 + Pf_{kk}^2\right) - Pf_{ke}^2\left(pu_{11}f_k^1 + u_{22}f_k^2\right)\right) < 0. \tag{5.33c}$$

$$\frac{dz}{dt^{c2}} = \frac{1}{\Delta}u_1\left(\left(f_{kk}^1 + Pf_{kk}^2\right)\left(sb^2 M' - (1-S)Z_P\right) + sb^2\left(f_k^2\right)^2\right) \tag{5.34a}$$

$$\frac{dz}{de^1} = sa^1 + \frac{(1-S)Z_P}{\Delta}\left(f_{ke}^1\left(pu_{11}f_k^1 + u_{22}f_k^2\right) - pu_{11}f_e^1\left(f_{kk}^1 + Pf_{kk}^2\right)\right),$$

$$+ \frac{sb^2}{\Delta}\left(f_k^2\left(f_{ke}^1(u_1 + pu_{11}(M + PM') + u_{22}M') - pu_{11}f_e^1 f_k^2\right)\right) \tag{5.34b}$$

$$- M'\left(\left(f_{ke}^1\left(pu_{11}f_k^1 + u_{22}f_k^2\right) - pu_{11}f_e^1\left(f_{kk}^1 + Pf_{kk}^2\right)\right)\right),$$

$$\frac{dz}{de^2} = sa^2 + sb^2f_e^2 - \frac{(1-S)Z_P}{\Delta}\left(Pf_{ke}^2\left(pu_{11}f_k^1 + u_{22}f_k^2\right) - pu_{11}f_e^1\left(f_{kk}^1 + Pf_{kk}^2\right)\right),$$

$$- \frac{sb^2}{\Delta}\left(f_k^2\left(Pf_{ke}^2(u_1 + pu_{11}(M + PM') + u_{22}M') - u_{22}f_e^2 f_k^2\right)\right) \tag{5.34c}$$

$$+ M'\left(Pf_{ke}^2\left(pu_{11}f_k^1 + u_{22}f_k^2\right) - u_{22}f_e^2\left(f_{kk}^1 + Pf_{kk}^2\right)\right).$$

The effects on the world market prices are straightforward. If a tax is levied on the consumption of a good, its demand will be reduced and the world market price goes down. If a sector-specific factor, e^1 or e^2, is taxed, then the supply of final goods of the industry is reduced. The world market price is increased. Equations (5.34a–c) denote the effects on pollution. The direct effect of the consumption tax rate is negative. Pollution tends to be reduced. However, there is a change in the terms of trade and therefore the foreign country is induced to change its emissions from consumption and production. This is the leakage effect, and it may be positive or negative. Similar considerations apply in the case of an emission reduction on the supply side. The direct effect is sa^i, i.e. pollution is reduced and environmental quality rises. The leakage effect is again ambiguous and it depends on whether the regulated sector is an import-competing or an export industry and on how the foreign country reacts to the change in the terms of trade. Moreover, it has to be taken into account that environmental regulation of the supply side affects the domestic consumption possibility set. This effect is a bit more complicated than in the small-country case considered in Section 4 of this chapter since environmental policies affect the consumption possibility set not only through the output expansion but also through the terms of trade.

Proposition 5.15. Tighter environmental regulation in the export industry improves the terms of trade. Tighter environmental standards in the import industry worsen the terms of trade. High consumption taxes on the exported (imported) good worsen (improve) the terms of trade. Leakage effects occur if the foreign emissions react to changes in the terms of trade.

Leakage effects can have different causes and we have identified three of them.

- The foreign consumption possibility set is increased if the foreign country's terms of trade are improved and the change in relative prices induces a substitution effect.
- If foreign taxes on production emissions are given, then a change in relative prices leads to increased foreign emissions if the good whose price has been increased is emission-intensive.
- In the case where environmental policies are adjusted by the foreign government, an additional effect has to be taken into account. If environmental quality is a superior good, emissions are a declining function of the terms of trade.

Leakage effects can be illustrated nicely by the example of the regulation of carbon dioxide emissions. A strict regulation of carbon dioxide emissions involves a tax on carbon products that can be used both for final consumption (e.g. heating) or for production. The consumption tax reduces the demand for these goods and therefore their prices. This implies that demand in the rest of the world tends to increase. But for exporters of carbon products, e.g. OPEC countries, the terms of trade will deteriorate and their own demand tends to decline. This may partially offset the substitution effect of the change in relative prices. The other, and probably more important effect, is caused by regulation of production activities and changes in the patterns of specialization. A carbon tax raises the production costs faced by the producers of carbon-intensive goods. They will reduce their supply and the world market price of these goods is increased. Given the increase in the price, producers of carbon-intensive goods in other countries expand their output and this expansion dominates the effect of the contraction of the less environmentally intensive industries. Thus, the foreign contribution to the global pollution problem tends to be increased in absolute terms. Foreign environmental regulation has up to now been assumed to be given. If, however, the foreign government adjusts its emission taxes, the leakage effect may be reduced. To countries exporting carbon-intensive goods their price increase is a terms-of-trade improvement and if environmental quality is a superior good, they will tighten their environmental standards and taxes.

There have been several attempts to quantify leakage effects and they have already been mentioned in Chapter 3, where carbon leakage was the result of international factor movements. Computable general-equilibrium models have been analysed by Oliveira-Martins *et al.* (1993), Felder and Rutherford (1993), Manne and Oliveira-Martins (1994), and OECD (1995). It turns out that the results are highly sensitive to the parameters assumed in the models, e.g. energy-demand elasticities and the future integration of China with its huge coal reserves into the world economy. Carbon-leakage figures derived from these models range from 3 to 40 per cent of original emission reductions. It should noted that these models do not consider the possibility of international factor movements that may accelerate carbon-leakage. International factor movements are taken into account by A. Ulph (1994a) in a non-competitive partial-equilibrium model. He calibrates it for the fertilizer industry and he finds even higher leakage figures of more than 60 per cent. The overall impression from this literature is that the empirical results are still a rather mixed bag and do not provide a reliable guideline for estimating the practical relevance of pollution leakage.

Given the terms-of-trade effects of environmental regulation and the problem of carbon leakage, how should a large country design its environmental policy? The optimality conditions are derived from the social-welfare function,

$$w = u(f^1 + PM(P), f^2 - M(P), -z).$$ (5.35)

The first-order conditions of environmental policy can be rearranged by means of the demand equations for final goods and capital, equations (5.31a) and (5.31b). Thus,

$$\frac{dw}{dt^{c2}} = u_1(M - t^{c2} M') \frac{dP}{dt^{c2}} - u_1 t^{c2} f_k^2 \frac{dk^1}{dt^{c2}} - u_3 \frac{dz}{dt^{c2}} = 0,$$ (5.36a)

$$\frac{dw}{de^1} = u_1 f_e^1 + u_1(M - t^{c2} M') \frac{dP}{de^1} - u_1 t^{c2} f_k^2 \frac{dk^1}{de^1} - u_3 \frac{dz}{de^1} = 0,$$ (5.36b)

$$\frac{dw}{de^2} = u_2 f_e^2 + u_1(M - t^{c2} M') \frac{dP}{de^2} - u_1 t^{c2} f_k^2 \frac{dk^1}{de^2} - u_3 \frac{dz}{de^2} = 0.$$ (5.36c)

Using the comparative-static results derived from equation (5.32), we obtain:

$$t^{c2} = sb2 \frac{u_3}{u_1} + \frac{\left(f_{kk}^1 + P f_{kk}^2\right)\left(M - (1 - S) Z_P(u_3/u_1)\right)}{M'\left(f_{kk}^1 + P f_{kk}^2\right) + \left(f_k^2\right)^2},$$ (5.37a)

$$t^{e1} = f_e^1 = sa1 \frac{u_3}{u_1} + \frac{f_k^2 f_{ke}^1\left(M - (1 - S) Z_P(u_3/u_1)\right)}{M'\left(f_{kk}^1 + P f_{kk}^2\right) + \left(f_k^2\right)^2},$$ (5.37b)

$$t^{e2} = P f_e^2 = sa2 \frac{u_3}{u_1} - \frac{f_k^2 f_{ke}^2\left(M - (1 - S) Z_P(u_3/u_1)\right)}{M'\left(f_{kk}^1 + P f_{kk}^2\right) + \left(f_k^2\right)^2}.$$ (5.37c)

It is seen that each tax consists of two components. The first one is the internalization of environmental damage and the second one is the terms-of-trade effect. An increase of the terms of trade is beneficial except in situations where it induces substantial pollution spillovers from abroad.[31] It is seen that the

---

[31] An example is the following scenario. The foreign country is specializes in the production of environmentally friendly goods. The improvement of the home country's terms of trade implies that the foreign country's export price is reduced. Thus it expands its import-substitution sector, which produces environmentally intensively. In the case of transfrontier pollution, this has an adverse effect on domestic environmental quality.

consumption tax rate on good 2 is negatively affected by the terms-of-trade component if this good is exported.[32] A small tax rate on the export good raises its domestic demand and, therefore, its global scarcity and price. Of course, if the good were imported, the tax should be high. Similar considerations apply to the regulation of emissions from production. A high tax rate improves the terms of trade if the good is exported and worsens the terms of trade if the good is imported. Thus, under the assumption that the carbon-leakage effects do not offset the pure terms-of-trade effects, one should underregulate the import-competing industry and overregulate the export industry compared to the Pigouvian scenario, where tax rates equal marginal environmental damages.

Similar considerations apply when emissions from consumption can be neglected. Then, the optimal emission tax rates are

$$t^{e1} = f_e^1 = sa^1 \frac{u_3}{u_1} - \left(M - (1 - S)Z_P \frac{u_3}{u_1} \right) \frac{dP}{de^1}, \tag{5.38a}$$

$$t^{e2} = Pf_e^2 = sa^2 \frac{u_3}{u_1} - \left(M - (1 - S)Z_P \frac{u_3}{u_1} \right) \frac{dP}{de^2} \tag{5.38b}$$

with $dP/de^1 > 0$ and $dP/de^2 < 0$ from equations (5.33b) and (5.33c). This confirms the results from the more general model.

Proposition 5.16. The optimal tax rate on the consumption of the exported good tends to be lower (higher) than the Pigouvian tax rate if the relative price of this good has a positive (negative) impact on domestic welfare. The optimal tax rate on emissions from the production of the exported good tends to be higher (lower) than the Pigouvian tax rate if the relative price of this good has a positive (negative) impact on domestic welfare. The welfare effect of the relative price is composed of a pure terms-of-trade effect and an environmental leakage effect.

Finally, one may wish to consider the question whether there will be a race to the bottom in environmental taxes if the other country behaves in a similar way. Such a scenario cannot be excluded here, although it is not a generic property of the model. Consider for instance a case where the pure terms-of-trade effects are small compared to the leakage problems. In this case, both countries tend to underregulate their pollution-intensive sectors with the intention of reducing environmental leakage effects.

Proposition 5.17. In the case of substantial leakage effects, optimal environmental policies tend to lead to too low emission tax rates.

It should be noted, however, that this effect depends on the comparative statics of a Nash equilibrium in an international policy game. The comparative statics of Nash equilibria, however, involve a lot of ambiguities such that this by no means a necessary consequence of the model (see Dixit (1986)).

---

[32] This argument is a bit heuristic. An analytical derivation of the impact of this component would involve the use of the implicit-function theorem. What one can do, however, is to start from a purely Pigouvian tax rate and then introduce a 'marginal' terms-of-trade component. The tax rate will then deviate from the Pigouvian tax rate and the direction of the deviation is determined by the sign of the additional effect.

5.9 Green Trade Interventions

If strict environmental policies have undesired consequences in that they may lead to increased emissions in the rest of the world, one is led to the idea that these measures need to be supported by the introduction of additional policy instruments that help to cope with the side-effects. The obvious candidates are trade interventions. If tighter environmental standards in the home country make domestic consumers (and downstream producers) think about satisfying their needs from imported goods that are cheaper since they have been produced under laxer environmental standards, the first instrument which comes into mind is a border-tax adjustment. The underlying idea is to raise the prices of imported goods by so much that tighter domestic production standards do not increase the demand for foreign, unsustainably produced goods any more. This would imply the introduction of a tariff. Additionally, it is possible that the regulated good is not imported but exported. The question then is whether one should introduce an export subsidy in order to avoid 'clean' domestic goods being crowded out by 'dirty' foreign goods.

It should be noted that the purpose of these border tax adjustments is not to protect domestic industries. However, such measures of course have a strong protectionist effect, and in reality the distinction between environmental protection and protectionism is difficult to make. Thus, the use of trade measures to avoid leakage effects will induce substantial rent-seeking. However, we will not take up this issue here. Protectionist lobbying will be addressed in Chapter 7 and some institutional implications of protectionist rent-seeking under the pretext of environmentalism will be discussed in Chapter 9.

If we leave the free-trade world of the previous section and allow the home country to use trade taxes and subsidies, its general-equilibrium conditions are changed slightly:

$$(P + t^{c2} + t^t)u_1 (f^1 + PM(P)) - u_2(f^2 - M(P)) = 0, \tag{5.39a}$$

$$f_k^1 - (P + t^t)f_k^2 = 0, \tag{5.39b}$$

$$z = sa^1e^1 + sa^2e^2 + sb^2(f^2 - M(P)) \\ + (1 - S)(A^1E^1(P) + A^2E^2(P) + B^2C^2(P)). \tag{5.39c}$$

The comparative-statics results are determined by

$$\begin{pmatrix} u_1 + pu_{11}(M + PM') + u_{22}M' & pu_{11}f_k^1 + u_{22}f_k^2 & 0 \\ -f_k^2 & f_{kk}^1 + \tilde{p}f_{kk}^2 & 0 \\ sb^2M' - (1-S)Z_P & sb^2f_k^2 & 1 \end{pmatrix} \begin{pmatrix} dp \\ dk^1 \\ dz \end{pmatrix}$$

$$= \begin{pmatrix} -u_1 & -u_1 & -pu_{11}f_e^1 & u_{22}f_e^1 \\ f_k^2 & 0 & -f_{ke}^1 & pf_{ke}^2 \\ 0 & 0 & sa^1 & sa^2 \end{pmatrix} \begin{pmatrix} dt^t \\ dt^{c2} \\ de^1 \\ de^2 \end{pmatrix}. \tag{5.40}$$

The effects of a tariff are:

$$\frac{dP}{dt^t} = -\frac{1}{\Delta}\left(u_1(f^1_{kk} + \tilde{p}f^2_{kk}) + f^2_k(pu_{11}f^1_k + u_{22}f^2_k)\right) < 0. \tag{5.41a}$$

$$\frac{dz}{dt^t} = \frac{1}{\Delta}\left(sb^2 M' \left(f^2_k(pu_{11}f^1_k + u_{22}f^2_k) + u_1(f^1_{kk} + \tilde{p}f^2_{kk})\right)\right.$$
$$-sb^2(f^2_k)^2 (pu_{11}(M + PM') + u_{22}M')$$
$$\left.-(1 - S)Z_P\left(f^2_k(pu_{11}f^1_k + u_{22}f^2_k) + u_1(f^1_{kk} + \tilde{p}f^2_{kk})\right)\right). \tag{5.41b}$$

Here Δ is different from the determinant in the previous section. The effect of a trade tax on the terms of trade is negative because good 2 is exported and a negative value of t^t denotes an export tax. The smaller t^t, the higher the export tax and the larger the price of the export good. The environmental effect of the trade tax is determined by the income and substitution effects of the changes in the terms of trade and by the leakage effect. The effects of emission and the consumption taxes on the terms of trade and on environmental quality are similar to those derived in the previous section.

The optimal environmental policy is determined by

$$t^t = \frac{M}{M'} - \frac{(1 - S)Z_P}{M'}\frac{u_3}{u_1}, \tag{5.42a}$$

$$t^{c2} = sb^2\frac{u_3}{u_1}, \tag{5.42b}$$

$$t^{e1} = sa^1\frac{u_3}{u_1}, \tag{5.42c}$$

$$t^{e2} = sa^2\frac{u_3}{u_1}. \tag{5.42d}$$

The environmental tax rates, t^{e1}, t^{e2}, and t^{c2}, equal the marginal environmental damages. The trade tax serves the purposes of improving the terms of trade and of dealing with the leakage effects.[33] To interpret equation (5.42a) assume that $M < 0$, i.e. foreign imports are negative and the good on which the trade tax is levied is imported by the home country. Then t^t is positive and an optimal tariff which improves the terms of trade. The second component corrects for the carbon leakage effect. It is positive if an increase in the relative price of good 2 raises environmental disruption. Note that an increase in the trade tax rate reduces P and, therefore, improves environmental quality in this case. Since the influence of the leakage effect on the optimal trade tax is decisively affected by the degree of pollution spillover, $(1 - S)$, one may be tempted to call t^t a green trade tax.

Proposition 5.18. Consider a large country. If trade taxes are available as instruments of environmental policy, they should be used to address transfrontier spillovers from abroad. The other taxes should be used to internalize the domestic environmental externalities.

[33] This result is not new. It was shown for the first time by Markusen (1975). See also Rauscher (1991a).

The result that the trade tax can be used for environmental purposes is explained by the fact that the variable through which domestic policies affect foreign emissions is the world market price ratio. And the most efficient policy instrument to influence this variable is a trade tax.

The set of policy instruments specified in equations (5.42a–d) is first best from a single country's point of view. This, however, does not mean that further improvements are not possible. A trade tax always creates a distortion and, thus, one can find better solutions to the problem of international environmental externalities. One could, for instance, negotiate an international agreement which removes the trade barriers and specifies the same level of emissions that have occurred in the case of trade interventions. Emissions would be unchanged, but the distortion would be removed. Thus, the pie to be shared would be increased and one could find a sharing rule that makes both parties better off compared to a situation in which one or both parties use trade restrictions.[34]

Proposition 5.19. Trade taxes generate distortions that can be avoided by an international environmental agreement involving side-payments.

5.10 Non-Traded Goods and Environmental Dumping[35]

The end of this chapter will be used to address the issue of environmental dumping again—now in a model framework with a non-traded good. The central question is in which circumstances a welfare-maximizing government may be interested in using lower emission tax rates in the tradables than in the non-tradables sector of the economy.

Let us therefore introduce a third consumption good, which is non-tradable. Let p^1 and p^2 be the domestic prices of commodities 1 and 2 in terms of the non-traded good which serves as the numéraire. In the absence of taxes on consumption and trade, $P = p^2/p^1$ again denotes the country's terms of trade. In order to keep the model tractable, we assume that the import good, commodity 1, is not produced at home. The welfare function now has four arguments and the fourth one is environmental quality:

$$w = u(c^1, c^2, c^3, -z). \tag{5.43}$$

The general equilibrium of the trading economy is described by

$$c^3 = f^3(k^3, e^3), \tag{5.44a}$$

$$f^2(k^2, e^2) - c^2 = M(P), \tag{5.44b}$$

$$p^1 c^1 = p^2(f^2(k^2, e^2) - c^2), \tag{5.44c}$$

$$k = k^2 + k^3. \tag{5.44d}$$

---

[34] A graphical illustration of the superiority of lump-sum payments over distorting instruments was towards the end of Ch. 3 for the case of international factor movements.

[35] This section of the chapter is based on my model developed earlier in Rauscher (1994a).

The first of these equations determines the equilibrium for the non-tradables sector, the second one the market equilibrium for the export good, the third equation is the balance-of-payments constraint, and the last equation represents the factor market equilibrium. In order to make the emission taxes used in different sectors comparable, let us assume that all sectors discharge the same pollutant. No distinction is made between a^2 and a^3. Then, the environmental disruption is

$$z = se^2 + se^3 + (1 - S)\left(A^1E^1 (P) + A^2E^2(P) + B^2C^2(P) \right). \tag{5.44c}$$

Inserting equations (5.44a–d) into the welfare function, we obtain

$$w = u(PM(P), f^2(k - k^3, e^2) - M(P), f^3(k^3, e^3), - z). \tag{5.45}$$

Moreover, we have the equations for determining consumer demand and the demand for capital:

$$Pu_1 - u_2 = 0, \tag{5.46a}$$

$$u_2 f_k^2 - u_3 f_k^3 = 0. \tag{5.46b}$$

In the small-country case, P is fixed and the optimal environmental policy is determined by the Pigouvian emission tax rates. Environmental dumping cannot be optimal. There exists no incentive to use environmental policy instruments for purposes other than the internalization of environmental externalities.

Matters may be different if the country under consideration is large. It has an impact on its terms of trade and this affects its welfare. The effect is

$$dw = (Mu_1 - (1 - S)Z_P u_4)dP. \tag{5.47}$$

As an exporter of good 2, the country will benefit from an increase in the relative price of this good compared to the imported good, provided that the leakage effect is not too large.

Using equations (5.46a) and (5.46b), one can derive the welfare effects of changes in sector-specific environmental policies. Optimal policies are determined by:

$$t^{e2} = p^2 f_e^2 = \frac{su_4}{u_3} - \left(M \frac{u_1}{u_3} - (1 - S)Z_P \frac{u_4}{u_3} \right) \frac{dP}{de^2}, \tag{5.48a}$$

$$t^{e3} = f_e^3 = \frac{su_4}{u_3} - \left(M \frac{u_1}{u_3} - (1 - S)Z_P \frac{u_4}{u_3} \right) \frac{dP}{de^3}, \tag{5.48b}$$

We can now easily determine a condition for ecological dumping defined in the sense of discrimination of non-traded goods production. Let us consider the case of negligible pollution leakage, i.e. $Z_P = 0$ or $S = 1$. Then, the condition for environmental dumping to occur is

$$t^{e2} < t^{e3} \quad \text{iff} \quad \frac{dP}{de^3} < \frac{dP}{de^2}.$$

Ecological dumping is optimal if the terms-of-trade effect of additional emissions in the non-tradables sector is smaller than the corresponding effect in the sector producing traded commodities. If this condition is met, the improvement in the terms of trade by an additional unit of emissions in the tradables sector exceeds the improvement achieved by increasing emissions in the non-tradables sector. Therefore, it is optimal to apply lower environmental standards to the export industry.

The terms-of-trade effects of sector-specific environmental policies can be determined by total differentiation of the private sector's optimality conditions, equations (5.45a) and (5.45b). This yields

$$
\begin{pmatrix} -M'u_{22}-u_1-P(M+PM')u_{11} & -u_{22}f_k^2 \\ M'u_{22}f_k^2 & u_3f_{kk}^3 + u_{33}(f_k^3)^2 + u_3f_{kk}^2 + u_{22}(f_k^2)^2 \end{pmatrix} \begin{pmatrix} dP \\ dk^3 \end{pmatrix}
$$
$$
= \begin{pmatrix} 0 & -u_2f_e^2 \\ -u_3f_{ke}^3 - u_{33}f_k^3 f_e^3 & u_2f_{ke}^2 + u_{22}f_k^2 f_e^2 \end{pmatrix} \begin{pmatrix} de^3 \\ de^2 \end{pmatrix}. \qquad (5.49)
$$

The sign of the determinant, Δ, of the matrix on the left-hand side is ambiguous, for the same reason as before. I will assume that it has the 'correct' sign which is positive here.

The terms-of-trade effects of sector-specific environmental policies can be determined by applying Cramer's rule to equation, (5.49). This yields

$$
\frac{dP}{de^2} = -\frac{1}{\Delta}u_{22}\left(f_e^2(u_3f_{kk}^3 + u_{33}(f_k^3)^2 + u_2f_{kk}^2) - u_2f_k^2f_{ke}^2\right) < 0, \qquad (5.50a)
$$

$$
\frac{dP}{de^3} = -\frac{1}{\Delta}u_{22}f_e^2\left(u_3f_{ke}^3 + u_{33}f_k^3 f_e^3\right). \qquad (5.50b)
$$

The terms-of-trade effect of an increase in emissions is negative in the traded commodities sector and ambiguous in the non-tradables sector. This can be explained as follows. An increase in the availability of environmental resources in sector 2 increases the supply of exportable goods and, in normal circumstances, their price will decline. For sector 3, which produces the non-traded good, there are two opposing effects. On the one hand, an increase in emissions raises the marginal productivity of capital since $f_{ke}^3 > 0$. If commodity prices are given, capital is moved from sector 2 to sector 3. This reduces the supply of the export good and tends to improve the terms of trade. On the other hand, the increase in the availability of the environmental factor of production in the non-tradables sector increases the supply of this good. Its price relative to that of the other good which is produced at home is reduced. For given productivities, capital tends to move from sector 3 to sector 2, this raises the supply of the exported good and leads to a deterioration of the terms of trade.

Given the terms-of-trade effects of sector-specific environmental policies, the policy implications can easily be derived. Since in normal circumstances the terms-of-trade effect of additional emissions in the export sector is negative, one should attempt to reduce these emissions below those of the reference scenario in which the terms-of-trade effects are not taken into account. The policy implication for the non-tradables sector is ambiguous. If capital and emissions are bad substitutes in this sector (if f^3_{ke} is large), then there is a positive terms-of-trade effect, and the environmental policy measures applied to the non-tradables sector should be relaxed. In this scenario the policy implication is the opposite of eco-dumping: discriminate against the sector which produces traded goods. It should be noted, however, that a number of different scenarios are imaginable some of which can indeed result in discrimination against the non-tradables sector. But such an outcome is not particularly likely.

Proposition 5.20. In an economy with a non-tradables sector and without an import-competing industry, the export industry is likely to be regulated in a tighter fashion if terms-of-trade considerations play a role than if they don't. The impact of the terms-of-trade motive on the non-tradables industry is ambiguous. It is possible, albeit unlikely, that the emission tax rate is higher than in the export industry.

Eco-dumping is possible, however only with particular parameter constellations. The reason is that the terms-of-trade motive always calls for restrictions on the supply of the export good. An import-competing industry, where the opposite policy recommendation would apply, does not exist in this model. Thus, the results derived here are to some extent artefacts of the special assumptions of this model.

In the case of substantial leakage problems, proposition 5.20 is turned around. Lax environmental policies in the export industry tend to reduce the world market price of the export good and this is beneficial to the home country if the foreign country produces this good environmentally intensively. This makes environmental dumping likely as an optimal policy. However, due to the general-equilibrium repercussions in this three-sector economy, it may also be possible that the objective to reduce leakage effects can be achieved by laxer environmental regulation in the non-tradables sector.

Another way to increase the likelihood of ecological dumping is a change in the policy-maker's objective function by the introduction of a concern about the well-being of the export industry. For example, the regulator may care about employment in this sector and it is not far-fetched to assume that employment is an increasing function of output. In order to keep terms-of-trade effects out of the picture, we consider the small-country case again, i.e. P is given and constant. Thus, starting from a Pigouvian policy, we have to look for an adjustment such that output is increased.

Changes in environmental policies have direct effect on output but also indirect effects since they change the allocation of capital. Total differentiation of equation (5.46b) yields

$$\frac{dk^3}{de^2} = \frac{u_2 f^2_{ke} + u_{22} f^2_k\, f^2_e}{u_3 f^3_{kk} + u_{33}\big(f^3_k\big)^2 + u_2\, f^2_{kk} + u_{22}\big(f^2_k\big)^2},$$

$$(5.51a)$$

$$\frac{dk^3}{de^2} = \frac{-u_3 f_{ke}^3 - u_{33} f_k^3 \, f_e^3}{u_3 f_{kk}^3 + u_{33}(f_k^3)^2 + u_2 \, f_{kk}^2 + u_{22} \left(f_k^2\right)^2}, \tag{5.51b}$$

An increase in emissions in sector 3 moves capital into this sector if F_{ke}^3. is large, i.e. if there is a substantial increase in capital productivity, or if $-u_{33}$ is small. The latter condition means that the price elasticity of demand is large and this implies that an increase in supply results only in a small price reduction. Thus the increase in e^3 has only a small effect on the marginal-value product of capital for a given level of the physical productivity. The same arguments apply for the other sector of the economy.

Starting from a situation of a social optimum in which $dw/de^1 = dw/de^2 = 0$, ecological dumping by discriminating the non-traded goods sector is beneficial to the government if

$$f_e^2 - f_k^2 \frac{dk^3}{de^2} > -f_k^2 \frac{dk^3}{de^3},$$

i.e. a marginal increase of emissions in the export sector leads to a larger increase in the output of this sector than an increase in emissions in the non-tradables sector. Using equations (5.51a) and (5.51b), we obtain

$$\frac{f_e^2 \left(u_3 f_{kk}^3 + u_{33}(f_k^3) + u_2 f_{kk}^2\right) - f_k^2 \left(u_3 \, f_{ke}^3 + u_2 \, f_{ke}^2 + u_{33} f_k^3 f_e^3\right)}{u_3 f_{kk}^3 + u_{33} \left(f_k^3\right)^2 + u_2 f_{kk}^2 + u_{22}(f_k^2)^2} > 0. \tag{5.52}$$

The last term in the numerator on the left-hand side of this equation may exhibit the 'wrong' sign. Thus it is possible that the export industry is supported best by applying more restrictive environmental policies there than in the non-tradables industry. This is just the opposite of ecological dumping defined as the preferential treatment of the export industry in terms of low emission tax rates. However, this result requires a very particular parameter constellation and in the normal case it is advisable to apply lower levels of environmental regulation in the export industry than in the non-traded goods sector.

Proposition 5.21. Usually an output increase in the export industry can be achieved by lax environmental standards that give this industry a cost advantage over other sectors. It can, however, not be excluded that it is better to give the non-tradables sector a cost advantage over the sector whose output is to be supported.

The reason for these ambiguities in the non-tradable goods models is its dimensionality. There is a second price besides the terms of trade and this additional degree of freedom generates the space for greater variability in the results. This example also shows that the generalization of the results derived in this chapter to higher-dimensional and more realistic models is not straightforward.

5.11 Summary of Results

The results of this chapter have been derived under a number of restrictive assumptions. In particular, it has been assumed that there are only two goods (except in section 9) and that environmentally policy is neutral in the sense that it does not affect the patterns of demand for private consumption goods. The results should be viewed with this qualification in mind.

1. With external effect on production the patterns of trade cannot be explained by factor abundance. Ricardian productivity effects need to be considered as well.
2. A country with a high degree of environmental concern tends to export goods that are relatively environmentally friendly in their production and relatively environmentally intensive when consumed.
3. For a highly regulated country, trade makes it possible to 'export' some of its environmental problems to the other country.
4. Trade liberalization may have negative welfare effects if environmental policies that regulate production and consumption are not at their optimal levels. In such cases trade interventions may be used for welfare-improvements and the achievement of second-best solutions. Tariffs are welfare-improving in situations with too low environmental taxes if, *ceteris paribus*, the imported good is environmentally unfriendly in its consumption or if the exported good is produced environmentally intensively. Trade interventions are, however, inefficient instruments.
5. Free trade is not the reason for disadvantageous trade liberalization effects in the case of environmental externalities. The reason is insufficient environmental policy and the first-best solution is to improve environmental policy.
6. With a move from autarky to trade, the country well-endowed with environmental resources will tighten its environmental regulation of production, the other country will relax its regulation. The country importing the good whose consumption is environmentally intensive should increase the consumption tax. The effect in the other country is unclear. Both countries should introduce measures to regulate the additional externalities of international transport.
7. In a trading economy, an environmental policy which reduces emissions from one set of economic activities may lead to increased emissions from other activities
8. In a small open economy, activities should be taxed according to the marginal environmental damage they cause.
9. Leakage effects may diminish (or sometimes advance) the effectiveness of unilateral environmental policy measures.
10. In the case of substantial leakage effects, optimal environmental policies tend to lead to too low emission tax rates.

11. Tariffs can be used to deal with leakage problems.
12. Tariffs are distortive. A first-best world is characterized by the internalization of *all* environmental damage and free trade.
13. The introduction of non-tradable goods into the model may lead to counter-intuitive results. In particular, ecological dumping is not optimal in all situations where this might be expected at first sight.

6
Imperfect Competition, Foreign Trade, and the Environment

6.1 An Overview

In the previous chapters, models have been discussed that are based on the assumption of perfect competition in all goods and factor markets. This assumption simplifies the analysis considerably and in many cases it is also a satisfactory approximation to real markets. However, not all markets are approximately competitive and this limits the applicability of perfect-competition models. For example, traditional models fail to explain the large share of intra-industry trade, i.e. trade in similar commodities between similar countries. Moreover, some of the policy implications derived from these models depend decisively on the assumption of price-taking behaviour and zero profits. In the late 1970s and early 1980s, a 'new' trade theory was established and one started to use the tools of modern industrial economics to look at non-competitive market structures. In the meantime, this approach has been incorporated into the main body of modern international trade theory. For surveys of the approach and the results see e.g. Bensel and Elmslie (1992), Helpman and Krugman (1985, 1989), Kierzkowski (1987), Krugman (1988a), and Vousden (1990, chs. 5–7).

The main differences between the new and the traditional approaches to international trade theory are threefold. First, the new approach explicitly concerns itself with non-competitive market structures whereas the majority of traditional models assume perfect competition. Second, in the new trade literature, one usually looks at single markets whereas the traditional approach is devoted to general-equilibrium analysis. Finally, the traditional approach has resulted in a unified framework of a many-countries, many-goods, many-factors version of the old Heckscher–Ohlin and Ricardo models that can be modified easily to include non-traded goods, endogenous factor supplies, etc. In contrast, the new theory of international trade still looks rather patchy and–like industrial economics–seems to lack a unified model framework. None the less, there are a number of 'core' models that have been influential in the economic-policy debate. They will be used here to discuss the effects of environmental policies on foreign trade in the case of non-competitive market structures.

The main focus of this chapter is to ask how instruments of environmental policy can be used to achieve trade-related policy objectives. Again, the underlying thought is that in an era of trade liberalization (albeit sometimes more on the regional that on the global level) the traditional instruments of trade policy are not available to the policy-maker and she may look for substitutes. The chapter is organized so that we start with the most non-competitive models and move to more competition in the course of the analysis. The first class of models to be presented considers monopolistic markets that are the subject of Sections 2 and 3. In Sections 4 and 5, we then increase the number of firms and look at oligopolies, mostly represented by two-firm models. Finally, in Section 6, monopolistic-competition models will be considered where the number of firms is large and there are no barriers to entry such that profits vanish as in the perfect-competition model. We will look at partial-equilibrium models during most of the investigation and, in the tradition of the analysis of non-competitive markets, we will use cost and demand functions to model the behaviour of firms and households instead of production and utility functions. Emissions that are generated during the production process can be determined by application of Shephard's lemma to the cost function $\tilde{c}(q,t^e, . , . , .)$. Thus, emissions, e, are given by the derivative of the cost function with respect to the emission tax rate:

$$e = \frac{\partial \tilde{c}(q,t^e, . , . , .)}{\partial t^e}$$

See Chapter 2. Moreover, the externalities due to transport activities will be neglected for convenience.

6.2 Monopolies, Foreign Trade, and Environmental Regulation

6.2.1 Introduction

Environmental policy in a non-competitive market differs from environmental policy in a competitive market. Buchanan's (1969) seminal paper has shown that imposing emission taxes on a hitherto unregulated monopolistic firm may lead to welfare losses. The reason is that a monopolist's supply is too small and taxes make it even smaller: the loss of consumer surplus in the goods market may exceed the welfare gains by the improvement of ambient quality. Optimal tax formulae that have been derived by Lee (1975) and Barnett (1980) elucidate the underlying problem. The environmental tax does not only depend on the marginal environmental damage but also on the price elasticity of demand, which is a measure of the monopolist's market power. The larger the market power of the firm, the lower the tax rate. The optimal emission tax may even turn out to be negative. The reason is that the emission tax is only a second-best policy instrument. There are two distortions, the environmental externality and the non-competitive market structure, and they would require two policy instruments. If the appropriate instrument to increase the output of the monopolist firm (e.g. a subsidy) is not available, the second-best emission tax will be biased downwards to raise the monopolist's supply.

Second-best considerations of this kind are also relevant if a monopolist is involved in foreign trade or competes against foreign suppliers in the domestic market. The investigation will start with the case of a foreign monopolist who produces for the domestic market. We will then turn to the opposite case where the domestic monopolist sells her output in the foreign market. Then, an import-competing firm with some monopoly power in the domestic market is considered. Finally, we will address the case where the firm supplies both markets but, before doing that, decides on the location of its plant. In this model, there will be internationally mobile capital and foreign trade.

6.2.2 Foreign Monopoly and Rent-Shifting Environmental Policies

Consider a foreign firm which enjoys monopoly power in a domestic market. By restricting its supply, this firm is able to raise the price above marginal costs and it will exploit the domestic consumers. The optimal response of the domestic government would be to regulate the monopoly by introducing a maximum price. However, this has rarely been observed in reality. So, Katrak (1977), Svedberg (1979), Tower (1983), and Brander and Spencer (1984) argued that a tariff might also serve the purpose of shifting some of the monopolist's profits back to the home country (see also Kowalczyk (1994)). On the one hand, tariffs will usually lead to an additional reduction of the supply and therefore will result in a reduction of consumer surplus. On the other hand, however, they create a tariff revenue which is paid by foreigners. This revenue may exceed the loss of consumer surplus.

Similar results can be obtained by environmental policy instruments. Let us consider a foreign monopolist selling (a part of) its output in the home country. Domestic consumption, c, is determined by the demand function, $d(p)$, where p is the price in the home market. The firm produces also for the foreign market and the foreign consumption is $C = D(P)$.[1] There may be market segmentation. If price discrimination is impossible, then $p = P$. Both demand functions are negatively sloped. The production costs, $\tilde{C}(Q, T^e)$ depend on the total output, $Q = d(p) + D(P)$, on the foreign emission tax rate, T^e, and on a number of other parameters that are not affected by domestic environmental policies. The domestic government imposes a tax on the domestic use of the good which pollutes the environment when consumed. Thus, the net price the monopolist can charge is $p - t^c$. Her optimization problem is to maximize the profits,

$$\Pi = (p - t^c)d(p) + PD(P) - \tilde{C}(d(p) + D(P), T^e). \tag{6.1}$$

The first-order conditions are

---

[1] We use demand functions instead of inverse-demand functions here since the algebra is tractable more easily in the case of no price discrimination.

$$pd' + d - \tilde{C}_Q d' = t^c d',$$
(6.2a)

$$PD' + P - \tilde{C}_Q D' = 0$$
(6.2b)

if price discrimination is possible and

$$pd' + d + PD' + D - \tilde{C}_Q(d' + D') = t^c d'$$
(6.2c)

if it is not. Marginal revenues equal marginal costs where the emission tax rate can be interpreted
as the cost of selling one unit of the output to domestic consumers. A change in domestic taxes results in the following price changes:

$$\frac{dp}{dt^c} = \frac{\Pi_{pp} d'}{\Pi_{pp} \Pi_{PP} - \left(\tilde{C}_{QQ} d' D'\right)^2} > 0,$$
(6.3a)

$$\frac{dP}{dt^c} = \frac{\tilde{C}_{QQ} D' d'^2}{\Pi_{pp} \Pi_{PP} - \left(\tilde{C}_{QQ} d' D'\right)^2}$$
(6.3b)

in the case of price discrimination and

$$\frac{dp}{dt^c} = \frac{dP}{dt^c} = \frac{d'}{\Pi_{pp}} > 0$$
(6.3c)

if there is no price discrimination.[2] A tax increase will lead to an increase in the domestic price if the second-order conditions are satisfied. In the price-discrimination scenario, the effect on the foreign price is ambiguous. It depends on the second derivative of the cost function. If there are increasing returns to scale, then the effect is positive, in the case of decreasing returns it is negative.

Given these results concerning the behaviour of the firm, the optimal environmental policy of the domestic government can be determined. The objective is to maximize the sum of consumer surplus (i.e. the integral under the demand curve),[3] tax revenue, and environmental quality. Thus:

$$w = \int_p^\infty d(\phi) d\phi + t^c d(p) + u\big(-sbd(p) - (1 - S)(A\tilde{C}_T + BD(P))\big),$$
(6.4)

where the quantity of pollutants generated by foreign production follows from Shephard's lemma. The first-order condition is

$$t^c = sbu' + \frac{d}{d'}\left(1 - \frac{1}{dp/dt^c}\right) + (1 - S)u'\left(A\tilde{C}_{TQ} + B\right)\frac{D'}{d'}\frac{dP/dt^c}{dp/dt^c}.$$
(6.5)

---

[2] Note that Π_{pp} in equation (6.3.c) differs from Π_{pp} in the previous two equations.

[3] Consumer surplus is a correct measure of the welfare accruing to a consumer only in the case of quasilinear utility functions (see Varian (1992, ch. 10)). For our purposes, however, the use of consumer surplus is appropriate even in the case of more general demand functions. In what follows, we will look predominantly at welfare effects of marginal changes in taxes and other policy instruments. And the marginal consumer surplus is a correct measure of the marginal change in the consumer's well-being. To see this, define the change in consumer's well-being as the negative value of the expenditure necessary to maintain the utility level υ after a price change. If $\varepsilon(p, \upsilon)$ is the expenditure function, then and since the derivative of the expenditure function with respect to a price is the Hicksian demand, it follows that $de = c\,dp$. Thus, the change in consumer's welfare is $-c\,dp$. This is exactly the result one gets from differentiating the integral under the demand curve.

The first term on the right-hand side is the marginal environmental damage due to the domestic consumption of an additional unit of the commodity. The second term is the profit-shifting element of the consumption tax. Finally, the tax affects the foreign production activities and can be used to reduce transfrontier pollution. The first component is straightforward but the other two terms deserve some additional explanation.

In a situation where the good under consideration is not produced domestically, a consumption tax is equivalent to a tariff. A tariff raises the price and this harms the consumers since their surplus is reduced. But it also generates revenues.[4] The increase in tax revenue may well dominate the reduction of consumer surplus. This is basically the Brander and Spencer (1984) profit-shifting argument. In order to give a graphical representation, we will look at a simplified version of the model where price discrimination is possible and where the foreign firm produces under conditions of constant returns to scale, i.e. the marginal-production cost is constant. This also implies that the quantity produced for the foreign market is not affected by domestic environmental policy. Figure 6.1 depicts the domestic demand curve, d, the monopolist's marginal-revenue curve for the case of a zero tax rate, MR, her marginal production cost, MC, and the domestic marginal environmental damage, med. The environmental damage is drawn such that it is added to the marginal production cost. The initial situation is characterized by a Pigouvian tax rate that equals the marginal environmental damage. According to equation (6.2b), the monopolist will decide to supply c^0 such that the price, p, equals the marginal revenue plus the tax rate. The introduction of a consumption tax now reduces the marginal revenue accruing to the monopolist by t^c. The supply will be reduced to c^1

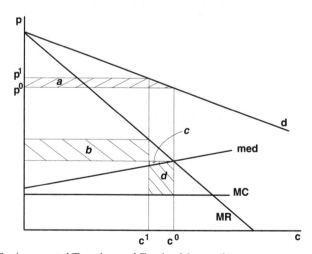

FIG. 6.1. Environmental Taxation and Foreign Monopoly

[4] Moreover, there will be a reduction in profits but this affects only foreigners and, therefore, is of no concern to the domestic government.

and the new price will be higher, namely p^1. The welfare effects are determined by areas $a, b, c,$ and d. Due to the higher price, the consumer surplus will be reduced by a. The change in tax revenues is $b-c-d$ and the improvement in environmental quality is d. Thus the net welfare effect is $b-a-c$ As has been shown by Brander and Spencer (1984), b is larger than a for small tax rates in normal circumstances. Moreover, $b-a$ will be greater than c in this case. This implies that an environmental tax on consumption can be used to shift profits from a foreign monopolist to the domestic economy if the tax rate is set such that it exceeds the marginal-environmental damage. The possibility of profit-shifting, however, depends on the parameters of the model. If the marginal-revenue curve is flatter than the demand curve, the opposite case is possible. Then dp/dt^c > 1 and the profit-shifting tax component is negative. This implies that the externality should not be fully internalized. Additional complications arise in the case of non-linear cost functions or the impossibility of price discrimination. Then, the optimal tax rate also depends on the shapes of the cost function and of the foreign demand curve.

Besides shifting profits, the consumption tax may be used to deal with transfrontier pollution problems. The third term in equation (6.5), which represents this effect, consists of two components. First, by reducing domestic demand, the consumption tax also reduces the foreign output and this is good for the domestic environment. Second, there may be spillover effects to the foreign market if the cost function is non-linear. If there are increasing returns to scale, a reduction in the output for the domestic market will raise the marginal cost of the production for the foreign market and the monopolist will reduce this part of her production as well. The effects to the domestic environment are beneficial since both production for the foreign market and foreign consumption are reduced. Matters are different in the case of declining returns to scale. A high tax rate, by reducing domestic demand, will reduce marginal-production costs and the output produced for the foreign market will be raised. This is detrimental to the domestic environment due to the pollution spillovers that are generated by production and consumption activities on the foreign market. In the small-country case and in situations where transfrontier pollution is negligible, these effects of course play no significant role and need not be considered.

Proposition 6.1. Under particular parameter constellations, it is possible to use an environmental consumption tax which exceeds the marginal environmental damage to shift profits from a foreign monopolist to the domestic economy. Moreover, the tax rate should be adjusted in order to deal with transfrontier pollution problems.

The first part of this proposition is a variation of the Brander and Spencer (1984) result. Compared to the original case of a profit-shifting tariff, an environmental tax has the advantage of not being as direct and obvious a barrier to trade as a tariff. By using the appropriate terminology, the policy-maker can advertise such a policy as environmental protection. The possibility of profit-shifting by high tax rates is, however, limited to particular parameter constellations. In general, it is not clear whether the tax rate should be larger or smaller than the marginal social cost. The transfrontier-pollution component also has an ambiguous sign, which depends on the technology used by foreign firms. Due to these ambiguities, the policy recommendations are highly sensitive with respect to the parameters. Since in the real world most of these parameters are unknown to the policy-maker, the consideration of profit-shifting motives in environmental policy design may in many situations lead to welfare losses rather than welfare gains. Thus, the standard Pigouvian tax may still be a useful rule of thumb for environmental policies in monopolistic markets.[5] Moreover, it is clear that this multipurpose tax is not first best. A better method to shift profits to the domestic economy would be to introduce a price ceiling and then tax consumption in order to internalize environmental externalities (see Helpman and Krugman (1989: 50–3)). Transboundary pollution spillovers may be addressed in the framework of international environmental agreements involving side payments.

6.2.3 A Domestic Monopolist in the Foreign Market

If environmental policies can be used to extract profits from a foreign monopolist who is active in the home market, one may be led to the conclusion that environmental policy may also be used to increase the profits of a domestic monopolist in the foreign market. This conclusion, however, is incorrect. To show this, we look at a very simple model of monopolistic behaviour. We assume here that the monopolist is not active in the home market. This allows us to neglect second-best environmental policies that would be used to correct the distortion due to monopoly power in the domestic market.[6] The instrument of environmental regulation is an emission tax, the tax rate being t^e. The policy-maker's objective function is

$$w = PD(P) - \tilde{c}(D(P),t^e) + t^e\tilde{c}_t + u(-sa\tilde{c}_t - (1-S)BD(P)), \tag{6.6}$$

where $PD(P) - \tilde{c}(D(P),t^e) = \pi$ denote the monopolist's profits, $t^e\tilde{c}_t$ is the tax revenue, and $u(.)$ is the utility derived from environmental quality. Differentiation with respect to t^e yields

$$\frac{dw}{dt^e} = \frac{d\pi}{dP}\frac{dP}{dt^e} - \tilde{c}_t + \tilde{c}_t + (t^e - sau')(\tilde{c}_{tt} + \tilde{c}_{tq}D'\frac{dP}{dt^e}) - (1-S)Bu'D'\frac{dP}{dt^e}.$$

[5] Similar conclusions have been drawn by Oates and Strassman (1984) in the case of regulation of a domestic monopolist in a closed economy. Using a calibrated model, they were able to show that after the introduction of an environmental tax the welfare gains due to improved environmental quality were much larger than the losses from reduced outputs. This led them to the conclusion that non-competitive market structures in general require only small deviations from Pigouvian tax rates.

[6] This issue has already been mentioned earlier. Since monopolist's supply in the domestic market is too small, the second-best environmental tax rate must be smaller than the marginal environmental damage. See again Lee (1975) and Barnett (1980).

Since the monopolist maximizes profits, $d\pi/dP = 0$, and the optimal tax rate turns out to be

$$t^e = sau' + \frac{(1 - S)Bu' \, D' \left(dP/dt^e\right)}{\tilde{c}_u + \tilde{c}_{tq}D'\left(dP/dt^e\right)} . \tag{6.7}$$

The first term is the direct environmental damage caused by an additional unit of emissions. The second term is an indirect effect. Since dP/dt^e is positive,[7] it is also positive. This component measures the environmental damage due to transfrontier pollution originating from the additional foreign consumption which becomes possible if domestic emissions are increased by one unit. Therefore, it is not misleading to interpret the right-hand side of equation (6.7) as the total marginal environmental damage. Proposition 6.2 follows immediately:

Proposition 6.2. The optimal environmental policy vis-à-vis *a domestic firm which is a monopolist in the foreign market is to use a Pigouvian emission tax.*

This result is not surprising. The marginal cost of improving the monopolist's profits in the foreign market is the marginal environmental damage. Thus it is optimal to signal to the monopolist the social cost of her behaviour by means of an appropriate tax. Unlike the case of perfect competition there is no correction for the terms of trade in the optimal tax rate. The domestic market power, necessary to raise the terms of trade is already exerted by the monopolist and, therefore, the government has no reason to adjust its environmental policy.

6.2.4 The Import-Competing Monopolist

Let us consider a market with a monopolist on the supply side who faces some competition from abroad. Environmental policies have two effects in this case. They internalize environmental externalities and they have an impact on output and demand and can therefore be used to deal with the distortions created by the monopoly. We will consider two cases. Case 1 deals with a good which causes environmental damage during its production and during its consumption. Therefore, two policy instruments are needed to deal with environmental problems. Case 2 considers production externalities only and it is assumed that consumption taxes or subsidies are not at the policy-maker's disposal. In both cases, we look at a market where the domestic monopolist is constrained by imports at a given world market price which is smaller than the price an unconstrained monopolist would charge. Thus, in the absence of taxes on consumption, the monopolist's supply would be $q = d(P)$ where P is the world market price. For the following analysis, it is assumed that the marginal cost of

---

[7] This can be shown algebraically by totally differentiating the monopolist's first-order condition. It also follows from the standard textbook diagram of a monopolistic market (see Fig. 6.1 for example). An increase in the tax rate raises the marginal cost and this in turn leads to a higher supply price.

production is smaller than the world market price: it is cheaper to produce at home than to import final goods. The opposite case is uninteresting since nothing would be produced at home.

If there are both production and consumption externalities and if final goods can be imported, the government has at its disposal up to three tax instruments: an emission tax, t^e, a tax on consumption, t^c, and a tariff, t^t. It will be seen that one of the latter two policy instruments is redundant. The domestic consumer price of the good is $p = P + t^c + t^t$ and the marginal and average revenue of the monopolist turns out to be $p - t^c$. Since the monopolist can undercut the world market price plus tariff marginally, she will supply the whole market and nothing will be imported. None the less, the competition from abroad matters since it restricts the monopolist's potential to raise the price. The policy-maker's objective is to maximize the sum of consumer surplus, profits, tax revenue, and utility derived from environmental quality:

$$w = \int_p^\infty d(\phi)d\phi + (p - t^c)d(p) - \tilde{c}(d(p),t^e) + t^c d(p) + t^e \tilde{c}_t + u(-sa\tilde{c}_t - sbd(p))$$

and this can be rewritten

$$w = \int_p^\infty d(\phi)d\phi + pd(p) - \tilde{c}(d(p),t^e) + t^e \tilde{c}_t + u(-sa\tilde{c}_t - sbd(p)). \tag{6.8}$$

Since p is a linear function of t^c and t^t, one of the tax instruments is redundant. $t^c + t^t$ has to be chosen correctly but the individual choices of t^c and t^t do not matter. Optimization with respect to $t^c + t^t$ and t^e yields

$$t^e = sau', \tag{6.9a}$$

$$p = \tilde{c}_q + sbu' \Rightarrow t^t + t^c = \tilde{c}_q + sbu' - P \tag{6.9b}$$

Proposition 6.3. In the case of an import-competing monopolist, the optimal policy is to use consumption taxes and/or tariffs such that the price equals the marginal cost of production plus the marginal environmental damage of consumption and to charge the Pigouvian tax rate from the monopolist.

Consumption taxes and tariffs are used such that the monopolist is forced to behave like a competitive firm. It is not necessary to discriminate against imports to achieve this goal. The firm is then taxed such that the tax rate equals marginal environmental damage.

Matters may be different in Case 2 where the government cannot tax or subsidize consumption. If the price of the imported good is low, then the optimal policy is to use environmental taxes only for the internalization of environmental externalities. The import price is the maximum price the monopolist can charge. She will act as a price-taker and the optimal environmental policy is to set the emission tax rate such that it equals marginal environmental damage, i.e. $t^e = sau'$ again. But if the import price is high, i.e. close to the monopolist's price, this policy may no longer be optimal. Using inverse-demand functions now,[8] the monopolist's problem is to maximize

[8] Here, the usual approach involving inverse-demand functions turns out to be more convenient for the computation of results.

$$\pi = p(q)q - \tilde{c}(q, t^e) \tag{6.10}$$

with respect to q for given t^e. In the optimum, marginal revenue equals marginal cost, and the effect of a change in the tax rate on supply, dq/dt^e is negative.[9] The policy-maker's objective function is

$$w = \int_0^q p(\phi)d\phi - p(q)q + \pi + t^e \tilde{c}_t + u(-sa\tilde{c}_t) \tag{6.11}$$

and the optimal tax rate is

$$t^e = sau' + qp' \left(\frac{dq}{dt^e} \bigg| \frac{de}{dt^e} \right), \tag{6.12}$$

where

$$\frac{de}{dt^e} = \tilde{c}_{tt} + \tilde{c}_{tq} \frac{dq}{dt^e} < 0.$$

This is exactly Barnett's (1980) result of the optimal taxation of a monopolist in a closed economy. The optimal tax rate equals the marginal environmental damage plus a negative term which is inversely related to the elasticity of demand.[10] The distortion due to monopoly power requires a subsidy and this is given indirectly via a reduction in the emission tax rate.

Proposition 6.4. In a second-best world where taxation of consumption is not possible, the optimal tax equals the Pigouvian tax if the import price is low and it is smaller than the Pigouvian tax if the import price is high.

The following diagram can be used to explain this result. It shows the demand function, d, the marginal revenue, mr, and the marginal-cost curve, mc. mc is evaluated for the case of the Pigouvian tax. Consider a situation in which the world market price, P, is rather high. If the emission tax is reduced now, then marginal costs will be diminished (mc'), the domestic firm is not constrained by the world market price and the new domestic price is p^m. What are the welfare effects? On the hand, there is an increase in the sum of profits and consumer surplus. This is measured by $a + b$. On the other hand, there is a deterioration in environmental quality and a change in the tax revenue. In the case of a small change in the environmental tax rate, this can be approximated by $-a$.[11] The net welfare effect is b and this is positive. If the world market price equalled p^m b would vanish. For world market prices lower than p^m, the effect would become negative. Thus, Pigouvian taxation would become preferable in this case.

---

9 $\dfrac{dq}{dt^e} = \dfrac{\tilde{c}_{tq}}{\pi_{qq}}.$

10 To see this, set $p'q = -p/\eta$ in equation (6.12) where η is the price elasticity of demand.

11 Environmental damage and tax revenue cannot be measured directly in this diagram since they are related to emissions but not to output. However, it is known that the marginal profit of an import-competing monopolist equals the marginal environmental damage plus the marginal tax revenue. This is just the first-order condition of welfare maximization. Thus, for small changes in the parameters of the model, the change in marginal profit, $-a$, is a good approximation of the welfare effect of the changes in tax revenue and environmental quality. If supramarginal parameters changes are considered, $-a$ underestimates the true welfare loss.

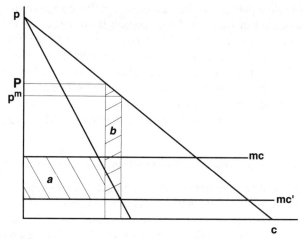

FIG. 6.2. Import-Competing Monopolist: The Second-Best Case

The low emission tax rate in the case of high import prices is, in principle, a closed-economy result. The deviation from marginal environmental damage is not a result of tough international competition but of a lack of competition. Thus, calling this environmental dumping would be misleading.

6.3 Environmental Policy and the Locational Decisions of a Monopolist Firm

6.3.1 Introduction

Up to now we have assumed that the monopolist firm is an established enterprise in the home or the foreign country. We will now look at the locational decision. In which country will a polluting plant be raised? Similar questions have already been addressed in Chapter 3, where the international allocation of capital has been discussed in a competitive framework. Chapter 3 has dealt with the economy as a whole and the term 'capital' has been used to characterize the capital stock of a country. We will now turn to sector-specific capital and look at non-competitive market structures. Moreover, indivisibilities will be important, i.e. a certain minimum size of an investment is required; otherwise no investment will be undertaken at all. Finally, there will be trade in final goods. Models of this type have been considered by Hoel (1994) and Rauscher (1995c), and Markusen et al. (1995). Markusen et al. (1995) consider a situation where there is one polluting firm which decides upon the location of its plants. High firm-specific fixed costs prevent the entry of additional firms. There are two kinds of fixed costs, that of being in the market and that of setting up a plant. The variable costs include pollution abatement and trade costs.

172   Imperfect Competition and Foreign Trade

The firm may build a plant in the home country, in the foreign country, in both of them or in neither of them, and the decision is influenced by the environmental policies in the two countries. This model turns out to be rather complex even in the case of only one firm. Markusen *et al.* (1995), therefore, use a numerical example to derive some results. Hoel (1994) and Rauscher (1995*c*) have tried to avoid this complexity by neglecting trade costs. The model can now be analysed by simple diagrammatic methods. In what follows, a two-country version of my original *n*-country model (*Rauscher* (1995*c*)) will be presented.

6.3.2 A Simple Model of Monopoly and Locational Choice

There are two countries, the home and the foreign country, and a single firm which supplies the world market with a consumption good. The fixed costs, $\bar{C}$, are assumed to be so high that there can be only one firm in the market. Consumption does not cause significant environmental problems as it did in the previous sections. This assumption is made for the sake of tractability. Since trade costs are negligible, the firm will open at most a single plant, and the decision where to open it depends only on the level of environmental tax rates imposed by the two countries. If emission taxes are very high, the firm will not build the plant at all since profits become negative.

It is assumed here that price discrimination is not possible, i.e. the law of one price holds. As will be seen later, the possibility of price discrimination would not alter the qualitative results. Here it turns out to be useful again to consider demand functions $c = d(p)$ and $C = D(p)$ instead of inverse-demand functions. Thus, the optimization problem of the firm is to choose its price such that

$$\Pi = p(d(p) + D(p)) - \tilde{C}\big(d(p) + D(p), \min(t^e, T^e)\big) - \bar{C} \qquad (6.13)$$

If Π is negative even for the best choice of p, the investment will not be undertaken. The first-order condition states that marginal revenues equal marginal costs and it follows that

$$\frac{dp}{dt^e} = \frac{\tilde{C}_{Qt}(d' + D')}{\Pi_{pp}} > 0 \qquad (6.14)$$

and this implies that consumption will be reduced in both countries if the host country raises its emission taxes. The emission tax rate at which the firm decides not to invest at all is determined by $\Pi = 0$.

The governments are assumed to maximize social welfare, which is the sum of consumer surplus, tax revenue, $t^e\tilde{C}_t$ or $T^e\tilde{C}_t$,[12] and the utility derived from environmental quality. Monopoly profits are not a part of the social-welfare function. This may be motivated by the assumption that the monopolist's well-being has a negligible weight in the social-welfare function or that her profits contribute to economic welfare in a third country.[13]

---

[12] Emissions are again determined by Shephard's lemma: $e = \tilde{C}_t$ or $E = \tilde{C}_t$.

[13] See Hoel (1994) for alternative assumptions.

The welfare of the two countries, depending on whether the monopolist invests in the home country (superscript h) or in the foreign country (superscript f) is

$$w^h = \int_p^\infty d(\phi)d\phi + t^e\tilde{C}_t + u(-sa\tilde{C}_t), \tag{6.15a}$$

$$w^f = \int_p^\infty d(\phi)d\phi + u(-(1-S)A\tilde{C}_t), \tag{6.15b}$$

$$W^h = \int_p^\infty D(\phi)d\phi + U((1-s)a\tilde{C}_t), \tag{6.15a'}$$

$$W^f = \int_p^\infty D(\phi)d\phi + T^e\tilde{C}_t + U(-SA\tilde{C}_t). \tag{6.15b'}$$

The joint welfare function is $w^h + W^h$ if the home country is the host or $w^f + W^f$ if the foreign country is the host. A necessary condition for the investment to be desirable is that welfare must be larger than the reservation welfare level that would be attained without the investment, i.e. $u(0) + U(0)$. If there is an interior solution to the optimization problem, the optimal environmental policy is characterized by

$$t^e = sau' + (1-s)aU' + \frac{(d(p) + D(P))\,(dp/dt^e)}{(de/dt^e)} - \frac{e}{(de/dt^e)}, \tag{6.16}$$

or

$$T^e = SAU' + (1-S)Au' + \frac{(d(p) + D(P))\,(dp/dt^e)}{(dE/dt^e)} - \frac{E}{(dE/dt^e)}, \tag{6.16'}$$

respectively. The optimal tax rates consist of four components. The first two are the marginal environmental damage in the home and the foreign countries. The third one represents the change in consumer surplus. It is negative since the higher the tax rate, the higher the price and the smaller the consumer surplus. The final component is related to the tax revenue. Components three and four together establish a kind of profit-shifting element in the optimal tax similar to that discussed in Section 2 of this chapter. The difference between this model and the previous one is that the tax is now raised on one of the inputs (the environmental resource) but not on the output. This gives the monopolist the possibility of tax evasion by reducing emissions. But the basic result is the same as before: depending on the shapes of the demand and cost functions, the optimal tax rate may be higher or lower than that internalizing the mere cost of pollution.

Figure 6.3 depicts a jointly optimal environmental policy, characterized by the optimal tax rate, t^*. There are four curves in this diagram. tr is the tax revenue accruing to the host country. This curve is assumed to be bell-shaped. $cs + CS$ is the sum of the consumer surpluses in the home and the foreign country. $tr + cs + CS$ results from adding up tax revenue and consumer surpluses. $ed + ED$ measures the total environmental damage at home and abroad.[14] It is

---

[14] Environmental damage is the negative value of the difference between the utility derived from environmental quality when the plant is built and the reservation welfare level.

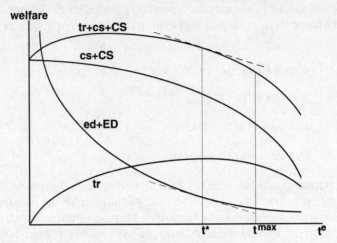

FIG. 6.3. Location of a Polluting Plant: The Co-operative Solution

a declining function of the tax rate. The optimal tax rate minimizes the distance between the $(tr + cs + CS)$ and the $(ed + ED)$ curves. If the tax rate exceeds, t^{max}, the investment will not be undertaken. In this diagram, this has been assumed to be a non-binding constraint. Otherwise, t^{max} would be chosen as a boundary solution or, if the damage exceeds the benefits, the optimal tax rate would be set at a level where no investment is undertaken.[15]

Where should the polluting plant be located? Since only the environmental damage depends on the location chosen by the investor, the answer is relatively simple. If the $(ed + ED)$ curve is lower for one location over the whole range of feasible tax rates, then the plant should be located in this jurisdiction. It is optimal to have the polluter in the location where she causes the least environmental damage.[16] If the $(ed + ED)$ curves for different locational choices intersect, the welfare levels for the two tax rates that satisfy the first-order conditions have to be compared.

6.3.3 Interjurisdictional Competition for Mobile Capital

We now turn to non-co-operative solutions. Let us assume initially that the countries are identical in all respects and that $s = S = 1$, i.e. there is no transfrontier pollution. A government deciding whether or not to host the plant has

---

[15] This case will not be considered here for the sake of brevity. See Rauscher (1995c) for some results.

[16] This proposition is plausible and it is simple to prove that it is also correct. Assume that the country with the higher environmental damage has been chosen and the tax rate is optimal. Then a move to the other country at this tax rate will always improve welfare since environmental damage is reduced whereas consumer surpluses and tax revenue remain constant. If the location-specific optimal tax rates differ across countries, additional improvements are possible by tax-rate adjustment.

to compare the additional benefits from being the host and the costs. Since the consumer surplus is independent of the location of the plant, the only benefit from being the host is the appropriation of the tax revenue. The cost, of course, is the loss of environmental quality. Loosely speaking, compared to the co-operative case the weight of the consumer surplus has been reduced and the weight of the tax revenue has been increased since it must not be shared with the other country. Moreover, marginal tax changes can lead to discrete changes in welfare. By slightly undercutting its neighbour's emission tax rate, a country can appropriate the whole tax revenue, but it also has to bear the full cost of environmental disruption. Figure 6.4 depicts the solution of the game.

Figure 6.4 represents the game from the view of the home country. The decisive variables are tax revenue, tr, and environmental damage, ed. It will be seen that the solution is affected by the level of the damage function, and four scenarios, ed^1 to ed^4, have been drawn into the diagram.

- Case 1. If the level of environmental damage is rather small, ed^1, then each of the two countries attempts to reap the net benefit by undercutting its competitor until the net benefit vanishes. The solution is t^1, i.e. a tax rate which is too low. This is the case of harmful interjurisdictional competition.
- Case 2. If the environmental damage is larger, ed^2, the tax rate may be too large, t^2.
- Case 3. If the environmental damage is increased even further, to ed^3, the environmental damage exceeds the tax revenue. It does not pay to be the host if the foreign country offers to be the host. The foreign country, however, faces the same problem. However, both of them would lose if no one became the host. This is a chicken game where the host country is the

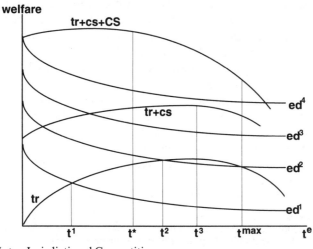

FIG. 6.4. Inter-Jurisdictional Competition

chicken. Such a game has two equilibria in pure strategies and it is not clear whether one of them will be attained (see Fudenberg and Tirole (1991: 18–19)). If mixed strategies are used, it is possible that the investment is not undertaken although everyone would benefit from it. If the plant is built, the tax rate t^3 will be offered by the chicken. This is the tax rate at which the country maximizes its national welfare. It is too high.[17] It should be noted that the relationship between the level environmental damage and the emission tax is non-monotonous. A reswitching phenomenon turns up as we move from Case 2 to Case 3.

- Case 4. Finally, if the environmental damage is very large (d^4), none of the countries benefits from being the host. The investment will not be undertaken because of the traditional prisoner's dilemma problem. It would be individually irrational to provide the consumer surplus to the citizens of other countries if this results in an individual welfare loss. Both governments agree that the plant be built but 'not in my backyard'.

Two effects generate the deviation from the desirable environmental policy. On the one hand, the host country appropriates the tax revenue. If this is large compared to the environmental damage, the jurisdictional competition will induce the governments to undercut tax rates imposed elsewhere. On the other hand, there is the consumer surplus of which the home country can appropriate only a share. Thus, by offering to be the host, a country provides a public good to the other country. This generates the potential for a prisoner's dilemma when the cost of being the host is large.[18]

Proposition 6.5. In an environmental tax competition amongst several countries for foreign direct investment, the resulting tax rate may deviate from the jointly optimal one. It is too low if the benefits of being the host are large to an individual country or it may be too high if the environmental cost is large.

The net benefit to the host country is zero if it has chosen a policy instrument which leaves the scarcity rent of environmental resources to the foreign investor, i.e. a maximum-emissions standard. In this case, scenarios 1 and 2 do not occur, and environmental legislation will be too restrictive. Either the chicken will host the plant at too-restrictive a regulation level, or the investment will not be undertaken at all.

Several extensions of the model are feasible. The introduction of country heterogeneity does not change the results significantly. In the case of mutual undercutting of environmental standards, however, the host country will usually experience a positive net benefit since the other country is likely to drop out of the rat race at an earlier stage. If countries are heterogeneous with respect to their environmental costs, the firm will always be located in the low-cost country and this is efficient (see Hoel (1994) and Rauscher (1995c)).

---

[17] The reason is that the foreign consumer surplus is a declining function of the tax rate. Therefore, the tax rate for which marginal environmental damage equals the global benefit is always smaller than the tax rate at which it equals the benefits accruing to a single country.

[18] This kind of prisoners' dilemma would occur also if price discrimination were possible.

Additional modifications are possible with respect to market structure. Hoel (1994) considers the case of monopolistic competition. It is shown that the same consideration applies in this case and the scenarios described before are still possible. Markusen *et al.* (1995) introduce trade costs and this in certain circumstances makes it profitable for the monopolistic firm to invest in both countries. They show that in a situation where it is optimal that only one plant be built legislational competition may lead to overinvestment (plants in both countries that produce too much pollution) or underinvestment (a single plant which is too small or no plant at all). The first scenario is the race to the bottom and the second one the 'not-in-my-backyard' solution. The underlying intuition is the same as in the simple one-plant model.

Duopoly models of this kind have been investigated by Markusen *et al.* (1993) and Motta and Thisse (1994). Due to the complexity of these models, it is not possible to consider the tax competition between countries but one can investigate policy changes in only one country given the environmental policy of the other country. Various kinds of market structure are imaginable in which both firms, one firm, or none of the firms invests in one of the countries or both of them. As before, these locational decisions affect consumer surplus, profits, tax revenue, and environmental pollution. Since marginal changes in environmental policy may produce discrete changes in market structure, they have also discontinuous effects on economic welfare.[19] A slightly mistaken environmental policy may result in large welfare losses. The difference between the approaches of Markusen *et al.* (1993) and Motta and Thisse (1994) is that the latter authors also consider sunk costs. Thus an incumbent plant has an advantage over a new plant. This has some consequences for environmental policy design. In the Markusen *et al.* (1993) model, the domestic firm can open a foreign branch if it is expelled from its original location by high emission taxes. In the Motta and Thisse (1994) model, this may not be possible since a part of the foreign incumbent's fixed costs are already sunk. The home country loses the domestic firm's profits and in addition, since the foreign firm is now a monopolist, a part of its consumer surplus. These losses are larger than in the other model. The gains of environmental quality, on the other hand, are the same in both models. Therefore, there is a higher likelihood in the Motta and Thisse model that strict environmental policies reduce welfare drastically and are, therefore, not chosen. The existence of sunk costs limits the desirable 'green' environmental policies.

Finally, A. Ulph (1994*a*) uses a generalized version of the Markusen *et al.* (1993) model. There is a larger number of firms and countries. The model is calibrated by using empirically determined data and different policy scenarios are simulated. A. Ulph shows that unilateral policy changes may have drastic relocation effects. In some cases emissions reductions in one country are offset

---

[19] This is a variation of the '*natura facit saltum*' result derived by Horstman and Markusen (1992) in their trade-policy model with endogenous market structure.

by more than proportional emission increases in the rest of the world. Thus, unilateral approaches to global environmental problems like global warming may be counter-productive. A. Ulph's carbon-leakage figures exceed those that have been derived from competitive models.

Some of the results derived here are rather different from those that have been obtained in the framework of the modified McDougall and Kemp model of international factor movements in Chapter 3. The underlying reason is the existence of fixed costs. In the McDougall–Kemp model, there are neither fixed costs nor increasing returns to scale. This implies that, first, capital is always productive and, secondly, that marginal units of capital can be moved between the home and the foreign countries. Therefore, the given capital stock is shared by the two countries such that rates of return to capital are equal. The policy-maker deciding on environmental taxes has to compare the marginal costs and benefits of changes in the allocation of capital. If there are substantial fixed costs, however, marginal changes in environmental policies will lead to supra-marginal changes in the allocation of capital and in welfare. Additionally, the possibility arises that no investment at all is undertaken. Therefore, the environmental policy decisions have to be based on criteria that are not marginal conditions. This is not only true for the simplistic one-firm one-plant model investigated here but also for other kinds of market structure (see Hoel (1994) and Markusen *et al.* (1995)).

Finally, consider the case of transboundary pollution spillovers. Transboundary pollution raises the opportunity cost of not being the host country. To show this, let us consider the changes in welfare that can be attained if the firm changes its locational decision. The welfare differentials for the home and the foreign countries are

$$w^h - w^f = t^e \tilde{C}_t + u(-sa\tilde{C}_t) - u(-(1-S)A\tilde{C}_t), \tag{6.17}$$

$$W^f - W^h = T^e \tilde{C}_t + u(-SA\tilde{C}_t) - u(-(1-s)a\tilde{C}_t), \tag{6.17'}$$

The net welfare effect is tax revenue plus the utility derived from environmental quality if the country under consideration itself is the host minus the utility derived from environmental quality if the other country is the host. The incentive to become the host is increased.

Proposition 6.6. Transfrontier pollution spillovers raise the opportunity cost of not being the host country for a foreign investor. Thus, the existence of transfrontier pollution raises the likelihood of a tax competition towards undesirably low levels of environmental regulation.

If transfrontier pollution effects are substantial, the net opportunity cost of appropriating the tax revenue approaches zero or even becomes negative. The result is a race to the bottom in environmental taxes. A sufficient condition for this to occur is $sa \leq (1-S)A$ and $SA \leq (1-s)a$. A special case where this condition is met is that of identical pollutants causing a global environmental problem, i.e. $a = A$ and $s = S = \frac{1}{2}$

6.3.4 Instrument Choice: Direct Subsidies vs. Emission Taxes

The environmental taxes discussed here are no first-best policies. Besides the internalization of the environmental externality, there are additional policy objectives that are taken care of by the emission tax, in particular the appropriation of the tax revenue. Thus, one may argue that it would be better to use more than one instrument, e.g. it would be advisable to introduce subsidies in order to attract the foreign firm. This possibility will be considered initially for the simple case of identical countries and no transfrontier pollution. Let σ be a lump-sum subsidy paid by the government to the foreign firm in case the investment is undertaken. If the investment is beneficial from a single country's point of view, the two countries will compete for the foreign firm as long as the tax revenue exceeds the costs of the investment, which consist of the loss of environmental quality and the subsidy that has to be paid. The game will come to an end when this net benefit approaches zero. In order to be able to attract the firm, the home government has to choose taxes and subsidies such that the monopolist's profit is maximized—subject to the condition that

$$t^e \tilde{c}_t - \sigma + u(-sa\tilde{c}_t) - u(0) = 0. \tag{6.18}$$

[20]

Differentiation of the corresponding Lagrangean function with respect to t^e and σ yields the optimal tax rate

$$t^e = sau'. \tag{6.19}$$

[21]

This is the Pigouvian tax, which equals the marginal environmental damage. The underlying reason is that direct subsidies are the most efficient way to attract a foreign investor.[22] If the same subsidy were given to the firm indirectly by means of low emission taxes, the increase in environmental damage would be an additional cost component which would have to be taken into account by the policy-maker. Therefore, lump-sum subsidies are better means to compete for a foreign investor. The Pigouvian tax rate is, however, not the jointly optimal tax rate since it does not take account of the distortion stemming from the market imperfection.

The same result would follow if the countries were different with respect to their perception of environmental damage. In this case, the country which is more conscious of environmental quality will drop out of the rat race earlier, i.e. when the net benefit to the other country is still positive ($t^e \tilde{C}_t - \sigma + u(-sa\tilde{C}_t)$ $- u(0) > 0$ if the home country turns is the host). None the less, the two policy instruments will still be used in the most efficient way. Only the subsidy that has to be paid by the host will be lower than in the case of identical countries. Even

---

[20] Of course, the same condition applies to the foreign country (which here is identical to the home country, however).

[21] The alternative method to compute the optimal tax rate and the subsidy is to maximize the net benefit with respect to a target level of profits. This produces the same result for the emission tax rate.

[22] In a perfect-competition model with mobile capital, Oates and Schwab (1988) come to a similar conclusion. Sub-Pigouvian environmental policies are optimal if the tax on capital is too high. In their model, the optimum tax rate is zero, in my model a lump-sum subsidy is optimal.

transfrontier pollution does not change the result. The environmental-quality component of the opportunity costs of not the being host country is reduced from $u(0)$ and $U(0)$ to $u(-(1 - S)A\tilde{C}_t)$ and $U(-(1 - s)a\tilde{C}_t)$ respectively. But it is still independent of the government's choice of the tax rate since they are determined solely by the environmental policy in the other country. Thus, they are exogenous to the policy-maker in the country under consideration and are taken as given. Then, the optimal policy is to maximize the monopolist's profits for given net benefits or vice versa and again the tax rate equals the domestic marginal environmental damage.

Proposition 6.7. The first-best policy is to use a subsidy to attract the foreign firm and to charge the Pigouvian tax rate for emissions.

If lump-sum subsidies are available, there will never be a race to the bottom in the field of environmental regulation. From a welfare point of view, lump-sum subsidies are cheaper than emission-tax reductions and, therefore, they will be used to attract foreign investors. In reality, however, there may be limits to the use of lump-sum subsidies and the policy-maker will search for alternative instruments. Environmental regulation is one candidate.

Finally, the 'not-in-my-backyard' case will be addressed briefly. Lump-sum subsidies do not prevent this possibility. It is still possible that a desirable investment is not undertaken. An individual country has no incentive to consider the foreign consumer surplus and this is not changed by the introduction of additional policy instruments.

6.4 International Oligopoly and Strategic Environmental Policy

6.4.1 Introduction

Strategic trade policy in general and export subsidization in particular have become the most debated issues of the new trade theory and policy during the second half of the 1980s. There are two main reasons for this. First, the theory of strategic trade policy seemed to offer explanations for phenomena that the traditional approaches failed to explain. For example, the success of the Japanese economy after the Second World War has often been attributed (at least in part) to an active government policy of export promotion. According to standard trade theory, such a policy would have caused welfare losses rather than welfare improvements. Secondly, and perhaps more importantly, this theory provided a new justification for industrial policy and other kinds of government intervention. Therefore, it became attractive to lobbyists and those politicians who believe in the neomercantilist proposition that exports are good and imports are bad.[23]

---

[23] 'In fact, the key to the influence of the Brander–Spencer model may be, not that it challenged conventional beliefs, but that it confirmed them.' (Krugman (1992)).

The original model of export subsidization is due to Brander and Spencer (1985). They look at a partial-equilibrium model in which two firms, a domestic and a foreign one, compete in a third country's market. The competition is of the Nash–Cournot type. It is shown that a firm produces more if it is subsidized by its home government. This leads to an increase in profits which exceeds the cost of subsidization (if the subsidy is not too large). The underlying reason is that subsidies may move a firm which behaves according to the Nash–Cournot conjecture into a Stackelberg position. There are two types of difficulties that arise if such a policy is implemented practically. First, the policy recommendations are not necessarily applicable to the real world. The Brander and Spencer model is based on a number of special assumptions (e.g. Cournot instead of Bertrand competition, perfect knowledge, no retaliation by the foreign government, etc.)[24] and the results turn out to be sensitive to changes in the assumptions. Second, even if the model were applicable to the real world, export subsidization would be considered as unfair trading and countervailing duties ought to be expected. To countries that have signed free-trade agreements, it is even less an option. Therefore, one has looked for ways to disguise strategic export subsidization. One possibility is public funding of export-related research. Spencer and Brander (1983) show that this policy leads to similar conclusions. Another approach is to give hidden subsidies by means of low pollution abatement requirements. This possibility has been considered by A. Ulph (1992), Conrad (1993a, b), Barrett (1994), and Kennedy (1994) (see A. Ulph (1994b) for a survey on strategic environmental policy). Here, we use Barrett's (1994) model and extend it by transfrontier pollution. The same road has been taken by D. Ulph (1994).[25] The domestic government knows and takes into account that environmental policies that increase foreign production may have a negative impact on domestic environmental quality.

6.4.2 The Model

Consider a situation where a domestic and a foreign firm compete in a third country's market.[26] It is assumed, that due to the partial-equilibrium character of this model, external effects on production can be neglected. However, the two firms affect environmental quality as a public consumption good. They play Nash–Cournot against each other and the governments play Stackelberg vis-à-vis the firms and Nash against each other. The strategic variable of the

---

[24] For surveys of the critique, see Grossman (1987), Siebert (1988), and *Brander* (1995).

[25] D. Ulph (1994) uses a linear cost function and considers abatement activities explicitly whereas my cost function is more general and abatement is implicit in the cost function.

[26] The third-country assumption simplifies the analysis considerably. It implies that a subsidy on production and a subsidy on exports are equivalent and that the consumer surplus does not have to be considered in the welfare analysis. This assumption has been introduced in the original Brander and Spencer (1985) model. For a model in which the third-country assumption is relaxed, see Conrad (1993a, b)

government is the emission tax rate.[27] In the first stage of the game, governments set the emission tax rates. Afterwards the firms decide on their outputs. The game is solved in the usual backward fashion. Each firm takes as given the quantity produced by the other firm. Profits can be written

$$\pi = p(q,Q)q - \tilde{c}(q,t^e), \tag{6.20}$$

$$\Pi = P(q,Q)Q - \tilde{C}(Q,T^e), \tag{6.20'}$$

$p(q,Q)$ and $P(q,Q)$ are inverse-demand functions, i.e. the prices of domestic and foreign goods, p and P depend on the produced quantities, q and Q. As a special case, one may assume that the domestic and the foreign goods are perfect substitutes and that their prices are identical. t^e and T^e are the emission taxes chosen by the governments.[28]

The first-order conditions for an optimum are

$$p_q q + p - \tilde{c}_q = 0, \tag{6.21}$$

$$p_q Q + P - \tilde{C}_Q = 0, \tag{6.21'}$$

It is assumed that the second-order conditions are satisfied, i.e. π_{qq} and Π_{QQ} < 0. The comparative-static results are obtained by application of Cramer's rule to

$$\begin{pmatrix} \pi_{qq} & \pi_{qQ} \\ \Pi_{qQ} & \Pi_{QQ} \end{pmatrix} \begin{pmatrix} dq \\ dQ \end{pmatrix} = \begin{pmatrix} \tilde{c}_t dt \\ \tilde{C}_T dT^e \end{pmatrix}.^{29} \tag{6.22}$$

Let us additionally assume that the cross-derivatives of the profit functions, $\pi_{qQ} = p_Q + p_{qQ}q$ and $\Pi_{qQ} = p_q + p_{qQ}Q$, are negative and the determinant $\Delta = \pi_{qq}\Pi_{QQ} - \pi_{qQ}\Pi_{qQ}$ is positive. Then, it follows that the reaction functions, $q = \check{r}(Q,t^e)$ and $Q = \check{R}(q,T^e)$ are negatively sloped in the (q,Q) space, i.e.

$$\frac{\partial \check{r}}{\partial Q} = -\frac{\pi_{qQ}}{\pi_{qq}} < 0, \tag{6.23}$$

$$\frac{\partial \check{R}}{\partial q} = -\frac{\Pi_{qQ}}{\pi_{QQ}} < 0, \tag{6.23'}$$

and that the domestic firm's reaction curve is steeper than the foreign firm's curve. (see Figure 6.5). The Nash equilibrium, N, is the point of intersection of the reaction curves denoted by r and R in Figure 6.5. It is assumed to exist and

[27] Other candidates for the choice of policy instruments are emission standards or technological standards that define minimum abatement equipment or a maximum emission-output ratio. It has been shown by A. Ulph (1992) and Verdier (1993) that the results may be affected by the choice of the strategic variables and that cost-inefficient instruments be useful for profit-shifting purposes. This problem area will, however, not be discussed here.

[28] These environmental taxes may be industry-specific, i.e. industries operating in other sectors of the economy may pay different tax rates may even if they discharge the same pollutant.

[29] See Dixit (1986) for a general treatment of comparative statics of the Cournot equilibrium.

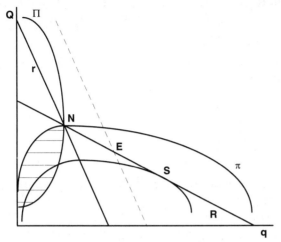

FIG. 6.5. Strategic Environmental Policy in the Cournot Model

to be unique. Moreover, the domestic and foreign firm's iso-profit curves are depicted in this diagram. Each firm would benefit if the other firm reduced its output. The shaded area represents the potential of profit increases that can be achieved by co-operation, i.e. by a cartel agreement. The reaction functions have been derived for given environmental tax rates. If the domestic tax rate is reduced, the domestic firm's reaction function is shifted outwards. This is depicted by the dashed line. If the domestic firm were the Stackelberg leader, it could attain point S where it maximizes its profits for a given reaction function of the foreign firm. In the Brander and Spencer (1985) model, this situation is achieved by government intervention.

Matters are a bit different if the domestic government cannot subsidize the firm directly but gives indirect subsidies in terms of low pollution-abatement requirements. Consider first, as a reference case, a situation in which the government does not behave strategically. It does not take account of the possibility of shifting profits to the domestic supplier from abroad. Thus, it behaves as if it did not have an impact on the foreign producer's supply, Q. This situation has already been dealt with in Section 6 where the regulation of a domestic monopolist who sells in a foreign market has been discussed. If pollution spillovers due to consumption of the exported goods are negligible, the optimal tax rate is the marginal social cost, i.e. $t^e = sau'$. Correspondingly, $T^e = SAU'$ for the foreign country. Let us assume that the reaction functions that are represented by solid lines in Figure 6.5 are based on this type of government behaviour. The shaded area indicates that tax increases in both countries could lead to increased profits. Such a policy would reduce the output and result in cartel-like behaviour. This again is a variation of Solow's (1974: 8) saying that environmentalists and monopolists are friends.

Let us now introduce strategic behaviour. The home government's objective function is

$$\pi + u(-sa\tilde{c}_t - (1-S)A\tilde{C}_T) + t^e\tilde{c}_t.$$

Differererentiation with respect to t^e and the use of the firm's first-order condition, $\pi_q = 0$, yield the optimal tax rate

$$t^e = sau' - \frac{p_Q q - (1-S)A\tilde{C}_{QT}u'}{\tilde{c}_u + \tilde{c}_{tq}q_t} Q_t.$$

$$T^e = SAU' - \frac{P_q Q - (1-s)a\tilde{c}_{qt}U'}{\tilde{C}_{TT} + \tilde{C}_{TQ}Q_T}$$

is the optimal tax rate in the foreign country. The derivatives of the outputs, q and Q, with respect to the tax rates, t^e and T^e, can be obtained by the application of Cramer's rule to equation (6.22). It follows that q^T and Q^t are positive. Together with the signs of the other terms this implies that the second terms on the right-hand sides of equations (6.25) and (6.25´) are positive. This results in:

Proposition 6.8. If the government uses environmental policy strategically, it should not completely internalize the environmental cost of production.

This is environmental dumping according to the first definition given in Chapter 2. Since there are no reasons why other sectors of the economy, in particular those which are not export industries, should be subsidized in this way, this is also a discriminating policy.[30] The second term on the right-hand side of equation (6.25) represents the incentive for using environmental policy strategically. There are two effects. First, if the government reduces the tax rate towards a level below the marginal damage, the domestic firm produces more and this leads to an increase in profits that exceeds the welfare loss due to increased environmental deterioration (provided that the tax rate is not reduced by too much). Second, low domestic emission taxes force the foreign firm to reduce its output and this reduces transfrontier pollution.[31]

Finally, the question arises as to how far the support for the domestic firm may go. Will the domestic government make the home firm the Stackelberg leader in the market? The following proposition is proved in the appendix:

Proposition 6.9. In the case of no pollution spillovers, the optimal environmental policy establishes an equilibrium which is located between the Nash

[30] This result is derived from a partial equilibrium approach where each market is dealt with as an entity separated from the rest of the economy. It may change if general-equilibrium interdependencies are introduced. This issue will be addressed below when the applicability of the model to the real world is discussed.

[31] Arguably, the transfrontier pollution problem is in most cases more severe in non-competitive models than in competitive ones. If, for instance the demand and cost functions are linear, the slope of the foreign firm's reaction curve is $-\frac{1}{2}$ which means that a reduction in domestic output by one unit is accompanied by an increase in foreign output by two units. Similar effects exist in competitive model frameworks as well but they tend to be much smaller. The implication is (i) that carbon-leakage problems tend to be more severe in oligopolistic markets than in competitive ones (see A. Ulph (1994a) for some results from calibrated models) and (ii) that the incentive to use lax environmental policies to avoid carbon leakage is larger.

equilibrium and the Stackelberg point. In the case of substantial transfrontier pollution, the domestic output may be increased towards a level beyond the Stackelberg point.

The first part of this proposition has been established by Barrett (1994), however without a rigorous proof. According to Barrett (1994: 333): 'The reason for this result is that weaker environmental standards offer an 'implicit subsidy' but one that is costly; society suffers because the subsidy worsens domestic pollution.' In my view, this explanation misses the point. The problem is not that pollution is increased by weaker environmental standards or lower emission taxes, the problem rather is that the marginal social cost of pollution exceeds the marginal benefit to the firm if the tax rate is reduced to a level lower than *sau'*, the Pigouvian tax rate. This may happen even in the case of constant marginal environmental damage as shown in the appendix. Thus, the first part of the proposition is due to the second-best properties of the instrument of subsidization. If the input of a factor of production (e.g. an environmental resource) is subsidized to promote exports, a deadweight loss has to be taken into account compared to a situation where the correct instrument (an export subsidy) is chosen. The marginal deadweight loss increases with the rate of subsidization and, therefore, the welfare maximum is attained at a lower level of exports. Thus, the Nash equilibrium with strategic choice of emission taxes is located between N and S in Figure 6.5, for instance in point E.

The second part of this proposition is an (inverse) carbon-leakage result. The deadweight loss due to the choice of the wrong policy instrument may be dominated by the benefit of foreign output reduction if there are substantial pollution spillovers from abroad. In this case, the optimum may be located beyond the Stackelberg point on the foreign firm's reaction curve. It is seen that the motive to shift rents from abroad to domestic suppliers may explain lax environmental policies. The optimality of such a policy, however, hinges on specific assumptions. Variations in the assumptions of the model may lead to drastic changes in the policy recommendations.

The first problem here is retaliation. Just as the home government supports its firm by means of lax environmental standards, the foreign government can also use environmental policy strategically. This may result in a rat race where each country responds to lower emission taxes abroad by reducing its own emission taxes. Each government reacts to a reduction in foreign emission taxes by relaxing its own environmental policy. The shapes of the reaction functions in this game amongst the governments are indeterminate in the general case; it is, however, plausible that their slopes are negative and that an equilibrium with positive tax rates exists.[32] None the less, these taxes are too low and at least one

[32] The optimal response to an outward shift in the domestic firm's reaction curve is a tax reduction abroad which shifts the foreign firm's reaction curve outwards. If we assume that very low taxes lead to disastrous effects on the environment whereas the change in profits remains comparatively low, then there will be limits to the reduction of taxes. A zero level of regulation will not be the outcome of the policy game.

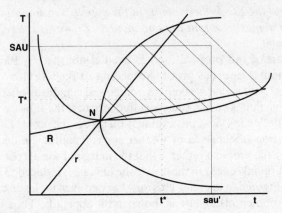

FIG. 6.6. Strategic Environmental Policy and Tax Consumption

country is worse off compared to a situation in which each country does not behave strategically but only internalizes the externalities created by its own firm.

See Figure 6.6 for a graphical representation of the tax competition. If one
country does not behave strategically, i.e. $t^e = sau'$ or $T^e = SAU'$, the other
country will implement its optimal tax rate, which is lower that the Pigouvian
tax. These tax rates are denoted by t^* and T^*, respectively. Under the conventional assumption that the home-country's reaction curve, r, is steeper than
the foreign-country's reaction curve, R, the Nash equilibrium, N, is stable and
the tax rates are too low. The shaded area represents potential Pareto improvements.[33]

6.4.3 Strategic Environmental Policy and Price Competition

One of the central points of critique against the original Brander and Spencer
(1985) model is that the policy implications are unstable with respect to conjectural variations. This has been shown by Eaton and Grossman (1986). Similar
considerations apply to the strategic-environmental-policy model. Consider
for instance a scenario in which prices rather than quantities are the strategic
variables used by the firms. This is the case of Bertrand oligopoly. The profits
are now determined by

$$\pi = p\,q(p,P) - \tilde{c} \tag{6.27}$$

and

$$\Pi = P\,Q(p,P) - \tilde{C}, \tag{6.27'}$$

where the quantities supplied by the firms are declining functions of their own
prices but increasing functions of the other firm's price. The first-order condition for an optimum can be established easily and the comparative statics can
be obtained by application of Cramer's rule to

---

[33] The jointly optimal solution requires even higher tax rates than sau' and SAU' (see Fig. 6.5).

$$\begin{pmatrix} \pi_{pp} & \pi_{pP} \\ \Pi_{pP} & \Pi_{PP} \end{pmatrix}\begin{pmatrix} dq \\ dP \end{pmatrix} = \begin{pmatrix} \tilde{c}_t dt^e \\ (\tilde{C}_T dT^e) \end{pmatrix}. \tag{6.28}$$

If the profit functions are strictly concave, if π_{pP} and Π_{pP} are negative, and if the determinant, $\pi_{pp}\Pi_{PP} - \pi_{pP}\Pi_{pP}$, is positive, then the reaction functions are positively sloped in the (p, P) space, the domestic firm's reaction curve is steeper than the foreign firm's curve, and a tax increase leads to an outward shift of the domestic curve. Again N is the Nash equilibrium, S is the Stackelberg point, and the equilibrium with a higher domestic tax rate is the intersection point of the foreign reaction curve and the dashed domestic reaction curve. See Figure 6.7. The shaded area represents the potential of profit increases for both the domestic and the foreign firms. This can be achieved by higher prices, e.g. by cartelization.

Let us start from a reference case where the domestic government imposes a tax equal to the marginal cost of pollution, i.e. $t = sau'$. Now, the home government raises the tax rate. Welfare is again the domestic firm's profit plus the tax revenue plus the utility derived from environmental quality:

$$w = \pi + t^e \tilde{c}_t + u(-sa\,\tilde{c}_t - (1 - S)A\,\tilde{C}_T). \tag{6.29}$$

A marginal change in the emission tax rate has the following welfare effect

$$\frac{dw}{dt^e} = \pi_p p_t + \pi_P P_t + (t - sau')\,(\tilde{c}_{tt} + \tilde{c}_{tq}(q_p p_t + q_P P_t))$$
$$- (1 - S)A\tilde{C}_T(Q_p p_t + Q_P P_t), \tag{6.30}$$

where p_t and P_t are the impacts of the tax change on the Nash-equilibrium prices. Both of them are likely to be positive as can be seen from Figure 6.7. In the initial situation, $t = sau'$ and $\pi_p = 0$. Therefore:

Proposition 6.10. If the transfrontier pollution spillover effect is small, an increase in domestic environmental taxes starting from the marginal environmental

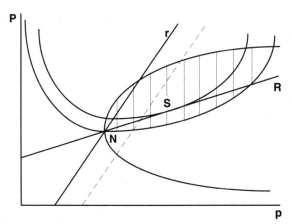

FIG. 6.7. Price Competition and Environmental Policy

damage increases the welfare. In the case of substantial transfrontier pollution, the optimal policy may, however, be characterized by lower taxes.

Proposition 6.10 follows from $\pi_p > 0$ and $P_t > 0$. Ecological dumping is no longer an optimal strategy. The same result has been derived by Barrett (1994) in his model without transfrontier pollution. This corresponds to the Eaton and Grossman (1986) result that exports should be taxed rather than subsidized if firms use prices as their strategic variables. The reason is that price competition leads to too much competition and both governments would benefit from restricting this competition and exploiting the consumers in the third country.[34] If there are substantial spillovers, however, ambiguities arise. This is due to the fact that both prices increase as a response to the tax increase. The resulting change in output is ambiguous and so is the foreign emission level. Thus it may happen that a tax increase raises foreign output and this has a negative effect on domestic environmental quality. For a government taking account of this effect, it may, therefore, turn out to be more sensible to reduce the tax rate as in the Cournot model.

The optimal tax rate can be obtained by rearranging the terms in equation (6.30):

$$t = sau' - \frac{\pi_P P_t - (1-S)A\tilde{C}_{TQ}(Q_p p_t + Q_P P_t)}{\tilde{c}_u + \tilde{c}_{tq}(q_p p_t + q_P P_t)} \tag{6.31}$$

From the signs of the derivatives, it follows that the sign of the denominator is ambiguous since the effect of the change in emission taxes on the domestic output is ambiguous. Nevertheless, if the iso-welfare curves have monotonous derivatives, it follows from proposition 6.10 that the tax rate exceeds marginal damage if the pollution spillover is small. It can be seen from Figure 6.7 that no profit-shifting takes place as it does in the Cournot model. High environmental taxes raise both firms' profits at the expense of the consumers in the third country.

This result may be interpreted a support for the hypothesis that tight environmental standards and high taxes improve the competitiveness of domestic firms. However, this view is mistaken. First, it is not clear whether or not the domestic firm can really increase its profits due to the tax increase.[35] And second, the domestic tax increase is beneficial to the foreign firm whose profits are an increasing function of the domestic emission tax rate. Such a policy can hardly be called pro-competitive.

---

[34] Barrett (1994) uses the argument that quantities usually are strategic substitutes whereas prices are strategic complements in the terminology of Bulow *et al.* (1985). See Klette (1994) for a generalized strategic trade policy model where quantities can be also strategic complements and prices can be strategic substitutes.

[35] The marginal effects of a tax increase are contained in equation (6.30). The effects on the domestic firm are an increase in production cost and a larger revenue (since the foreign firm's price is increased). Which one of these effects dominates, depends on the parameters of the model.

6.4.4 Additional Extensions of the Model and Policy Implications

Besides the problem of tax competition in the Cournot model and the change in the results when one turns from Cournot to Bertrand competition, there are several other reasons as to why the strategic use of environmental policy is problematic (see also Grossman (1986) and Siebert (1988) for summaries of the critique). The following issues are to be noted:

- Not only do conjectural variations, e.g. the move from Cournot to Bertrand competition, affect the results drastically. The number of firms is also a decisive variable. If there is more than one domestic firm, there will be benefits from cartelization. Cartelization can be mimicked by the government if it uses high environmental taxes to reduce the output of domestic firms (see Barrett (1994)). This is closely related to the traditional terms-of-trade argument which calls for high emission taxes in the export industry as the previous chapter has shown. This has to be weighed against the profit-shifting motive, and the policy implications become unclear.

- Subsidies given directly or indirectly by means of lax environmental standards raise the profits of the incumbent firm and this may cause entry by new firms. Horstman and Markusen (1986) show that too many firms may enter the market and that the benefits of the increased market share can be offset by the increase in average costs.

- Domestic consumers have been neglected in this model by the utilization of the third-country assumption. If they were reintroduced, some of the policy implications would be affected. In the Bertrand model, a high tax on output always implies a loss of consumer surplus. In the Cournot model, the effects are unclear since the change in environmental taxes moves the domestic and the foreign supplies into opposite directions. See Conrad (1993b) and Kennedy (1994) for models that take account of the demand side.

- Due to the partial-equilibrium nature of this game, other sectors have been neglected in the analysis. Dixit and Grossman (1986), for instance, show that strategic trade policy for one sector may turn out to be strategic trade policy against other sectors of the economy. Rauscher (1994a, b) looks at general-equilibrium models where the domestic export industry consists of only one firm which plays Nash–Cournot against a foreign competitor. Strategic environmental policy does not always require ecological dumping but may, in some cases, imply emission tax rates that exceed the marginal environmental damage and/or tax rates that are larger than those applied to the non-tradables sectors of the economy.

- One of the major problems in strategic trade policy is information. In order to be able to choose its optimal environmental policy, the government does not only need to have information about marginal environmental damage but also on the shape of the reaction curves, which themselves depend on the cost functions. If the government does not assess the parameters of these functions correctly, a too low emission tax rate may be chosen and the strategic trade policy may lead to welfare losses. Asymmetric information may cause additional problems. The firms tend to have better knowlegde than the government on the relevant parameters, and thus the government relies to some extent on signals given by the private firms. If signalling is costly, in particular if it results in a rent-seeking contest for subsidies, the mere announcement that environmental policies will be used strategically can induce welfare losses.

The conclusion to be drawn here is that the policy implications of the model are not robust with respect to changes in the assumptions. Thus, one would be misled in deriving general conclusions from the model. One is, therefore, driven to do case-studies in order to identify sectors where particular policies may be useful. Thus, the data ultimately have to decide on which policies are advisable. A number of this kind of study has been carried out since the appearance of the original Brander and Spencer (1985) argument, some of them in a volume edited by Krugman and Smith (1994). The basic idea underlying these studies is to modify the original model such that it fits well to a particular industry, to calibrate it, and then do policy simulations. Three of these case-studies will be mentioned briefly. Venables (1994) looks at a general model that may be applied to various industries and shows that the effects of strategic subsidies are very small. Smith (1994), dealing with the car industry, shows that the effects of strategic trade policy are minuscule. Klepper (1994) investigates the aircraft market, which is said to be *the* example where strategic trade policy should be applied and he shows that the welfare impact of subsidizing Airbus has been negative for Europe and for the world as a whole. On the whole, these studies reveal that the welfare effects of strategic export promotion are positive but marginal or negative. Since indirect subsidies by means of lax environmental standards are more costly in welfare terms than the direct subsidies studied in the empirical models, it is highly unlikely that the strategic use of ecological dumping will do anything good to an economy.

6.5 International Oligopoly and the Strategic Choice of Environmental Product Standards

6.5.1 Introduction

The standard argument concerning the impact of environmental regulation on international competitiveness is that tight environmental standards and high emission taxes are harmful because they raise costs. However, some industries in highly regulated countries, such as Japan and Germany, are doing very well in spite of these standards. This is often explained by the fact that Japan and Germany introduced tight standards earlier than other countries and, thus, forced domestic firms to develop new environmentally friendly products and technologies. In the longer term, when other countries also started to tighten their environmental standards, German and Japanese firms had a first-mover advantage over their foreign competitors.[36] This is the so-called 'early home-demand effect'.[37] If this effect is relevant in practice, one is led to the conclusion that the government should adjust its environmental policy such that domestic firms are forced to innovate. The costs of such a policy, so the argument goes, will in the longer term be dominated by the benefits of increased competitiveness. This idea has been refered to as the 'Porter hypothesis' in the recent literature due to Porter's (1991) article in the *Scientific American*.[38] However, the question arises whether government intervention is really necessary for the enhancement of competitiveness. Why don't the firms themselves take care of their competitiveness? And if they do, why should the government do better? As Oates *et al.* (1993) correctly argue, a price-taking firm cannot be made better off by the imposition of a restriction in its choice set (e.g. a tighter standard or tax). There are, however, basically four arguments as to why firms may fail and government intervention is beneficial nevertheless:[39]

- First, X-efficiency theory tells us that firms tend to operate inside their production possibility spaces for reasons of intrafirm inefficiencies in organization and co-ordination (see Leibenstein (1966) and Frantz (1989)). Not intrinsic motivations like the profit motive but rather extrinsic pressure like increased competition from abroad can induce improvements in efficiency. In these circumstances, almost any change in the economic environment that makes entrepreneurs think about cost reduction or product innovation tends to move the firm towards the edge of the production possibility space. However, if X-inefficiency were the reason for the potential to enhance productivity, a better performance could be achieved by any kind of exogenous shock and there may be better policy instruments than a change in environmental policy.

[36] See Blazejczak *et al.* (1993, ch. 4) for a discussion of the German experience. Porter (1990: 346–7) argues that Sweden also has an important advantage in the production of environmentally friendly goods due to its large home demand and the strict environmental regulation.

[37] See Porter (1990: 95). The idea is not new, however. It goes back to Vernon (1966) and the product-cycle theory of international trade.

[38] The European Commission in its White Book on 'Growth, Competitiveness, and Employment' (Commission of the European Communities (1993, ch.2)) expresses similar views. Clean technologies and products are regarded as one of the keystones of Europe's future competitiveness and the Commission argues that governments should actively support the development of these technologies and products. See also Carbaugh and Wassink (1992) for simple arguments in favour of the Porter hypothesis.

[39] The popularity of the Porter hypothesis may also be explained by political-economy arguments. Even if it is not true, it can be politically helpful because it may be used as political propaganda to reduce the resistence against sound environmental policy by industry lobbyists. Even if it is not true that tight environmental standards enhance international competitiveness, the belief that they do may help to achieve a social consensus on environmental policy which enables a society to harvest the true fruit of tight emission policies, namely a clean environment and higher non-pecuniary living standards.

- Second, one may argue that the government possesses better information on future environmental policies in other countries and the future attitude of foreign consumers towards environmentally friendly goods. In my view, this argument is not convincing. A state bureaucracy will rarely be better informed about a private firm's economic environment than the owners and managers of the firm themselves. Anyway, even if there were an informational advantage for the government, the first-best policy would of course not be to fiddle about with environmental policy but instead to pass this information to the private sector.
- Third, the development of environmentally friendly products requires research and development and there are some good arguments in industrial-organization theory in favour of the hypothesis that externalities in the R&D competition lead to less than optimal research activities.[40] The solution to this problem would, however, be to support R&D rather than to tighten environmental standards.
- The fourth candidate for an explanation is that the strategic interaction of firms in oligopolistic markets results in products with low-quality standards and that domestic firms would be better off if they could credibly commit themselves to high-quality products.[41] If such commitments are not credible, the government has to intervene and restrict the private entrepreneurs' choice set. This is another application of strategic trade policy argument.

The fourth line of arguing will be followed here. We will look at a simple duopoly model that considers the product innovation aspect of the Porter hypothesis.[42] There is a domestic and a foreign firm. Each of them produces a single good. For the sake of simplicity, it is assumed again that the output is exported to a third country. The demand in this country depends on the quality of the product which is measured by the emissions discharged during its consumption or its utilization as an input in downstream industry. Buyers of the good are willing to pay more for 'clean' than for 'dirty' goods, whether because they just derive utility from behaving in an environmentally conscious way, or because they are forced by the government which taxes the use of pollution-intensive goods. The pollution-intensity parameters b and B that have been

---

[40] Underinvestment in R&D occurs if there are substantial knowledge spillovers across firms such that the benefits of an innovation can be appropriated only partially by the inventor. In the case of perfect appropriability, however, there tends to be overinvestment in R&D (see *Reinganum* (1981)).

[41] This argument is closely related to the previous one if the introduction of better product qualities requires R&D.

[42] For the process innovation aspect, i.e. the question whether tight standards may induce firms to use better technologies rather than to produce better products, see D. Ulph (1994) and Ulph and Ulph (1994). Their models involve a three-stage game, where the government chooses environmental taxes in the first stage and the firms determine their R&D levels and outputs in the second and third stages. In contrast, the product innovation model considered can be treated as a two-stages game. The results of these rather different models are, however, quite similar as will be seen soon.

assumed to be given and constant up to here can now be chosen by the firms. There is a trade-off because the better the final good the higher the production cost. The structure of the game is as follows. Initially, the firms choose the quality of the products they supply. Given this, they decide on the quantities they produce if they play Nash-Cournot or on the prices they charge if they play Bertrand. Under the assumption of subgame perfection[43], the game can be solved in the usual backward fashion. The role of the government is to intervene in the first stage by using an environmental product standard to restrict the strategy set of 'its' firm. This may be viewed as stage zero of the game. The investigation will start with quantity competition à la Cournot; afterwards we will look at price competition.

The model is simplistic in that it neglects the domestic market and does not consider product-improving R&D explicitly. At a first glance this appears to be a serious shortcoming. In a model without a home market, there cannot be an early home-demand effect, which is said to be so important for international competitiveness. However, the basic strategic interactions that are relevant here can be represented also without considering the home market. What is important here is that the competitiveness argument induces the government to choose an environmental policy which deviates from the policy which would be chosen if only environmental considerations mattered. The direction of the deviation is independent of the existence of a home market. If tight environmental policies can improve the competitiveness of domestic firms, there will always be a bias towards stricter standards independently of which share of their output domestic producers sell in the home market.[44] The intertemporal aspects of an R&D competition are captured by the model implicitly since it involves two stages. In the first stage, the product quality is chosen and the cost of choosing a high quality may be interpreted as an R&D cost. In the second stage, prices and quantities are determined. The discount factor can be regarded as being implicit in the cost function.

6.5.2 Quantity Competition

The domestic and the foreign firms produce quantities q and Q of differentiated goods. Let the qualities of the goods be ω and Ω, respectively. ω and Ω are negatively related to the pollution-impact parameters b and B, e.g

$$\omega = -b, \tag{6.32}$$

$$\Omega = -B. \tag{6.32'}$$

---

[43] For definitions of subgame perfection, see Friedman (1989: 77–82) and Fudenberg and Tirole (1991: 92–100).

[44] Moreover, a model without a home market has an important advantage over a more complicated model: in the reference case where competitiveness is not taken into account by the government, the optimal policy is simply *laissez-faire* and this mitigates analytical problems considerably. A model which does not neglect domestic consumption has been developed by Motta and Thisse (1993) but they do not look at the strategic considerations that are addressed here.

Thus, high values of ω and Ω denote environmentally friendly goods. The higher w and Ω, the higher the price that can be charged for the good. However, developing and producing the environmentally friendly goods is costly and the cost functions are increasing functions of ω and Ω. The profits of the firms are

$$\pi = p(q,Q,\omega,\Omega)q - \tilde{c}(q,\omega), \tag{6.33}$$

$$\Pi = P(q,Q,\omega,\Omega)Q - \tilde{C}(Q,\Omega), \tag{6.33'}$$

where

$$p_q < 0, p_Q < 0, p_\omega > 0, p_\Omega \le 0;\ \tilde{c}_q > 0,\ \tilde{c}_\omega > 0,\ \tilde{c}_{q\omega} \ge 0,$$

$$P_q < 0, P_Q < 0, P_\omega \le 0, P_\Omega > 0;\ \tilde{C}_Q > 0,\ \tilde{C}_\Omega > 0,\ \tilde{C}_{Q\Omega} \ge 0.$$

$\tilde{c}_{q\omega}$ and $\tilde{C}_{Q\Omega}$ are zero if only the development but not the production of high-quality products is costly compared to that of lower-quality goods. The signs of the other cross-derivatives need not be specified here. One may, however, assume that their signs equal those of the products of the two corresponding single derivatives. Moreover, it is assumed that all second-order conditions of profit maximization are satisfied.

We start with stage two of the firm's profit-maximization problem and determine the optimal outputs for given levels of product quality. The first-order conditions are $p_q q + p - \tilde{c}_q = 0$ and $P_Q Q + P - \tilde{C}_Q = 0$, respectively, and the comparative statics can be derived from

$$\begin{pmatrix} \pi_{pp} & \pi_{pQ} \\ \Pi_{pQ} & \Pi_{QQ} \end{pmatrix} \begin{pmatrix} dq \\ dQ \end{pmatrix} = \begin{pmatrix} \tilde{c}_{q\omega} - p_\omega - p_{q\omega}q & -p_\Omega - p_{q\Omega}q \\ -p_\omega - p_{Q\omega}Q & \tilde{C}_{Q\Omega} - P_\Omega - P_{Q\Omega}Q \end{pmatrix} \begin{pmatrix} d\omega \\ d\Omega \end{pmatrix}. \tag{6.34}$$

Let us assume that there exists a Nash equilibrium in which each firm chooses its best response to the other firm's output decision. If $\pi_{qq}\Pi_{QQ} - \pi_{qQ}\Pi_{qQ} > 0$, then the domestic reaction curve is steeper than the foreign curve and the Nash equilibrium is stable. Moreover, assume that the strategic variables are substitutes, i.e. $\pi_{qQ} < 0$ and $\Pi_{qQ} < 0$. Then the reaction curves are negatively sloped in the (q, Q) diagram. A change in domestic product quality will have the following impacts on domestic and foreign equilibrium outputs:

$$\frac{dq}{d\omega} = \frac{\Pi_{QQ}(\tilde{c}_{q\omega} - p_\omega - P_{q\omega}q) - \pi_{qQ}(P_\omega + P_{Q\omega}Q)}{\pi_{qq}\Pi_{QQ} - \pi_{qQ}\Pi_{qQ}} \tag{6.35}$$

$$\frac{dQ}{d\omega} = \frac{\Pi_{qQ}(\tilde{c}_{q\omega} - p_\omega - P_{q\omega}q) - \pi_{qq}(P_\omega + P_{Q\omega}Q)}{\pi_{qq}\Pi_{QQ} - \pi_{qQ}\Pi_{qQ}} \tag{6.35'}$$

Similar results can be derived for variations in the quality of the foreign product. The signs $dq/d\omega$, $dQ/d\Omega$, and $dQ/d\Omega$ of are in general ambiguous. To give an economic intuition, one may decompose these effects into the shifts of the two reaction functions. $P_\omega + P_{Q\omega}Q$ is the impact of a change in domestic product quality on the foreign firm's marginal revenue. Its sign is ambiguous ($P_{Q\omega}$ may well be positive), but let us assume that it is negative. If its marginal revenue is reduced, the foreign firm will reduce its output. The reaction curve is shifted inwards. This is denoted by the dashed line R' in Figure 6.8. The effect on the domestic firm's reaction curve is ambiguous. An increase in product quality may raise the marginal production cost and this is an incentive to reduce output. On the other hand, a better quality will result in a higher price and probably in a higher marginal revenue, provided that $p_\omega + p_{q\omega}q > 0$. This would be a reason to increase the output. Figure 6.8 shows inward and outward shifts of the home firm's reaction curve, r' and r'', respectively. The effect of the increase in quality on the location of the equilibrium is ambiguous (N' or N'').[45] What can be said is that, except in the case of a positive effect on foreign marginal revenue (which is not depicted here), at least one firm's output will be reduced as a result of an increase in domestic product quality. If the effect of quality improvements on marginal production cost, $\tilde{c}_{q\omega}$, is low, then an equilibrium like N' is likely to be the result of the quality improvement. A small value of $\tilde{c}_{q\omega}$ means that the major cost component of introducing a better quality is the R&D cost. Then high-quality products have the same marginal production costs as low-quality goods and domestic (foreign) output is an increasing (decreasing) function of the level of product quality. Of course, a similar diagram can be drawn for an increase in foreign product quality and the conclusions to be drawn are basically the same.

Now consider stage one of the game, the optimal choice of the product quality. Maximization of the profit function yields

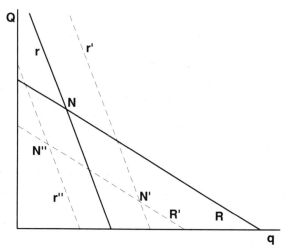

FIG. 6.8. Effects of Quality Changes in the Cournot Game

---

[45] In the case where high-quality goods are only costly in their development but not in their production, N' is likely to be the new Nash equilibrium. In this case, high product-quality requirements improve a firm's position in the final-goods market. As will be seen soon, however, this does not have the policy implication that the government should introduce tight minimum product standards to support the domestic producer.

$$q\left(P_\omega + P_Q \frac{dQ}{d\omega}\right) - \tilde{c}_\omega = 0 \qquad (6.36)$$

$$Q\left(P_\Omega + P_q \frac{dq}{d\Omega}\right) - \tilde{C}_\Omega = 0 \qquad (6.36')$$

Assume that a unique Nash equilibrium exists. The slopes of the reaction functions are

$$\frac{\partial \breve{r}}{\partial \Omega} = - \frac{qP_{\omega \Omega} + qP_{Q\Omega}\dfrac{dQ}{d\omega} + \left(qP_{q\omega} + qP_{qQ}\dfrac{dQ}{d\omega} + \dfrac{\tilde{c}_\omega}{q} - \tilde{c}_{q\omega}\right)\dfrac{dq}{d\Omega}}{\pi_{\Omega\Omega}}$$

$$+ \frac{q\left(P_{Q\omega} + P_{QQ}\dfrac{dQ}{d\omega}\right)\dfrac{dQ}{d\Omega} + P_Q\dfrac{d^2Q}{d\omega d\Omega}}{\pi_{\Omega\Omega}} \qquad (6.37)$$

$$\frac{\partial \breve{R}}{\partial \omega} = - \frac{QP_{\omega\Omega} + QP_{q\omega}\dfrac{dq}{d\Omega} + Q\left(P_{q\Omega} + P_{qq}\dfrac{dq}{d\Omega}\right)\dfrac{dq}{d\omega}}{\Pi_{\Omega\Omega}}$$

$$+ \frac{\left(QP_{Q\Omega} + QP_{qQ}\dfrac{dq}{d\Omega} + \dfrac{\tilde{C}_\Omega}{Q} - \tilde{C}_{Q\Omega}\right)\dfrac{dQ}{d\omega} + QP_q\dfrac{d^2q}{d\omega d\Omega}}{\Pi_{\Omega\Omega}} \qquad (6.37')$$

Their signs are ambiguous. There are four reasons for this:

- The signs of the cross-derivatives of the functions are generally not known, but let us assume that they are either zero or have the 'normal' signs, i.e. equalling those of the corresponding single derivatives.
- The effects of changes in product quality on the Nash-equilibrium outputs are ambiguous. An increase in domestic product quality induces an increase in domestic output and a reduction in foreign output if the effect of quality on marginal production cost is small.
- If $\tilde{c}_{q\omega}$ and $\tilde{C}_{Q\Omega}$ are large, then the signs of the longest terms in brackets in equations (6.37) and (6.37') are reversed. In this case the impact of product quality on marginal costs should dominate the impact on average costs. However, this is unlikely to happen (though not impossible) since usually a substantial part of the cost of a better product quality is R&D cost, which does not affect marginal production costs.
- The last term in the numerator contains third derivatives of the demand and cost functions and their signs are ambiguous.

Thus, in general the signs of the slopes of the reaction curves are ambiguous. If the cross-derivatives of the functions have the 'normal' signs, if the costs of better product qualities are primarily R&D costs, and if the revenue and cost functions are nearly quadratic, then the slopes of the reaction curves are negative.

In this model, the government has a very simple objective function. It maximizes profits as well. Consumer surpluses can be neglected because of the third-country assumption. In order to keep the model tractable and to concentrate on the essentials it is assumed that production does not cause significant environmental harm. Although the government and the firm have the same objective function, they differ in one important aspect. The government can define a product standard before the firm decides on the kind of product it wishes to produce. It therefore has the first-mover advantage and can act as a Stackelberg leader *vis-à-vis* the firms.

The Stackelberg solution will be illustrated graphically. In order to be able to do this, one has to determine the shapes of the iso-profit contours. The shape of the home firm's iso-profit curve is decisively affected by the externality originating from the strategy chosen by the foreign firm. It is

$$\frac{d\pi}{d\Omega} = \left(p_\Omega + p_Q \frac{dQ}{d\Omega}\right)q, \tag{6.38}$$

where $dQ/d\Omega$ is determined by equation (6.34). Since its sign is ambiguous, the direction of the external effect is ambiguous as well. It is, however, plausible to assume that the direct effect dominates the indirect effect and that $d\pi/d\Omega$ is negative: an increase in the competitor's product quality reduces domestic profits. In this case, the iso-profit curve is concave; otherwise, it is convex.[46] The same two cases are possible for the foreign firm's iso-profit contours. Thus, four scenarios can be distinguished.[47] They are depicted in Figure 6.9.

Figure 6.9 shows potential Nash equilibria in product qualities. Note that each point in this figure is a Nash equilibrium in quantities. Parts (a) and (b) of the figure show the case of a negative externality of foreign product quality, (c) and (d) depict the case of a positive externality. In parts (a) and (c) the product qualities are strategic substitutes; in parts (b) and (d), they are complements. N always denotes a Nash equilibrium, S a Stackelberg point. Since the firms make their decisions simultaneously, none of them has a first-mover advantage and, thus, a commitment to choose the product quality such that the Stackelberg solution can be achieved, is impossible. The government, however, possesses a first-mover advantage since it can impose a restriction on the quality to be chosen by its firm. It is seen from Figure 6.9 that this restriction is a minimum quality standard in cases (a) and (d) and a maximum quality standard in cases (b)

[46] Concavity or convexity can be established only as local properties in the neighbourhood of the intersection points of the reaction curves and the iso-profit curve. It is assumed here that the concavity or convexity hold globally.

[47] There are four additional cases in which the slopes of the domestic and the foreign reaction curves have the opposite signs. However, these scenarios do not provide any additional insights here since the slope of the domestic reaction curve is irrelevant for the action taken by the government of the home country.

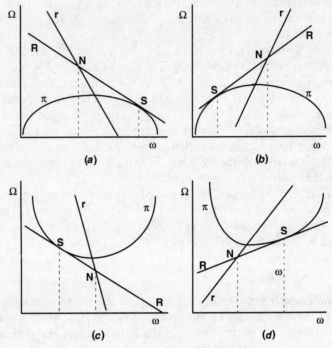

FIG. 6.9. Strategic Use of Environmental Quality Standards

and (c). Case 1 can be the result of a situation where $\tilde{c}_{q\omega}$ is small, i.e. where the major cost component of quality improvement is the R&D cost but not production cost. This is a situation where the Porter hypothesis is likely to be supported by the model.

Proposition 6.11. Assume that foreign and domestic firms behave according to the Cournot conjecture. Depending on whether product qualities are strategic substitutes or complements and on whether the domestic firm gains or loses if the foreign firm increases its product quality, the optimal policy of the government can consist in a minimum or a maximum product quality standard. The Porter hypothesis that tight environmental standards improve competitiveness is likely to hold in the case where these standards raise the marginal cost of production only marginally. If this cost increase is substantial, the opposite policy implication has to be drawn.

This result is not particularly satisfactory. Even if the less plausible case (the positive effect of foreign product quality on domestic profits) is ruled out, the ambiguity does not vanish. If qualities are strategic substitutes, the optimal policy is a high minimum quality standard which forces the firm to produce higher qualities than in the unregulated case. The opposite policy recommendation results if the product qualities are strategic complements. Whether they are complements or substitutes, depends on the shape of the cost functions and on the behaviour of the demand side and no a priori judgements are possible as to which scenario may be more relevant for practical purposes. Hence, making a good policy requires a very profound knowledge of markets and technologies and it is questionable whether this knowledge exists. Similar conclusions have been reached by D. Ulph (1994) in his model where environmental regulation affects process innovation rather than product innovation. Depending on the shape of the R&D success function which specifies the impact on R&D on emissions, high emission taxes may either reduce or raise the profits of the regulated firm.

6.5.3 Price Competition

In the case of heterogeneous goods, it is usually more realistic to model firm behaviour as a competition in prices than in quantities. The purpose of this section is to consider this case of Bertrand behaviour and to find out whether the policy implications are changed and, in particular, whether some more clear-cut results can be obtained.

If prices are the strategic variables in stage two of the game, the profit functions of the two firms are

$$\pi = q(p,P,\omega,\Omega)p - \tilde{c}(q(p,P,\omega,\Omega),\omega), \tag{6.39}$$

$$\Pi = Q(p,P,\omega,\Omega)P - \tilde{C}(Q(p,P,\omega,\Omega),\Omega), \tag{6.39'}$$

where

$$q_p > 0, q_P < 0, q_\omega > 0, q_\Omega < 0; \tilde{c}_q > 0, \tilde{c}_\omega > 0,$$

$$Q_p < 0, Q_P > 0, Q_\omega < 0, Q_\Omega > 0; \tilde{C}_Q > 0, \tilde{C}_\Omega > 0,$$

It is assumed that the second-order conditions of profit maximization are satisfied. The first-order conditions are $(p - \tilde{c}_q)q + q = 0$ and $(P - \tilde{C}_Q)Q_P + Q = 0$, respectively, and the comparative statics can be derived from

$$\begin{pmatrix} \pi_{qq} & \pi_{pP} \\ \Pi_{pP} & \Pi_{PP} \end{pmatrix} \begin{pmatrix} dp \\ dP \end{pmatrix} = \begin{pmatrix} q_p \tilde{c}_{q\omega} - q_\omega + \dfrac{q_{p\omega}q}{q_p} & -q_\omega + \dfrac{q_{p\Omega}q}{q_p} \\ -Q_\omega + \dfrac{Q_{P\omega}Q}{Q_P} & Q_P \tilde{C}_{Q\Omega} - Q_\Omega + \dfrac{Q_{P\Omega}Q}{Q_P} \end{pmatrix} \begin{pmatrix} d\omega \\ d\Omega \end{pmatrix}. \tag{6.40}$$

Assume that there exists a Nash equilibrium. If $\pi_{pp}\Pi_{PP} - \pi_{pP}\Pi_{pP} > 0$, the domestic reaction curve is steeper than the foreign curve and the Nash equilibrium is stable. Moreover, assume that prices are strategic complements, i.e. $\pi_{pP} > 0$ and $\Pi_{pP} > 0$. Then the reaction curves are positively sloped in the (p,P) diagram. The comparative-static results concerning the effects of changes in product qualities are still ambiguous. If, however, the cross-derivatives of the demand functions with respect to prices and qualities are sufficiently small, i.e. if the last terms of the matrix elements of the right-hand side of equation nearly vanish, and if the cross derivative of the cost function is non-negative, then the comparative static effects can be signed. For a given price of the foreign good, an increase in domestic product quality will lead to an increase in the price of the domestic product. In Figure 6.10, the domestic reaction curve, r, is shifted to the right.[48] The foreign reaction curve is shifted downwards since the price foreign producers can charge for their output is reduced if domestic producers sell higher-quality products at a constant price. The Nash equilibrium is moved from N to N'. The direction of this movement is indeterminate. It is plausible that the domestic price is raised and the foreign price is reduced, but it is also possible that both prices increase or decline. The only case which can be excluded is a reduction of the domestic price and an increase in the foreign price.

Given these ambiguities in stage two of the game, it is not amazing that the outcome of stage one is ambiguous as well. Maximization of the profit functions yields

$$pq_\omega - \tilde{c}_\omega + (p - \tilde{c}_q)q_P\frac{dP}{d\omega} = 0, \tag{6.41}$$

$$Q_\Omega - \tilde{C}_\Omega + (P - \tilde{C}_Q)Q_p\frac{dp}{d\Omega} = 0. \tag{6.41'}$$

The slopes of the reaction functions, $\check{r}(.)$ and $\check{R}(.)$ are ambiguous.[49]

Again, the external effect of a change in foreign product quality can be determined. It is

$$\frac{d\pi}{d\Omega} = (p - \tilde{c}_q)\left(q_\Omega + q_P\frac{dP}{d\Omega}\right), \tag{6.42}$$

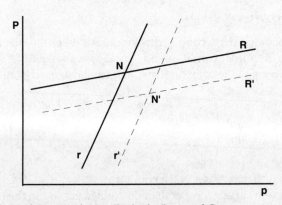

FIG. 6.10. Effects of Changes in Quality in the Bertrand Game

[48] It is plausible that goods of higher quality become more expensive since (1) the willingness to pay is higher and (2) their production is more costly.

[49] Again, one reason for this is the occurrence of third derivatives. The first-order conditions of stage-two optimization are constraints that have to be considered in stage-one optimization. Therefore, the first-order conditions of stage one will contain second derivatives of the cost and demand functions. Additional differentiation to obtain comparative-static results yields third derivatives.

where $dP/d\Omega$ can be determined from equation (6.40). The sign of the external effect is ambiguous. If one assumes that the direct effect dominates the indirect effect, then $d\pi/d\Omega$ is negative: an improvement in foreign product quality reduces domestic profits. As in the case of Cournot competition we arrive at the four scenarios depicted in Figure 6.9 in the previous section. The following conclusion can be drawn:

Proposition 6.12. Assume that foreign and domestic firms behave according to the Bertrand conjecture. Depending on whether product qualities are strategic substitutes or complements and on whether the domestic firm gains or loses if the foreign firm increases its product quality, the optimal policy of the government can consist in a minimum or a maximum product quality standard.

The policy recommendation in the Bertrand case is as ambiguous as in the Cournot case. Thus one cannot derive simple policy recommendations from this model. It shows that tight environmental standards may be beneficial to domestic producers but they may also be harmful. Matters would become even more complicated if the model were extended by relaxing some of its unrealistic assumptions. For example, one may introduce domestic consumption, look at more general market structures, or consider general-equilibrium repercussions. It is unlikely that an extended model will be more clear-cut in its policy implications.[50] Given the discrepancy between the amount of knowledge necessary to find the optimal product standard and the knowledge which exists, one may conclude that policy-makers should refrain from using environmental policy instruments to shift profits to the home economy.

6.6 Monopolistic Competition and Intra-Industry Trade

6.6.1 Introduction

A great disadvantage of the Heckscher–Ohlin approach is that it explains only a part of international trade, namely that part which is due to differences in factor endowments between countries. One of the predictions of the

[50] The models investigated by Reitzes (1992) and Motta and Thisse (1993) produce less ambiguous results despite the existence of domestic consumption. The Motta and Thisse model differs in various respects from the present one. They consider an intra-industry trade model in which various qualities are produced in each country and they use specified demand and cost functions. With these demand and cost functions they derive unambiguous results in favour of minimum environmental quality standards. It is, however, questionable whether their results are generalizable to other demand and cost functions. A similar critique applies to Reitzes (1992). Due to the rather special assumptions on consumer behaviour, many ambiguities vanish, and he arrives at the result that firms choose socially optimal product qualities unless there are 'set-up' costs in raising product qualities. These set-up costs are equivalent to the R&D costs mentioned in the preceding paragraphs of this chapter. If there are set-up or R&D costs, the government should intervene by setting minimum quality standards in the Reitzes model. This result is compatible with the conclusions derived from our model.

Heckscher–Ohlin model is that the more different the countries and the more different the commodities the larger are the gains from the international division of labour and the larger the volume of international trade. In reality, however, the biggest share of international trade is trade between industrialized countries, which are relatively similar in their factor endowments. And much of this is trade in commodities that are similar with respect to their factor intensities.[51] This is in sharp contrast with the predictions of the traditional trade models. Thus, new approaches have been developed to explain this intra-industry trade. None of them uses comparative advantage as an explanation any more. In all these models, trade is a result of imperfect competition and increasing returns to scale. There are basically three modelling approaches to intra-industry trade:[52] (1) the love-of-variety approach by Krugman (1979, 1980) and Dixit and Norman (1980) based on the Spence (1976) and Dixit and Stiglitz (1977) models of monopolistic competition; (2) the specific-preferences approach by Lancaster (1980), and Helpman (1981) based on Hotelling's (1929) model of spatial competition; and (3) the Cournot oligopoly model of Brander (1981), Brander and Krugman (1983), and Venables (1985). The last category deals with trade in commodities that are (literally) identical and to me this seems to be the least interesting case. Models of category (2) assume that commodities are different and that each consumer prefers a particular variety of the good whereas models of category (1) assume that consumers wish to buy as many different varieties of the good as possible. The basic difference between these models is that in those of the first type a variable has to be introduced that measures the degree of difference between varieties whereas in models of the second category it is sufficient that these variants just differ somehow.[53] The specific-preferences model appears to be more useful since it is not only more plausible and realistic but it also offers the possibility of assigning contents like 'environmental friendliness' to the measure of difference. Unfortunately, however, these models turn out to be intractable rather easily and, therefore, the less satisfying approach of the love-of-variety model will be chosen here.[54]

An important aspect of the model to be discussed here is the endogeneity of market structure. The number of firms is not fixed but it may vary if changes in the economic environment (e.g. the introduction of emission taxes) induce new firms to enter the market or incumbents to go out of business. In this respect, the model is much more satisfactory than the monopoly and oligopoly models

[51] For more detailed country-specific evidence see Greenaway and Milner (1986, ch.7) and Helpman (1987).   [52] See also Greenaway and Milner (1986, chs. 2–3).
[53] In special circumstances, the love-of-diversity model may be viewed as a reduced form of the specific-preferences model. If each individual consumer prefers a specific variety of a good, the representative or average consumer who aggregates all individual preferences behaves as if she derived utility from product diversity (see Anderson et al. (1992, ch. 5)).
[54] As an example of the difficulties that arise if economic policies are discussed in the specific-preferences model, see Lancaster (1984). Another example of how environmental friendliness can be introduced into a trade model has been given in the previous section, but for a different market structure.

presented earlier. However, this advantage comes at a price. For the sake of tractability, some very restrictive assumptions will have to be made, in particular on preferences. Thus, the model will be very stylized and should not be mistaken for a realistic picture of what is going on in the real world. None the less, it is useful for giving some impression of what can happen in a world where increasing returns to scale and product diversity play a role. Even this simplistic model provides new insights that go beyond what can be achieved in the framework of traditional trade models. In less restrictive and less stylized models, a number of additional interesting observations would be possible. Some of the issues will be touched upon here, albeit in a rather speculative way of reasoning. Further research into this kind of imperfectly competitive models is definitely needed.

We will start with the presentation of the basic model. Then the question will be raised whether trade is good for the environment and for economic welfare. Afterwards, we will look at the effects of environmental policies in the presence of intra-industry trade and transfrontier pollution spillovers. Unlike in the previous sections, optimal policies will not be derived explicitly since the model is too complex.

6.6.2 A Model of Intra-Industry Trade

There are again two countries, the home country and the foreign country. Both countries are identical in all respects: consumer behaviour, technology, and factor endowment. The model is a modified version of the Dixit and Stiglitz (1977) model of a monopolistically competitive economy. There is a differentiated commodity with potentially infinitely many varieties. It will, however, be seen that only a finite number of varieties is actually produced, n in the home country and N in the foreign country. We assume that the two countries are identical with respect to the demand side, i.e. preferences are the same. Moreover, all commodities are produced with the same technology and they are equally desirable from the point of view of the consumers.[55] For the consumers, the characteristics of a variant do not matter; what matters is that each variant is different from all the others in some respects. They wish to consume as many different varieties as possible. This love of diversity is introduced via the representative consumer's utility function, which is composed of identical subutility functions for each variant:

$$\sum_{i=1}^{\infty}(c^i)^{\theta} + u(-z) \qquad \text{with } 0 < \theta < 1.[56] \tag{6.43}$$

[55] It would be an interesting extension of the model to introduce different technologies for different varieties. For instance, one could distinguish environmentally intensive and less intensive products. This, however, would fortify the complexity of the model and therefore this approach is not followed here. None the less, some non-formal thoughts on the effects of economic integration in the case of different technologies will be presented below.

[56] Since only a limited number of varieties, say n, will be available, many of the c_is will be zero.

with θ is the elasticity of substitution between different varieties and it makes sense to assume that this elasticity is a non-decreasing function of the number of varieties available.

$$\theta'(n + N) \geq 0. \tag{6.44}$$

Utility maximization under the usual budget constraint yields the demand functions

$$c^i = \xi y(p^i)^{1/(\theta-1)}, \tag{6.45}$$

where y is the income and ξ is a price index:

$$\xi = \left(\sum_{i=1}^{n+N} (p^i)^{\frac{\theta}{\theta-1}} \right)^{-1}.$$

See Helpman and Krugman (1985: 118) or the appendix to this chapter. The corresponding inverse-demand function is

$$p^i = \psi(c^i)^{\theta-1}. \tag{6.46}$$

Foreign consumers have the same utility function and the same demand functions.

The firms maximize profits for given demand functions. The number of firms is assumed to be large. Thus, every single firm treats the parameters ξ and ψ as given.[57] Due to increasing returns to scale, each good is produced by only one firm. Let us first consider the profit maximization of a domestic firm i for the case of no trade. The variable cost of production depends on the quantity produced and on the factor prices, i.e. the emission tax rate, t^e, and the rate of interest. The external effect on production will be neglected for the sake of tractability. The other factor of production is capital. Like in other intra-industry trade models, it is assumed here that the variable costs are linear in output. The unit costs are $\hat{c}(t^{e,i},r)$. Moreover, we assume that some fixed capital, k^o, is required for the production of each variety. Thus, there is a fixed cost rk^o which is independent of the output. All firms are assumed to use the same technology and, thus, their cost functions are identical. A single firm's optimization problem is to maximize its profits,

$$\pi^i = \psi(q^i)^\theta - \hat{c}(t^e,r)q^i - rk^o. \tag{6.47}$$

The first-order condition is that marginal revenue equals marginal cost and this implies:

$$p^i = \frac{\hat{c}}{\theta}. \tag{6.48}$$

---

[57] This is not an innocent assumption as Heijdra and Yang (1993) and Yang and Hejidra (1993) have shown since it is based on the existence of a very large number of firms (going to infinity). But the number of firms is a variable to be determined in the model and it turns out to be finite. Nevertheless, for the sake of simplicity we will also use this assumption.

The second-order condition is satisfied.[58] Free entry by other firms drives profits to zero and this implies

$$(1 - \theta)\hat{c}q^i - \theta r k^o = 0. \tag{6.49}$$

It is assumed here that n is so large that integer problems do not arise and the entry of the nth firm makes profits go 'very close' to zero. Moreover, n will be dealt with as a continuous variable in the following sections and integer problems are neglected. To simplify notation, we can drop the superscript i since all firms are identical with respect to their relevant parameters. Thus, we now consider the behaviour of a representative firm.

The model is closed by the factor-market equilibrium. Each firm demands capital. As factor of production, however, is available only in limited supply. As in the Heckscher–Ohlin model its supply, k, is assumed to be inelastic. So the factor-market equilibrium is determined by Shephard's lemma:

$$n(\hat{c}_r q + k^o) = k. \tag{6.50}$$

Equations (6.48) to (6.50) determine the equilibrium in this economy. There are four unknowns in these three equations, p, q, r, and n. The rental rate, r, can be used as a numéraire.

The foreign country's autarky equilibrium is given by the same equations. The foreign country's variables will be characterized by uppercase letters except for the preference parameter, θ, which is identical for both countries.

$$P = \frac{\hat{C}}{\theta}. \tag{6.48'}$$

$$(1 - \theta)\hat{C}Q - \theta R K^o = 0. \tag{6.49'}$$

$$N(\hat{C}_R Q + K^o) = K. \tag{6.50'}$$

In the case of international trade, equations (6.48) to (6.50) and (6.48') to (6.50') continue to hold. It has to be taken into account, however, that demand for each good now comes from two countries. Therefore

$$q = (\xi y + \Xi Y)(p)^{1/(\theta - 1)}$$

$$Q = (\xi y + \Xi Y)(P)^{1/(\theta - 1)}$$

but this does not affect the decisions of a single producer since the income variables and the price indices do not occur in equations (6.48) to (6.50) and (6.48') to (6.50'), which determine the supply sides of the two economies.

Environmental pollution in autarky is due to emissions from production (again determined by Shephard's lemma) and consumption

$$z = ns(a\hat{c}_t q + bc) + N(1 - S)(A\hat{C}_t Q + BC), \tag{6.51}$$

$$Z = n(1 - s)(a\hat{c}_t q + bc) + NS(A\hat{C}_t Q + BC). \tag{6.51'}$$

---

[58] Since the variable-cost function is linear in q, the slope of the marginal-revenue curve gives the second-order condition. It is $\theta(\theta - 1)(q^i)^{\theta - 2} < 0$.

In a situation with trade, one has to distinguish between the consumption of domestic and of foreign goods. Since the prices may differ, demand may differ as well. In order to be able to make this distinction, two new variables are introduced. m denotes the domestic imports of a foreign variety and M the foreign imports of a domestic variety. Thus, $q - M$ is the domestic consumption of a domestic variety and m is the consumption of a foreign variety. Correspondingly, $Q - m$ represents the consumption of foreign varieties in the foreign country and M the consumption of a domestic variety by foreigners. Then

$$z = s(an\hat{c}_t q + bn(q - M) + bNm) + (1 - S)(AN\hat{C}_t Q + BN(Q - m) + BnM) \\ + \gamma(nM + Nm), \tag{6.52}$$

$$Z = (1 - s)(an\hat{c}_t q + bn(q - M) + bNm) + S(AN\hat{C}_t Q + BN(Q - m) + BnM) \\ + \gamma(nM + Nm). \tag{6.52'}$$

On some occasions in the following analysis, we simplify the model by assuming that the pollution coefficients of the two countries are the same: $a = A$, $b = B$ and $s = S$.

6.6.3 Gains and Losses from Trade

Will the gains from trade be diminished by increased pollution? Assume for simplicity that both countries are completely identical, i.e. they have chosen the same environmental policy and, therefore, firms in both countries face identical cost structures.

Matters are relatively simple if the elasticity of consumption substitution is independent of the number of available alternatives, i.e. if $\theta' = 0$, and if all autarky prices are identical across goods and across countries because of identical emission tax rates. Merging the two economies increases the number of available varieties for all consumers but does not alter the profit-maximization and zero-profit conditions of the firms. Total output and total consumption remain unchanged (see Krugman (1980)). Gains from trade originate from the increased number of varieties available in each country. Losses may be due to transport externalities. However, it is possible to design an international environmental agreement such that the net gains from trade are positive. The optimum transport tax will never be prohibitive. This follows from the specification of the utility function: the utility derived from a marginal unit of a new imported good is infinity whereas the welfare loss due to increased pollution from transporting this marginal unit is finite. Thus, it is always better to have some foreign trade instead of autarky despite the existence of transport costs. In this respect, this intra-industry-trade model differs from the Heckscher–Ohlin model, where all goods are already available in autarky. Note, however, that this result is a direct implication of the choice of the utility function. If the introduction of a new good had only a finite marginal welfare effect, a prohibitive trade tax could not be excluded.

Now consider the case where θ is an increasing function of the number of variants available. If foreign products appear on the market, the choice set of the consumers is enlarged; their possibilities to substitute between different consumption goods is increased. To each single producer this is an exogenous change in θ. Total differentiation of equations (6.49) and (6.50) yields

$$\begin{pmatrix} (1-\theta)\hat{c} & 0 \\ n\hat{c}_r & \hat{c}_r q + k^0 \end{pmatrix} \begin{pmatrix} dq \\ dn \end{pmatrix} = \begin{pmatrix} (\hat{c}q + rk^0)d\theta \\ 0 \end{pmatrix}.$$
(6.53)

It follows that

$$\frac{dq}{d\theta} = \frac{\hat{c}q + rk^0}{(1-\theta)\hat{c}} > 0,$$
(6.54a)

$$\frac{dn}{d\theta} = -\frac{(\hat{c}q + rk^0)n\hat{c}_r}{(1-\theta)\hat{c}(\hat{c}_r q + k^0)} < 0.$$
(6.54b)

The number of domestic firms will be reduced but the remaining firms will increase their output if the number of varieties is increased by foreign trade. The total output in this economy, nq, will be increased:

$$\frac{d(nq)}{d\theta} = \frac{(\hat{c}q + rk^0)nk^0}{(1-\theta)(\hat{c}_r q + rk^0)\hat{c}} > 0.$$
(6.54c)

This is a normal result in the case of increasing returns to scale. Better substitutability of consumption goods implies a reduction in the demand for diversity. Some firms will disappear from the market. With a smaller number of firms the share of fixed costs of the total costs in this economy is reduced and, therefore, total output can be raised.[59]

What does this mean to the environment? On the one hand, there are emissions from the production process. They follow from Shephard's lemma, $e = n\hat{c}_r q$ and are proportional to the economy's total output. Thus, emissions from production will rise at a given emission tax rate. On the other hand, consumption also causes pollution. A part of the output is consumed and the rest is exported in exchange for foreign goods that are equally polluting when consumed. Thus, pollution from consumption will be increased as well. Since the foreign country is affected by increased openness in the same fashion, there will also be an increase in transfrontier pollution. Finally, transportation causes environmental damage, but with an appropriate tax the net welfare effect will be positive.

Proposition 6.13. In the case of constant marginal cost, international trade will raise the externalities due to production and consumption if the elasticity of substitution between consumption goods is an increasing function of the number of available varieties. The environmental costs of trade may be internalized by a non-prohibitive tax.

[59] If k^0 were zero, the total output would remain unchanged.

As mentioned earlier, the result that it is never optimal to prevent international trade is an artefact of the model assumptions. With other kinds of utility functions, one may arrive at different conclusions.

Up to here, it has been assumed that the commodities are produced in identical production processes. What would happen if a distinction between environmentally friendly and environmentally unfriendly goods were made? Environmental friendliness would be reflected in product-specific emission taxes that could lead to differences in production costs. If the demand side is modelled as before, then producers would specialize on production of the 'cleanest' goods. The producer of the dirtiest of these clean goods would make zero profits and the other producers would earn Ricardian rents. One can now imagine different scenarios for the autarky situation. If both countries produce the same commodities in autarky, then half of the incumbent producers have to give up their production when trade commences. The reason for this is the fixed cost: it is inefficient to have a commodity produced by more than a single firm. When the number of firms has been halved, profits are increased and even the marginal producer makes a positive profit. New entrants appear in the market. Since the niches of clean products are already occupied by incumbents, however, the new firms have to produce less environmentally friendly goods. The pollution intensity of production is raised. Besides this pessimistic scenario, an optimistic one is also conceivable. Assume, that domestic and foreign firms produce different goods in autarky. With realistic assumptions on substitutability between consumption goods, there may be a concentration process when trade commences and some firms leave the market. In this case, the firms producing the least environmentally friendly goods disappear and production becomes environmentally less intensive. One may argue that the second scenario is more realistic since there is no reason why commodities produced in different countries in an autarky situation should be identical from a consumer's point of view. Thus, there would be environmental gains from trade.

6.6.4 The Effects of Environmental Policies in an Open Economy

Environmental policies affect relative prices and, therefore, the allocation of factors of production, the supply of and demand for final goods, and the patterns of trade and world market prices. In a first step, trade restrictions are assumed to be absent. Consumption needs not be taxed since the environmental impact of all goods via consumption is identical and as long as transportation costs are negligible. Thus, the only policy instrument is the taxation of emissions generated during the production process.

The integrated general equilibrium of the two trading economies is characterized by the following system of equations:

$$pq - \hat{c}q - rk^o = 0, \tag{6.55a}$$

$$\theta p - \hat{c} = 0, \tag{6.55b}$$

$$n(\hat{c}_r q + k^o) = k,$$ (6.55c)

$$PQ - \hat{C}Q - RK^o = 0,$$ (6.55a')

$$\Theta P - \hat{C} = \hat{O},$$ (6.55b')

$$N(\hat{C}_R Q + K^o) = K,$$ (6.55c')

$$pm^{\theta-1} - P(q - M)^{\theta-1} = 0,$$ (6.55d)

$$PM^{\theta-1} - p(Q - m)^{\theta-1} = 0,$$ (6.55d')

$$npM - NPm = 0.$$ (6.55e)

Equations (6.55a) and (6.55a') are the zero-profit conditions, (6.55b) and (6.55b') represent monopolistic pricing, (6.55c) and (6.55c') denote the capital-market equilibria, and (6.55d) and (6.55d') reflect the demand conditions: the price ratio between domestic and imported goods equals the marginal rate of substitution. Algebraically this follows from equation (6.46). Finally, (6.55e) is the balance-of-payments equation. These nine equations contain ten unknowns, q, Q, p, P, n, N, r, R, m, and M. We take the price of the foreign good as a numéraire, $P = 1$; then p represents the home country's terms of trade. Moreover, in order to keep the model tractable, it is assumed that q is constant and does not depend on the number of varieties. A number of additional simplifications are possible. Equations (6.55a'–c') contain just three unknowns: the variables of the foreign country's supply side, Q, R, and N. They are independent of the domestic environmental policy. Of course, the domestic variables are also independent of foreign policies.[60] This can be seen if equations (6.55a, b) are divided by p. Since the cost functions are linear homogeneous in factor prices,[61] this implies:

$$q - \hat{c}(r/p, t^e/p)q - (r/p)k^o = 0,$$ (6.56a)

$$\theta - \hat{c}(r/p, t^e/p) = 0.$$ (6.56b)

Moreover, equation (6.55c) can be rewritten

$$n(\hat{c}_r(\hat{c}(r/p, t^e/p)q + k^o) = k.$$ (6.56c)

These three equations determine the variables of the domestic supply side, q, n, and r/p, as a function of the real emission tax rate, t^e/p. Imports, exports, and the terms of trade can be obtained by rearranging equations (6.55d, d', e):

$$q - Qp^{\frac{1}{\theta-1}} = 0.$$ (6.57a)

$$m = \frac{nq^\theta Q}{NQ^\theta + nq^\theta},$$ (6.57b)

$$M = \frac{NQ^\theta q}{NQ^\theta + nq^\theta}.$$ (6.57c)

---

[60] Similar results have been obtained by Gros (1987a, b) who considered the effects of trade policy in an intra-industry trade model of this type.   [61] See Varian (1992: 76).

The terms-of-trade equation, (6.57a), is straightforward. It also follows from the demand functions for different varieties of the good (see equation (6.45)). Equation (6.57a) allows the determination of the terms-of-trade effect of environmental policy once the impact on the output of a representative domestic firm has been obtained. The other two equations determine imports of a representative good as a function of the number of firms and the output per firm. The consumption levels can be obtained from equations (6.55a, b).

With these simplifications, the derivation of comparative-static results is rather simple. The impact of a change in domestic emission taxes is determined by total differentiation of equations (6.56a–c):

$$
\begin{pmatrix} 1-\theta-\hat{c}_r q - k^o & 0 & 0 \\ 0 & -\hat{c}r & 0 \\ n\hat{c}_r & n\hat{c}_{rr}q & \hat{c}_r q + k^o \end{pmatrix} \begin{pmatrix} dq \\ d(r/p) \\ dn \end{pmatrix} = \begin{pmatrix} \hat{c}_r q d(t^e/p) \\ \hat{c}_r d(t^e/p) \\ -n\hat{c}_{rt} q d(t^e/p) \end{pmatrix}
\tag{6.58}
$$

and it follows that

$$
\frac{dq}{d(t^e/p)} = \frac{k^o \hat{c}_t}{(1-\theta)\hat{c}_r} < 0
\tag{6.59a}
$$

$$
\frac{d(r/p)}{d(t^e/p)} = -\frac{\hat{c}_t}{\hat{c}_r} < 0,
\tag{6.59b}
$$

$$
\frac{dn}{d(t^e/p)} = -\frac{n\hat{c}_r \hat{c}_t k^o - (1-\theta)nq(\hat{c}_r \hat{c}_{rt} - \hat{c}_t \hat{c}_{rr})}{(1-\theta)\hat{c}_r (\hat{c}_r q + k^o)}.
\tag{6.59c}
$$

An increase in the emission tax rate reduces the output of the representative firm and it reduces the income of the other factor. These effects are straightforward. The effect on the number of firms is ambiguous. There are three subeffects. The increase in emission tax rate has a negative impact since it raises $\hat{c}_r$. The reduction in the interest rate has the same effect. Finally, the impact of the reduction in output per firm has the opposite effect: less firms demand less capital and, thus, there is a tendency towards an increase in the number of firms. Which one of these effects will dominate is unclear. None the less, the effect on total output is unambiguous:

$$
\frac{d(nq)}{d(t^e/p)} = -\frac{n\hat{c}_t(k^o)^2 + (1-\theta)nq^2(\hat{c}_r \hat{c}_{rt} - \hat{c}_t \hat{c}_{rr})}{(1-\theta)\hat{c}_r(\hat{c}_r q + k^o)}.
\tag{6.59d}
$$

Total output will be reduced. Since emissions per unit of output, $\tilde{c}_t$, are a declining function of the emission tax rate,[62] the total emissions from production will be reduced.

Some additional results can be derived by using (6.58a–d) in the equations that determine world market prices and trade.

[62] $\dfrac{d\hat{c}_t}{d(t^e/p)} = \hat{c}_{tt} - \dfrac{\hat{c}_t}{\hat{c}} \hat{c}_{rt} < 0$

- Terms of trade. The terms-of-trade effect follows from (6.56a). Since the output of domestic firms is reduced whereas the output of a representative foreign firm remains constant, the domestic terms of trade will be improved by a strict environmental policy.
- Consumption. The effects on domestic and foreign consumption are ambiguous. Their shares in global consumption are

$$\frac{nq^\theta}{nq^\theta + NQ^\theta} \quad \text{and} \quad \frac{NQ^\theta}{nq^\theta + NQ^\theta} .$$

The derivative of nq^q with respect to the real tax rate is likely to be negative but it may be positive if the change in the number of domestic firms is positive and θ is small. In the first case, the share of domestic consumption will be reduced. Since worldwide consumption is reduced, domestic consumption is reduced as well. This is good for the environment. However, other scenarios are also possible where domestic consumption is increased or where foreign consumption rises and causes transfrontier pollution. In a world where the pollution-impact parameters of both countries are the same, environmental disruption will always be reduced.
- The volume of trade. It is not clear whether trade will be increased or reduced by strict environmental standards.

Proposition 6.14. In an intra-industry trade framework, many of the effects of changes in environmental policy are ambiguous. Outputs will be reduced, but the number of varieties may rise. Foreign production remains unaffected as long as the substitutability of varieties does not depend on the number of varieties.

Results become even more ambiguous if θ is not constant. Not only will the foreign industry be affected by a change in domestic environmental policy; also the results on domestic output effects will become ambiguous.[63]

It would be desirable to move on from here and discuss optimal environmental policies. But this road will not be taken. Even the simple Dixit and Stiglitz (1977) model soon turns out to be very complex. Even in the closed-economy case, the derivation of optimal environmental policies can pose serious difficulties (see Katsoulacos and Xepapadeas (1994) and Xepapadeas and Katsoulacos (1994), for instance). One may expect that the terms-of-trade effect of environmental policy will lead to an upward bias in the environmental tax rates. Gros (1987a, b) has shown that there exists a positive optimal tariff even in the small-country case. Every country supplies goods that are not produced elsewhere and, therefore, enjoys some monopoly power in the world market. Applying this idea to environmental policy suggests the conclusion that even small countries should use tight environmental standards to improve their terms of trade. This would be the opposite of ecological dumping.

---

[63] To see this, insert θ' instead of 0 in the second-row third-column element of the matrix on the left-hand side of equation (6.58). However, this gives only an incomplete impression of the effects since foreign and domestic supply sides are now connected and a 6 x 6 matrix has to be considered.

Like the location model of Section 3, the intra-industry model shows that the effects of environmental policy on market structure (i.e. on the number of firms in the market) are important. Future research into this field is desirable since models with a limited number of firms and with entry and exit are much more realistic and relevant to the environmental regulation of the production sector than the alternative approaches involving either atomistic competition or a fixed number of firms in an oligopolistic market. Calibration may help to overcome the problems that originate from the complexity of models with endogenous market structure.

6.7 Summary of Results

1. Under normal demand and cost conditions, high environmental consumption taxes may be used to shift a foreign monopolist's profits to the domestic economy.
2. A domestic firm which is a monopolist in the foreign market should be charged the Pigouvian environmental tax rate.
3. An import-competing monopolist should be subsidized by low emission taxes since this raises output. If other policy instruments to regulate the monopolist are available, the emission tax rate should equal marginal environmental damage.
4. In the case of low environmental damage or substantial pollution spillovers, environmental tax competition for foreign direct investment may result in too low emission taxes. If the environmental damage the host country has to bear is large, the emission tax rate may be too high. If lump-sum subsidies to attract the foreign firm are availabe, there will not be a race to the bottom in emission taxes.
5. In an international Cournot duopoly, the strategic use of environmental policy requires an emission tax rate below the marginal domestic environmental damage. In an international Bertrand duopoly, the strategic use of environmental policy requires an emission tax rate above the marginal domestic environmental damage if the transfrontier pollution spillover is small.
6. Product standards can be used strategically to shift foreign profits to the home economy. Depending on the kind of competition and on the shape of demand and cost functions, the optimal product standard may either be a minimum quality standard, which forces producers to raise product quality, or a maximum quality standard, which constrains the firms in developing better products.
7. In an intra-industry trade framework with endogenous market structure, free trade may be harmful to the environment since it creates transport and since output is raised due to concentration processes and increasing returns

to scale. The concentration process may also be beneficial if firms that use environmentally intensive technologies leave the market.

8. Tighter emission taxes in the intra-industry trade model lead to terms-of-trade improvements. Even a small country may improve its terms of trade. Output will be reduced both on the firm level and economy-wide. The effects on consumption and trade are ambiguous.

Appendix

6.A1 Location of the Nash Equilibrium with Strategic Environmental Policy

Proposition 6.9 is proved by comparing the slopes of the domestic firm's iso-profit curve and the foreign firm's reaction curve in the Nash equilibrium with strategic choice of emission taxes. We assume that the marginal environmental damage is fixed, i.e. u' is constant. The profits of the domestic firm can be expressed as

$$\pi(t^{e,s}) = \pi(sau') + \tilde{c}(sau') - \tilde{c}(t^{e,s}),$$

where $t^{e,s}$ is the strategic tax rate, given by equation (6.24). The profits of a firm subject to this taxation equal the profits of a firm subject to the Pigouvian tax rate, sau', plus the subsidy which is the cost with Pigouvian taxation minus the cost with strategic taxation. The other arguments of the functions have been omitted for convenience. The profit maximum is determined by:

$$\pi_q(sau') + \tilde{c}_q(sau') - \tilde{c}_q(t^{e,s}) = 0. \tag{6.A1}$$

Using a Taylor series approximation, one obtains

$$\pi_q(sau') - (t^{e,s} - sau')\tilde{c}_{qt}(t^{e,s}) - \zeta = 0. \tag{6.A2}$$

ζ is a positive term for the correction of the error which is due to the approximation of the non-linear concave function by a linear one. For $t^{e,s} - sau'$, one can use equation (6.24) and after some rearranging of terms, one arrives at

$$-\frac{\pi_q}{\pi_Q} = \frac{1 - \dfrac{(1-S)A\tilde{C}_T u'Q_t}{\pi_Q}}{\dfrac{\tilde{c}_{tt}}{Q_t\tilde{c}_{qt}} + \dfrac{q_t}{Q_t}} - \frac{\zeta}{\pi_Q}. \tag{6.A3}$$

where the arguments of the functions have been omitted for convenience. It follows from equation (6.22) that the slope of the foreign firm's reaction curve can be represented by $\check{R}_q = Q_t/q_t < 0$. Moreover, π_q/π_Q is the slope of the iso-profit curve (for a firm subject to Pigouvian taxes). The numerator of the first term on the right-hand side equals one if there is no transfrontier pollution. In this case the isoprofit curve is flatter than the foreign firm's reaction curve. In the case of substantial transfrontier pollution the numerator is greater than one and the iso-profit curve may be steeper. This proves proposition 6.9. If the environmental-damage function is non-linear and the marginal damage is increasing, then the first effect is reinforced and a scenario where the strategic Nash equilibrium is located left of the Stackelberg point becomes more likely.

6.A2 Demand Functions in the Intra-Industry Trade Model

The demand functions of the Dixit and Stiglitz (1977) model are usually presented without an explicit derivation. Examples are Dixit and Stiglitz (1977) but also Helpman and Krugman (1985, 1989). The derivation of the demand functions is straightforward but a bit tedious. Therefore, I decided to present it here.

The Lagrangean of the optimization problem is

$$L = \sum_i c_i^\theta + \lambda\left(y - \sum_i p_i c_i\right).$$

The first-order condition for the consumption of commodity i is

$$\theta c_i^{\theta-1} = \lambda p_i \tag{6.A4}$$

and this can be rewritten such that

$$c_i = \left(\frac{\lambda p_i}{\theta}\right)^{\frac{1}{\theta-1}}. \tag{6.A5}$$

This can be multiplied by p_i. Summing up over i, one arrives at

$$y = \sum_i p_i c_i = \left(\frac{\lambda}{\theta}\right)^{\frac{1}{\theta-1}} \sum_i p_i^{\frac{\theta}{\theta-1}} \tag{6.A6}$$

If this is used in (6.A4), one obtains

$$c_i = \frac{y}{\sum_i p_i^{\frac{\theta}{\theta-1}}} p_i^{\frac{1}{\theta-1}}. \tag{6.A7}$$

This is equation (6.45) in the main text.

Matters are a bit more complicated if we want to use the representation of the demand function given by Dixit and Stiglitz (1977). λ and y have to be eliminated. Equation (6.A4) can be rewritten if we multiply by c_i and take the sum:

$$\lambda \sum_i p_i c_i = \lambda y = \theta \sum_i c_i^\theta. \tag{6.A8}$$

Using (6.A6) to eliminate y and rearranging terms, one obtains

$$\lambda = \left| \frac{\sum_i c_i^\theta}{\sum_i p_i^{\frac{\theta}{\theta-1}}} \right|^{\frac{\theta-1}{\theta}}. \tag{6.A9}$$

This can be inserted in equation (6.A1) and one arrives at the original Dixit and Stiglitz (1977) formula:

$$c_i = \left(\sum_i c_i \theta\right)^{\frac{1}{\theta}} \left(\frac{\left(\sum_i p_i^{\frac{\theta}{\theta-1}}\right)^{\frac{\theta-1}{\theta}}}{p_i} \right)^{\frac{1}{1-\theta}} \tag{6.A10}$$

6.A3 Demand Conditions and Balanced Trade

Equations (6.55h–j) can be rewritten

$$mp^{\frac{1}{\theta-1}} = q - M, \tag{6.A11a}$$

$$m = \frac{n}{N} pM, \tag{6.A11b}$$

$$M = (Q - m)p^{\frac{1}{\theta-1}} \tag{6.A11c}$$

Inserting for m from (6.11b) yields

$$M = \frac{q}{1 + \dfrac{n}{N} p^{\frac{\theta}{1-0}}}, \tag{6.A11a'}$$

$$M = \frac{Qp^{\frac{1}{1-\theta}}}{1 + \dfrac{n}{N} p^{\frac{\theta}{1-\theta}}}. \tag{6.A11c'}$$

Then, equation (6.54h') is straightforward.

7

The Political Process and Environmental Policy in Open Economies

7.1 The Problem

This chapter introduces the dimension of political economy into the analysis. The issue has been touched upon earlier, e.g. in Chapter 3, where the aspect of labour market objectives has been considered in the framework of the capital mobility model. In this chapter, a similar exercise will be performed in the framework of an international trade model. The difference between this chapter and the two preceding ones, that dealt with trade issues, is the set of questions addressed. In Chapters 5 and 6, we were concerned with the impacts of various policy instruments on factor allocation, trade, and welfare. The ultimate objective was to derive normative policy implications in terms of what should be done by a benevolent government. What are the emission tax rates or environmental standards that maximize social welfare? This chapter, in contrast, is an attempt to show why these measures are not taken. I will use a public-choice approach and have a closer look at the process of policy formation. The main objective is to show in which direction the outcome of the political process is likely to deviate from what is being regarded as optimal by welfare theorists. In particular, I wish to reconsider the question of ecological dumping. Given that benevolent governments have only limited incentives to engage in eco-dumping, can too lax environmental standards be explained by the particularities of the political process of environmental policy formation in open economies? Moreover, I wish to address the question whether there are incentives to abuse environmental regulation as an instrument of disguised protection and whether or not such measures will be taken.

The optimal policies derived in the previous chapters may serve as a benchmark of what can be achieved; this chapter is a (modest) attempt to explain what is. The economic approach to modelling this is public-choice theory, nowadays often called political economy. We will start the analysis with a summary of some basic insights gained by public-choice theorists. This summary serves the purposes of providing the theoretical background underlying the analysis and of motivating the particular modelling framework used in the remainder of the chapter. This framework will be a partial-equilibrium model, which neglects some of the interdependencies across markets that have been

218   Lobbies and Environmental Policy

considered in Chapter 5. As a first step, welfare-maximizing policies will be derived as a benchmark. Then we will look at the outcomes of political processes, firstly for the case of a small open economy and afterwards for the case of two large economies.

7.2 Representative Democracy and the Capture of Environmental Regulation in an Open Economy

Public-choice theory offers basically two explanations for non-welfare-maximizing public policies. The first one is the decisive role of the median voter in a direct democracy, the second one the capture of the policy-making process by idiosyncratic interest groups in a representative democracy.

The median-voter model abolishes the idea of the representative individual which has been an important tool of traditional welfare economics. Individuals are viewed as being different, in particular with respect to their initial endowments. And these endowments decide on their voting behaviour. In a direct democracy, policies are in the end determined by the preferences or perceptions of the median voter.[1] Since income and wealth distributions are usually skewed to the right, the majority of the voters (and the median voter as well) are relatively poor. Therefore, this theory would predict a tendency of redistribution from the rich to the poor. As long as the proposal is a lump-sum redistribution scheme, this does not cause inefficiencies. If, however, the policy instruments to be decided upon affect the allocation of resources in the economy (like tariffs and environmental taxes), the resulting policy tends to be distortive. For an application to the theory of tariff formation see Mayer (1984). He has shown that the median voter overrepresents the interests of the more equally distributed factor. This idea can be applied to the problem of environmental policy in an open economy. Since environmental quality is a public consumption good, the distribution of environmental harm across the population is rather equal. However, the distribution of ownership of sector-specific factors or capital in general is rather uneven and the median voter is to be expected to be endowed with less than the per-capita capital stock of the economy. Thus, she tends to be biased towards environmentalism and, it would be difficult to derive ecological dumping as a result in a median-voter model.

The median-voter model is useful in explaining economic and environmental policies in direct democracies like Switzerland, where voters themselves can decide on issues they consider to be relevant. However, I do not think that the median-voter model is a satisfactory representation of what is going on

[1] In order to get a majority, a proposal needs the support of at least 50 per cent of the electorate plus one vote. In an ideal world, the proposal is formulated in such a way that just this majority is attained. Thus, the median voter does not only decide the vote but also determines the shape of the proposal which is subjected to the referendum. See Mueller (1989, ch. 5) for a survey of the properties of median voter models and on the conditions under which they function.

politically in most countries. In representative democracies, the basic problem is that of regulatory capture: powerful subgroups of society gain influence on the political process and succeed in modifying to serve their idiosyncratic interests.[2] Often, this leads to discrimination against competitors and to the adoption of inefficient policies.

The precondition for regulations to be captured by idiosyncratic interests is that voters are not perfectly informed. If they were, any politician not acting on behalf of the voters would be punished by not being re-elected. Downs (1957, chs. 11–13) has argued that a rational voter will indeed be uninformed to some extent because the costs of being well informed are high. This rational ignorance results in an imperfect control of the policy-making process by the electorate and it gives the politician some discretion in her decisions. The discretion is utilized by particular interest groups who are then able to affect political decisions in a way the electorate would not tolerate if it were fully informed. The basic questions to be answered by a theory of regulatory capture are threefold:

1. Who is interested in influencing the political decision-making process?
2. Who is able to influence the political decision-making process?
3. How is the influence over the political decision-making process exerted?

The first question has a simple answer. Everyone should have an interest in influencing the political process in her favour. However, the willingness to spend resources on exerting this influence is unevenly distributed. In many cases, the group of beneficiaries of a policy intervention is rather small whereas the group of losers is large.[3] In a direct democracy with majority voting, such a policy would not be adopted. In a representative democracy this may be different. The willingness to spend resources on lobbying activities depends on a number of parameters that are unevenly distributed among different subgroups of society. The most important one is group size. If the gains from a policy intervention are highly concentrated, i.e. they are appropriated by a small group, then the gains accruing to an individual member of this group are large. If the welfare losses are widely dispersed, the share of the costs to be borne by an individual member of the losing group is small. Thus, an individual belonging to the first group has a large incentive to place effort and resources on activities directed towards an influence on politics whereas the incentive is small in the case of a member of group two. Typically, group one consists of the producers that are active in a particular industry; group two usually consists of consumers or tax payers. The consumers of environmental quality constitute a special case. About twenty years ago, they would have fallen into category two. However, this has changed with the rising influence of

---

[2] The term 'regulatory capture' is due to Stigler (1971) and his paper contains some good examples of the shapes that regulatory capture can take.

[3] An example is trade protection of an industry by tariffs or subsidies. The gains accrue to workers and capital owners in this particular industry whereas the costs have to be borne by the economy as a whole and by its trading partners.

non-governmental environmental organizations and green lobbying is becoming increasingly important.[4]

For the construction of a model in which interest groups matter, a decision has to be made whether to use a partial- or a general-equilibrium framework. In the partial- equilibrium framework, one neglects the possibility that the general-equilibrium repercussions of policy measures may offset their direct and straightforward effects.[5] This is not unrealistic since lobbyists are usually unaware of the general-equilibrium effects of their activities. Moreover and more importantly, the model framework is decisive for the identification of what constitutes an interest group. The Heckscher–Ohlin model argues that sectoral effects of policy changes are irrelevant because, in the long run, factors are perfectly mobile across sectors. They are completely indifferent where to be employed. As a conclusion, the Heckscher–Ohlin model predicts that factors of production should constitute economy-wide interest groups. Empirical evidence presented by Magee (1980) suggests, however, that industry-specific rather than factor-specific lobbying coalitions are formed when trade policy is at disposal.[6] This indicates that interest-group formation is based mainly on short-term objectives and that the potential to move to another sector if one's own industry is hit by a policy measure is not considered to be a realistic alternative. Therefore, we will choose a model framework where factors are tied to a particular sector of production.

If a group of persons is interested in achieving a policy change, this is a necessary but not a sufficient condition for the change actually taking place. Each interest group faces an internal free-rider problem. By fighting for her own interest, a group member also fights for the other group members. Thus, she provides a public good and like all public goods this public good will be underprovided: the marginal benefit to the individual is smaller than the marginal benefit to the group. Interest groups have to overcome this free-rider problem to be influential. The conditions for this are that the group be small, that the group be homogeneous and have a common interest (see Olson (1965)).[7] A

---

[4] It may be true that the power of green lobbies has been overemphasized in the past. Peirce (1991: 282), for instance, shows that out of more than 500 pressure groups that are formally represented at the European Communities only seven represent consumers' or environmentalists' interests.

[5] See Rauscher (1994a) for a model where interest groups lobbying for 'competitiveness' benefit from stringent environmental policies because the general-equilibrium effects of such a policy are positive and dominate the direct increase in production costs. The general-equilibrium framework has been used by Young and Magee (1986) and Magee et al. (1989) for the investigation of trade barriers.

[6] Magee (1980) uses the Summary of Testimony for the Hearings before the Committee on Ways and Means in the US House of Representatives on the Trade Reform Act of 1973 as a database. This summary contains the views of twenty-nine trade associations and twenty-three unions on trade liberalization vs. protection. The different positions of owners of different factors predicted by the Heckscher–Ohlin model can be observed in only two industries whereas capital and labour take the same position in twenty-one industries.

[7] In some cases, large groups have invented institutions that limit free-riding behaviour. Olson (1965: 66–97) illustrates this by examples of labour unions in different countries.

relatively small and homogeneous group like a dozen steel producers in a single country may be more effective in overcoming their free-rider problem than the large and heterogeneous group of downstream producers, consumers, and taxpayers that may be negatively affected if the government decides to support the steel industry by means of tariffs, subsidies, or administered prices.

The relationship between the policy-maker and a lobbyist may be thought of as one of mutual exchange of gifts or of supply and demand.[8] The lobbyist demands economic support from the policy-maker and can help the policy-maker to increase her political support. The policy-maker is desirous of political support and can supply economic support to the lobbyist. There is a potential for gains from trade. The exchange of gifts may take the following shape. In a situation where voters are imperfectly informed about what is going on in politics, the politician can increase her political support, e.g. the probability of being re-elected, by spending money on advertising. This money is offered by specific interest groups that are ready to contribute to the politician's election campaign if the politician recognizes the needs and aims of these interest groups in a sufficient manner.

The exchange of gifts can be modelled in various ways (see Ursprung (1991)). The most realistic framework is the multi-lobby multi-party model. In this model, also referred to as the interest-group-cum-electoral-competition model, two games take place at the same time. Interest groups play against each other by giving campaign contributions to different candidates. The candidates themselves play against each other by choosing their policies such that their probabilities of being elected are maximized. These two games are linked because the probabilities of being elected depend on the campaign contributions the lobbies are willing to make. For applications of this model framework to trade policy see Young and Magee (1986) and Hillman and Ursprung (1988, 1992, 1994).[9] A simpler way of modelling interest-group influence on public policies is to assume that political platforms are given. In this case, the whole problem reduces to a probabilistic voting model which can be thought of as a special case of a rent-seeking game. See Tullock (1980) for the original contribution and Brooks and Heijdra (1989), Mitchell and Munger (1991), and Nitzan (1994) for surveys. This modelling framework has been applied to environmental policy by Bartsch et al. (1993). An even simpler category of models emerges if the so-called political-support function approach is considered. It is assumed that the policy-maker is influenced by various interest groups and the policy maker's objective function is a weighted average of the welfare functions of the individual lobbies. This approach is due to Peltzman (1976) who used it to model regulatory capture. The political-support function

---

[8] The title of a recent article by Grossman and Helpman (1994), 'Protection for Sale' illustrates this relationship.

[9] A special variation of this type of models has been considered by Laffont and Tirole (1991) who distinguish the government as a legislator and the public administration as the government's agent. Both may be subject to lobbying activities by interest groups and *Laffont/Tirole* derive policy equilibria with regulatory capture.

model may be thought of as a reduced form of a more complicated model involving games between interest groups and policy-makers who wish to maximize the probability of being elected.[10]

Finally, the government and the members of state bureaucracy have some independent goals and may be able to follow them due to the lack of control by the voter. These goals include maximization of the tax revenue, shirking, and unproductive status-signalling activities[11] (see Niskanen (1973), for instance). Of course, these objectives are not limited to the public sector and its employees. Employees of private firms have similar interests but they are often better controlled and the incentives to perform well are usually stronger. Although the leviathan state is an interesting subject of economic analysis, it will not be addressed here. The activities of a leviathan government in a trading economy are not much different from those in a closed economy[12] and, therefore, their consideration would not contribute much to the analysis of regulatory capture of environmental policies in a trading economy.[13]

For the following analysis, I have chosen a partial-equilibrium framework. A single import-competing industry is considered. The foreign industry produces a similar good which the home country imports. These goods are close substitutes and, therefore, the possibilities to pass increases in the production costs through to the consumers are limited. In order to keep the model tractable, I assume that the firms act as price-takers. If there were non-price-taking behaviour, the optimal emission tax rate should contain components that correct for the market imperfection. In order to avoid this, we will start from a competitive

---

[10] For a model showing that a political contest leads political parties to maximize a political-support function see Coughlin *et al.* (1990). However, their model does not consider lobbying activities but voting behaviour of interest-group members. Moreover, their result that the political programmes of different parties converge and, therefore, can be represented by a political-support function is not a general property of political-contest models. See Ursprung (1991) who gives conditions for the convergence of political programmes. Another approach to provide a behavioural foundation of a political-support function has been chosen by Grossman and Helpman (1994). They do not model a political contest but look at an incumbent government maximizing its political support. Instead of using the standard political-support-function approach, they assume that interest groups determine contribution schedules to give the government the incentive to act on their behalf. Employing game-theoretic arguments, Grossman and Helpman (1994) manage to show that in the equilibrium the government acts as if it maximizes a simple political-support function.

[11] Status may be signalled for instance by a large number of subordinates and this contributes to Parkinson's law.

[12] There are, however, some good arguments in favour of the hypothesis that the leviathan is tamed to some extent in an open economy because with increased openness, tax bases tend to become more mobile and the threat of increased tax evasion forces the policy-maker to use more-efficient policy instruments (see Brennan and Buchanan (1980, ch. 9.2), Sinn (1992), and Edwards and Keen (1994)).

[13] Moreover, many of the results would be ambiguous anyway. If, for instance, one includes the target of administering a large budget in the policy-maker's objective function, the effect on the optimal tax rate may be positive or negative, depending on whether tax revenue is an increasing or declining function of the tax rate. In the case of a hill-shaped Laffer curve, the effect on the optimal tax rate depends on whether the tax rate which generates the maximum tax revenue is located to the left or to the right of the welfare-maximizing tax rate.

setting.[14] The lobbies represent an industry-specific factor of production and an environmentalist interest group. The environmental-policy instruments that are subject to regulatory capture in this model are taxes on emissions from production and consumption and a minimum environmental product quality standard.[15]

7.3 A Partial-Equilibrium Model Regulatory Capture

Consider a domestic market where two goods are traded. One good is produced in the home country, but not exported, and the other one is imported from abroad.[16] These goods are substitutes. Firms maximize their profits and take prices as given. The government can use its environmental policy to give protection to domestic industries that compete in international markets. It can do this in three ways. First, taxes that internalize consumption externalities can be modified such that they discriminate against foreign products. This is nothing else but a tariff policy. Secondly, the government may relax emission taxes or environmental standards and pollution-abatement requirements for particular production processes or industries. This reduces production costs and, therefore, has the character of a hidden subsidy. Thirdly, environmental product standards may be used to discriminate against foreign suppliers of goods. It is assumed here (as in Section 4 of Chapter 6) that the pollution intensity of consumption is not exogenous but is determined by the producer who decides on the design of the final product. Since environmentally friendly goods are more expensive in their production than less environmentally friendly goods, the government has to restrict the choices of the producer by imposing an environmental product standard.[17] Product standards are subtler means of protection than tariffs and they have been a continuous source of international trade disputes. Often it is only a matter of interpretation whether

[14] Hillman and Ursprung (1992, 1994) have looked at models with non-competitive producers. They lobby for increases in profits and the paper shows that the lobbying equilibria depend, *inter alia*, on the market structure, i.e. on the number of firms.

[15] The issue of choice of instruments will be neglected e.g. there are good reasons as to why industries as well as environmentalists may prefer quantitative instruments of environmental policy to taxes or tradable-permits schemes, in particular under non-competitive market conditions (see Hoekman and Leidy (1992) and Leidy and Hoekman (1994)). However, these arguments are not altered by the existence of trade and the desire for protection from foreign competition and, therefore, this issue will not be taken up here.

[16] This set-up of the model is simplistic and it does not allow the analysis of export promotion. However, as will be seen below, even the analysis of the protection of the import-competing industry is a difficult task.

[17] Alternatively, the government could use a variable scheme for the taxation of consumption goods, where the tax rate depends on environmental friendliness. Although environmental quality standards are non-price instruments, they are equivalent to such a tax scheme. If there were uncertainty or problems of rationing in the model or if we considered the possibility of environmental innovation, pecuniary instruments would do better that the command-and-control approach (see Pearce and Turner (1990, ch. 7) or Siebert (1995, ch. 8)).

a specific product standard is primarily a measure of environmental protection or consumer safety or a means of discrimination against imports.[18] From the view point of the policy-maker, these standards have the great advantage of providing protection in a rather discreet way.[19] Environmental protection and environmental protectionism are difficult to disentangle.

Let us assume that there are constant returns to scale. The unit-cost function $\hat{c}(.,.,.)$ has as its arguments the environmental tax rate, t^e, the remuneration of the specific factor of production, r, and the environmental product standard, ω, which is measured by the negative pollution intensity of consumption, b, as in the previous chapter: $\omega = -b$. Thus the smaller b, the larger ω and the stricter the environmental regulation. The properties of the unit-cost function are

$$\hat{c}_t > 0, \hat{c}_r > 0, \hat{c}_{tt} < 0, \hat{c}_{rr} < 0, \hat{c}_{rt} > 0, \hat{c}_{rr}\hat{c}_{tt} - \hat{c}_{rt}^2 \geq 0,$$

$$\hat{c}_\omega > 0, \hat{c}_{\omega\omega} > 0, \hat{c}_{r\omega} > 0, \hat{c}_{t\omega} > 0.$$

The foreign industry's unit-cost function, $\hat{C}(R,T^e,\Omega)$ has the same properties and $\Omega = -B$ is the domestic quality standard for foreign products.

The demand side is characterized by (domestic) demand functions for domestic and foreign products, $d(p,P)$ and $D(p,P)$, respectively, where p and P are the prices of domestic and foreign goods. The demand functions satisfy

$$d_p < 0, d_P > 0, D_p > 0, D_P < 0, d_pD_P - d_PD_p > 0,$$

i.e. none of the goods is a Giffen good, the goods are substitutes, and the final inequality is a stability condition which is satisfied if the own-price effects dominate the cross-price effects.

The equilibrium in this market is determined by six equations. Free entry and exit together with profit maximization imply that the producer prices equal the marginal costs of production, which here equal the unit costs. The final goods prices are determined by adding the consumption tax rates, t^c and T^c. The factor market equilibrium requires that the industry-specific factor is fully employed. Factor demand follows from Shephard's lemma and factor supply (k in the home country and K abroad) is exogenously given and fixed. Finally, there are the goods-markets equilibria: supply equals demand, i.e. $q = d(p,P)$ and $Q = D(p,P)$. Two of these equations can be eliminated by combining the conditions for the goods-market equilibrium and the factor market equilibrium. Thus, we have

$$p = \hat{c}(r,t^e,\omega) + t^c, \tag{7.1}$$

$$P = \hat{C}(R,T^e,\Omega) + T^c, \tag{7.1'}$$

---

[18] See Hoekman and Leidy (1992), for instance. European examples are the Danish-bottle case and the purity laws for German beer and Italian pasta that have all been subject to the jurisdiction of the European Court of Justice.

[19] See Magee *et al.* (1989, ch. 18) for the importance of voter obfuscation as a goal of economic policy.

$$d(p,P)\hat{c}_r(r,t^e,\omega) = k, \qquad\qquad (7.2)$$

$$D(p,P)\hat{C}_R(R,T^e,\Omega) = K. \qquad\qquad (7.2')$$

Most of the following analysis will be restricted to the small-country case, i.e. it is assumed that the foreign country's resource constraint, equation (7.2′), is not binding. This implies that the price of the foreign good depends on the foreign environmental policy and on the domestic quality requirement for foreign goods in a very simple fashion:

$$\frac{dP}{dT^c} = 1 \qquad\qquad (7.3a)$$

$$\frac{dP}{dT^e} = \hat{C}_T, \qquad\qquad (7.3b)$$

$$\frac{dP}{d\Omega} = \hat{C}_\Omega \qquad\qquad (7.3c)$$

Total differentiation of equations (7.1) and (7.2) gives

$$\begin{pmatrix} 1 & -\hat{c}_r \\ d_p\hat{c}_r & -\hat{c}_{rr} \end{pmatrix}\begin{pmatrix} dp \\ dr \end{pmatrix} = \begin{pmatrix} 1 & \hat{c}_t & \hat{c}_\omega & 0 \\ 0 & -q\hat{c}_{rt} & -q\hat{c}_{r\omega} & -dp\hat{c}_r \end{pmatrix}\begin{vmatrix} dt^c \\ dt^e \\ d\omega \\ dP \end{vmatrix} \qquad (7.4)$$

The comparative statics follow from Cramer's rule and the detailed results are reported in the appendix.

Finally, pollution is considered. In order to concentrate on the effects of interest-group influence in the following analysis, we assume that transfrontier pollution is negligible and that trade, i.e. international transport, does not cause additional environmental harm:

$$s = S = 1, \quad \gamma = 0,$$

for the remainder of this chapter. Thus environmental pollution in the home and foreign countries is

$$z = ae + bq + BQ,[20] \qquad\qquad (7.5)$$

$$Z = AE. \qquad\qquad (7.6)$$

The comparative-static effects on prices, quantities, emissions, and pollution are summarized in Table 7.1 and in proposition 7.1.

Proposition 7.1. Tight environmental taxes or standards in the home country raise the price of domestic goods, reduce the output of the domestic industry, and raise imports. Tight-quality standards on imported goods raise the prices, reduce the demand for imported goods, and raise the demand for domestic goods. The effect on the income of the domestic industry's specific factor is ambiguous. Foreign

---

[20] Note that unlike in the previous chapters BQ here denotes the impact of domestic consumption of the foreign good on the domestic environment.

TABLE 7.1 Comparative Statics of the Partial-Equilibrium Model

on	Effects of a change in					
	t^c	T^c	t^e	T^e	ω	Ω
p	+	+	+	+	+	+
P	0	+	0	+	0	+
q	−	+	−	+	−	+
Q	+	−	+	−	+	−
r	−	+	?	+	?	+
e	−	+	−	+	?	+
z	?	?	?	?	?	?
E, Z	+	−	+	−	+	?

emissions from production are raised. Domestic emissions from production are reduced in the case of an emission tax. The effect of a product standard on domestic emissions is ambiguous.

These results can be explained as follows:

- Prices. Tight environmental standards and emission taxes raise the costs of the firms who are subject to these standards and taxes. Part of this is passed through to the consumers in the shape of higher prices. This results in an increased demand for the other good, which is a substitute, and therefore its price rises as well. Environmental consumption taxes raise the price of the affected good and of its substitute. Some of the domestic-policy variables do not have an impact on the price of the foreign good due to the small-country assumption.

- Output. Tight environmental standards and taxes lead to output reductions in the industry affected by these standards and taxes. The producers of the substitute commodity will raise their output since their price has risen.

- Rate of return to capital. High taxes and quality standards raise the remuneration of the specific factor of the industry producing the substitute commodity. The increase in the price of the output of this industry induces output expansion and an increase in the demand for the specific factor. Since the supply of this factor is inelastic, its price goes up. The effect on the income of the specific factor of the industry affected directly by the tighter policies is ambiguous in some cases. High consumption taxes unambiguously reduce the remuneration of the specific factor. However, the effects of policy instruments that affect the production costs, i.e. emission taxes and quality standards, are indeterminate. There are two effects, a substitution effect and a demand effect. On the one hand, an increase in emission taxes induces a substitution process: capital for environmental resources. With increased demand for capital and fixed supply, this factor tends to become dearer. On the other hand, the increase in production costs is passed through to the consumer and the consumer reacts by reducing demand. If demand is elastic, the decline in output makes the specific factor more abundant. Its price tends to decline. If equations (7.A1c) and (7.A1e) in the appendix to this chapter are rewritten, it can be seen that the signs of the changes in r are determined by

$$\frac{\hat{c}_{rt}t^e}{\hat{c}_r} + \frac{\hat{c}_t t^e}{p}\frac{d_p p}{p}$$

and

$$\frac{\hat{c}_{r\omega}\omega}{\hat{c}_r} + \frac{\hat{c}_\omega \omega}{p}\frac{d_p p}{p}$$

respectively. The first term is the elasticity of the demand for capital with respect to the emission tax rate (product quality standard). The second term is negative and equals the share of emission taxation (product quality) in the final good price times the price elasticity of demand for the final good. Thus, if demand is elastic, then the specific factor is harmed by tighter environmental regulation. Otherwise, the substitution effect dominates and the specific factor gains. To make this effect more plausible, imagine capital in this model consisting of two components, production capital and abatement capital. The owners of production capital lose if emission taxes are increased, the owners of abatement capital gain.

- Emissions. Higher emission taxes induce emission reductions in the industry directly affected. This is plausible. The emissions of the industry in the other country are increased. This is due to the increase in output and to the increase in the price of the specific factor. The latter effect induces a substitution of environmental resources for the specific factor. The same argument can be used to explain the effect of a tighter product standard on the emissions of the industry producing the substitute. However, the effect of a tighter product standard on the emissions from the directly affected industry is ambiguous. The output is reduced but the emission intensity of production may be increased.
- Pollution. The effects on foreign pollution are the same as on foreign emissions because they are the only cause of pollution in that country. The effects on domestic pollution are ambiguous since the consumption of domestic and foreign goods are affected in opposite directions. However, if the direct impacts of the instruments dominate, then we have negative effects of all policy instruments except foreign emission taxes.

Many of these results are plausible. It is, however, remarkable that even in this simple partial-equilibrium framework some counter-intuitive results are possible. Environmentalists may find ambient quality being negatively affected by tight productstandards.[21] Moreover, industry lobbies may be surprised to gain from tight environmental standards even if there are foreign competitors that are not subject to these standards. In this context, it is interesting to note among the domestic policy instruments that address the supply side of the economy (emission taxes and product standards) the only instrument which has an unambiguous effect on the remuneration of the specific factor of the domestic industry is the quality standard of foreign goods. The stricter this standard, the higher the income of the specific factor.

7.4 Optimal Environmental Policies

In a first step, we will look at a scenario where lobbies do not influence the political decision making process. The difference between this model and the model discussed in Chapter 5 is (i) that we now look at a partial equilibrium, (ii) that domestic and foreign goods are not perfect but only imperfect substitutes, and (iii) that product standards are considered as means of environmental policy.

The utility derived from environmental quality is $u(-z)$ and the utility function has the usual properties. The benevolent government maximizes the sum of consumer surplus, profits, the income of the specific factor, the tax revenue, and the utility derived from environmental quality.

$$w = -\varepsilon(p, P; \upsilon) + (p - t^c)q - \hat{c}(r, t^e, -b)q + rk + t^c q + T^c Q + t^e e$$
$$+ u(-ae - bq - BQ),[22] \tag{7.6}$$

The policy instruments of the home government are t^c, T^c, t^e, b, and B. The foreign government decides on the foreign emission tax rate, T^e, but this will not be discussed here. Differentiation of w and the use of Shephard's lemma and the first-order conditions of profit maximization to eliminate some of the terms yields the following necessary conditions for an optimal environmental policy.

$$(t^e - au')\frac{de}{dt^c} + (t^c - bu')\frac{dq}{dt^c} + (T^c - Bu')\frac{dQ}{dt^c} = 0, \tag{7.7a}$$

---

[21] This is not an artefact of the model but this phenomenon is relevant for real-world problems. Improvements of environmental quality in one dimension may cause environmental disruption in another one, and it is not clear that the net effect is always positive. It has been argued, for instance, that policies which encourage the recycling of used materials can be counterproductive from an environmental point of view. It is not a priori clear that recycling processes are less environmentally disruptive than the storage or combustion of waste plus the production of final goods involving new raw materials rather than recycled ones. See Klepper and Michaelis (1995) for a case-study which deals with recycling schemes for metal scrap containing cadmium.

[22] Here we do not use the conventional notion of consumer surplus but the negative value of the expenditure necessary to attain a certain level of consumer satisfaction, υ. The vector product of the derivative of this function with respect to the prices and the changes in the prices gives the equivalent variation, which is an exact measure of the change in consumer well-being (see Varian (1992: 162)).

$$(t^e - au')\frac{de}{dT^c} + (t^c - bu')\frac{dq}{dT^c} + (T^c - Bu')\frac{dQ}{dT^c} = 0, \tag{7.7b}$$

$$(t^e - au')\frac{de}{dt^e} + (t^c - bu')\frac{dq}{dt^e} + (T^c - Bu')\frac{dQ}{dt^e} = 0, \tag{7.7c}$$

$$(t^e - au')\frac{de}{db} + (t^c - bu')\frac{dq}{db} + (T^c - Bu')\frac{dQ}{db} + \hat{c}_\omega q - u'q = 0, \tag{7.7d}$$

$$(t^e - au')\frac{de}{dB} + (t^c - bu')\frac{dq}{dB} + (T^c - Bu')\frac{dQ}{dB} + \hat{C}_\Omega Q - u'Q = 0. \tag{7.7e}$$

It is assumed that the second-order conditions are satisfied. Equations (7.7a) to (7.7e) can be rewritten in matrix notation:

$$\begin{vmatrix} \dfrac{dq}{dt^c} & \dfrac{dQ}{dt^c} & \dfrac{de}{dt^c} & 0 & 0 \\ \dfrac{dq}{dT^c} & \dfrac{dQ}{dT^c} & \dfrac{de}{dT^c} & 0 & 0 \\ \dfrac{dp}{dt^e} & \dfrac{dQ}{dt^e} & \dfrac{de}{dt^e} & 0 & 0 \\ \dfrac{dp}{db} & \dfrac{dQ}{db} & \dfrac{de}{db} & q & 0 \\ \dfrac{dp}{dB} & \dfrac{dQ}{dB} & \dfrac{de}{dB} & 0 & Q \end{vmatrix} \begin{pmatrix} t^c - bu' \\ T^c - Bu' \\ t^e - au' \\ \hat{c}_\omega - u' \\ \hat{C}_\Omega - u' \end{pmatrix} = \begin{pmatrix} 0 \\ 0 \\ 0 \\ 0 \\ 0 \end{pmatrix}$$

Since the matrix on the left-hand side has full rank[23], the optimal policies turn out to be

$$t^e = au', \tag{7.8a}$$
$$t^c = bu', \tag{7.8b}$$
$$T^c = Bu', \tag{7.8c}$$
$$\hat{c}_\omega = u', \tag{7.8d}$$
$$\hat{C}_\Omega = u'. \tag{7.8e}$$

In the home country, the optimal tax rates equal the marginal environmental damage and the optimal product standard is chosen such that the marginal cost of increasing product quality equals the marginal improvement in environmental quality. It should be noted that even commodities that are very similar from the viewpoint of the consumer can be subject to significantly different quality standards. These differences can be justified from the cost side. Goods whose quality improvement is cheap should be subject to stricter standards than products whose improvement is costly. If the second category of goods were subject to the same regulation as the first one, the loss of consumer surplus due to the high price would exceed the gain in environmental quality.

---

[23] This follows from the fact that, according to equations (7.A2a, b, c, d, g, h) and (7.A3a, b, d)

$$\frac{dq}{dt^c} \left| \frac{dq}{dt^c} = \frac{dQ}{dt^c} \right| \frac{dQ}{dt^e} \neq \frac{de}{dt^c} \left| \frac{de}{dt^e} \right. \quad \text{and} \quad \frac{dq}{dt^c} \left| \frac{dq}{dP} = \frac{de}{dt^c} \right| \frac{de}{dP} \neq \frac{dQ}{dt^c} \left| \frac{dQ}{dP} \right. .$$

7.5 Lobbies that Influence Single-Policy Instruments

Within the framework of the political-support function approach, one can assume that powerful interest groups can capture either environmental policy as a whole or only certain aspects and instruments of environmental policy, e.g. merely the regulation of production or of final-goods design. We start the analysis of regulatory capture by looking at the second case. The more general and more complicated scenario will be discussed later on. Moreover, we will restrict most of the analysis to the case of a single country, the home country. The interactions of lobbying activities in different countries will also be discussed later.

It is assumed that all environmental policy instruments except the one captured by the interest group remain at their optimal levels and that their optimal levels are not affected by the change in the captured variable. This is only possible if the utility of environmental quality is a linear function of pollution, $u'' = 0$. It is assumed that this is the case for the remainder of this section.[24]

There are two lobbies here, the industry-specific factor and the environmentalists. The specific factor is interested in increasing its income, rk. The environmentalists are concerned about environmental quality. In the same way as Hillman and Ursprung (1992, 1994), I distinguish 'greens' and 'supergreens'. The normal green lobby cares about the domestic environmental quality only; supergreens in contrast take a more global view and are concerned about the environment in the foreign country as well. Thus, the political-support function turns out to be

$$\tilde{w} = w + \lambda^k rk + \lambda^g(-z) + \lambda^s(-Z), \tag{7.9}$$

where w is the social-welfare function defined in equation (7.6), λ^k and λ^g are the weights of the interest-group stakes in the policy-maker's objective function. λ^s/λ^g is the importance the green lobby places on foreign environmental quality compared to domestic environmental quality. It is reasonable to assume that $0 \leq \lambda^s \leq \lambda^g$. The extreme cases represent the interests of the simple greens and the supergreens, respectively. According to Grossman and Helpman (1994), the parameters also reflect the technology the policy-maker uses to transform lobbyist contributions into votes or political support:[25]

- λ^k is the relative increase in the political support in case a sum of money previously used in the private sector is given to the policy-maker in the shape of a campaign contribution. For example if $\lambda^k = 0.5$, then an increase in campaign contributions by one dollar raises political support by 1.5 times as much as a one-dollar increase in the disposable income of the private sector.

[24] Note that this assumption implies that the technology and the preferences over the consumption goods are convex enough to assure that the second-order conditions of optimization hold.

[25] Grossman and Helpman (1994) use a slightly different notation. The following propositions follow from their equations (5) and (11) and from footnote 5 if the notation is adapted properly.

- λ^q/λ^k is the marginal and average utility the environmentalists derive from domestic environmental quality.
- λ^s/λ^k is the marginal and average utility the environmentalists derive from foreign environmental quality.

Under the assumption that only one policy instrument is captured by the lobbies, the support maximizing policies can be derived easily:

$$t^e = au' + \left(-\lambda^k k \frac{dr}{dt^e} + \lambda^g \left(a \frac{de}{dt^e} + b \frac{dq}{dt^e} + B \frac{dQ}{dt^e}\right) + \lambda^s A \frac{dE}{dt^e}\right) \bigg/ \frac{de}{dt^e}, \qquad (7.10a)$$

$$t^c = bu' + \left(-\lambda^k k \frac{dr}{dt^c} + \lambda^g \left(a \frac{de}{dt^c} + b \frac{dq}{dt^c} + B \frac{dQ}{dt^c}\right) + \lambda^s A \frac{dE}{dt^c}\right) \bigg/ \frac{dq}{dt^c}, \qquad (7.10b)$$

$$T^c = Bu' + \left(-\lambda^k k \frac{dr}{dT^c} + \lambda^g \left(a \frac{de}{dT^c} + b \frac{dq}{dT^c} + B \frac{dQ}{dT^c}\right) + \lambda^s A \frac{dE}{dT^c}\right) \bigg/ \frac{dQ}{dT^c}, \qquad (7.10c)$$

$$\tilde{c}_\omega = qu' + \lambda^k k \frac{dr}{d\omega} - \lambda^g \left(a \frac{de}{d\omega} + b \frac{dq}{d\omega} + B \frac{dQ}{d\omega} + q\right) - \lambda^s A \frac{dE}{d\omega}, \qquad (7.10d)$$

$$\hat{c}_\Omega = Qu' + \lambda^k k \frac{dr}{d\Omega} - \lambda^g \left(a \frac{de}{d\Omega} + b \frac{dq}{d\Omega} + B \frac{dQ}{d\Omega} + Q\right) - \lambda^s A \frac{dE}{d\Omega}. \qquad (7.10e)$$

Notice that equations $(7.10a)$ to $(7.10e)$ represent five different scenarios in which only one policy instrument is captured by the interest groups. For each of these scenarios, there exist four additional optimality conditions like equations $(7.8a)$ to $(7.8e)$ which determine the policy variables that are not captured by the interest groups.

The results summarized in Table 7.1 can be used to determine the biases in environmental policies that caused by regulatory capture:[26]

Emission taxes. The view of the specific factor is ambiguous. On the one hand, emission taxes are bad because they raise costs and prices and reduce the demand for the domestic good. On the other hand, substitution processes are induced and there may be an increased demand for factors that are substitutes for environmental resources. It seems as if in the present discussion of environmental policy much more emphasis is placed on the first argument. If this is true, the specific factor is anti-green. The view of the greens is ambiguous as well. Of course, domestic emissions will be reduced and the demand for domestic goods will decline. This is good for the environment. But here will be substitution processes on the demand side. The demand for foreign goods will be increased and since consumption is environmentally harmful, the environmentalists may have an interest in avoiding too high tax rates.[27] If the greens

---

[26] The formal procedure to determine the impacts of the λ parameters is to differentiate the optimality conditions with respect to them. It is clear that these comparative statics contain third derivatives and are, therefore, in general ambiguous. They are unambiguous if the intial λ values are close to zero. The following results are subject to this caveat.

[27] Equations $(7.A2c)$ and $(7.A2d)$ reveal that besides the pollution-intensity parameters b and B, the values of the own-price elasticity of demand for the domestic good and the cross-price elasticity of the foreign good decide on the sign of the net effect of the changes in consumption on environmental quality.

care about foreign environmental quality as well, the emission tax rate is reduced even further.

Taxes on the consumption of the domestic good. The specific factor opposes these taxes since they reduce its income. The view of the environmentalists is ambiguous again. Domestic emissions and consumption of the home good are reduced but production of and consumption of the foreign good are increased.

Taxes on the consumption of the foreign good. The specific factor gains from these taxes. The green position is ambiguous. Foreign emissions and consumption are reduced by a large tax rate, but domestic emissions and consumption are raised.

Quality standards for domestic goods. The position of the specific factor is ambiguous for the same reason as in the case of emission taxes. The position of the greens is indeterminate as well. High environmental quality standards reduce the pollution per unit of the goods consumed as well as the number of the units of good itself, but the demand for foreign goods is raised and foreign emissions in the production process are increased. The effect of emissions from domestic production is ambiguous. It is possible, though unlikely, that they are increased by tight-quality standards.

Quality standards for foreign goods. The specific factor will always benefit from this non-tariff barrier to trade. The green position depends on the model parameters again. Tight product standards reduce the pollution impact parameters and reduce demand for the regulated good. However, the domestic substitute will be produced and consumed in greater quantities and this causes additional environmental disruption. The effect on foreign emissions is ambiguous, but in normal circumstances, they tend to decline.

The positions of the two interest groups towards the various policy instruments are less obvious than one would guess after a first thought. In particular, the green position always depends on the parameters of the model since policies that reduce domestic emissions and consumption of the domestic good tend to raise foreign emissions and the consumption of the foreign good. If, however, the own-price elasticities of the goods are substantially larger than the cross-price elasticities, then the indirect effects of a policy, which affect the production and consumption of the substitute good, are dominated by the direct effects and the green position is unambiguous.

Proposition 7.2. If the power of the specific factor in the lobbying process is large, then the quality requirements foreign goods have to meet are too high, the tax on consumption of foreign goods is too high and the tax on consumption of domestic goods is too low. If the direct effects of environmental regulation dominate its indirect effects, strong green lobbies tend to bias the environmental policy towards high emission taxes, high consumption taxes, and high environmental product standards.

As a corollary, we obtain

Proposition 7.3. If the direct effects of environmental regulation dominate its indirect effects, then industrial and green lobbies have a common interest in strict standards for the quality of foreign goods and high taxes on the consumption of foreign goods. They are opposed to each other in the case of taxation of consumption of domestic goods. They may be opposed to each other in the cases of emission taxation and domestic product quality standards but it is also possible that both of them lobby for high domestic emission taxes and strict quality standards for domestic goods.

This result has the following implications:

- High taxes on foreign consumption goods may be in the interest of domestic producers and environmentalists, but tax differences (which are nothing else but tariffs) are very obvious instruments of protection and, therefore, resistance by foreign producers and the foreign government has to be expected.
- High environmental quality standards for foreign goods serve the interests of domestic industry lobbies and tend to be supported by environmentalists. Moreover, and this is important for real-world issues, they are often not easy to be detected as protectionist devices.
- The last part of the proposition is a bit surprising. Industry-specific factors profit from tight regulation if the price elasticity of demand is small. Then the substitution effect dominates the demand effect and strict environmental policies raise the factor income. This result is a consequence of the introduction of aggregate capital as a homogeneous factor of production. The share of this capital which is used for pollution abatement will profit from tight environmental standards but it is questionable whether in reality this effect is strong enough to offset the negative impact of tight taxes and standards on the remuneration of normal production capital.[28]

Thus, the implication of this model for practical purposes is that of the instruments discussed here the discriminative use of environmental product standards is the only one which (i) is likely to be supported by a coalition of lobbies in the home country and (ii) whose protectionist content can be obfuscated rather easily. Thus, such standards seem to be first choice if environmental and trade protection are to be combined.

7.6 Regulatory Capture of More than One Policy Instrument

Let us now turn to the more general case where the lobbies influence environmental policy as a whole. Again the policy-maker's objective is to maximize her political support, defined by the political-support function, equation (7.9). In matrix notation, the first-order conditions are

[28] It should be noted that this is not a phenomenon specific to open economies; it is also relevant for industries that are not affected by international trade.

$$
\begin{vmatrix}
\dfrac{dp}{dt^c} & \dfrac{dQ}{dt^c} & \dfrac{de}{dt^c} & 0 & 0 \\[2mm]
\dfrac{dp}{dT^c} & \dfrac{dQ}{dT^c} & \dfrac{de}{dT^c} & 0 & 0 \\[2mm]
\dfrac{dp}{dt^e} & \dfrac{dQ}{dt^e} & \dfrac{de}{dt^e} & 0 & 0 \\[2mm]
\dfrac{dp}{db} & \dfrac{dQ}{db} & \dfrac{de}{db} & q & 0 \\[2mm]
\dfrac{dp}{dB} & \dfrac{dQ}{dB} & \dfrac{de}{dB} & 0 & Q
\end{vmatrix}
\begin{vmatrix}
t^c - bu' - b\lambda g \\[1mm]
T^c - Bu' - B\lambda g \\[1mm]
t^e - au' - a\lambda g \\[1mm]
\hat{c}_\omega - u' - \lambda g \\[1mm]
\hat{C}_\Omega - u' - \lambda g
\end{vmatrix}
=
\begin{vmatrix}
\lambda^s A\dfrac{dE}{dt^c} - \lambda^k k\dfrac{dr}{dt^c} \\[2mm]
\lambda^s A\dfrac{dE}{dT^c} - \lambda^k k\dfrac{dr}{dT^c} \\[2mm]
\lambda^s A\dfrac{dE}{dt^e} - \lambda^k k\dfrac{dr}{dt^e} \\[2mm]
\lambda^s A\dfrac{dE}{db} - \lambda^k k\dfrac{dr}{db} \\[2mm]
\lambda^s A\dfrac{dE}{dB} - \lambda^k k\dfrac{dr}{dB}
\end{vmatrix}
\tag{7.11}
$$

The second-order conditions are assumed to be satisfied. Due to equations (7.A1b, d, f, h), (7.A2a, c, e, g), and (7.A4a) to (7.A4e) in the appendix to this chapter, this can be rewritten

$$
\begin{vmatrix}
\dfrac{dp}{dt^c} & \dfrac{dQ}{dt^c} & \dfrac{de}{dt^c} & 0 & 0 \\[2mm]
\dfrac{dp}{dT^c} & \dfrac{dQ}{dT^c} & \dfrac{de}{dT^c} & 0 & 0 \\[2mm]
\dfrac{dp}{dt^e} & \dfrac{dQ}{dt^e} & \dfrac{de}{dt^e} & 0 & 0 \\[2mm]
\dfrac{dp}{db} & \dfrac{dQ}{db} & \dfrac{de}{db} & q & 0 \\[2mm]
\dfrac{dp}{dB} & \dfrac{dQ}{dB} & \dfrac{de}{dB} & 0 & Q
\end{vmatrix}
\begin{vmatrix}
t^c - bu' - b\lambda g - \dfrac{\hat{c}_r}{q\hat{c}_{rr}} k\lambda^k \\[2mm]
T^c - Bu' - B\lambda g A\hat{C}_T\lambda^s \\[1mm]
t^e - au' - a\lambda g \\[1mm]
\hat{c}_\omega - u' - \lambda g \\[1mm]
\hat{C}_\Omega - u' - \lambda g
\end{vmatrix}
=
\begin{vmatrix}
0 \\[1mm]
0 \\[1mm]
\lambda^k k\dfrac{\hat{c}_{rt}}{\hat{c}_{rr}} \\[2mm]
\lambda^k k\dfrac{\hat{c}_{r\omega}}{\hat{c}_{rr}} \\[2mm]
\lambda^s A\hat{C}_{T\Omega}Q
\end{vmatrix}
\tag{7.12}
$$

Using results from the appendix, one can conclude that:

$$
t^c = bu' + b\lambda g + \frac{\hat{c}_r\hat{c}_{tt} - \hat{c}_t\hat{c}_{rt}}{q(\hat{c}_r r\hat{c}_r - \hat{c}_{rt}^2)} k\lambda^k,
\tag{7.13a}
$$

$$
T^c = Bu' + B\lambda g + A\hat{C}_T\lambda^s,
\tag{7.13b}
$$

$$
t^e = au' + a\lambda g + \frac{k\hat{c}_{rt}}{q(\hat{c}_{rr}\hat{c}_{tt} - \hat{c}_{rt}^2)}\lambda^k,
\tag{7.13c}
$$

$$
\hat{c}_\omega = u' + \lambda g + \frac{k(\hat{c}_{rt}\hat{c}_{t\omega} - \hat{c}_{r\omega}\hat{c}_{rt})}{q(\hat{c}_{rr}\hat{c}_{tt} - \hat{c}_{rt}^2)}\lambda^k,
\tag{7.13d}
$$

$$
\hat{C}_\Omega = u' + \lambda g - A\hat{C}_{T\Omega}\lambda^s.
\tag{7.13e}
$$

If u' is constant, the impact of the lobbying activities can be derived directly from these equations (with the same caveat as before expressed in footnote 26):

- The taxation of domestic consumption goods is affected positively by environmental lobbies and negatively by the lobby of the specific factor. This result is intuitive. Concerns about foreign environmental quality do not influence the taxation of domestic goods.
- Taxes on foreign consumption goods are increased if domestic concern about environmental quality at home and abroad rises. The interests of the industry-specific factor have no impact on the tax rate. At a first glance,

this is surprising since domestic industries would get protection by high tax rates on foreign goods. This is nothing else but a tariff. However, it is well known that the same degree of protection can be achieved more efficiently by means of direct subsidies, i.e. by lowering the consumption tax rate of the good the industry produces itself. Since the policy-maker maximizes her political support, she will always choose the most efficient means of supporting the lobbies.

- Emission taxes are positively influenced by domestic environmental lobbies and by the specific factor of production. They are not affected by concerns for foreign environmental quality. That the influence of green lobbies on the policy-making process raises emission taxes is not surprising. The positive effect of industry lobbying, however, is counter-intuitive and deserves an explanation. As has been shown earlier, a high emission tax rate has two effects on the remuneration of capital. There is a negative effect due to the decline in demand and a positive effect due to substitution. The efficient policy to deal with the demand effect is a subsidy on consumption. A lower emission tax rate achieves the same objective in a more costly way and is, therefore, not chosen by a rational policy-maker. However, the efficient way to induce substitution processes that benefit the specific factor is a high emission tax. This result becomes more intuitive if the specific factor is interpreted as an aggregate of two factors one of which is used for output expansion and the other one for pollution abatement. The pollution-abating factor gains from strict regulations. The capacity factor benefits from lax regulation but it can be helped in a more efficient way by means of low consumption taxes.[29]

- Domestic product standards are positively affected environmentalists and by industry lobbies. That industry lobbies seem to like tight environmental standards is for the same reason as in the case of emission taxes. The demand effect can be addressed in a more cost-effective way by relaxing consumption taxes. However, high-quality goods require more of the specific factor for their production than low-quality goods and this raises its remuneration.

- Standards on foreign product quality are influenced by the concerns of domestic environmentalists about domestic and foreign environmental quality. Surprisingly, the influence of supergreen lobbies leads to less restrictive environmental product standards. To interpret this result, recall

---

[29] The result that a competition among pressure groups favours efficient policy instruments has been established by Becker (1983: 386). For the present model, it can be shown that the combined effects of low consumption taxes and high emission taxes are indeed beneficial to the specific factor. Consider an initial situation without lobbying, i.e. $\lambda^k = 0$. Then a marginal increase in λ^k reduces the consumption tax rate and increases the emission tax rate. Using equations (7.A1b) and (7.A1c) from the appendix, one can establish that

$$\frac{dr}{d\lambda^k} = \frac{-d_p\hat{c}_r^2\hat{c}_{tt} - q\hat{c}_{rt}^2}{(\hat{c}_{rr}\hat{c}_{tt} - \hat{c}_{rt}^2)(q\hat{c}_{rr} - d_p\hat{c}_r^2)} \, k/q > 0.$$

that an increase in the product quality has two effects. On the one hand, demand is reduced, output goes down, and this improves environmental quality. On the other hand, cleaner products have higher production costs, i.e. they require more inputs. Since one of these inputs is an environmental resource, tighter product standards tend to raise the emission intensity of production. The efficient way to deal with the first effect is a tax on consumption, but not a quality standard (see equation (7.13b)). The remaining second effect can be addressed by a reduction in the product quality standard.

The results reached here can be summarized as follows:

Proposition 7.4. Lobbying activities of the industry-specific factor result in low consumption taxes on domestic goods, high emission taxes, and high environmental quality standards of domestic goods. Green lobbying leads to high taxes on production emissions, on the consumption of domestic and foreign goods, and to tighter product quality standards. The influence of supergreen lobbies leads to higher taxes on the consumption of foreign goods and to less restrictive quality standards for these goods.

The results concerning the influence of the industry-specific factor are counter-intuitive and perhaps also counterfactual. They are due to the assumption that the government acts completely rationally and always uses the most efficient instrument to provide protection to the interest group. Owners of pollution-abatement capital are supported by standards and taxes that influence the production process. Owners of usual production capital are subsidized by means of low consumption taxes but not by means of any other instruments since their use would cause greater income losses to the general public than subsidization. Anecdotal evidence, however, suggests that industry lobbies tend to lobby for lax emission taxes and product standards rather than for the converse, the only exception being standards that affect the foreign competitors more severely than the domestic industry itself. The results derived from the theoretical model, therefore, raise the question as to whether the political-support-function model is a realistic description of the impact of idiosyncratic interest groups on the policy-making process.

There are (at least) three candidates for an explanation of the differences between theory and the stylized facts. Two of them concern the foundations of the theoretical model and the third one concerns the empirical evidence. In regard to the empirical evidence, one has to note that observed lobbying activities do not provide a genuine test of the predictions of the model. The model does not predict that industry lobbies are interested in tight standards and taxes but that tight standards and taxes are what they get as a outcome of the political process. And this is a different matter. It is very difficult—if not impossible— to test such a hypothesis empirically. As far as the model framework is concerned, two types of shortcomings may be responsible for counter-intuitive results. On the one hand, real economic agents may act in a much less rational way than the model underlying the political-support-function approach assumes. If this is the case, the rationality assumption has to be substituted by something else. On the other hand, the model lacks some of the aspects that are important in the real policy-making process. Probably the most important of these is obfuscation (see Magee *et al.* (1989, ch. 18)). The political support a policy-maker acquires does not only depend on the gains and losses that accrue to different groups in society but also on the visibility of these gains and losses. From the point of view of the policy-maker, inefficient policy instruments may be useful if they allow the costs of distortive policies to be hidden. For this purpose, environmental quality standards and technological product standards may be much more useful than price instruments such as taxes that make the costs and benefits of a policy measurable and, thus, more obvious. Obfuscation could be introduced into this model in an *ad hoc* fashion rather easily, but a behavioural model which models the voter's information problems explicitly would be preferable, albeit more difficult to construct and to solve.

This discrepancy between theoretical results and anecdotal evidence is not only a deficiency of the model under consideration here. In general, the problem as to why in reality inefficient policy instruments are often preferred over efficient ones is one of the puzzles that remains to be solved by political-economy models of regulation. See Rodrik (1994) for an overview. Further research into this direction is needed.

7.7 Lobbying Activities in the Large-Country Case

Up to now, it has been assumed that the home country is small, i.e. the foreign country is so large that is faces no constraint on the use of the specific factor. This constraint is introduced now. In order to keep the model tractable, assume that consumption now does not affect environmental quality significantly and there are no taxes on consumption and no environmental quality standards.

Total differentiation of equations (7.1), (7.1′), (7.2), and (7.2′) yields

$$
\begin{pmatrix}
1 & 0 & -\hat{c}_r & 0 \\
0 & 1 & 0 & -\hat{C}_R \\
dp\hat{c}_r & dp\hat{c}_r & q\hat{c}_{rr} & 0 \\
D_p\hat{C}_R & D_p\hat{C}_R & 0 & Q\hat{C}_{RR}
\end{pmatrix}
\begin{pmatrix}
dp \\
dP \\
dr \\
dR
\end{pmatrix}
=
\begin{pmatrix}
\hat{c}_r & 0 \\
0 & \hat{C}_T \\
-q\hat{c}_{rt} & 0 \\
0 & -Q\hat{C}_{RT}
\end{pmatrix}
\begin{pmatrix}
dt^e \\
dT^e
\end{pmatrix}.
\tag{7.14}
$$

The results of the comparative-statics analysis are given in the appendix to this chapter. They are straightforward and intuitive:

- Prices are raised by high emission taxes. Production of the good affected directly by such a tax becomes more costly and part of this cost increase is passed through to the consumer. This raises demand for the substitute good and, therefore, its price is raised as well.
- Higher emission taxes reduce emissions by the industry affected directly and raise the emissions in the country producing the substitute good. The

first effect is intuitive and the second one can be explained by the increased demand for the substitute good.

- High emission taxes raise the remuneration of the specific factor of the industry producing the substitute good. The effect on the remuneration of the specific factor employed in the industry directly affected by the tax increase is ambiguous. The underlying rationality is the same as in Section 7.3. There is a positive substitution effect and a negative demand effect.

A benevolent government maximizes the sum of consumer surplus, profits, the income of the specific factor, the tax revenue, and the utility derived from environmental quality. In the foreign country's welfare function, the consumer surplus does not turn up since it is assumed that the commodity is consumed only in the home country.

$$w = -\varepsilon(p, P; \upsilon) + pq - \hat{c}(r, t^e, b)q + rk + t^e e + u(-ae), \tag{7.15}$$

$$W = PQ - \hat{C}(R, T^e, B)Q + RK + T^e E + U(-\hat{A}E). \tag{7.15'}$$

Each country chooses its emission tax rate, t^e and T^e, respectively. Differentiation of w and W and the use of Shephard's lemma and of the first-order conditions of profit maximization to eliminate some of the terms yields the necessary conditions for optimal environmental policies:

$$t^e = au' + Q \frac{dP}{dt^e} \bigg/ \frac{de}{dt^e}, \tag{7.16}$$

$$T^e = AU' - Q \frac{dP}{dT^e} \bigg/ \frac{dE}{dT^e}. \tag{7.16'}$$

Environmental policy has a terms-of-trade effect. Similar results have been derived in Chapter 5 in a general-equilibrium framework. The foreign country uses high emission taxes to raise its export price. The home country has an incentive to use low emission tax rates in order to keep the import price low. This may be called environmental dumping since the emission tax rate does not cover the marginal environmental damage. However, this policy is applied to an import-competing industry that does not sell its output on foreign markets. Thus the term 'dumping' is somewhat misleading.

Equations (7.16) and (7.16') constitute a Nash equilibrium in which both governments take as given the emission tax rates in the other country and choose their best responses. This non-co-operative equilibrium is not efficient since there are external effects of environmental policies in one country on the other country's welfare. These external effects are

$$\frac{dw}{dT^e} = -Q \frac{dP}{dT^e} < 0, \tag{7.17}$$

$$\frac{dW}{dt^e} = Q \frac{dP}{dt^e} > 0. \tag{7.17'}$$

Thus, we have

Proposition 7.5. Benevolent governments choose a less than Pigouvian emission tax rate in the home country and a higher than Pigouvian emission tax rate in the foreign country. The home country would benefit if the foreign government reduced the tax rate. The foreign country would benefit if the home government raised the emission tax rate.

This is represented graphically in Figure 7.1. It is assumed here that emission taxes are strategic substitutes, i.e. the reaction curves are negatively sloped.[30] This may be interpreted as aggressive behaviour by the two governments. An increase in the foreign country's emission tax rate is bad for the home country. The home government reacts by reducing its own emission tax rate, which is bad for the foreign country. The foreign country reacts in a similar 'tit-for-tat'-fashion to tax reductions in the home country.[31] This is shown in a (t^e, T^e) diagram where r and R are the reaction functions of the home and the foreign governments, respectively, N is the Nash equilibrium, and w and W are the corresponding iso-welfare lines whose shapes follow from equations (7.17) and (7,17'). The shaded area denotes the potential of Pareto improvements. Both countries could be better off if the home country increased its emission tax rate and the foreign country reduced its tax rate.

Now the effects of regulatory capture are investigated. The domestic and foreign political-support functions are

$$\tilde{w} = w + \lambda^k rk + \lambda^g(-ae) + \lambda^s(-AE), \tag{7.18}$$

$$\tilde{W} = W + \Lambda^k rk + \Lambda^g(-AE) + \Lambda^s(-ae), \tag{7.18'}$$

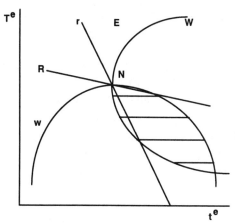

FIG. 7.1 Non-cooperative Environmental Policies

[30] See Rauscher (1991*b*) for a condition that is sufficient for negatively sloped reaction curves in a simpler model with only one food and international factor mobility. This condition is that the objective functions are nearly quadratic such that third derivatives can be neglected in the computation of the comparative-static results.

[31] The term 'tit for tat" does not have a game-theoretic meaning here. Tit-for-tat strategies in a game theoretic sense are possible only in repeated games but not in this static one-shot game.

Maximization with respect to the emission tax rates, t^e and T^e, yields the following results.

$$t^e = \left[au' + Q \frac{dP}{dt^e} \middle/ \frac{de}{dt^e} \right] + \lambda^g + \lambda^s A \frac{dE}{dt^e} \middle/ \frac{de}{dt^e} - \lambda^k k \frac{dr}{dt^e} \middle/ \frac{de}{dt^e}, \quad (7.19)$$

$$T^e = \left[AU' - Q \frac{dP}{dT^e} \middle/ \frac{dE}{dT^e} \right] + \Lambda^g + \Lambda^s a \frac{de}{dT^e} \middle/ \frac{dE}{dT^e} - \Lambda^k k \frac{dR}{dT^e} \middle/ \frac{dE}{dT^e}. \quad (7.19')$$

The impacts of the lobbies on the outcome of the political process follow directly the comparative-static results:

Proposition 7.6. Green lobbying tends to bias emission taxes upwards. This is mitigated if environmentalists care about foreign environmental quality. The impact of the specific-factor's lobbying on emission taxes is ambiguous.

The first part of this proposition is intuitive. The consideration of supergreen interests in the policy-making process leads to lower taxes since low emission taxes in one country reduce the demand for the substitute commodity and, therefore, the emissions discharged in the other country. The ambiguity in the impact of the specific-factor interests follows from the opposite signs of the two effects that tax changes have on the remuneration of the specific factor.

The results stated in proposition 7.6 refer to the case where the emission tax rate in the other country is given, i.e., the proposition shows into which direction the a country's reaction curve is moved by the process of regulatory capture. The effect on the non-co-operative equilibrium can be investigated most easily by means of diagrammatic methods. This is done in Figure 7.2 where it has been assumed that emission taxes are strategic substitutes and where only one country is affected by regulatory capture. Regulatory capture in both countries can be analysed easily by looking at combinations of the shifts in the reaction curves.

In Figure 7.2, the solid lines represent welfare-maximizing behaviour and the dashed lines represent shifts in the reaction curves due to the influence of idiosyncratic interests on the policy-making process. Four scenarios are depicted:

1. Domestic greens and/or industry lobbies are successful in driving the emission tax rate up. The new equilibrium represents a Pareto improvement. Both countries are better off. The reason is that the home country's welfare-maximizing tax rate is too low. It is raised by interest-group influence. This is beneficial for the foreign country and it reacts by raising its own emission tax rate and this in turn is beneficial to the home country. If the shift in the reaction curve were larger than in the diagram, the home country or both countries could lose.

2. Domestic industry lobbies and/or supergreens are successful in reducing the emission tax rate. Both countries are worse of in the new Nash equilibrium. By reducing the emission tax rate, the home country increases the negative externality it imposes on the foreign country and the foreign country reacts in a way detrimental to the home country's welfare.

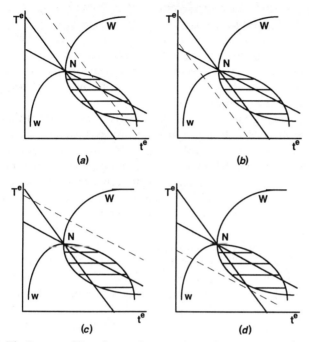

FIG. 7.2 The Impact of Regulatory Capture on Environmental Policy in the Nash
Equilibrium

3. Foreign lobbies raise emission taxes. Since they have been too large already,
this is bad for the home country and the home country reacts by reducing its tax
rate in order to mitigate the terms-of-trade effect of the foreign tax increase.
Both countries are worse off.
4. Foreign lobbying reduces emission taxes. This is beneficial to the home
country. The home country raises its tax rate, which is beneficial to the foreign
country. In this diagram, however, this positive effect is not sufficient to offset
the negative effect which is due to the deviation from the socially optimal policy
in the foreign country but a case in which both countries are better off is also
conceivable (as in a scenario in which both countries lose).

Additional scenarios are conceivable if there are lobbies in both countries. For
instance, if green lobbies are strong in both countries and are able to accom-
plish tax increases, then the foreign country is likely to be better off and the
home country is likely to be worse off than in a scenario where both governments maximize social welfare. If, on the other hand, industrial lobbies benefit
from low emission tax rates and their lobbying is successful, then the home
country may benefit whereas the foreign country may lose.
    *Proposition 7.6. The effects of regulatory capture on in an international en-
vironmental policy game are ambiguous. Both countries may gain, both countries*

may lose or one country may gain whereas the other loses compared to a situation without regulatory capture.

It is interesting that lobbying activities can lead to Pareto-superior results compared to situations in which lobbies are inactive and a benevolent government maximizes social welfare. The underlying reasons is that these lobbies internalize a part of the externalities resulting from the international policy game—of course, without the intention to do so.

As a corollary, one can conclude that institutional settings that reduce interest-group influence in the policy-making process are undesirable in such a situation. But is this realistic? Probably not. The reasons are the following. First, the behavioural model underlying the political-support function approach is a model of bribery in which lobbying activities take the shape of mere transfers. The costs of rent-seeking, i.e. the allocation of productive resources towards the non-productive activity of influencing the distribution of wealth and income, are neglected. Thus an important source of welfare losses is missing in this model. Secondly, it is questionable whether real governments use environmental policies to influence the terms of trade. If they don't, there are no externalities in the international policy game that could be internalized by the lobbies. Thirdly, the empirical evidence suggests that the trade effects of environmental regulation are rather small. This implies that areas of Pareto improvements are small as well and that it becomes unlikely that they are reached when lobbies enter the arena. Finally, one may argue that emission tax rates are not the first-best policies and that additional policy instruments could be introduced into the model. If export taxes and subsidies are feasible, then they are used to affect the terms of trade. Industrial lobbies interested in high tariffs or large export subsidies would aggravate the prisoners' dilemma of optimal tariff policies. Environmentalists would lobby for inefficiently high emission taxes. This suggests that in a first-best world lobbying is not beneficial.

7.8 Summary of Results

1. If single policy instruments are captured by environmentalist interest groups or the lobby supporting the interests of specific factors of production, the biases in environmental policies take the expected directions in most of the cases. Environmentalists lobby for tight product standards and high environmental tax rates. Industry-specific factors are interested in low taxes on consumption. They, however, may benefit from high emission taxes and high product standards if these policies raise the demand for these factors.

2. If environmental regulation as a whole is captured, the policy-maker chooses the most efficient means to support the interest groups. The specific factor is supported by low taxes on consumption and high taxes on emissions. Green interests are supported by high taxes on both consumption and

emissions from production and by strict product quality standards. Supergreen interests are supported by high taxes on the consumption of foreign goods and lax quality standards for these goods.

3. In the large-country case where the governments play a non-co-operative game in emission tax rates, regulatory capture may mitigate or amplify the problems arising from the prisoners' dilemma of the tax game. With regulatory capture, none, one, or both of the countries may be better off than without.

4. In a setting where rent-seeking costs are taken into account and where first-best policies are available, regulatory capture tends to reduce the welfare of all countries involved.

Appendix:
Comparative-Static Results

7.A1 The Small-Country Case

From equation (7.4), we have

$$\frac{dp}{dt^c} = \frac{q\hat{c}_{rr}}{q\hat{c}_{rr} + d_p\hat{c}_r^2} \begin{cases} > 0 \\ < 0 \end{cases} \qquad \frac{dr}{dt^c} = \frac{-d_p\hat{c}_r}{q\hat{c}_{rr} + d_p\hat{c}_r^2} < 0, \qquad \text{(7.A1}a),(\text{7.A1}b)$$

$$\frac{dp}{dt^e} = \frac{q(\hat{c}_t\hat{c}_{rr} - \hat{c}_r\hat{c}_{rt})}{q\hat{c}_{rr} + d_p\hat{c}_r^2} > 0, \qquad \frac{dr}{dt^e} = \frac{q\hat{c}_{rt} + d_p c_r\hat{c}_t}{q\hat{c}_{rr} + d_p\hat{c}_r^2}, \qquad \text{(7.A1}c),(\text{7.A1}d)$$

$$\frac{dp}{dt^e} = \frac{q(\hat{c}_\omega\hat{c}_{rr} - \hat{c}_r\hat{c}_{r\omega})}{q\hat{c}_{rr} + d_p\hat{c}_r^2} > 0, \qquad \frac{dr}{d\omega} = \frac{q\hat{c}_{r\omega} + d_p\hat{c}_r\hat{c}_\omega}{q\hat{c}_{rr} + d_p\hat{c}_r^2}, \qquad \text{(7.A1}e),(\text{7.A1}f)$$

$$\frac{dp}{dP} = \frac{-d_p\hat{c}_r^2}{q\hat{c}_{rr} + d_p\hat{c}_r^2} > 0, \qquad \frac{dr}{dP} = \frac{-d_p\hat{c}_r}{q\hat{c}_{rr} + d_p\hat{c}_r^2} > 0. \qquad \text{(7.A1}g),(\text{7.A1}h)$$

The effects on the quantities are obtained via the demand functions, i.e.

$$\frac{dq}{dt^c} = \frac{qd_p\hat{c}_{rr}}{q\hat{c}_{rr} + d_p\hat{c}_r^2} < 0 \qquad \frac{dQ}{dt^c} = \frac{qD_p\hat{c}_{rr}}{q\hat{c}_{rr} + d_p\hat{c}_r^2} > 0, \qquad \text{(7.A2}a),(\text{7.A2}b)$$

$$\frac{dq}{dt^e} = \frac{qd_p(\hat{c}_t\hat{c}_{rr} - \hat{c}_r\hat{c}_{rt})}{q\hat{c}_{rr} + d_p\hat{c}_r^2} < 0, \qquad \frac{dQ}{dt^e} = \frac{qD_p(\hat{c}_t\hat{c}_{rr} - \hat{c}_r\hat{c}_{rt})}{q\hat{c}_{rr} + d_p\hat{c}_r^2} > 0, \qquad \text{(7.A2}c),(\text{7.A2}d)$$

$$\frac{dq}{d\omega} = \frac{qd_p(\hat{c}_\omega\hat{c}_{rr} - \hat{c}_r\hat{c}_{r\omega})}{q\hat{c}_{rr} + d_p\hat{c}_r^2} < 0 \qquad \frac{dQ}{d\omega} = \frac{qD_p(\hat{c}_\omega\hat{c}_{rr} - \hat{c}_r\hat{c}_{r\omega})}{q\hat{c}_{rr} + d_p\hat{c}_r^2} > 0, \qquad \text{(7.A2}e),(\text{7.A2}f)$$

$$\frac{dq}{dP} = \frac{qd_p\hat{c}_{rr}}{q\hat{c}_{rr} + d_p\hat{c}_r^2} > 0, \qquad \frac{dQ}{dP} = \frac{\hat{c}_r^2(d_pD_p - d_pD_p) + qD_p\hat{c}_{rr}}{q\hat{c}_{rr} + d_p\hat{c}_r^2} < 0. \qquad \text{(7.A2}g),(\text{7.A2}h)$$

Domestic emissions, e, are determined by Shephard's lemma: $e = \hat{c}_t q$. It follows that

$$\frac{de}{dt^e} = q\hat{c}_{tt} + q\hat{c}_{tr}\frac{dr}{dt^e} + \hat{c}_t\frac{dq}{dt^e},$$

and the effects of the other policy parameters can be determined in an analogous fashion. It follows that

$$\frac{de}{dt^c} = \frac{qd_p(\hat{c}_t\hat{c}_{rr} - \hat{c}_r\hat{c}_{rt})}{qc_{rr} + d_p\hat{c}_r^2} < 0, \qquad \text{(7.A3}a)$$

$$\frac{de}{dt^e} = \frac{q^2(\hat{c}_{rr}\hat{c}_{tt} - \hat{c}_{rt}^2) + qd_p(\hat{c}_t^2\hat{c}_{rr} + \hat{c}_r^2\hat{c}_{tt} - 2\hat{c}_r\hat{c}_t\hat{c}_{rt})}{q\hat{c}_{rr} + d_p\hat{c}_r^2} < 0, \qquad \text{(7.A3}b)$$

$$\frac{de}{d\omega} = \frac{q^2(\hat{c}_{rr}\hat{c}_{t\omega} - \hat{c}_{rt}\hat{c}_{r\omega}) + qd_p(\hat{c}_\omega\hat{c}_t\hat{c}_{rr} + \hat{c}_r^2\hat{c}_{t\omega} - \hat{c}_r\hat{c}_\omega\hat{c}_{rt} - \hat{c}_r c_t\hat{c}_{r\omega})}{q\hat{c}_{rr} + d_p\hat{c}_r^2}, \qquad \text{(7.A3}c)$$

$$\frac{de}{dP} = \frac{qd_p(\hat{c}_t\hat{c}_{rr} - \hat{c}_r\hat{c}_{rt})}{q\hat{c}_{rr} + d_p\hat{c}_r^2} > 0. \qquad \text{(7.A3}d)$$

For the effects on foreign emissions, we obtain

$$\frac{dE}{dt^c} = \hat{C}_T \frac{dQ}{dt^c} > 0, \tag{7.A4a}$$

$$\frac{dE}{dt^e} = \hat{C}_T \frac{dQ}{dt^e} > 0, \tag{7.A4b}$$

$$\frac{dE}{d\omega} = \hat{C}_T \frac{dQ}{d\omega} > 0, \tag{7.A4c}$$

$$\frac{dE}{d\Omega} = \hat{C}_T \hat{C}_\Omega \frac{dQ}{dP} + \hat{C}_{T\Omega} Q, \tag{7.A4d}$$

$$\frac{dE}{dT^c} = \hat{C}_T \frac{dQ}{dP}, \tag{7.A4e}$$

$$\frac{dE}{dT^e} = \hat{C}_{TT} + \hat{C}_T^2 \frac{dQ}{dP}. \tag{7.A4f}$$

7.A2 The Large-Country Case

From equation (7.14), we have

$$\frac{dp}{dt^e} = \frac{q(\hat{c}_t\hat{c}_{rr} - \hat{c}_{rt}\hat{c}_r)(Q\hat{C}_{RR} + \hat{C}_R^2 D_P)}{q\hat{c}_{rr}(Q\hat{C}_{RR} + \hat{C}_R^2 D_P) + \hat{c}_r^2(d_p Q\hat{C}_{RR} + \hat{C}_R^2(d_p D_P - d_P D_p))} > 0, \tag{7.A5a}$$

$$\frac{dP}{dt^e} = \frac{-q\hat{C}_R^2 D_p(\hat{c}_t\hat{c}_{rr} - \hat{c}_{rt}\hat{c}_r)}{q\hat{c}_{rr}(Q\hat{C}_{RR} + \hat{C}_R^2 D_P) + \hat{c}_r^2(d_p Q\hat{C}_{RR} + \hat{C}_R^2(d_p D_P - d_P D_p))} > 0, \tag{7.A5b}$$

$$\frac{dr}{dt^e} = \frac{-q\hat{c}_{rt}(Q\hat{C}_{RR} + \hat{C}_R^2 D_P) - \hat{c}_t\hat{c}_r(d_p Q\hat{C}_{RR} + \hat{C}_R^2(d_p D_P - d_P D_p))}{q\hat{c}_{rr}(Q\hat{C}_{RR} + \hat{C}_R^2 D_P) + \hat{c}_r^2(d_p Q\hat{C}_{RR} + \hat{C}_R^2(d_p D_P - d_P D_p))}, \tag{7.A5c}$$

$$\frac{dR}{dt^e} = \frac{\hat{C}_R D_p q(\hat{c}_t\hat{c}_{rt} - \hat{c}_t\hat{c}_{rr})}{q\hat{c}_{rr}(Q\hat{C}_{RR} + \hat{C}_R^2 D_P) + \hat{c}_r^2(d_p Q\hat{C}_{RR} + \hat{C}_R^2(d_p D_P - d_P D_p))}. \tag{7.A5d}$$

Using the demand functions, we obtain

$$\frac{dq}{dt^e} = \frac{q(\hat{c}_t\hat{c}_{rr} - \hat{c}_{rt}\hat{c}_r)(d_p Q\hat{C}_{RR} + \hat{C}_R^2(d_p D_P - d_P D_p))}{q\hat{c}_{rr}(Q\hat{C}_{RR} + \hat{C}_R^2 D_P) + \hat{c}_r^2(d_p Q\hat{C}_{RR} + \hat{C}_R^2(d_p D_P - d_P D_p))} < 0, \tag{7.A5e}$$

$$\frac{dQ}{dt^e} = \frac{q d_p Q\hat{C}_{RR}(\hat{c}_t\hat{c}_{rr} - \hat{c}_{rt}\hat{c}_r)}{q\hat{c}_{rr}(Q\hat{C}_{RR} + \hat{C}_R^2 D_P) + \hat{c}_r^2(d_p Q\hat{C}_{RR} + \hat{C}_R^2(d_p D_P - d_P D_p))} > 0. \tag{7.A5f}$$

Finally, emissions, e and E, are determined by Shephard's lemma. $e = \hat{c}_t q$ and $E = \hat{C}_T Q$. It follows that

$$\frac{de}{dt^e} = q\hat{c}_{tt} + q\hat{c}_{tr}\frac{dr}{dt^e} + \hat{c}_t\frac{dq}{dt^e},$$

$$\frac{dE}{dt^e} = Q\hat{C}_{TR}\frac{dR}{dt^e} + \hat{C}_T\frac{dQ}{dt^e}.$$

The previous results can be inserted and this yields

$$\frac{de}{dt^e} = \frac{q^2(\hat{c}_{rr}\hat{c}_{tt} - \hat{c}_{rt}^2)(Q\hat{C}_{RR} + \hat{C}_R^2 D_P)}{q\hat{c}_{rr}(Q\hat{C}_{RR} + \hat{C}_R^2 D_P) + \hat{c}_r^2(d_p Q\hat{C}_{RR} + \hat{C}_R^2(d_p D_P - d_P D_p))}$$

$$+ \frac{q(\hat{c}_{tt}\hat{c}_r^2 + \hat{c}_t^2\hat{c}_{rr})(d_p Q\hat{C}_{RR} + \hat{C}_R^2(d_p D_P - d_P D_p))}{q\hat{c}_{rr}(Q\hat{C}_{RR} + \hat{C}_R^2 D_P) + \hat{c}_r^2(d_p Q\hat{C}_{RR} + \hat{C}_R^2(d_p D_P - d_P D_p))} < 0, \qquad (7.\text{A}6a)$$

$$\frac{dE}{dt^e} = \frac{q Q D_p(\hat{c}_r\hat{c}_{rt} - \hat{c}_t\hat{c}_{rr})(\hat{C}_R\hat{C}_{RT} - \hat{C}_T\hat{C}_{RR})}{q\hat{c}_{rr}(Q\hat{C}_{RR} + \hat{C}_R^2 D_P) + \hat{c}_r^2(d_p Q\hat{C}_{RR} + \hat{C}_R^2(d_p D_P - d_P D_p))} > 0. \qquad (7.\text{A}6b)$$

The last effect is a carbon-leakage effect. The impacts of the regulation of the foreign industry, T^e can be obtained by analogous reasoning since the model is symmetric.

8

Intertemporal Trade and the Environment: The Foreign-Debt Problem

8.1 Introduction

So far we have been occupied with the static aspects of international trade and the environment. In Chapters 4 and 5, where the issue has been addressed in a general-equilibrium framework, it has been assumed that the value of exports equals the value of imports and that there is no trade deficit nor a trade surplus. This is not particularly realistic and it neglects the important dimension of time. In what follows, this dimension will be introduced and intertemporal aspects of foreign trade and the use of environmental resources will be addressed.

In a world where international trade does not always balance, some countries are debtors and some countries are lenders. During the 1970s and 1980s, this process of borrowing and lending has driven developing countries into what has been called the foreign-debt crisis (see Gutowski (1986), Lomax (1986), Krueger (1987), and Sachs (1989a) for surveys). Much of the debt crisis is attributed to loose conditions of lending by international organizations and private banks that faced problems of petro-dollar recycling during the 1970s and early 1980s. Many credits were used to satisfy consumption needs but not to invest into profitable projects and in some countries capital flight has played an additional role. Moreover, in some countries loaned money was invested into resource projects in the expectation of ever-increasing real resource prices. Thus, a substantial share of the credits have not been allocated to productive uses, i.e. to projects whose rate of return would have allowed the servicing and repayment of the debt. In the beginning of the 1980s, therefore, many developing countries found themselves in situations where their debt burdens had increased whereas no substantial additional investments had been undertaken in production capacity. Since the debt burden tended to exceed the ability (or in some cases the willingness) to pay, the debt crisis became apparent. On the one hand, developing countries became subject to severe balance-of-payments problems. On the other hand, the Western banking system was under threat by the possibility of default of some of the major debtor countries.

Here, we do not wish to analyse the reasons underlying the debt crisis and ways in which it could have been avoided. Rather, we start from a situation in which a developing country has inherited a substantial external debt from the past and now has to find a way to cope with this problem. The main question here is how this affects the environment and which policy instruments may be used to solve the problems arising in this context. It has frequently been argued that the balance-of-payments problems associated with the indebtedness situation induce indebted countries to overexploit their natural resource bases, i.e. to sell the family jewels in order to be able to service the debt and to retain the reputation of being a reliable debtors. Environmentalists have argued that this may have been one of the main reasons for the increase of environmental disruption and the quick destruction of the resource bases in many indebted countries. In particular, tropical deforestation has been attributed to the foreign-debt crisis (see Adams (1991), Miller (1991), and George (1992)). An alternative line of arguing has been proposed by Hansen (1989). He suggested that it would also be possible for an indebted country to solve its problems not by increasing its exports but by reducing its imports. If a large part of these imports consist of environmentally disruptive technology and capital goods (e.g. felling and wood processing equipment), then the balance-of-payments problems of an indebted country would be beneficial to the environment. Thus, the first question to be dealt with in this chapter is whether and in which circumstances a high level of foreign debt is harmful to the environment.

Secondly, the—perhaps more important—question arises which instruments can be used to deal with environmental problems in an indebted country. In the late eighties, debt-for-nature swaps have been invented to deal with the debt crisis and with environmental disruption simultaneously (see Hansen (1989) and Sarkar and Ebbs (1992) for an overview). This business was initiated by non-governmental organizations such as the World Wildlife Fund who purchased a part of the debt in the secondary market and offered the debtor country a debt relief in exchange for an environmental agreement by which the government of the indebted country committed itself to restrain from the commercial exploitation of a part of the country's natural-resource base. In tropical countries, such an agreement usually involved the declaration as natural reserves of a part of the rain-forest area (see Page (1989)). More recently, debt-for-nature swaps have been proposed to solve environmental and indebtedness problems of non-tropical countries like the emerging market economies of Eastern Europe (see Manser (1993: 122–3) and Zylicz (1993)). Besides debt-for-nature swaps, there exist additional instruments to deal with the environmental problems of indebted countries. For instance, if the over-exploitation of environmental resources is really caused by foreign indebtedness, an unconditioned debt relief could mitigate the pressure on an indebted country's natural-resource base. Finally, there exists the possibility of addressing environmental issues without linking them to the indebtedness situation. It is interesting to compare these instruments with respect to the feasibility of their implementation and their efficiency.

This chapter is organized as follows. In Section 2, a simple model of an indebted country will be introduced. The relationship between the level of indebtedness and the exploitation of environmental resources will be addressed in Section 3. Sections 4 and 5 are devoted to extensions of the model. We will introduce imports of resource-extraction equipment to be able to discuss Hansen's (1989) hypothesis that balance-of-payments constraints may reduce the pressure on the indebted country's resource base. Moreover, the impact of suboptimal environmental policies will be investigated. The following three sections then look at the lender country and at the instruments it can use to preserve the environmental-resource base in the debtor country. We will consider debt forgiveness, debt-for-nature swaps, and side-payments that are not linked to the foreign debt.

8.2 The Indebted Country

Consider an open economy which has inherited a foreign debt from the past. This country faces an intertemporal balance-of-payments constraint, it has to pay back (a part of) its debt over a given time horizon. The model to be used here is a modified version of the one-good model that has been used to investigate international capital movements in Chapter 3. However, as the introduction of intertemporal linkages complicates the analysis considerably, the static allocation aspects will be modelled in a much less detailed way. In particular, it is assumed that neither consumption nor international trade cause environmental disruption and that the capital stock is constant.

The first assumption implies that the analysis will be restricted to externalities arising from production activities only. This is consistent with what has been written on the linkages of environmental and foreign-debt problems. Environmental disruption in indebted countries is attributed mainly to the increased effort to produce exportable goods. Of course, these goods have to be transported but this appears to be less problematic. Consumption externalities will probably even be reduced in highly indebted countries since the higher the debt the lower the consumption path.[1] However, this effect tends to be of minor importance compared to that of production externalities. As far as the capital stock is concerned, it is difficult to justify the assumption of fixed supply in an intertemporal framework. This is a simplification made predominantly for the sake of tractability. The consideration of the endogenous growth of the capital stock would require the introduction of a second state variable in addition to foreign debt and two-state-variable intertemporal optimization problems are difficult to solve[2] (see Rauscher (1989) for an example).

[1] A large foreign debt means a tight budget constraint. Therefore, aggregate consumption tends to be reduced if the debt is increased. This effect may be turned around if the debt situation induces a switch from expensive environmentally friendly consumption goods to cheaper and dirtier ones.

[2] Only if foreign assets/debt and physical capital were perfectly malleable, a model with capital accumulation could be represented in a one-state-variable fashion. This variable would represent the total-assets position of the country and in each period the static-allocation problem of the composition of the portfolio would have to be solved. This also complicates the analysis but, with

Let $v(t)$ be the foreign-assets position of the country at time t. Its change through time is denoted by $v^{\cdot}(t)$[3] and it depends on the trade balance and on the interest payments the country receives or has to make. Output is $g(-sae(t))f(k,e))$ and the trade surplus is output minus consumption, $g(-sae(t))f(k,e)) - c(t)$. Interest payments are a function of the asset position. Usually a fixed interest rate is assumed. See, for example, Bardhan (1967) and Siebert (1987) for the standard framework of a foreign-borrowing model where this assumption is made. However, if the interest rate is fixed, Fisher's separation theorem applies. This theorem states that production decisions are independent of the decisions on saving, lending, and borrowing if the capital market is perfect. See Fisher (1930) for the original contribution and Siebert (1985, ch. 4), who uses it in the analysis of trade in exhaustible resources. Applied to the problem under consideration here, Fisher's separation theorem would imply that environmental disruption is independent of a country's foreign-asset position. Foreign debt and environmental problems would be separate issues. However, the requirements of Fisher's separation theorem are unlikely to be met in reality. Capital markets are usually not perfect. This is taken into account here by modelling interest payments as a non-linear function of the foreign-assets position, $h(v(t))$, with the following properties:

$$h(0) = 0, h'(v(t)) > 0, h''(v(t)) < 0. \qquad (8.1)$$

This function is depicted in Figure 8.1. The interest rate relevant for the last unit of foreign assets, $h'(v(t))$, is a declining function of the stock of foreign assets. Or, to put it the other way around, the interest rate to be paid for an

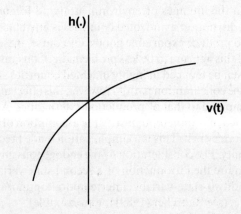

FIG. 8.1 The $h(.)$ Function

the usual assumptions on the shape of production and utility functions, it does not provide additional insights into the problem area discussed here. Moreover, the assumption of perfect malleability is not much less unrealistic than the assumption of a fixed capital stock.

[3] A dot above a variable denotes its derivative with respect to time.

additional unit of foreign debt is an increasing function of the level of indebtedness. This shape of the $h(.)$ function may be motivated by two types of arguments:

- Lenders charge a risk premium if the borrowing country is highly indebted since the default risk raises with the level of indebtedness.[4]
- Highly indebted countries may be required to adopt structural adjustment programmes which are supervised by borrower organizations like the International Monetary Fund. These programmes constrain the discretion of the government and are, therefore, viewed as an additional cost of a high foreign debt by the policy maker in the indebted country.

Both these arguments imply that the marginal cost of being indebted is an increasing function of the debt level. The $h(.)$ function represents this relationship. Moreover, one may argue that a high foreign debt may have a negative impact on welfare or–at least–on the utility of the policy-maker. The effects of such an assumption will be discussed later on.

The change in the country's foreign-assets position is given by:

$$\dot{v}(t) = g(-sae(t)) f(k,e(t)) - c(t) + h(v(t)). \tag{8.2}$$

The initial foreign-assets position at time $t = 0$ is

$$v(0) = v_o < 0, \tag{8.3}$$

i.e. the country has inherited a foreign debt. In order to make the borrowing constraint binding, one has to assume that the country cannot accumulate an infinite foreign debt. If the time-horizon is infinite, this implies that

$$\lim_{t \to \infty} v(t) \geq v_1 > -\infty. [5] \tag{8.4}$$

The government's objective is to maximize the present value of welfare by choosing the appropriate consumption and emission paths over an infinite time-horizon. The arguments of the utility function, $u(.,.)$, are consumption and environmental quality. It has positive partial derivatives and is strictly concave. The foreign-assets position is not included since although the utility of the policy-maker may be affected by the indebtedness situation. But it will be argued later on that such an extension of the model would not change the results significantly. Future utility is discounted at a rate δ. Thus the optimization problem is to

$$\max_{c(t),e(t)} \int_0^\infty u(c(t), -sae(t)) e^{-\delta t} dt \tag{8.5}$$

subject to the constraints (8.2), (8.3), and (8.4).

---

[4] See Strand (1990) for a model where this risk is considered explicitly.
[5] In an overlapping-generations framework, Mohr (1991) came to the conclusion that a Ponzi game where an infinite debt is accumulated is possible and sustainable in a borrower–lender relationship. However, even in that model each generation faces a binding budget constraint and the shadow price of foreign assets is positive. In the present model, linkages across generations cannot be represented and, therefore, we rely on a constraint like (8.3).

8.3 Optimal Environmental Policies in an Indebted Country

The derivation of optimal paths requires the application of Pontryagin's maximum principle. See Feichtinger and Hartl (1986), Seierstad and Sydsœter (1987), Kamien and Schwartz (1991), Chiang (1992) and Léonard and Long (1992), for this method. Initially, we will look at a simplified version of the model where $u(.,.)$ is additively separable in its arguments.

The current-value Hamiltonian turns out to be

$$\tilde{h} = u(c, -sae) + \lambda(g(-sae)f(k,e) - c + h(v)), \tag{8.6}$$

where the argument t of the time-dependent variables has been omitted for convenience. λ is the shadow price of foreign assets and it represents the value attached to a marginal improvement in the foreign-assets position. The necessary optimality conditions are

$$\dot{\lambda} = (\delta - h')\lambda, \tag{8.7}$$

$$u_1 = \lambda, \tag{8.8}$$

$$\lambda(gf_e - sag' f) = sau_2. \tag{8.9}$$

Using equation (8.8) one can rewrite condition (8.9) such that

$$u^1(gf_e - sag' f) = sau_2. \tag{8.10}$$

Moreover, a complementary-slackness condition (or transversality condition at infinity) has to be met

$$\lim_{t \to \infty} e^{-\delta t} \lambda(t)(v(t) - v_1) \geq 0. \tag{8.11}$$

The second-order conditions of optimality are satisfied due to the assumptions on the shapes of the production and utility functions, i.e. the Hamiltonian function is strictly concave in (v,e,c).

Equation (8.7) states that the shadow price of foreign assets grows at a rate equalling the discount rate minus the marginal rate of interest. This is a standard result of optimal-borrowing and optimal-growth models. Equation (8.8) is a condition for an optimal-consumption path: the marginal utility of consuming a marginal unit of income equals the value of the marginal improvement in the foreign-assets position if this unit of income were saved. Equation (8.10) is the condition for the equality of the marginal benefits and the marginal damage due to emissions. The same condition would be obtained in a static model framework. See the results in Chapter 3, for instance.

c and λ can be eliminated from these equations. It follows from equation (8.10) that along an optimal path

$$\frac{dc}{de} = -\frac{u_1(gf_{ee} - 2sag' f_e + (sa)^2 g'' f) + (sa)^2 u_{22}}{u_{11}(gf_e - sag' f)} < 0 \tag{8.12}$$

That dc/de is negative, follows from the assumptions on the utility function. Linear separability implies that both the consumption good and environmental quality are normal goods, i.e. their demand is an increasing function of income. Thus an exogenous increase in income, e.g. a transfer from abroad, will raise consumption and environmental quality. Emissions are reduced. This result is an artefact of the models assumptions but it is also realistic. Aggregate consumption in an economy should be an increasing function of income. And empirical results on the demand for environmental quality on the micro and macro levels suggest that the willingness to pay for environmental quality is increased if income is raised.[6] One can now establish growth rates in equation (8.9) and use (8.7) to eliminate $\dot{\lambda}$ and λ. This procedure yields

$$\left(\frac{gf_{ee} - 2sag'f_e + (sa)^2 g''f}{gf_e - sag'f} + \frac{sau_{22}}{u_2}\right)\dot{e} = h' - \delta$$

Equations (8.2) and (8.13) describe the behaviour of the paths of the variables e and v that satisfy the first-order conditions of optimality. An equilibrium, in which neither e nor v changes is determined by

$$h' = \delta, \tag{8.14a}$$

$$gf + h = c^*, \tag{8.14b}$$

the asterisk denoting the equilibrium value of a variable. Equation (8.14a) states that the interest rate and the discount rate are equal in an equilibrium. Equation (8.14b) states that all income is consumed such that saving is zero. Total differentiation of equations (8.2) and (8.12) in the equilibrium yields

$$\begin{pmatrix} \dot{v} \\ \dot{e} \end{pmatrix} = \begin{pmatrix} \delta & gfe - sag'f - \frac{dc}{de} \\ h''/\zeta & 0 \end{pmatrix} \begin{pmatrix} v - v^* \\ e - e^* \end{pmatrix}, \tag{8.15}$$

where e^* and v^* denote the equilibrium values of v and v, respectively, and $\zeta < 0$ represents the complicated term in brackets on the left-hand side of equation (8.13).

These results can be used to represent the paths satisfying the optimality conditions in a (v,e) phase diagram (see Figure 8.2). From equation (8.15) we have the following results:

- The line along which $\dot{e} = 0$ is vertical. If v is larger than the value at which $h' = \delta$, then $\dot{e} > 0$. If v is smaller, then $\dot{e} < 0$.
- The line along which $\dot{v} = 0$ is negatively sloped. Above this line, $\dot{v} > 0$, below, $\dot{v} < 0$.

The system derived from the necessary optimality conditions is stable in the saddle-point sense (which can also be verified via the eigenvalues of the matrix on the left-hand side of equation (8.15)). The saddle path is the optimal path since all other paths either lead to an infinite debt or to over-accumulation of

[6] See Walter and Ugelow's (1979) cross-country study for the macro level and the survey of contingent-valuation studies by Kriström and Riera (1996) for the micro level.

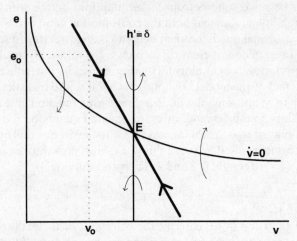

FIG. 8.2 Optimal Paths of Assets and Emissions

foreign assets.[7] It is negatively sloped. The saddle path determines the optimal starting-point of the paths of emissions and consumption. It is seen that the larger the stock of foreign assets, or the smaller the foreign debt, the smaller are the initial emissions. In the long-run, all optimal paths approach the same steady state (denoted by E in the diagram). Thus, long-run emissions are independent of the initial debt situation.

Proposition 8.1. In a simple intertemporal framework with increasing marginal costs of foreign indebtedness, the initial emissions are an increasing function of the initial debt level. Long-run emissions are not affected by initial indebtedness.

The same result has been established by Strand (1990), who has modelled the default risk explicitly instead of using a reduced-form $h(.)$ function for interest payments. The intuition underlying the result is the following: the higher the foreign debt, the higher the marginal cost of being indebted. Repaying the debt requires exports, which require environmentally harmful production. Due to this relationship, there is a trade-off between a strict environmental policy and a quick solution of the debt problem. A large foreign debt raises the opportunity costs of tight environmental policies. Therefore, there is a positive relationship between the initial debt and the initial emissions. In the long run, the equilibrium level of foreign debt or assets will be approached and, therefore, the long-run opportunity costs of strict environmental policies are independent of the initial conditions.

Two types of question may be raised at this point. One of them is whether the result derived from this simple model is robust or whether extensions of the model may lead to different results. The other one concerns the policy implications to be drawn from this analysis. Some extensions have been looked at in

[7] An additional condition which has to be met here is that the debt limit, v_1, is not exceeded by the equilibrium debt level.

earlier papers, e.g. Rauscher (1989, 1990*a*). It has been shown there that the introduction of intertemporal aspects of pollution into such a model does not affect the main conclusion—as long as the effects of environmental disruption on the consumption-vs-saving decision are not unrealistically high.[8] Moreover, one may introduce an effect of the debt situation on the objective function in order to capture non-pecuniary costs of being indebted such as the policy-maker's loss of standing and discretion if the country becomes subject to externally supervised adjustment programmes. This changes the canonical equation (8.7) such that

$$h' + \frac{\partial u}{\partial v} \Big/ \frac{\partial u}{\partial c} = \delta.$$

i.e. the total rate of return to foreign assets equals the discount rate. How does this affect the dynamics of the optimum path? The ($\dot{e} = 0$) line can have a negative slope and one could conceive of multiple intersection points of the ($\dot{v} = 0$) and ($\dot{e} = 0$) lines. But it follows from a theorem by Gale and Nikaido (1965: 91) that this is impossible. The ($\dot{v} = 0$) line always intersects the ($\dot{e} = 0$) line from below (see also Feichtinger and Hartl (1985, ch. 4.3)). Thus the optimal path remains stable in the saddle-point sense and approaches a unique steady state. This saddle path is negatively sloped and, therefore, the positive relationship between initial debt and the use of environmental resources is maintained. However, other extensions that capture relevant aspects of reality are conceivable and they will be considered in the following two sections. Afterwards policy implications will be discussed.

8.4 Suboptimal Environmental Policies

It has been shown that, in this simple model, there is a unique equilibrium which is stable in the saddle-point sense. Therefore, the long-run steady state will always be independent of the initial conditions and the initial indebtedness situation has an impact on the environment only in the short to medium term. This result qualifies the thesis of the negative side-effects of the debt crisis on the environment. But is it a robust result? Models from other areas of economic research that use similar methods suggest that multiple equilibria and instability may occur if externalities are not internalized. In economic geography, for example, it has been shown in agglomeration models that multiple stable equilibria are possible if there are positive spillovers between firms that locate in the same area.[9] Which one of the equilibria will be attained in the long run,

---

[8] In this case, optimal paths may be cyclical (see Rauscher (1990*a*) and Feichtinger and Novak (1991)).

[9] See Krugman (1991). Another example is endogenous-growth theory, where knowledge spillovers drive economic growth (see Romer (1986)). In his original model, Romer (1983: 131–4) showed that unstable spiralling growth paths are feasible in the case of particularly strong knowledge spillovers across firms.

depends on the starting point. Thus, history, i.e. the inherited initial conditions, may matter in the long run as well (see Krugman (1993), for instance). In the preceding section, we have assumed that all externalities are internalized since the government of the debtor country maximizes social welfare. Albeit being conventional and convenient, this assumption is not particularly realistic. Especially developing countries suffer from ill-defined property rights in natural resources (see Chichilnisky (1994)) and from enforcement deficits in environmental policy. Thus, it is not far-fetched to modify the basic model by assuming that the government does not take the social cost of environmental disruption fully into account.

Thus assume that the government behaves as if the pollution impact parameter was β instead of a with $\beta < a$. Thus, β/a measures the degree of internalization. The first-order condition for the optimal environmental policy turns out to be

$$u_1(gf_e - s\beta g' f) = s\beta u_2 \tag{8.17}$$

instead of equation (8.10). Equations (8.12) and (8.13) are modified such that

$$\frac{dc}{de} = \frac{u_1(gf_{ee} - s(a+\beta)g' f_e + s^2 a\beta g'' f) + s^2 a\beta u_{22}}{u_{11}(gf_e - s\beta g' f)} < 0, \tag{8.18}$$

$$\left(\frac{gf_{ee} - s(a+\beta)g' f_e + s^2 a\beta g'' f}{gf_e - s\beta g' f} + \frac{sau_{22}}{u_2}\right)\dot{e} = h' - \delta. \tag{8.19}$$

The equilibrium is again determined by equations (8.14a) and (8.14b). v^*, the long-run level of foreign assets, remains the same as in the previous section but e^* and c^* will be different. Does this affect the dynamics of the optimal path? Since e^* and c^* are changed, the location of the ($\dot{v} = 0$) locus in the phase diagram is shifted. Moreover, the adjustment speed of the horizontal component of the system changes since the term by which $\dot{e}$ is multiplied in equation (8.19) is different from that in equation (8.13). The Jacobian matrix, which determines the behaviour of the system near the equilibrium, is

$$J = \begin{pmatrix} \delta & gfe - sag'f - \dfrac{de}{dc} \\ h''/\xi & 0 \end{pmatrix},$$

where $\xi < 0$ represents the term in brackets on the left-hand side of equation (8.19).

Since this matrix has the same structure as that of equation (8.14), the system is structurally stable, i.e. its qualitative behaviour remains unchanged by the introduction of suboptimal environmental policies into the model.

Proposition 8.2. Suboptimal environmental policies do not alter the qualitative behaviour of optimal paths.

The underlying reason is that the ($\dot{e} = 0$) line in figure 8.2, defined by $h' = \delta$, remains unaffected by this change in the model structure. The model is structurally stable with respect to deviations from welfare-maximizing environmental policies.

8.5 Inferior Consumption and Imported Inputs: Foreign Debt Can Reduce Environmental Problems

The preceding section has shown that the equilibrium remains stable in the case of non-internalized externalities. We will now address the second specificity of the model: the positive slope of the saddle path. There may be basically two reasons why this result may be reversed:

- On the one hand, there may be a possibility that a high debt level leads to reductions in consumption that are so substantial that no increase in emissions is necessary to solve the balance-of-payments problem.
- On the other hand, economic activities that generate emissions may rely on imported inputs. If these imports are reduced due to the debt crisis, emissions tend to be reduced and the environmental situation will be the better the larger the foreign debt.

The first hypothesis can be investigated if we use a more general utility function than in Section 3 of this chapter. Let utility be still independent of foreign debt but do not let the utility function be additively separable any more. Total differentiation of the first-order condition, equation (8.10), then yields

$$\frac{dc}{de} = \frac{u_1\left(gf_{ee} - 2sag'\,f_e + (sa)^2\,g''f\right) + (sa)^2\,u_{22} + u_{12}\left(gf_e - sag'f\right)}{u_{11}\left(gf_e - sag'f\right) - sau_{12}} \tag{8.20}$$

and the sign of this fraction is indeterminate. dc/de may be positive. In this case either consumption or environmental quality is inferior. dc/de has an impact on the movement of the state variable, v, along the optimal path. As can be seen from the Jacobian matrix in equation (8.15), the ($\dot{v} = 0$) line has a positive slope if dc/de is larger than the marginal productivity of the environmental resource, i.e. if the marginal increase in consumption exceeds the marginal increase in output. This is true if

$$\frac{d(gf-c)}{de} = \frac{u_1\left(gf_{ee} - 2sag'\,f_e + (sa)^2\,g''f\right) + (sa)^2\,u_{22} + u_{12}\left(gf_e - sag'f\right)^2}{u_{11}\left(gf_e - sag'f\right) - sau_{12}} \tag{8.21}$$

is negative. This may happen if u_{12} is negative and comparatively large.[10] Economically, this means that the consumption good is inferior, i.e. its demand is reduced when income is raised.[11] But this is not the only change in the dynamics of the system. The e component is affected as well $\dot{e}$ changes its sign at the same parameter constellation at which $d(gf - c)/de$ changes its sign.[12] Thus

---

[10] Although the standard utility functions like Cobb–Douglas have $u_{12}>0$, the opposite sign cannot be excluded.

[11] To show this, consider the static-optimization problem where utility, $u(c,-sae)$, is maximized subject to the condition that $c = g(-sae)f(k,e)+ \sigma$ where σ is the income from an exogenous source, i.e. a transfer such as unconditioned foreign aid. The condition for consumption to decline if this exogenous income is increased is $sau_{12}<u_{11}(gf_e-sag'f)$.

[12] This can be shown if growth rates are established in equation (8.9) and it is taken into account that u_{12} is different from zero and that c can be represented as a function of e according to equation (8.20).

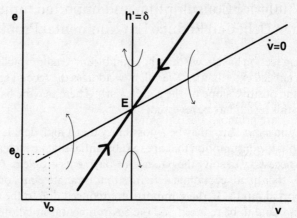

FIG. 8.3 A Saddle Path with Positive Slope

both off-diagonal elements change their signs at the same time, the determinant remains negative and the equilibrium remains stable in the saddle-point sense. However, the saddle path is now positively sloped (see Figure 8.3). At a small initial debt (high value of v_0), the emissions are larger than at a large initial debt (lower value of v_0).

Thus, one can state the following result:

Proposition 8.3. If the consumption good is inferior, initial emissions are a declining function of the initial debt.

Albeit interesting from a theoretical point of view, this result is unlikely to be of major relevance in practice. In this model, c does not represent the consumption of a particular commodity but the level of aggregate consumption in this economy. And a situation where the aggregate consumption is reduced when the disposable income rises seems to be rather strange and there is no evidence that such a phenomenon has been observed in the real world.

Let us now turn to the case where environmentally intensive production requires imported inputs. An example is sawing and transport equipment in countries that exploit their tropical rain forests. It is rather obvious, however, that in a one-good model of the economy the introduction of such an imported input does not alter the results significantly. To see this, assume that each unit of emissions requires imports of a unit of a foreign good at a price p^e. The first-order condition is changed such that

$$\lambda(gf_e - sag'f - p^e) = sau_2. \tag{8.22}$$

Since p is exogenously given in the small-country case, it cannot affect the dynamic structure of the optimal solution. As long as the marginal productivity of the environmental resource, $gf_e - sag'f$, exceeds the price of the imported good, resource exploitation and exports serve the purpose of debt service. Thus, the larger the foreign debt, the larger the rate of resource exploitation and the environmental disruption. If, however, the price of the imported input were larger than the marginal productivity of the environmental resource, then there would not exist any path satisfying the boundary conditions. Foreign debt could never be repaid.

One may argue that the saddle path would change its slope and that environmental quality could be an increasing function of debt if there were additional goods in the model. The underlying reasoning would be as follows: if goods that are primarily consumed at home are relatively dirty in their production and goods that are primarily exported are relatively clean, then the combined effect of the reduction in domestic consumption and the expansion of exports that are necessary to solve the balance-of-payments problem may be less pollution. This hypothesis will be examined under the assumption that the utility function is additively separable in aggregate consumption and environmental quality. Since it has been shown earlier that inferiority of aggregate consumption may lead to the reversal of the relationship between resource use and debt, this possibility will be excluded here. If there are n goods, the balance-of-payments equation turns out to be

$$\dot{v} = \sum_{i=1}^{n} g^i(-z)f^i(k^i,e^i) - p^i c^i - p^{e,i}e^i + h(v), \tag{8.23}$$

where p^i and $p^{e,i}$ represent the (exogenous) world market prices of the good i and of the input in industry i, respectively. Some goods will be exported and other goods may be imported, depending on domestic demand and world market prices. The first-order conditions of maximization with respect to c^i and e^i are

$$\lambda p^i = u_i, \quad \forall i \in \{1, \ldots, n\}, \tag{8.24}$$

$$\lambda(g^i f_e^i - sa^i \sum_j g^{j'} f^j - p^{e,i}) = sau_{n+1}, \quad \forall i \in \{1, \ldots, n\}, \tag{8.25}$$

where environmental quality is now the $(n + 1)$st good in the utility function. It can be shown now that the result of a positive correlation between debt and environmental damage remains unchanged. Since the proof is rather complicated and requires the introduction of matrix notation, it is given in the appendix to this chapter.

Proposition 8.4. In the case of free trade and superiority of aggregate consumption of goods, environmental pollution is an increasing function of foreign debt even in the many-goods case.

This is a strong result. A crucial assumption, however, is that there is free trade in all goods. If trade is restricted, the result may be reversed. To show this, let us assume that good i is not traded, i.e.

$$c^i = g^i(-z)f^i(k^i,e^i).$$

This can be inserted into the utility function and the first-order condition for the optimal e^i is

$$u_i(g^i f_e^i - sa^i \sum_j g^{j'} f^j) - sa^i u_{n+1} = \lambda p^{e,i}. \tag{8.27}$$

This can be differentiated with respect to time and growth rates can be established:

$$\left(\frac{u_{ii}\left(g^i f_e^i - sa^i \sum_j g^{j} f^{j}\right)^2 + (sa^i)^2 u_{n+1,n+1}}{u_i\left(g^i f_e^i - sa^i \sum_j g^{j} f^{j}\right) - sa^i u_{n+1}} \right.$$

$$\left. + \frac{u_i\left(g^i f_e^i - 2sa^i g^i f_e^i + (sa^i)^2 \left(\sum_j g^{j''} f^{j}\right)\right)}{u^i\left(g^i f_e^i - sa^i \sum_j g^{j} f^{j}\right) - sa^i u_{n+1}} \right) \dot{e}^i + \left\{ \ldots \right\} = \delta - h'. \qquad (8.28)$$

The last term on the left-hand side, represented by braces, contains the time-derivatives of the emissions of all the other sectors and of the consumption of all the other goods in this economy. This term vanishes if the cross-derivatives of the utility function are zero and if the other sectors do not use environmental resources in their production or if their resource inputs are constant for whatever reason. Since one example is sufficient to show that there are exceptions to the rule that foreign debt is bad for the environment, we assume that this is the case. The remaining term has a positive denominator and a negative numerator. Thus, $(\dot{e} > 0)$ if $h' > \delta$, i.e. if v is small. The Jacobian matrix is

$$J = \begin{pmatrix} \delta & -p^{e,i} + \ldots \\ -h''/\chi & 0 \end{pmatrix},$$

where χ represents the complicated term in brackets on the left-hand side of equation (8.28) and where the dots denote the effects of changes of e^i on the exports and imports of the other goods. It is possible that the overall effect of an increase in e^i on the balance of payments is negative (e.g. if the cross derivatives of the utility function are zero and the resource inputs in the other sectors are fixed). Therefore, the $(\dot{v} = 0)$ line can be positively sloped in this case. It follows that the phase diagram is the same as in Figure 8.3. The saddle path is positively sloped. Thus we have

Proposition 8.5. If the production of a non-traded good requires the use of environmental resources and if the utilization of the environmental resource requires intermediate inputs, then emissions and environmental disruption may be a decreasing function of foreign debt.

To give an example, we look at a tropical country in which a substantial part of the landless rural population moves to rain-forest areas, cuts the forests, and uses the land for subsistence production of agricultural goods. In such a situation, one may argue that import restrictions adopted to solve the debt problem can have a positive environmental impact on the environment if these restrictions affect mainly intermediate goods that are used to convert the forest into arable land. Whether this effect can offset the tendency of increased utilization of environmental resource in other sectors of the economy, is an empirical matter. One should note that it is essential that the good under consideration is non-tradable. And even agricultural goods produced for subsistence are tradable in principle. An increase in subsistence production can help to reduce the import dependency on agricultural goods. If this is true, we again arrive at the conclusion that the relationship between debt and environmental pollution or deforestation is positive.

To conclude: the result that a debt problem makes a country increase the utilization of its environmental resources is a rather robust one. The opposite relationship is possible theoretically but the conditions under which it may occur seem to be of little empirical relevance. There is, however, an additional caveat. The model framework that has been used here is based on the assumption of welfare maximizing behaviour by the government of the indebted country. One may wonder whether this is a realistic assumption. Deviations from welfare-maximizing behaviour may be caused by regulatory capture and, more trivially, by errors and lack of rationality. If, however, this were taken into account, almost any policy outcome would become explainable. And in order to avoid eclecticism, we have concentrated on the case of a benevolent optimizing government. A final reason for carrying on with the assumption that debt aggravates the environmental problem has to do with the research-strategic considerations. A number of interesting (and relevant) questions would vanish or have trivial answers. For example, a debt relief would always be counterproductive and an increase in foreign debt which would benefit the lender in economic and environmental terms would be infeasible. Debt-for-nature swaps would simply be the wrong policy instrument because they would be inferior to all other kinds of environmental agreements that do not affect the debt situation. If, however, the relationship between environmental disruption and foreign debt is a positive one, the policy implications will be less trivial.

8.6 Debt Forgiveness: The Lender's View

If it is true that a high foreign debt may have harmful environmental consequences, people in other countries who care about environmental disruption may be willing to act and improve the debt situation. Whether this concern is due to real spillovers like greenhouse warming or biodiversity loss or to psychological externalities like the killing of baby seals does not matter here. What matters is that there is some welfare loss and some willingness to pay. Thus the lending country may be willing to write off some of the debt in order to reduce the spillover. Alternatively (but equivalently), interested parties like environmentalist organizations may purchase a part of the debt and then write it off. During the investigation, we will concentrate on the debt–environment relationship and neglect other reasons that would make it profitable to the lender to write off parts of the credits.[13]

Let us assume that the net interest rate from the view of the lender is $r = h'(0)$. Of course the marginal interest rate an indebted country has to pay is

[13] It may be true that the willingness or ability to repay foreign debt depends on the level of indebtedness. If this function exhibits the bell-shaped curvature of a Laffer curve, the repayment may be increased if a part of the debt is relieved (see Krugman (1988) and Sachs (1989b)).

larger since h' increases with the debt. But the difference, $h'(v) - h'(0)$, is the premium which compensates the lender for the risk of default. We avoid the explicit modelling of risk here and take a short cut by assuming that r is the lender's rate of discount for the future benefits of a debt relief.[14] The lender (or the environmentalist group) has to trade off the reduction of claims against the improvement of environmental quality. Let the face value of the debt in the books be $(-\bar{v})$. If $(-v_0)$ is the level of indebtedness after the debt relief, the cost of forgiving this debt is $(\bar{v} - v_0)$. Obviously, $v_0 > \bar{v}$, i.e. the lender can implement a debt relief but never a unilateral increase in the debt. The environmental damage the lender is exposed to in each period is $Z = (1 - s)ae$,[15] and this is evaluated by an additively separable and strictly concave utility function $U(C, -Z)$. For the moment, the lender's consumption path is assumed to be exogenously given. Since the emissions in the foreign country are negatively related to the foreign-assets position of the indebted country along the saddle path, they may be expressed as

$$e = \psi(v) \tag{8.29}$$

with $\psi' < 0$ as the slope of the saddle path. Finally the dynamic properties of the saddle path can be described by $\dot{v} = \phi(v, v^*)$ where the equilibrium level, v^*, is determined by $h'(v^*) = \delta$ and where $\phi_v < 0$ and $\phi_v^* > 0$. In the linearized version of the model, the shape of $\phi(., .)$ depends on the second derivatives of the $h(.)$ function and of the indebted country's production and utility functions.

Under these assumptions, the lending country's optimization problem is to maximize

$$\bar{v} - v_0 + \int_0^\infty U(C, -(1-s)a\psi(v))e^{-rt}\,dt \tag{5.30}$$

with respect to v_0 and subject to the state condition

$$\dot{v} = \phi(v, v^*). \tag{8.31}$$

The current-value Hamiltonian of this problem is

$$\tilde{H} = U(C, -(1-s)a\psi(v)) + \Lambda(\phi(v, v^*)) \tag{8.32}$$

The second-order conditions are assumed to be satisfied, i.e. $\tilde{H}$ is concave in v. The shadow price, Λ, evolves according to

$$\dot{\Lambda} = (r - \phi_v)\Lambda + (1-s)aU_2\psi' \tag{8.33}$$

and its equilibrium value is determined by

$$\Lambda^* = -\frac{(1-s)aU_2\psi}{r - \varphi_v}. \tag{8.34}$$

---

[14] This is equivalent to assuming that the value of the debt is determined by the expected future interest payments, rv, that are derived from the future interest payments the country is obliged to make, $h(v)$, by use of a correction factor that incorporates the default risk

[15] Note that this implies that the lending country's emissions are not affected by a debt relief. The underlying assumption is that the lender's interest rate is not changed by a change in its foreign-assets position, i.e. Fisher's separation theorem holds for the lending country.

From the concavity of the Hamiltonian, it follows that Λ^* is a declining function of the indebted country's foreign-assets position, v.

In an optimum, the lender's welfare loss due to a marginal reduction of the debt must equal the marginal welfare gain due to the improvement in environmental quality associated with the debt relief. The marginal welfare loss equals 1, the marginal gain is measured by the shadow price of foreign assets at time 0. Thus, the optimality condition is

$$\Lambda(0) = 1. \tag{8.35}$$

The optimal solution is depicted in Figure 8.4. It shows a (v,Λ) diagram with the $(\dot{v} = 0)$ line, the $(\dot{\lambda} = 0)$ line, and the saddle path, which is negatively sloped. The initial value of v has to be chosen such that the corresponding value of Λ on the saddle path equals 1. If the historically inherited debt is larger than this optimal initial debt, i.e. $\bar{v} < v_0$, then a debt relief is optimal from the lending country's point of view. If the inherited debt is smaller than the optimal one, it would be optimal to increase the debt until the marginal value of foreign assets equals the marginal environmental damage. However, such an intervention into the foreign-assets position of the indebted country is not possible since the lender cannot unilaterally increase the debt.

The results can be summarized as follows

Proposition 8.6. There may exist incentives for a lender to adopt an unconditioned debt relief for environmental reasons. The weaker the relationship between debt and the environment the weaker the incentives to adopt a debt relief.

In the case of only a small impact of the debt on the emissions, even a large debt relief results in only small improvements in the environmental situation

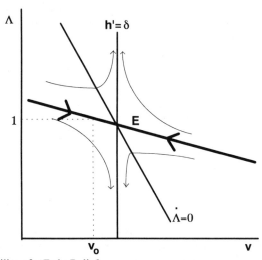

FIG. 8.4 Desirability of a Debt Relief

and its net welfare effects for the lender country may therefore be negative. Thus, the lender's willingness to use an unconditioned debt relief as an instrument of environmental policy is limited. Since the borrower, however, always benefits from a relief, it may wish to take some additional measures to improve its environmental policy and to raise the incentives to the lending country to forgive some of the foreign debt.

8.7 The Economics of Debt-for-Nature Swaps

A debt-for-nature swap is a conditional debt relief where the debt is forgiven subject to the condition that the indebted country takes measures to improve the conservation of its natural and environmental resources. Often, these measures have taken the shape of declaring tropical-forest areas as natural reserves. Although this instrument has became rather popular towards the end of the 1980s, it has not become a major subject of economic analysis. Studies concerned with the issue are Borregaard and Meyer (1988), Pillarisetti (1991), and Strand (1994). Borregaard and Meyer (1988) look at the indebted country only. They argue that the debt relief has an impact on the discount rate and that this reduces the utilization of renewable environmental resources. An additional resource-conserving effect comes from the constraint on the resource-extraction rate which is negotiated as part of the swap. This model suffers from two shortcomings: the effect of the external debt on the discount rate lacks a foundation and the incentives of the lender to participate in the swap are not analysed. Pillarisetti (1991) also looks at the debt-for-nature swap from the point of view of the indebted country and addresses the questions as to how the consumption, investment, and resource-conservation profiles are affected by the swap. The model framework is a two-period model where measures of environmental conservation are undertaken in period one and the compensation payment is made in period two. Although this payment is called a debt relief, it could also be any other kind of compensation payment which is not linked to the external debt. A genuine debt-for-nature swap is analysed by Strand (1994). In contrast to the model used in this chapter, Strand's approach takes account of default risks explicitly in a two-periods model setting. The debt-for-nature swap takes the shape of debt forgiveness in exchange for a part of the indebted country's resource stock. We will have to take a slightly different modelling framework here since our basic lending model does not contain a resource stock. We will, therefore, assume that the debt-for-nature swap allows the borrower to influence the time profile of the extraction of environmental resources.

The borrower and the lender countries are modelled as before. They are connected via a debt-for-nature arrangement and we will ultimately address the question whether this is an efficient way of compensating a resource-rich country for restricting its resource utilization or whether other types of side payments achieve the same environmental objective at a lower price.

The objective of the lending country is again to maximize the present value of welfare which is composed of the loss due to the debt relief and the discounted sum of future utility derived from environmental quality:

$$\bar{v} - v_0 + \int_0^\infty U(C(t), -(1-s)ae(t))e^{-rt}\, dt. \tag{8.30}$$

The lender proposes to the government of the indebted country a reduction in the external debt in exchange for a loss of sovereignty in its environmental policy. The indebted country is willing to accept this proposal if its welfare level is not diminished compared to a situation without a debt-for-environment agreement. We assume here that any agreement following the acceptance of the proposal is binding, i.e. issues of default and renegotiation are neglected. Thus, the constraints under which the objective function, (8.30), is maximized are:

$$\dot{v}(t) = g(-sae(t))f(k,e(t)) - c(t) + h(v(t)), \tag{8.2}$$

$$\lim_{t\to\infty} v(t) \geq v_1 > -\infty, \tag{8.4}$$

$$\dot{w} = e^{-\delta t}u(c(t), -sae(t)), \tag{8.36}$$

$$\lim_{t\to\infty} w(t) \geq \bar{w}. \tag{8.37}$$

$\bar{w}$ is the reservation level of welfare of the indebted country. Welfare has to be at least as large as in the unconstrained case without a debt-for-nature agreement.[16] Moreover, the lending country is unable to unilaterally increase the debt, i.e. $\bar{v} \leq v_0$.

The control variables are the initial debt, v_0, the rate of utilization of the environmental resource, $e(t)$, and the consumption path, $c(t)$. That the lender can determine the initial debt level is plausible. Moreover, the debt-for-nature contract gives the lender the possibility to influence the indebted country's environmental policy. The consumption path cannot be chosen by the lender, but if she could choose the consumption path, she would choose the same one the benevolent government of the indebted country would consider to be optimal.[17]

The current-value Hamiltonian of this maximization problem is

$$\tilde{H} = U(C, -(1-s)ae) + \Lambda^v(g(-sae)f(k,e) - c + h(v)) + \Lambda^w u(c, -sae), \tag{5.38}$$

where Λ^v and Λ^w are the shadow prices denoting the values of the indebted country's assets position and welfare, respectively, to the lending country. The first-order optimality conditions are

---

[16] The indebted country may even be able to negotiate an agreement with an even higher welfare level if its bargaining power is large enough, i.e. $\bar{w}$ may be larger than the welfare level attainable without the swap. But this would not change the following results. Of course, it would be interesting to determine $\bar{w}$ endogenously in the model. The adequate way of doing this would be a Nash bargaining model (see Friedman (1989, ch. 5)). However, this route will not be taken here since bargaining power is not of major concern here.

[17] Otherwise, the reservation welfare level could only be attained if a larger part of the debt were forgiven. Of course, this would be inefficient.

$$\dot{\Lambda}^v = (r - h')\Lambda^v, \tag{8.39a}$$

$$\dot{\Lambda}^w = (r - \delta)\Lambda^w, \tag{8.39b}$$

$$\Lambda^v = u_1\Lambda^w, \tag{8.39c}$$

$$\Lambda^v(gf_e - asg'f) - sau_2\Lambda^w = (1 - s)aU_2, \tag{8.39d}$$

$$\Lambda^v(0) = 1. \tag{8.39e}$$

Equations (8.39a) to (8.39c) can be used to determine the consumption growth path:

$$\frac{\dot{c}}{c} = \varsigma(h' - \delta), \tag{8.40}$$

where $\varsigma = -u_1/(cu_{11})$ is the intertemporal elasticity of substitution for consumption goods. This is Ramsey's rule, which is a standard result of optimal-growth models. Consumption is growing if the rate of return to the asset exceeds the discount rate (see Ramsey (1928)). Moreover, we have from equations (8.39c) and (8.39d) that

$$gf_e = sag'f + sa\frac{u_2}{u_1} + (1 - s)a\frac{U_2}{\Lambda^w u_1}. \tag{8.41}$$

The right-hand side of this equation represents the total social cost of environmental disruption due to the production in the indebted country. The last term denotes the transfrontier environmental damage. It is evaluated by the marginal utility of consumption times the costate variable, i.e. shadow-price, of the indebted country's welfare. The higher the reservation level of welfare, the larger is this costate variable and the smaller the effect of transboundary pollution on the environmental tax rate in the indebted country. Anyway, the emission tax rate, gf_e, is higher (at a given level of consumption) than without the debt-for-nature swap.

The long-run equilibrium is given by

$$h' = r, \tag{8.42a}$$

$$gf + h = c^*. \tag{8.42b}$$

It follows from equations (8.40) and (8.42a) that consumption grows at a rate $\varsigma(r - \delta)$ in the steady state. In order to avoid complications with non-stationary control variables in the long run, it is assumed here that

$$r = \delta \tag{8.43}$$

and this implies that Λ^w is constant along the optimal path. As in Section 8.3 we can show that the ($\dot{v} = 0$) line is declining in the (v, e) phase space and that c and e are negatively related to each other along the optimal path. In the long-run equilibrium, e and c are smaller than in the case without the debt-for-nature swap.[18]

[18] This follows from equations (8.41) and (8.42b). Total differentiation of these equations with respect to $e, c,$ and U_2 yields the result that both emissions and consumption in the indebted country are decreasing functions of the lender's environmental concern.

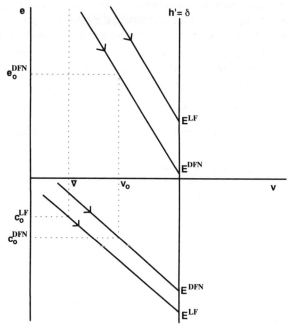

FIG. 8.5 The Impact of a Debt -for-Nature Swap on Emissions and Consumption in the Indebted Country

The optimal paths of emissions and consumption in the cases of a debt-for-nature agreement (DFN) and of *laissez-faire* (LF) are depicted in Figure 8.5. The long-run equilibrium with a debt-for-nature swap is characterized by lower emissions and lower consumption than in the *laissez-faire* case. The indebted country is compensated for taking account of the lender's environmental concerns by a reduction in the initial debt which allows a higher consumption path in the initial periods.

The effects of a successful debt-for-nature swap can be summarized as follows:

Proposition 8.7. A debt-for-nature swap leads to the consideration of transfrontier pollution by the indebted country. Long-run emissions and consumption will be reduced. In the initial periods, the debt relief leads to higher consumption.

8.8. General Side Payments

A debt-for-nature agreement involves a very particular scheme of side payments. There is a single once-and-for-all compensation payment at the beginning of the time-horizon. The question arises as to whether there are more efficient ways of making the indebted country take account of the transboundary spillovers of its environmental-resource use. In order to investigate this, we look at a general compensation scheme where the pollutee agrees to compensate the polluter for the emission reduction at a variable rate in each period, $\sigma(t)$. A special case of this general compensation scheme is the debt-for-nature swap, where $\sigma(t)$ is very large for $t = 0$ and zero afterwards.

The lender's objective function is

$$\int_0^\infty U(C(t) - \sigma(t), -(1-s)e(t))e^{-\delta t}\,dt \tag{8.44}$$

and it is maximized with respect to $e(t)$, $c(t)$, and $\sigma(t)$ and subject to the constraints

$$\dot{v}(t) = g(-ae(t))f(k,e(t)) - c(t) + \sigma(t) + h(v(t)), \tag{8.45}$$

$$\lim_{t\to\infty} v(t) \geq v_1 > -\infty, \tag{8.4}$$

$$\dot{w} = e^{-\delta t}u(c(t), -sae(t)), \tag{8.36}$$

$$\lim_{t\to\infty} w(t) \geq \bar{w}. \tag{8.37}$$

The Hamiltonian is

$$\tilde{H} = U(C, -\sigma, -(1-s)ae) + \Lambda^v(g(-sae)f(k,e) - c + \sigma + h(v)) \tag{8.46}$$
$$+ \Lambda^w u(c, -sae),$$

and the first-order optimality conditions are

$$\dot{\Lambda}^v = (\delta - h')\Lambda^v, \tag{8.47a}$$

$$\dot{\Lambda}^w = 0, \tag{8.47b}$$

$$\Lambda^v = u_1\Lambda^w, \tag{8.47c}$$

$$\Lambda^v(gf_e - asg'f) - sau_2\Lambda^w = (1-s)aU_2, \tag{8.47d}$$

$$\Lambda^v = U_1. \tag{8.47e}$$

Compared to the previous section, where the debt-for-nature swap has been discussed, there is only one major change in the optimality conditions. Equation (8.47e) holds for the whole time-horizon, whereas equation (8.39e) determined only the initial value for the costate variable. By establishing growth rates in equation (8.47e), one can easily determine the optimal time-profile of the compensation payments:

$$\dot{\sigma} = \frac{U_1}{U_{11}}(h' - \delta). \tag{8.48}$$

In the case of a perfect capital market, h' and δ would be equal during the whole time horizon and the optimal side payment would be constant along the optimal path. In the case of capital market imperfection, however, this equality only holds in the long run. For an indebted country, $h' > \delta$ during the initial periods and this implies:

*Proposition 8.8. In the case where side payments are an argument in the pollu-
tee's welfare function and the polluter is a problem-debtor country, the optimal
side payment is declining through time and approaches a constant equilibrium
level in the long run.*

The constancy of the long-run side payment would hold even in the case
where the discount rates of the two countries differ.

Finally, note that the side-payments scheme as it has been introduced into
the model here included the possibility of a debt-for-nature swap, i.e a large initial side payment and zero payments afterwards. However, the debt-for-nature
swap has not turned out to be the optimal way of compensating the indebted
country. This implies:

Proposition 8.9. A debt-for-nature swap is an inefficient way of compensation.

This kind of inefficiency would also occur if the lender appropriated a part
of an environmental resource stock as in Strand's (1994) paper. However,
Strand (1994) did not compare the debt-for-environment swap with other
kinds of side payment schemes.

Proposition 8.9 does not mean, however, that the idea of the debt-for-nature
swap is totally wrong. Like the optimal compensation scheme, the debt-for-
environment swap involves a high payment in the first period and smaller (i.e.
zero) payments in the longer term. If external indebtedness of developing
countries aggravates the environmental problems, an optimal compensation
scheme must always include a debt-reducing component in the initial periods.
Thus, if debt-for-nature swaps are the initial measures of a longer-term environmental agreement, they may be interpreted as a part of an efficient compensation scheme.

8.9 Summary of Results

1. Highly indebted countries tend to use their environmental resources at
   higher rates then countries with low debt levels.
2. A positive impact of foreign debt on environmental quality can be expected
   under the unrealistic assumptions of (i) the inferiority of aggregate consumption or (ii) the existence of very pollution-intensive non-traded goods.
3. Unconditioned debt reliefs may mitigate environmental problems, but the
   incentives to use these instruments are very small.
4. Debt-for-environment swaps tend to reduce environmental disruption in
   the short and the long run. The indebted country is compensated for lower
   long-run consumption possibilities by higher consumption levels in the
   initial periods.
5. Debt-for-environment swaps are inefficient means of compensation. The
   time-path of the efficient compensation scheme is smoother than that of a
   genuine debt-for-environment swap.

Appendix:
Many Goods in the Debt Model

The proof that environmental disruption is an increasing function of foreign debt will proceed as follows. We will represent the optimal values of emissions and consumption as functions of the shadow price λ. Then the canonical equations, (8.2) and (8.4), will be linearized in the equilibrium and the initial results will be used to eliminate e and c from this system, such that there are only two differential equations in two variables. The shape of the saddle path will be examined. Then environmental pollution, z, will be expressed as a function of λ and from this we can infer the desired relationship between z and v.

Equation (8.25) can be rewritten in matrix notation:

$$\lambda \vartheta = su' a \qquad (8.A1)$$

where ϑ is a column vector whose ith component is $(g^i f_e^i - p^i - sa^i \sum_j g^{j\prime} f^j)$, a is a vector of the same dimension containing the a^is as its components. Moreover u' is used to represent u_{n+1} for notational brevity and convenience. Total differentiation yields

$$\vartheta \, d\lambda + \lambda \Theta de = -(sa)u'' A \, de.$$

e is the vector of emission rates, e^i. Θ is matrix with elements equalling the second derivatives of gf with respect to e. They are all negative and the matrix is negative definite since all f^is are strictly concave in the e^is and the externalities, represented by the g^i functions, are negative. A is a matrix whose ith-row jth-column element is $a^i a^j$. It is symmetric and its rank is 1. Finally, u''. has been used to replace $u_{n+1,n+1}$. The equation can be solved for de:

$$de = -(\Theta + s^2 u'' A)^{-1} \vartheta d\lambda. \qquad (8.A2)$$

The matrix in the right-hand side of this equation is symmetric. It consists of negative elements and its diagonal elements are dominant (i.e. their absolute values exceed the absolute values of the off-diagonal elements in the same row or column). Thus this matrix is negative definite.

In the same fashion, we can derive

$$dc = U^{-1} p d\lambda, \qquad (8.A3)$$

where U is the matrix of second derivatives of the utility function, which is negative definite, and p is the vector of goods prices.

These results can be used to linearize the state equation (8.2) in the equilibrium and the dynamics of the optimal path are characterized by

$$\begin{pmatrix} \dot{v} \\ \dot{\lambda} \end{pmatrix} = \begin{pmatrix} \delta & -\vartheta^T(\Theta + s^2 u'' A)^{-1} \vartheta - p^T U p \\ h''/\lambda & 0 \end{pmatrix} \begin{pmatrix} v - v^* \\ e - e^* \end{pmatrix}, \qquad (8.A4)$$

where the superscript T denotes the transpose of a matrix or a vector. Due to the definiteness properties of the matrices, the first-row second-column element of the matrix on the right-hand side of this equation is positive. The system is stable in the saddle-point sense and saddle path has a negative slope in the (v, λ) phase space. This is shown in Figure 8A.1.

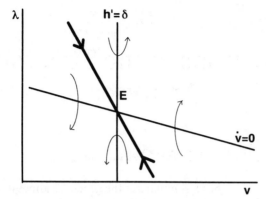

FIG. 8A.1 Optimal Paths of Foreign Assets and the Shadow Price

Pollution is the sum of the pollution impacts of all sectors:

$$z = sa^T c,$$ (8.A5)

and it follows that

$$dz = -sa^T (\Theta + s^2 u'' A)^{-1} \vartheta \, d\lambda.$$ (8.A6)

Now equation (8.A1) can be used and we obtain

$$dz = -\frac{\lambda}{u'} \vartheta^T (\Theta + s^2 u'' A)^{-1} \vartheta d\lambda.$$ (8.A7)

Since $(\Theta + s^2 u'' A)^{-1}$ is negative definite, this implies that z is an increasing function of λ and, therefore, a declining function of the stock of foreign assets. Thus, the larger the foreign debt, the worse the environmental situation.

9

Implications of the Theoretical Analyses

9.1 An Overview

This final chapter of this book summarizes the general findings of the theoretical inquiry and attempts to derive some policy implications. In the previous chapters a large number of results have been derived from different models some of which have been very specialized. These many results add up to a more general perspective on the links between international economic relationships and the environment and on the problems associated with these links. After the summary of the main findings, policy implications of the theoretical analysis will be discussed. This will be done in two parts. The first part is devoted to policies, i.e. the determination of emission taxes, tariffs, and interventions into capital markets. The second part deals with institutions that define the frameworks in which trade and environmental policies are made. We look at national institutions and at supranational ones. In particular, we will be interested in how the delicate issue of green trade conflicts can be settled in the framework of international trade and environmental agreements.

9.2 Summary of Results

The general conclusion from the previous analyses is that second-best considerations are essential for an understanding of the links between trade and environmental policies. A first-best world would be characterized by Pigouvian environmental policies that internalize all environmental externalities and by unrestricted trade and factor movements. This ideal state of the world may serve as a benchmark to which the second-best results can be compared. All results that are not pro-free-trade or that state the optimality of non-Pigouvian environmental policies are based on the existence of distortions. With the first best in mind, one will find it easier to identify the distortions that are responsible for deviations from the ideal environmental or trade policies.

9.2.1 The Patterns of Trade and Factor Movements

The results that have been established on the direction of foreign trade and factor movements are hardly surprising. A distinction has been made between the 'true' endowment of a country with environmental resources or the *de facto* endowment. The 'true' endowment represents the scarcity of environmental resources derived from the physical and technological characteristics of a country and the preferences of its residents. The *de facto* endowment is defined by the environmental policy of the government which may be biased in one direction or the other. It is seen that countries with lax environmental standards usually tend to specialize on pollution-intensive goods and that they attract foreign capital and hazardous waste. However, there are exceptions to this rule if production activities are negatively affected by environmental pollution. If these externalities on production are substantial, the patterns of trade may be reversed or a country with tight environmental policies may attract the mobile factors of production. The consideration of the 'true' endowment leads to the expected results as well. High pollution-impact parameters and an environmentally conscious population will lead to tight environmental standards and taxes and to the corresponding patterns of trade and factor movements.

From an economic theory point of view, there is no need to harmonize environmental taxes and standards. The endowments of different countries with environmental resources are determined by technological parameters and the preferences of the residents. An artificial levelling of the playing-field would cause inefficient factor allocations and smaller (if not negative) gains from trade.[1] There is only one case in which the harmonization of environmental standards is desirable. This is the global environmental problem, e.g. global warming or destruction of the ozone layer, where the environmental damage is independent of the location of the source of emissions. That this kind of harmonization is not observed in reality, however, is not problem of international trade but that of the global commons. Each country has an incentive to care only about the share of the damage it has to bear itself. And these shares are small and may well differ across countries.

9.2.2 *Environmental Disruption and the Gains from Trade*

The debate on the environmental consequences of international trade has produced opposing views on the desirability of free trade and factor movements. Here, we will address this question from a single country's point of view. The important issue whether trade causes a race to the bottom when countries use their environmental regulations to compete against others will be addressed later on.

The results derived on the environmental impact of trade and factor movements are rather diverse. In contrast to what is claimed by some environmentalists, foreign trade (even in toxic waste) is not generally bad for the environment. But even if it increases environmental disruption, openness can be good for an

---

[1] Anyway, the theoretical analysis predicts that there will be a kind of a voluntary harmonization after trade has commenced.

economy. There is usually a trade-off between environmental quality and the availability of private consumer goods and a social consensus may be reached that some environmental quality is sacrificed for better material living standards. Therefore, the result that some countries tend to be more polluted with than without trade is by itself not yet a reason to complain about the destructiveness of trade. One should look at a more general welfare measure than mere environmental quality. Trade liberals claim to do just this, but the extreme view held by some free-traders that openness is always beneficial is wrong as well. Openness is better than autarky if all environmental externalities, including transfrontier pollution spillovers, are perfectly taken care of by environmental policy, i.e. if individual producers and consumers are signalled the total social cost of their activities.

However, real-world environmental policies are often far from correctly internalizing environmental externalities and, therefore, the first-best scenario is of limited practical relevance. What can go wrong?

First, there are no—or only limited—incentives to a policy-maker to care about environmental damage occurring across the border. In contrast, it is desirable to her to rather externalize as many environmental problems as possible. An example is the policy of the high smoke-stacks followed in the 1960s and 1970s to reduce local air pollution problems—at the expense of long-distance environmental damage caused by acid rain. Free international trade and factor movements may aggravate these problems. The relocation of the factors of production to pollution-intensive sectors in less regulated countries may increase the environmental problems of a highly regulated country, particularly in border regions. This was one of the important environmental issues during the NAFTA negotiations. Of course, it would be desirable to internalize these environmental problems, but this may be rather difficult because there exists no supranational entities which enforce the internalization of the environmental damage occurring on the other side of the border.

The second problem is that environmental policies usually do not even internalize the domestic social costs of pollution correctly. Even in the absence of transboundary pollution, environmental policies tend to be distorted. These distortions can take both directions: underinternalization or overinternalization of the social costs of environmental disruption. The underlying reasons are the influence of idiosyncratic interest groups on the political process and informational deficiencies due to the difficulty to correctly assess environmental damage. If environmental policy is biased in one direction or another, the gains from trade are not always positive any more. In the case of the country which attracts mobile capital, specializes on pollution-intensive goods, or becomes an importer of hazardous waste, environmental pollution from production activities is likely to be increased after trade. Moreover, the specialization effects may make higher consumption levels possible, which in turn causes additional environmental harm. If the environmental policy in this country does not internalize the damages to a sufficient degree, the increase in pollution may be so large that the net welfare effect is negative despite the enlargement of the consumption possibility set. The other country may also be worse off if its environmental policy is too tight. Then the price changes induced by openness can lead to a reduction in emissions by so much that its negative output effect dominates the positive effects of free trade or factor movements.

Thirdly, additional problems may arise if we consider market entry and exit. In industries with increasing returns to scale, freer trade will induce concentration processes, i.e. some firms will have to leave the market. Usually, these are high-cost firms. In the case of insufficient environmental regulation, however, private and social costs diverge and the wrong firms may have to leave the market, in particular those that use environmentally friendly but expensive production processes. With a sound environmental policy, high taxes would be imposed on firms producing with a larger pollution intensity and they would be the ones that would fall victim to the concentration process. Thus, an incorrect environmental policy may cause an adverse selection on the supply side of the market. The survival of the dirtiest, however, is not a problem of trade liberalization but of the deficiencies of environmental regulation.

Moreover, there is the issue of instrument choice. It has been shown that a move from autarky to capital mobility may cause welfare losses if the environmental policy leaves rents to capital owners. This policy is an indirect subsidization of capital and, therefore, leads to an inefficient allocation if capital is mobile. It may happen that a country which originally is capital-rich attracts foreign direct investments since foreign capital owners are paid more than the marginal product of their factor. If the movement of capital takes the correct direction, the gains will always be positive, however smaller than they could be.

Finally, transportation is a source of environmental disruption. Transportation activities tend to be increased by foreign trade and they may be harmful to the environment. In particular, if these activities are performed in international environmental media like the oceans or the international air spaces, there are not sufficient incentives to internalize the corresponding environmental externalities. Thus, the social costs of transportation may easily dominate the private benefits. Again, this is a problem of second-best policies. If the environmental externalities were internalized perfectly, only those transportation activities would be undertaken that provide a non-negative net benefit to society as a whole.

The review of the empirical literature has revealed an additional aspect of openness which has not been addressed in the theoretical chapters of the book. Openness provides access to foreign technological knowledge. If new technologies have been developed under tighter environmental requirements than old technologies, the dissemination of new technologies tends to improve environmental quality. Moreover, for firms investing in foreign countries the relevant environmental regulation is not necessarily that of the host country. Fixed and sunk costs may make it cheaper to use environmentally friendly technologies, that have been developed for domestic plants elsewhere than to redesign them for laxer standards. Thus, in many real-world situations the binding restriction is not the environmental regulation of a pollution haven but that of a highly regulated country. This tends to reduce the environmental problems created by trade; it even may turn them into the converse. Foreign trade and factor movements may promote environmental quality by the dissemination of environmentally friendly technologies and products.[2]

So far, we have discussed the issue under the premiss of given environmental policies. What will happen if environmental policies are adjusted after a country has been opened to trade or factor movements? It has been shown that, in general, the country well endowed with environmental resources faces the necessity to use tighter environmental taxes and standards, and the capital-rich countries may wish to relax their environmental policies. Due to the changes in the allocation of the factors of production, the demand for environmental resources is increased in the country attracting pollution-intensive production. This scarcity should be reflected in prices, for instance in emission taxes. In contrast, the pressure on environmental resources is reduced in capital-rich countries because these countries tend to export their environmental problems. This should be reflected in lower prices. In reality, these comparative-static results tend to be overlaid by a general trend towards tighter regulation everywhere. So the speed at which environmental standards are tightened should be faster in former pollution havens.

The conclusion to be drawn from the exercise is that trade is not always beneficial when environmental externalities matter. But if the gains from trade are negative, the cause is not trade liberalization but the insufficiency of environmental regulation.

9.2.3 Environmental Policy in Open Economies: Is Ecological Dumping a Problem?

One of the central questions addressed in all of the chapters of this study has been to what extent environmental policies are influenced by trade-related policy objectives. In particular, we have tried to address the issue of ecological dumping. What may make a government use lax environmental policies to affect international trade and/or factor movements? It has been shown that quite a few candidates exists as an explanation of biased environmental policies in open economies. The policy outcome, however, is not always environmental dumping but often the converse.

In perfectly competitive economies that are small in international markets, only a few reasons exist as to why trade-related policy goals may lead to deviations from Pigouvian environmental taxes. First of all, there may be distortions due to failure in the choice of environmental policy instruments. If a

---

[2] The effect of the availability of new goods tends to be much larger than the traditional static gains from trade. See Romer (1994) for the theoretical argument and a calibrated model showing the practical relevance of this consideration.

command-and-control approach to environmental regulation is chosen that allows foreign capital owners to appropriate rents that are due to the scarcity of domestic environmental resources, then it is usually optimal to use very tight environmental standards. The reason is that the opportunity costs of tight environmental standards are reduced if a part of the scarcity rent goes to foreigners. However, the opposite case is also possible since the (hypothetical) emission tax revenue curve may be bell-shaped, and therefore tighter standards may actually raise the incentive to invest. A completely different argument in favour of biased environmental policies has been identified in the foreign-debt model. If the marginal cost of being indebted is not constant but increasing, then environmental resources tend to be over-used. The underlying problem is the capital market imperfection which makes it desirable for an indebted country to pay back the foreign debt as soon as possible. In order to achieve this goal, environmental quality is sacrificed during the initial periods.

Additional reasons for an influence of trade considerations on environmental policies turn up if we move from small competitive economies to large or imperfectly competitive ones. Initially, we will look at the first case, where firms have no market power.

A large country has potential monopoly power in international markets. If firms and households act as price-takers, they are unable to exert this market power. This is a reason for a benevolent government to intervene. The conventional (and first-best) policy instrument is a trade tax or, if there are international factor movements, a tax or subsidy on the domestic utilization of the mobile factor. However, if these instruments are not available, e.g. if their use is prohibited by trade agreements, then environmental regulation provides a more indirect means to influence international prices. The policy objective is to improve the terms of trade, i.e. to raise the relative prices of domestic export goods, or to change the remuneration of the mobile factor such that the return on investment is increased if the country is a capital exporter and decreased if it is an importer. The economic means to achieve this can be either tight or lax environmental standards depending on the position of a country in the international division of labour. A country well endowed with environmental resources should increase the scarcity of environmental resources by using tight standards, the resource-poor country should use lax environmental standards. These policy recommendations may be reversed if factor productivities are affected severely by environmental quality. In the monopolistically competitive model with differentiated goods and intra-industry trade, a country can exert the market power in the niches occupied by domestic firms by tight standards. Thus, as far as the issue of ecological dumping is concerned, no unambiguous results can be derived. Finally, as a caveat, one should note that the empirical relevance of the terms-of-trade argument is probably insignificant. The impact of environmental regulation on final goods prices is very small and, therefore, it is unlikely that governments really take account of potential terms-of-trade improvements when designing their environmental policies.

Another trade effect which may lead to biased environmental policies is carbon leakage. A large country which introduces higher emission taxes or tighter standards will induce factor movements and/or changes in the global division of labour. Usually this leads to increased emissions in the rest of the world. In applied general-equilibrium models, this effect has been estimated to be about 10 per cent of the initial emission reduction (albeit the variance of the results is substantial). In the case of pollution spillovers, particularly for global pollution spillovers, this reduces the incentives to tighten environmental regulation. The result will be what has been called ecological dumping in Chapter 2. In theory, these considerations are valid for large countries only, since small countries have no incentive at all to care about global environmental problems. None the less, they may be applied to small countries as well if these—for whatever reasons—wish to contribute, if only marginally, to the solution of global environmental problems.

In the case of imperfect competition, there may be additional reasons to use environmental policies for the achievement of trade objectives. Foreign monopoly profits can be shifted to the home country by high consumption taxes. In the case of international oligopolies, the policy implications are ambiguous. Lax environmental regulation provides an incentive to domestic producers to produce more and this may raise their profits by more than low emission taxes cost in terms of environmental deterioration. However, this result may no longer hold if the oligopolists' strategic variables are prices rather than quantities and if the model is extended by market interdependencies or entry by new firms. Moreover, high taxes may induce process innovation and can be beneficial in the longer term. Similarly, tight environmental product standards may promote product innovation and, thus, increase the competitiveness of domestic firms. However, since tight environmental standards always raise costs, it is not certain that the strategic innovation effect dominates the cost effect. This is another reason why no clear-cut policy implication can be derived from international oligopoly models with strategic environmental policy. Finally, it should be mentioned that carbon-leakage effects are relevant in these models as well. An environmental policy which makes foreign firms raise their outputs tends to aggravate transfrontier pollution. As in the competitive case, the consideration of this effect leads to laxer regulation of domestic firms, i.e. to environmental dumping.

Additional issues arise in the case of foreign direct investment if there are indivisibilities, e.g. if only one plant will be built in one out of two or more potential host countries. In this case, the environmental policy will usually not be determined by marginal conditions. A country wishing to be the host simply has slightly to undercut its competitors' environmental tax rates; a country not desirous of being the host has to chose its regulation such that the investor moves to somewhere else. Usually neither of these policies will lead to a tax rate which correctly internalizes the environmental externality.

Besides the welfare considerations that underlie the environmental policies discussed up to here, the capture of political processes by pressure groups may explain much of the biases in environmental and trade policies that we observe in reality. If protection of domestic producers is achieved by means of efficient policy instruments, we should expect low taxes on domestic consumption goods and tight regulation of production processes and product quality. The reason is that low taxes on consumption are equivalent to output subsidization and this is the cost-efficient instrument of protection. Tight regulation of production processes and product quality benefit those factors of production that are needed for the achievement of these goals, e.g. owners of pollution-abatement capital and of inputs needed for product improvement. Matters are different if inefficient means of protection are chosen. Then it is more likely that the regulation of production is relaxed and that product standards are used to discriminate against foreigners. It has been shown, moreover, that environmental interest groups follow interests which are sometimes in harmony and sometimes in conflict with those of the regulatees. Particularly if tight environmental standards are applied to foreign goods that are imported into domestic markets, there tends to be a coalition of environmentalist and protectionist interests.

On the whole, we have identified many good reasons for environmental dumping but about equally many good reasons to expect the converse. A general conclusion into which direction environmental policy will be biased by the consideration of trade-related objectives cannot be drawn.

9.2.4 The 'Race to the Bottom' versus 'Not in My Backyard'

Since it is not clear whether or not foreign trade leads to ecological dumping, the outcome of the interjurisdictional competition in the field of environmental regulation is ambiguous as well. Strategic behaviour by national regulating entities may lead to regulatory levels that are higher or lower than the optimal ones. If they are too low, the question arises how low may they be: does the race to the bottom come to an end before zero regulation is reached? The answer to this question depends on the model parameters, in particular on the relationship between environmental disruption and emission taxation. If the social costs of environmental disruption go to infinity as emission taxes go to zero, as in many theoretical models, the race towards the bottom will come to a halt before the bottom is reached. However, if the social costs are finite, the race may even go through the bottom and stop only at negative tax rates, i.e. subsidies for the use of environmental resources.[3] By the same line of argument one can establish that there is no generally valid upper-bound for environmental regulation. Whether or not emission taxes are chosen that are prohibitively high, again depends on the parameters of the damage function

---

[3] The subsidization of the use of coal, the dirtiest of all fossil fuels, in many countries illustrates the practical relevance of this possibility.

but also on economic parameters of the demand and supply sides of the economy. Keeping this in mind, we will use the terms 'race to the bottom' and 'not in my backyard' to illustrate the cases where interjurisdictional competition leads to too low and too high levels of environmental regulation, respectively.

A race towards too low levels of environmental regulation may have the following reasons:

- Carbon-leakage effects diminish the efficiency of an individual country's environmental policy. Thus all countries have incentives to use their environmental policies to attract mobile capital or to specialize on the production of pollution-intensive goods themselves. The global environmental problem is aggravated.[4]
- If there are interest groups in all countries that lobby successfully for lax environmental standards (and if terms-of-trade effects are sufficiently small), countries tend to compete with each other down to undesirably low levels of regulation.
- Lax environmental standards may be used to give indirect subsidies to strategic industries. If other countries retaliate and themselves act strategically, environmental standards tend to be too low.
- Lax environmental standards can help to attract foreign direct investment. If the investment is indivisible (e.g. a single plant), then a tax competition is possible which makes the net benefits of being the host vanish. Transboundary pollution aggravates the problem since it raises a country's cost of not being the host.

Interjurisdictional competition can also cause too tight environmental taxes and standards. This has one of the following explanations:

- If environmental regulation uses instruments that do not skim off the scarcity rent of environmental resources but leave it to the owners of the mobile factor of production, then an increase in foreign direct investment into a country makes an increasing share of this rent leave the country. Thus, there is an incentive to repel foreign capital. Since one country's attempt to repel foreign direct investment increases the costs of the other countries doing the same, there is an externality and the level of regulation tends to be too tight.
- If a foreign direct investment is beneficial not only to the host country but also to other countries, there can be incentives to free-ride on the host country. No one wants to host the polluter although everyone agrees that the polluting plant should be built somewhere. This is the classical case of 'not in my backyard'.

---

[4] It should be noted that scenarios where only some of the countries use too lax environmental policies are also possible, depending on the positions and shapes of the reaction curves.

- If tight environmental taxes and standards improve the position of domestic firms in international oligopolistic markets, it is possible that all governments use tighter than the Pigouvian regulations. Since benefits from this policy are reduced if other countries retaliate, there is an externality and emission taxes or environmental standards tend to be too strict.

Moreover, there is a case in which some countries tend to choose too-lax policies whereas others tend to choose too stringent policies. This is likely to happen if governments are concerned about the terms of trade or about the remuneration of the mobile factor of production. In a two-country world, one government is interested in increasing the relative price of the pollution-intensive good whereas the other one prefers to have it reduced. One country prefers a high rate of return to the mobile factor, the one other a low rate of return. If both governments use their environmental policies to achieve these goals, one of them will relax its standards, the other one will tighten its standards.

Finally, there is a large number of cases where neither a race to the bottom nor the opposite have to be expected. If the countries are small and if they use efficient means to achieve their economic-policy goals, there is no reason to expect a substantial interjurisdictional competition.

On the whole, one cannot conclude that the liberalization of trade and factor movements will inevitably induce a harmful competition among jurisdictions which erodes environmental quality. The converse is also possible as is the scenario in which environmental policies are not biased at all. Which of these cases is the most realistic, is an empirical issue. However, this is difficult to decide. On the one hand, it is problematic to define what too low environmental standards are empirically. On the other hand, even if one agreed on what too lax environmental standards are, it would be hard if not impossible to identify whether a regulatory deficit is to be attributed to foreign trade or to other reasons.

9.2.5 Green Barriers to Trade

Are there good environmental arguments in favour of barriers to trade and policy interventions that affect factor movements? They exist, but there are fewer of them than environmentalists and 'pro-competitive' lobbyists would believe.

The first argument in favour of barriers to trade is transportation. Like all other economic activities, transportation should bear its true social cost. Since transport causes negative externalities, it should be taxed. Of course, this raises transport costs and high transport costs restrict the possibility of trade. None the less, such type of regulation is not a barrier to trade in the literal sense. Its primary objective is not to reduce trade but to get the prices right.

As long as environmental problems are purely national, there is only one single and rather weak second-best argument in favour of trade interventions. A country may benefit from them if its environmental policies are mistaken. Depending on the characteristics of the country and of the policy failure, the correction may be achieved either by a restriction on trade or factor movements or by their promotion.[5] It is rather obvious, however, that such a 'solution' to the problem of a mistaken environmental policy is not inefficient. The first-best policy is to remove the original distortion by correcting the environmental policy and, if this is done, the optimal policy is *laissez-faire* in the policy area of trade and international factor movements.

One of the standard arguments in favour of trade restrictions used by environmentalists but also by sector-specific industry lobbies is that these measures be used as countervailing duties in the case of environmental dumping. Lax environmental standards are often are said to give foreign producers an unjustified advantage in international markets and, thus, are regarded as a practice of unfair trade. From a welfare-economic point of view, trade interventions should not be used in this case. As long as transfrontier pollution problems are of minor relevance, a country will always be better off with free trade and factor movements than with policy interventions.[6] From a purely national point of view, environmental dumping by other countries is no reason to restrict trade or international factor movements.

Matters are different if there is transfrontier pollution, particularly if the environmental problem is global. Tight environmental policies can cause leakage problems and these can be solved at least partially by policy interventions that affect trade and the movements of capital. As an example, consider a large country which unilaterally introduces a carbon tax. The competitiveness of its carbon-intensive industries is reduced and the patterns of trade will be changed: imports of carbon-intensive goods are increased or exports of carbon-intensive are reduced. In any case the rest of the world will increase its output of carbon intensive goods and, thus, its carbon emissions. The appropriate measure to take care of this undesired side-effect of the carbon tax is to tax the imports of carbon-intensive goods or to promote their exports by subsidization. Similar considerations apply in the case of environmental capital flight. It can be reduced or avoided by subsidies for the domestic use of capital.

What has not been considered in this monograph, is the use of trade restrictions as sanctions to stabilize international environmental agreements. Trade sanctions do not need to be tied to environmentally intensive commodities although precisely this approach has been taken in some international

---

[5] e.g. a country with a too lax environmental regulation should restrict capital movements if it is an importer of capital, or promote capital movements if it is an exporter. In both cases, the policy objective would be to drive polluting industries out of the country. Of course, the adequate policy would be to improve environmental regulation.

[6] Of course there is the standard terms-of-trade argument in favour of tariffs in the large-country case, but this has nothing to do with environmental issues.

agreements.[7] In an ideal world, sanctions are credible threats and they will never be used.

It should be kept in mind that trade measures are not the first-best instruments to deal with the impact of trade and factor movements on global environmental problems. The first-best policy is a co-operative approach in the field of environmental regulation and *laissez-faire* in the field of international trade and factor movements. However, this is difficult to achieve in reality.

9.2.6 *Areas of Future Research*

Although I have tried to address as many as possible of the issues that I regard to be relevant, the seven theoretical chapters of this book have by no means exhausted the subject. What remains to be done? Of course, every model can be refined and extended and this is one of the directions in which scientific progress proceeds. However, I would like to raise some points where I think it needs more than only refinements of existing research.

Given that we have quite a lot of theoretical results from various types of economic models, I feel that additional empirical research is necessary. In particular, we need realistic values for the parameters of our models. Many of the policy-relevant results that have been established in this study and elsewhere depend on the parameters. An example is the theory of strategic environmental policy, which offers good arguments for lax environmental policies but also good arguments for strict policies. As long as the relevant parameters are not known, economic theory provides a menu of policy recommendations from which everybody can pick what she likes. In this area of economic research, the marginal benefits from empirical work will probably exceed those from theoretical investigations.

However, there are still some issues where there is a lack of theoretical knowledge and where fruitful research is possible.

One of these is the differentiated-goods model of international trade, which has been used to explain intra-industry trade. Our knowledge on the interaction of trade and environmental policies in perfectly competitive markets is very well developed. Similarly, a lot of insights have been gained from the consideration of monopoly and oligopoly models. Differentiated-goods models with monopolistically competitive market structures, in contrast, have by and large remained unexplored in the environmental-economics literature. However, these models have some conceptual advantages over the other models. They are realistic in that they deal with markets with a finite number of firms rather than with atomistic competition. But they do not take the number of firms as given as do the standard oligopoly models. Entry and exit are taken into account and, therefore, the effects of trade and environmental policies on

---

[7] See Esty (1994*a*. 249–56) for a taxonomy of 'green' trade measures.

market structure. Finally, the differentiated-goods models of the Hotelling–Lancaster type would allow consideration of qualitatively differentiated goods and one could use them to analyse the impact of environmental product standards on international trade. I, therefore, think that the potential of these models could be fruitfully exploited.

Other issues that deserve additional consideration are intertemporal aspects of trade and the environment, e.g. the process of diffusion of environmentally relevant technological knowledge, and the role of trade restrictions as economic sanctions to stabilize international environmental agreements.

The diffusion of knowledge is important in two respects. On the one hand, environmental gains from trade are said to be at least partially caused by the access to foreign technological knowledge of environmentally friendly technology and goods. A theoretical model of these spillover effects is not yet available. On the other hand, one may have the impression that developed countries wish to close the markets for environmentally intensively produced goods once they have developed environmentally friendly technologies. An example is the Montreal Protocol with its restrictions on the trade in CFC intensive goods. The question here is whether, besides fairness and equity considerations, there are also economic-efficiency arguments in favour of giving developed countries access to the new technologies.

Sanctions and the linking of different issues have already been considered in the literature as means to stabilize international environmental agreements (see Barrett (1994a) and Folmer et al. (1993)). However, trade sanctions are special since trade issues are in many respects economically linked to environmental issues. For instance, the trade barriers proposed by the Montreal Protocol are, on one hand, sanctions that can be used to discipline deviants. On the other hand, they are green barriers to trade that are in the self-interest of countries that want to solve leakage problems. Usually, punishment strategies, as known from the theory of repeated games, impose a cost on the party that wants to punish. Here they generate a benefit and, therefore, they tend to be more credible. It is to be expected that the consideration of the economic links between environmental and trade issues in repeated games will provide some additional insights on how the incentive problems to participate in the solution of global environmental problems can be solved.

Intertemporal issues also include the impact of environmental disruption on future generations and the impact of current pollution and foreign trade on the assimilative capacity of eco-systems. However, the theoretical consideration of these issues requires differential-games techniques, and the question is whether models with a sufficient degree of realism are still tractable.

Finally, the area where I think future research may provide the highest returns is the modelling of regulatory capture. Public-choice theory has provied valuable insights on processes of regulatory capture in open economies. However, there remain unanswered questions. For instance, why does it happen so rarely that efficient instruments are chosen when protection is granted to idiosyncratic pressure groups in society? The idea to include 'obfuscation' in the policy-maker's objective function is promising, but a behavioural model of obfuscation is not yet available. If the process of regulatory capture could be understood better, a normative component might be added to the currently predominant positive analysis of modern public-choice theory. On top of explaining the discrepancy between the policy suggestions we derive from our models and what we observe in reality, we may be able to suggest ways in which institutions (and perhaps also constitutions) can be designed such that the capture of economic policy by powerful lobbies is reduced and that more efficient policy instruments are chosen.

9.3 Policy Implications for a Single Country

9.3.1 Environmental Policy

Optimal environmental policies should always equate the marginal benefits and the marginal costs of environmental-resource use. However, as the theoretical chapters and the preceding summary of results have revealed, there exist some good reasons why these benefits and costs in an open economy are different from those in a closed economy. Trade-policy objectives like the terms-of-trade motive, the idea of rent-shifting in oligopolistic markets, the avoidance of carbon leakage, and the attraction of mobile capital can have an impact on environmental policies. The question is whether or not these objectives should be taken into account in the process of environmental policy-making.

One of the central arguments against strict environmental standards is that they reduce the competitiveness of an open economy and drive mobile factors out of the country. Therefore, so the argument goes, they should be relaxed if openness is increased. The theoretical analyses do not support this view. The optimal environmental policy is almost always a Pigouvian policy which imposes the marginal cost of environmental disruption on the polluter. This rule is usually not changed by the threat of foreign competition in goods or factor markets. The demand for environmental quality should always be respected and the appropriate environmental tax rates be used. This may be changed in the case of distortions. If the government taxes the mobile factor, there tend to be fiscal externalities because of an interjurisdictional competition for a part of the tax base. In this case it would be optimal to use lax environmental standards to keep the tax base inside the country. But it would be even better to change the mode of taxation or to eliminate the fiscal externality by an international agreement. The other case in which lax environmental standards may be beneficial to a country is that of indivisibilities. If there is one foreign investor who wants to build one single plant in one out of many countries and if the investment decision depends on the environmental regulation, then the environmental policy of a potential host country does not depend on marginal considerations any more and there may be a rat race towards either very lax or very strict regulation levels. From the point of view of a single country, it is of course desirable to participate in this competition as long as the net benefits are positive. The country would, however, be better off if it switched from environmental standards to direct subsidies since these are the efficient instruments in this case. Then the emission tax rate would again equal marginal environmental damage.

The standard welfare-theoretic argument for policy interventions in open economies is that they may improve a large country's terms of trade. This is true also in the case of environmental policy, at least in theory. How relevant is this in practice? There are only very few industries where environmental regulation has a really significant impact on the prices of traded goods. However, the utilization of tight emission taxes and standards in these industries for terms-of-trade improvements is often limited by high import demand elasticities that are due to the availability of close substitutes in international goods markets. On the aggregate level of the economy as a whole, environmental regulation contributes only around 2 or 3 per cent to the costs of production. This implies that environmental regulation is probably one of the most inefficient means to achieve improvements in the terms of trade or favourable changes in the prices of internationally mobile factors of production. Thus, it is not amazing that these considerations have not played any significant role in the public environmental policy discussion. And there is no need to put them on the agenda.

Another reason for adjusting environmental policies to trade objectives is the improvement of the position of domestic firms that compete with foreign firms in international oligopolistic markets. The basic idea is to shift rents from abroad into the home country and this is beneficial if the additional rent exceeds the dead-weight loss from the inefficient allocation of domestic resources. The analysis in Chapter 6 has shown that the policy implications that can be derived from the theoretical models are indeterminate. There are good reasons for tight environmental standards and good reasons for lax standards. Which strategy is the correct one depends on the strategic variables used by the oligopolists (quantities or prices), on the number of firms, on the shapes of the cost and revenue functions, and on some variables that have not been considered explicitly in the model. In reality, this is information that a regulating entity rarely has access to. Thus, the theoretical models are not of much guidance to the policy-maker. Given the informational deficits, their message is merely that Pigouvian taxes may be too low or too high if firms compete in international oligopolistic markets. This insight is not of much use as advice on policy. Moreover, it should be noted that environmental policies are not the best instruments to shift rents. Efficient instruments, i.e. subsidies, have been investigated in several empirical studies and the general finding was that the gains from strategic trade policy are often minuscule and sometimes even negative. It is unlikely that indirect instruments like environmental taxes will perform better. Thus, as a rule of thumb, one may conclude that a government should abstain from using environmental regulation as strategic trade policy.

Another source of policy failure is the choice of the wrong policy instrument. In an open economy, a command-and-control approach allows foreigners to appropriate rents that are due to the scarcity of domestic environmental resources. The laxer the environmental policy, the larger the foreign direct investments from abroad and the larger the share of the rent appropriated by foreigners.[8] Thus a part of the benefits of a lax environmental policy, i.e. the increased consumption possibilities, goes to foreigners. The opportunity costs of strict environmental regulation are reduced and it is a good policy to introduce strict environmental standards. However, it would be even better to eliminate the distortion and use a mode of environmental regulation that skims off the scarcity rent of environmental resources and redistributes it to residents of the country. On top of all other arguments against the command-and-control approach to environmental policy, this is another reason to move to emission taxes or tradable discharge permits.

Finally, there is the leakage problem in the case of global environmental externalities. Strict environmental policies induce international capital movements and changes in the patterns of trade such that foreign emissions are raised. This reduces the efficiency of such a policy. What a government should do is to relax emission taxes or standards until they equal marginal benefit from the *net* reduction in pollution. What does that mean in reality? Up to now, there has not been much empirical evidence that environmental policy had significant relocation effects in the past. This is good news. However, simulation studies addressing the effects of greenhouse policies have provided a large range of estimates ranging from close to zero to more than 60 per cent carbon leakage. Thus, no one knows exactly whether or not this will be a significant problem in the future. As before, the environmental regulation is not the best policy instrument to deal with the problem. It would be better from the point of view of a single country to use trade interventions or to subsidize the domestic use of the mobile factor of production. None the less, these policies are themselves only second best and further improvements are possible. This will be the subject of the next section.

To conclude, in an open economy there are no strong arguments in favour of either very lax or very tight environmental standards. In all the cases considered here, the deviations from the standard rules of environmental economics are caused by distortions that can more efficiently be addressed by other policy instruments. In cases where these instruments are not available, changes in environmental policy can be suggested from an economic-theory point of view. However, the welfare effects are likely to be very small since environmental regulation is a very indirect instrument to affect trade and factor

---

[8] Since the rent itself depends on the level of environmental regulation, the rent itself may decline with laxer environmental policies. This is neglected here. For details, see Ch. 3, Sect. 12.

movements. The smaller the gains from such a policy, the larger the precision in their application to achieve some if not the maximum benefits. Due to informational deficits and uncertainty, these policy instruments may easily miss their targets.

9.3.2 Trade Policy

From a welfare-economic point of view, there are two cases in favour of green trade restrictions: the carbon-leakage problem and insufficient environmental regulation.[9] Trade interventions cannot be justified on welfare grounds if other countries just use different environmental policies, e.g. lower emission tax rates and laxer environmental standards. This 'levelling of the playing-field' is beneficial only to owners of sector-specific factors but harmful to a society as a whole.[10]

Trade restrictions can be justified on welfare grounds in the case of insufficient environmental policies. Of course, the most direct response to such a distortion is the improvement of environmental policy. But this may not always be a practicable solution in reality. An example is the importation of toxic waste and other hazardous substances by countries that lack appropriate safety regulations or the careful enforcement of these standards. In many countries, the border control is the only place where a serious inspection is possible. Knowing that these substances will remain uncontrolled after having entered the country, it is better to refuse their importation at the border. This argument is applicable to many developing countries and the emerging market economies of Eastern Europe. Sometimes, it may be even better and more efficient to locate the point of control in the waste-exporting country and use export restrictions.[11]

Leakage problems in the case of global environmental problems are another reason for the use of green tariffs and factor-market interventions. A large tax on carbon dioxide, for instance, would make carbon-intensive production very expensive in the country imposing the tax. Its comparative advantage will be affected and mobile capital may leave the country. Thus, in the extreme case, the effect of such a tax is merely a change in the location of production but not a change in total emissions. The optimum response would be a policy which

---

[9] Trade restrictions as sanctions will not be discussed here: they may stabilize international environmental agreements, but they are not effective if applied by a single country.

[10] Matters may be different if the ruling class of a foreign dictatorship imposes health and environmental risks on the population without providing appropriate compensation. In this case, altruistic motives may justify restrictions on the importation of the goods whose production is responsible for the damage. However, it is difficult to decide what the appropriate compensation is in another country. Due to this interpretatorial margin, the human-rights argument can be abused easily for protectionist interests.

[11] The exporting countries may agree to participate in such a control scheme because they incur some costs e.g. loss of international reputation, if their hazardous waste is recovered in a developing country where it causes environmental and health problems due to improper treatment.

prevents capital from moving to less regulated countries and/or imposes import restrictions on environmentally intensively produced foreign goods.

There are three major practical problems with green trade interventions and a theoretical one.

- The first problem is the determination of the tariff rate. The pollution contents of the imported good ought to be the decisive criterion for the import tax rate. In a simple trade model without intermediate goods, this variable can be determined rather easily. In reality, however, one needs to know the input–output matrix of the other country. Even goods that themselves have been produced by environmentally friendly methods may contain intermediate inputs that originate from environmentally very disruptive production. In reality, it will be almost impossible to compute the appropriate tariff rates.[12] Even scholarly calibrated models taking into account the market interdependencies show a large variation in their results on pollution leakage. Given these difficulties and the lack of knowledge on the decisive parameters, almost anything can be claimed to be a green tariff.
- The second problem is that import goods from different countries will usually differ in their pollution content. This requires a differentiation of import tax rates with respect to the country of origin. But such a policy violates the non-discrimination principle embodied in most international-trade agreements.
- Thirdly, green barriers to trade, even if they themselves can be justified, may open a Pandora's box of protectionism. A government declaring that it will use trade policy for environmental objectives invites rent-seekers at home and induces retaliation abroad. In the long run, the reduction in the gains from trade may offset the initial gains from better environmental quality.
- The theoretical obstacle to such a policy is that green trade taxes are not the best instruments to deal with carbon leakage. Any trade intervention causes a dead-weight loss. The first-best policy would directly address the activities that cause environmental damage. This is only possible with international cooperation in the field of environmental regulation. Thus international co-ordination of environmental policies is better than unilateral trade interventions.

To summarize, a case for green trade policies can be made in simple theoretical models. But in reality, the problems of practical implementation are substantial. For this reason, trade interventions should be viewed as a means of

---

[12] To make the issue more complicated, consider non-traded goods whose production in the foreign country causes negative spillovers to the home country. The home country may then find it optimal to choose a trade intervention that affects the foreign price of a traded good which is a substitute or complement of the non-traded good. The cross-price effect may then have a negative effect on the demand for the pollution-intensive good.

last resort and should be applied only if there exists sufficient knowledge on their effects. To date, this knowledge does not seem to be available.

9.3.3 Institutions of Trade and Environmental Policies

The borderline between environmental protection and environmental protectionism is difficult to draw. We have seen that trade taxes and subsidies to domestic industries can be justified for environmental reasons in certain circumstances. But these instruments also protect specific groups from international competition. The potential beneficiaries have incentives to lobby and influence the policy-making process in favour of trade barriers and subsidies. But not only trade barriers provide protection. Environmental regulation as well affects the distribution of income and environmental standards can also be abused to discriminate against foreign goods.

The negative consequences of lobbyism are twofold. On the one hand, the possibility of increasing one's own share of the pie—or the necessity to defend it against other claimants—makes economic agents relocate resources from productive activities (that augment the pie) to unproductive rent-seeking (that augment one's own share of the pie). From a societal point of view, these resources are wasted. On the other hand, if some interest groups are more successful in their attempt to capture regulation than others, then the policy outcome will be inefficient in the Pareto sense: it would be possible to design alternative policies that make everyone better off. Thus, an institutional framework has to be found in which the incentives for rent-seeking and the likelihood of regulatory capture are minimized—subject to the constraint that this framework be compatible with a democratic constitution.[13] The institutional framework serves the purpose of tying the policy-maker's hands by providing rules in which circumstances certain policy measures can be taken and how they have to be implemented. With their hands tied, policy-makers and the executive bureaucracy are less susceptible to the demand for trade protection. In a first step, we shall deal with trade interventions, afterwards with environmental policies.

One way to avoid regulatory capture is to restrict the choice of the policy instruments. The extreme and simple case is that a country commits itself to free trade and does not use trade interventions. Given the uncertainties involved with the use of green barriers to trade, this may be the best idea at the moment. Why open a Pandora's box of protectionism in order to make use of an instrument which (i) is inefficient and (ii) addresses what may be a non-problem empirically?

---

[13] Attempts to influence government decisions are inherent in pluralistic and democratically organized societies and lobbying is just one of them. Prohibition of lobbying by law would come close to a denial of the right of free speech.

However, this extreme position may not be politically acceptable everywhere and at every time.[14] Thus, less radical alternatives are sought. One of them is to use trade-policy instruments that are less likely to be captured by lobbyists than tariffs. From an economic-theory point of view, there are different ways of implementing environmentally motivated barriers to trade. In the two-country, two-commodity world, the effect of a tariff can also be achieved by an export tax and for any export subsidy there exists a corresponding import subsidy with the same allocative effect. And it is rather unlikely that domestic producer lobbies support export taxes or import subsidies. Similar arguments can be applied to interventions in capital movements. A subsidy going to those who invest their capital in the home country can be substituted for by a tax on the repatriated capital income of domestic residents and/or by a subsidy on the return on the investment made by foreigners in the home country. Theoretically, these instruments are equivalent but in the perception of the public, including the lobbies, they are not. This may make it possible to have trade measures that protect the environment but do not generate incentives for rent-seeking behaviour. The constitutional framework could be designed such that only these instruments are feasible—at least in theory. However, the idea—as fascinating it may be for a theorist—is unlikely to function in reality. In a multi-commodity world, an import tariff or export subsidy for one commodity has as its equivalent a complete set of trade interventions in all other markets. The informational requirements for getting all these tax or subsidy rates right are enormous. In the case of factor market interventions, taxes on repatriated profits may not work very well since tax evasion is rather simple. Thus, if interventions into free trade or factor movements are used, one relies on the policy instruments that are attractive to lobbyists as well and other ways out of the dilemma of regulatory capture have to be sought.

If it is not possible to restrict the instrument set, one can subject the implementation of policy instrument to binding rules. A possibility is to make the use of green barriers to trade conditional on the joint decision of the signatory parties to a multilateral environmental agreement.[15] In the case of multilateral sanctions, the governments of numerous countries have to agree on a common policy. Therefore, the outcome of the negotiation process is less likely to be dominated by national protectionist forces than in the case of measures taken unilaterally by a single government. The larger diversity of interests, perhaps including counter-lobbies in other countries, restricts the capability of domestic protectionists to influence environmental policy-making process. This increases the probability that the trade-restricting measure is implemented really

[14] There are for instance countries that have signed international environmental agreements which provide for trade restrictions. Moreover, future research may establish that carbon leakage is indeed a severe problem. Then, countries that are willing to take unilateral action *vis-à-vis* global environmental problems are in need of instruments that reduce the undesired relocation effects of such a policy.

[15] Article 104 of the North-American Free-Trade Agreement is an example for such a rule. It will be considered below in more detail.

for environmental reasons. However, environmentalists will not agree to such a rule. A laxer rule agreeable to environmentalists could include strict definitions of the environmental targets and of the time-frame of the trade intervention. The time-frame should be limited but renewable and the effects of the policy should be monitored periodically. If and when the policy measures become obsolete, e.g. at the time the foreign government introduces stricter environmental policies, they should be withdrawn at once.

Besides the instruments that intervene in trade and factor movements directly, there are other, more subtle ones and they include the regulation of environmentally disruptive production processes and, particularly, products. The capture of such instruments for protectionist purposes appears to be omnipresent and has already been a source of dispute in international trade negotiations. The proceedings of the European Court of Justice are an almost inexhaustible source witnessing the fantasy that is being used to justify ridiculous product standards that discriminate against foreigners. Another kind of regulatory capture is the use of lax environmental process standards as a means of indirect subsidization to support exporting or import-competing industries.[16]

One way to reduce regulatory capture in the environmental policy sphere is to dilute the power of idiosyncratic interest groups and I argue that environmental regulation is a policy area where this approach can be fruitful to some extent. According to Olson (1965), small interest groups with specific interests gain influence over government decision-making because (i) they can appropriate large rents whereas the costs of providing these rents are widely dispersed and (ii) these groups are relatively homogeneous and, therefore, are able to solve their internal free-rider problem more easily. This explains why producers' lobbies are more influential than groups that lobby for the interests of the consumers of commodities and ambient quality. If one aims at keeping the influence of special interest groups small, one should attempt to organize the policy-making process so that the groups affected by these policies are large and heterogeneous. If they are large, the potential costs of providing rents to them are large and this may raise the resistance of those who have to pay. Moreover, large and heterogeneous groups face higher transaction costs and internal free-rider problems. Interestingly, environmental policies that help to achieve these objectives are also efficient from the purely allocative point of view. Thus, there is no conflict between policy objectives.

According to the standard result of environmental economics, the polluters should be signalled the environmental costs of their activities. For instance, they should pay an emission tax which equals the marginal environmental damage. This Pigouvian tax does not depend on the kind of activity which causes the damage and is, therefore, also independent of who is the polluter. Thus, environmental policy should be directed primarily at pollutants but not

---

16 The Porter hypothesis, claiming that tight environmental standards are good for competitiveness, is probably not that convincing to lobbyists.

at polluters. The regulatory approach predominantly used in industrialized countries often does the converse. Sector or plant-specific process standards are used rather than environmental taxes or tradable-permit schemes that could be applied on a broader basis. Specific standards, however, tend to be more susceptible to interest-group influence than more general policies that affect various sectors of the economy at the same time. A group of producers who are active in different sectors of the economy is rather heterogeneous and will therefore face larger transaction costs and free-rider problems if it wishes to organize lobbying activities than a group of producers whose production activities are very similar. The probability of regulatory capture is smaller if environmental policy instruments are used that are not industry- or plant-specific. For this reason, environmental policies that are directed at pollutants and use emission taxes or tradable-permits schemes should be given priority over the command-and-control approach wherever this is possible.

Another aspect of the choice of policy instruments is that the regulatory approach to environmental policy as applied in many industrialzed countries often uses grandfather clauses and thus favours incumbent firms over new entrants. This serves to stabilize non-competitive market structures. But it does not only lead to inefficiencies but it also raises the power of the incumbents *vis-à-vis* the government. Market-orientated environmental policy instruments, in contrast, would result in a more dynamic structure of the industry and fluctuations in the composition of an industry make it more difficult to organize protectionist lobbying activities.

Similar considerations as in the case of process standards can be applied to product standards. These standards as well can easily be used to discriminate against foreigners and, thus, it makes sense to replace them by environmental consumption taxes where possible. Since these taxes are directed at the pollution contents of the goods, they discriminate against those who should be discriminated against: the users of environmentally unfriendly goods. Groups interested in influencing the outcome of the political process will face more difficulties co-ordinating their activities if the environmental policy measure addresses the pollution contents of a large variety of different goods than if environmental policies use specific standards for goods that are produced by particular industries.

Not only does the choice of policy instruments have an impact on regulatory capture; the organizational framework in which environmental policy is taking place is also important. In many countries, environmental policy is the responsibility of different ministries and bureaucracies some of which are closely linked to particular industries of the economy. With such an organizational structure, managers and owners of regulated firms have strong incentives and opportunities to collaborate and to influence the regulation process. Additionally, close relationships between the representatives of the administration and of the regulated groups develop over time. Therefore, the regulation process is likely to be captured by those who are regulated. One may, therefore, wish to—loosely speaking—maximize the distance between environmental policy institutions and protectionist interest groups. An extreme way of doing this would be to leave the decisions on environmental policies to an independent council. In the same way that the central bankers decide (more or less) independently on a country's money supply, this council would decide on the supply of environmental resources. However, the exemption of such an important and controversial policy area from the political process would be against the spirit of democracy. Thus, one should try to achieve the objective of a large distance between regulator and regulatee in an alternative way. In the case of environmental policy, the responsibility for environmental regulation should lie with the ministry of the environment and its affiliated institutions but not with, for example, the ministries of development, agriculture, energy, or specific industries.

None the less, although market-orientated environmental policies possess many advantages over the command-and-control approach, it will neither be possible nor desirable to abolish environmental product and process standards completely. In many situations, administration and monitoring costs may be much lower than in the case of taxes and tradable permits. Moreover, even environmental taxes and tradable-permits schemes are not necessarily free from protectionist influence. Since no one exactly knows the true social cost of environmental disruption, environmental policy inherently involves a high degree of discretion and the regulatees will attempt to influence the information-gathering process. Thus, environmental taxes may also be captured by protectionist interests. Domestic producers can be protected from foreign competition by low emission taxes and environmental consumption taxes can be used to discriminate against foreigners.[17] For these reasons, it is desirable that the public be informed about the protectionist content of environmental regulation. Usually, the majority of voters are (rationally) uninformed about existing protectionist measures and about the true costs of protection and this is a necessary condition for regulatory capture to take place. Therefore, it is advisable to create institutions that have the task of making hidden protection public and thereby act as the advocates of the consumer. Such an institution should review environmental regulation (but also other kinds of regulation) with respect to their protectionist contents and report its findings on a regular basis. It would be desirable to have the committee consist of independent experts such as natural scientists and economists but also of representatives of the groups that are disadvantaged in the process of regulatory capture, i.e. consumers and perhaps foreign producers.

Finally, it may be useful to introduce elements of direct democracy into the process of environmental policy-making. The underlying rationale is that representative democracy creates the discretionary space the policy-maker can

[17] As an example consider a government that wishes to protect the domestic automobile industry and has at its disposal a tax on fuel. Everything else being equal, the tax rate will be high if the industry produces a large share of small cars and low if the share of large cars is large.

use to distribute rents. Direct democracy tends to reduce the discretion and, therefore, on average will lead to a policy outcome in which pressure groups with idiosyncratic interests are less overrepresented.[18] This may turn out to be useful to prevent non-tariff barriers to trade and the indirect subsidization of some producers by means of lax environmental standards. However, in many countries there are constitutional limits to the use of direct-democracy elements in the political decision-making process.

9.4 Regulation of Environmental Scarcity and Foreign Trade on the Supranational Level

9.4.1 Basic Principles for the Design of Environmental and Trade Agreements[19]

In environmental and trade affairs, countries have incentives to free-ride on one another. This is obvious in the case of transfrontier pollution, but externalities play an important role in international trade, too. Individual countries can achieve welfare improvements by trade interventions that reduce global allocative efficiency. International treaties intend to reduce this kind of behaviour. Moreover, they serve the purpose of tying the policy-makers' hands. They restrain the use of certain policy instruments and, therefore, the policy-makers' discretion to use trade and environmental policy to support idiosyncratic interest groups.

Existing environmental and trade agreements are based on a number of basic principles and it may be useful to review them before looking at some particular agreements on trade and environmental issues.

- The *subsidiarity principle* is widely accepted in the theory of federalism and in practical policy-making and it has been used extensively as a guiding principle of European integration (see European Commission (1992), Cass (1992), and Begg *et al.* (1993)). According to the subsidiarity principle, political decisions should be made at the level closest to the citizen, e.g. local environmental problems should be dealt with by local authorities and national environmental problems by national authorities. Decentralized decision-making reduces administrative costs and tends to raise the quality of decisions since they are made on levels closer to the citizen. Only if there are substantial transfrontier pollution spillovers or other international externalities, supranational authorities should coordinate environmental policies.

[18] As has been argued in Ch. 7, it does not mean that direct democracy will always be 'unbiased' or orientated towards free trade.
[19] This section uses material from an earlier paper of mine, Rauscher (1995d: 1992–5).

- The *origin principle* demands that goods which are in agreement with national regulations in one country must also be tradable in other countries. This is a restriction on sovereignty since it limits a country's right to refuse imports of commodities that the ruling authorities wish to keep out of the country. On the other hand, it serves as a measure to eliminate disguised protection.[20] The *destination principle*, in contrast, is based much more on the ideal of national sovereignty. According to this principle, the regulation of the country of destination is decisive for the standards a commodity has to meet in order to be importable.

- The *non-discrimination principle* may be viewed as a compromise. It states that individual countries are sovereign in their decisions on national regulations but these regulations have to be designed such that they do not discriminate against foreigners. International trade agreements often use the notion that environmental policy measures should be applied in the least distortionary way.

- This leads us to the *principle of the appropriateness of the means*. The policy instruments should be chosen such that unnecessary distortions be avoided. For instance, a trade restriction as an instrument of environmental policy would be regarded as inappropriate if an emission tax were available that addressed the environmental problem directly.

- *Extraterritorialism* is another issue which is important in the framework of international trade agreements when environmental issues are of concern. Many environmentalists, particularly West Europeans and North Americans, argue that highly regulated countries should be able to enforce their environmental standards outside their jurisdictions if foreign standards are too lax (whatever that may mean). Often, trade restrictions are demanded for this purpose. It has been shown in the previous chapters that this may make sense if issues of global pollution are concerned where the environmental damage is independent of the source of emission. But in all other cases, extraterritorialism aims at unnecessary and undesirable harmonization of environmental laws. Third-world representatives are correct in calling this 'green imperialism'.[21]

- The *polluter-pays principle* is generally regarded as a good and unquestionable foundation of environmental policies. At a first glance, the application of this principle in environmental policy-making seems to have nothing to do with international trade issues. This impression is, however, wrong. The choice of the polluter-pays principle as the basic principle of environmental policy is based on a value-judgement rather than on efficiency considerations. According to Coase (1960), the application of

[20] This is documented by several decisions of the European Court of Justice starting with the famous Cassis-de-Dijon ruling. The European Court, however, has also acknowledged the limits of the origin principle in the Danish bottle case. Denmark has been allowed to restrict the use of non-refillable bottles and cans for environmental reasons although importers of beverages argued that this policy raised their costs by much more than that of domestic producers.

[21] For a developing-country's position, see Kisiri (1992).

the *pollutee-pays principle*—under certain assumptions—leads to the same allocation of environmental resources and it may in some cases be superior in solving environmental problems. I will argue later on that the inconsistencies between international trade agreements on the one hand and international environmental agreements on the other are basically due to different views on who should be compensated when environmental problems are solved.

- *Sustainability* is *the* catchword of the 1990s in the field of environmental policy. Having been coined in the Brundtland report, the term 'sustainable' describes a situation in which current economic development and growth do not restrict the opportunities of future generations. While economic theorists still debate alternative definitions of the concept, it has already been used in multilateral agreements. In most cases sustainablity shows up in the preamble of an agreement where the contracting parties express their will to avoid unsustainable policies. Usually, these declarations are so general that they do not lead to concrete obligations for the contracting parties. From the point of view of an economist, the value of such a preamble is mainly a cosmetic one and the important regulations are to be found in what follows the preamble.

The next section will review some existing international environmental and trade agreements to show how these principles are implemented and how the conflict between trade and environmental goals is solved.

9.4.2 Environmental Agreements with Trade Provisions

There exist many international environmental agreements some of which contain provisions for international trade.[22] These are reviewed briefly by *Esty* (1994*a*: 275–81). The most prominent ones are probably the Convention of Trade in Endangered Species of Wild Flora and Fauna (CITES), the Montreal Protocol on Substances that Deplete the Ozone Layer (hereafter: Montreal Protocol), and the Basle Convention on the Control of Transboundary Movements of Hazardous Waste and Its Disposal (hereafter: Basle Convention). I will review these three agreements here in order to give an impression how the trade-and-environment issue is handled by international environmental agreements. Before that, however, we will have a look at the trade provisions of the Declaration on Environment and Development adopted at the 1992 Earth Summit in Rio de Janeiro.

---

[22] The GATT's Annual Report 1990/91 states that from 1933 to 1990 125 multilateral environmental agreements were in force, 17 of which included trade provisions (see GATT (1992: 25)). Esty (1994*a*: 275–81) finds that 20 international environmental agreements of this time-period allow for trade restrictions.

The Rio Declaration on Environmental and Development

The Rio Declaration adopted by the United Nations Conference on Environment and Development is literally not an environmental agreement. It does not define rights and obligations of signatory parties precisely, but rather it is a general (and hardly enforceable) declaration of will. Its ingredients that are relevant for international trade are:

- Sovereignty (Principle 2). Each country has the sovereign right to exploit its resources and to pursue its own environmental policy but is also responsible to ensure that it does not cause environmental damage outside its own jurisdiction.
- Avoidance of trade distortions (Principle 12). States should promote an open international economic system. Trade measures for environmental purposes should be non-discriminating and should not constitute a means of disguised protection. Extraterritorialism should be avoided. Transboundary or global environmental problems should be solved by consensus.
- Polluter-pays principle (Principle 16). Polluters shall bear the costs of pollution.

None of these principles is enforceable. The second part of Principle 2 is even impossible to be achieved in practice. Moreover, these principles are so general that they offer a wide range for interpretation. One should note that trade restrictions are not excluded as a means of environmental policy. Principle 12, however, also states that consensus rather than unilateralism and extraterritorialism should be the way in which international environmental problems are solved.

The Convention on Trade in Endangered Species

CITES went into force in 1973. It is a multilateral agreement which regulates the trade in rare species of animals and plants or in products made from them. Recognizing that many species of fauna and flora are threatened by extinction, the signatory parties to this agreement agreed to slow down this process by taking economic measures. The view taken by the parties was that in many cases species' extinction was not caused by domestic demand in the countries where these animals and plants were endemic, but by import demand in the rest of the world. Examples are the demand for rhino horn and tiger products, particularly in East Asia. Moreover, these species were regarded as a common heritage of mankind and, therefore, an outside intervention was viewed as justifiable if the exporting countries were unable or unwilling to protect these resources in an adequate manner. The instruments used to monitor and restrict the trade in endangered species are export and import permits.

CITES Article III states that import permits are required for the trade in species that are threatened by extinction. Import permits are subject to the condition that the primary purpose of the imported animal, plant, or good is not commercial. Article IV regulates the trade in species that may become threatened by extinction if their trade were unrestricted. In cases where Article IV applies, the importation of the animal, plant, or good to the signatory state is conditional on the export permit of the country of export. Special articles regulate the trade in species that originate from extraterritorial areas, e.g. the international waters of the high seas. It is obvious that Articles III and IV of CITES constitute the basis for substantial trade interventions. Something like free trade in the sense of unrestricted exchange of commodities between suppliers in one country and consumers in another one has been made impossible (or at least illegal). The overall impression is that these trade restrictions are regarded as being justified not only in environmentalist circles but also in the international-trade community.

The Montreal Protocol

The Montreal Protocol, which was launched in 1987, regulates the use of substances that deplete the ozone layer, in particular CFCs. The signatory parties agree to participate in a schedule of CFC reduction until a complete phase-out.

The Montreal Protocol contains interesting trade provisions (see Enders and Porges (1992) for a more detailed discussion). Signatory parties to the Protocol are requested to ban imports and exports from non-parties of different types of goods relevant to the process of ozone depletion. The ban proceeds in a number of steps that are defined in Article 4 of the Protocol. First, imports of controlled substances themselves are banned. In a next step, the parties have to elaborate a list of products containing controlled substances and parties that have not objected to this list shall ban the imports of these goods from non-parties. The third step then establishes the same procedure for commodities that have been produced with, but do not contain, controlled substances. Article 4 sets up a time-schedule for these measures to be taken.

From the view point of the trade economist, two aspects are of major interest. Firstly, the introduction of trade restrictions is based not only on properties of a good as such but also on the way in which it has been produced.[23] As we shall see, this may conflict with some of the GATT's principles. Secondly, this measure catches two birds with one stone. On the one hand, it reduces leakage effects. On the other hand, it creates incentives for other countries to become signatory parties to the agreement and, thus, serves as a sanction to discipline free-riders. This is an intelligent combination since here a way has been found to design sanctions such that they do not hurt the punishing party. In contrast, they even tend to be profitable. This increases the credibility of the sanction and reduces the likelihood of non-compliance.

---

[23] Among the international environmental treaties with trade provisions, only one other one provides for trade restrictions in case the commodity is unsustainably produced: the Convention of the Prohibition of Fishing with Long Drift Nets in the South Pacific of 1989 (see Esty (1994a: 280)).

The Basle Convention

The Basle Convention constrains international trade in hazardous waste. Its basic principles are the requirement of written consent by the authorities of the importing, exporting and transit states, the duty to re-import, and the prohibition of waste movements to non-parties (see Douma (1991: 37–45) and Esty (1994a: 280)). Article 6 of the Convention specifies the obligations and rights of the signatory parties in the international waste trade. It demands that all international waste trade be supervised by the authorities of the states in question. Purely private transactions, without involvement of state authorities, are not allowed. The exporter of hazardous waste shall, through the authorities of its own state, notify the authorities of the importing states of the transboundary movement of waste. The transaction should be possible only with the written consent of the authorities of the importing and the transit countries. The exporting state must not allow the export of toxic waste until the consent has been received. According to Article 8, the exporting country is responsible for reimporting the toxic waste if the movement cannot be completed in accordance with the terms of the contract and if no alternatives are available for an environmentally sound disposal. Article 4(5) prohibits the export of toxic waste to non-parties. But this principle is diluted by Article 11, which allows signatory parties to export toxic waste to countries with which it has made bilateral or multilateral agreements—subject to the constraint that these agreements contain no provisions that are less environmentally sound than the Basle Convention itself.

It should be noted that what has been called an export restraint here is in reality an import restraint. Hazardous waste is not a good but a bad and the traded good is the service of waste treatment and disposal. Thus the refusal to export waste to non-parties is not something like a voluntary export restraint but an import ban.

The environmentalist critique of the Basle Convention is that the definition of what is hazardous waste is to some extent ambiguous and that trade with non-parties is reintroduced through the back door by Article 11. Moreover, one may argue that too strict requirements on international waste movements tend to increase illegal exports. From the view point of a trade economist, the Basle Convention is interesting in that it eliminates all purely private trade in one group of commodities. All transboundary movements of hazardous waste are state controlled and to some extent also state-managed. Finally, the group of non-signatory states is excluded from trade. These are important trade restrictions, which are even discriminatory. The reason to use such restrictions is the uneven availability of information and enforceability of safety requirements of the importing and exporting states. A part of the responsibility for the environmentally sound treatment of hazardous waste is moved to the exporting country, which may even be required to reimport. The restrictions to trade inherent in this agreement are of course not in accordance with the general spirit of inter-national free-trade agreements and the question arises how these agreements are made compatible with each other.

9.4.3 Existing Trade Agreements and Environmental Issues[24]

The GATT and the WTO[25]

The General Agreement on Tariffs and Trade was formulated at a time when environmental issues were not yet a major concern. Therefore, the environ-ment is not mentioned explicitly. The main purpose of the GATT has been to promote the free exchange of goods. Its main principle is non-discrimination and the instrument for its implementation is the most-favoured-nation clause (Articles I and III). Trade restrictions may take the shape of tariffs only; non-tariff barriers to trade are prohibited (Article XI). Countervailing duties are possible in the cases of foreign dumping and subsidization. However, these measures are not applicable to environmental dumping.[26] Other barriers to trade may be used if one of the escape clauses in the GATT applies. One of them is Article XX, which has often been interpreted to cover environmental issues. It states:

Subject to the requirement that such measures are not applied in a manner which would constitute a means of arbitrary or unjustifiable discrimination between countries where the same conditions prevail, or a disguised restriction on international trade, nothing in this Agreement shall be construed to prevent the adoption or enforcement by any con-tracting party of measures:

(b) necessary to protect human, animal or plant life or health; . . . .

(g) relating to the conservation of exhaustible natural resources if such measures are made effective in conjunction with restrictions on domestic production or con-sumption;

The original intention of section (b) of Article XX was to allow signatory par-ties to restrict the imports of goods for sanitary and health reasons. These goods include for instance addictive drugs and infected animals that could cause the spillover of diseases from abroad to the importing country. Section (g) was meant to cover export restraints on scarce energy and mineral re-sources whose supply for domestic use has been rationed. Both paragraphs, however, allow a broader interpretation that would cover environmental issues like those discussed in the current debate.

---

[24] This section uses material from an earlier paper of mine, Rauscher (1995d: 194–9).

[25] For a comprehensive survey of GATT and environmental issues, see Rege (1994). See also Arden-Clarke (1991: 12–21), Charnovitz (1991), Pearce (1993: 8–21), Sorsa (1992a, b), and Esty (1994a: 46–52),

[26] See Rege (1994: 157). Environmental dumping does not fall into the categories of dumping or subsidization as defined by the GATT.

The problem with this article—besides the fact that the term 'environment' is not mentioned explicitly—is its vagueness. For instance, it does not specify the location of individuals, animals, or plants to be protected and of the resources to be conserved. Is a country allowed to use trade measures to protect animals, plants, humans, and exhaustible resources that are not located in its own territory? Moreover, it is unclear whether or not trade in goods may be restricted not only because of their properties and characteristics but also because of the ways in which they have been produced. At the time of the formulation of this article, these possibilities had not been taken into account. It is also far from clear in which circumstances discrimination becomes arbitrary or unjustifiable.

Some GATT Panels offer insights on how the relationship of free trade and environmental protection is being viewed by the GATT. The tuna dispute between Mexico and the USA is the most prominent case.[27] The GATT Panel decided that a ban on Mexican tuna imports by the USA was incompatible with GATT rules. The US Marine Mammals Protection Act limits dolphin kills and the ban on Mexican tuna was launched by the USA since the Mexican fishing fleet used less dolphin-safe fishing methods. The USA argued that this measure was in accordance with Article III (which states that imported goods should be treated in the same way as similar or competing domestic goods) and with Article XX. The USA claimed that Mexican tuna was sufficiently different from tuna caught by US fishermen since Mexico used different (less dolphin-safe) fishing methods and that, therefore, the non-discrimination principle of Article III was not applicable. Article XX was used to justify the import ban as a means of environmental policy. The GATT decided that Article III referred to products but not to methods of production and that the ban, therefore, was not in accordance with the non-discrimination principle. This can be interpreted as an acknowledgement of the origin principle.[28] Differences across countries in the regulation of production processes do not constitute a justification to intervene in foreign trade. The GATT Panel's main arguments concerning Article XX were that the measure was discriminatory, that it was a disguised barrier to trade, and that less distorting measures of environmental policy would have been possible in this case.[29] Moreover, the Panel argued that Article XX does not permit a country to take measures to enforce its own environmental standards outside its jurisdiction.

The GATT Panel decision on the tuna case, however, provides only one of

[27] For a more detailed discussion, see the original GATT Panel, GATT (1993) but also Pearce (1993).

[28] This point has been made by the German Council of Economic Advisers in its 1994 report (see Sachverständigenrat (1994: 243)).

[29] A similar decision was made in the case of Thailand's import ban on foreign cigarettes which had been launched under the pretext of national health reasons (see Pearce (1993). In that case, it was much more obvious than in the tuna dispute that the health arguments were used only as a pretext to justify trade restrictions. Local cigarettes, which are no less injurious to health than imported ones, have not been subject to any comparable restrictions.

the feasible interpretations of Article XX. This article does not explicitly prohibit the extraterritorial use of environmental-policy measures. One should
note that this decision has never been adopted by the GATT council and,
therefore, cannot be used as a precedent. This would have bound future GATT
Panels, dealing for instance with disputes concerning the application of
Montreal Protocol trade restrictions. It may have been a policy of the GATT
to leave such controversial environmental issues open and undecided to some
extent. In this context, it should be mentioned that trade bans on certain animal products like ebony, rhino horn, and crocodile leather were launched after
CITES had gone into force. Neither the GATT itself nor its signatory parties
have intervened to declare that these policies are not in accordance with the
agreement.

Ambiguities like the ones discussed here suggest an amendment of the
GATT with the objective of clarifying the relationship between environmental
policies and free trade. Environmental issues have been discussed during the
Uruguay Round but they have not been included in the key negotiations since
this would have been an additional source of conflict. However, it has been decided that the first meeting of the new World Trade Organization (WTO)
should be directed to the establishment of a Committee on Trade and Environment whose purpose is to suggest refinements and amendments to the international trading system that take account of environmental issues. Thus, the
WTO does not only have the objective of sustainable development in its preamble, but also has environmental issues on its agenda.

The Treaty of Rome and European Community Law[30]

Like the GATT, the 1957 Treaty of Rome establishing the European Economic
Community was formulated at a time when environmental concerns were not
yet on the agenda and its Article 36 on the exemptions of trade liberalization
has the same content as GATT Article XX. Since then, the Treaty of Rome has
been amended in several respects. Article 130r, which has been in force since
1987, defines targets and measures of the common environmental policy of the
European Community. One of these is the use of the principle of subsidiarity.
It as been re-enforced in the Maastricht Treaty, Article 3b, as a general principle defining the division of labour between Brussels and the member states.[31]
However, the subsidiarity principle has not been applied in all areas of environmental regulation. An example is the regulation of drinking-water quality by
the Council's Directive 80/778/EC of 1980, which defines minimum drinking-
water standards that the member states have to enforce. Articles 9 and 10 of the
Directive allow for exemptions from the rules in particular circumstances, but
countries making use of the articles have to notify the EC Commission of

[30] See Folmer and Howe (1991), Siebert (1991), and Smith (1993) for a more detailed discussion
of European environmental regulation.

[31] See Corbett (1993) for a comprehensive survey of the Maastricht Treaty and its history.

these deviations. This violates the subsidiarity principle. Drinking-water quality is neither an international environmental problem nor does its national or even regional regulation entail any fiscal externalities. See Begg *et al.* (1993) for a more detailed discussion.

The origin principle has been used by the European Court of Justice to eliminate protectionist measures in the area of product standards.[32] However, the superiority of environmental considerations over free-trade considerations has been acknowledged by the ruling on the Danish bottle case, which has been mentioned earlier.

The North American Free-Trade Agreement

The North American Free-Trade Agreement (NAFTA) which was signed by Canada, Mexico, and the USA in 1993 may serve as a prototype for future international agreements involving countries at different levels of economic development and with different perceptions on how strict environmental regulation ought to be. The NAFTA is the first trade agreement whose negotiations have been influenced to a large extent by environmental concerns (see Esty (1994*b*)). US environmentalists expected that NAFTA would lead to major delocation of US industries to Mexico, where environmental regulations are relatively lax, and that this would cause substantial environmental problems. This point was taken up by unions and industry lobbies that feared delocation as well—though, for different reasons. The problem of the negotiating parties has been to distinguish between justified environmental concern and protectionist interests that would have undermined the spirit of NAFTA.

Like signatory parties to the WTO Treaty, the NAFTA parties state in the Agreement's preamble their willingness to perform the process of economic integration in a manner consistent with environmental protection and conservation and to promote sustainable development. The Agreement then specifies the obligations and rights of the signatory parties in the process of achieving this objective.[33]

Article 104 is an 'environmental window' or environmental escape clause to the free-trade provisions of NAFTA. It states that international environmental agreements like the Montreal Protocol, the Convention of Trade in Endangered Species, and the Basle Convention that propose restrictions on international trade, are given prevalence over the NAFTA in the case of inconsistencies. This Article represents a major change in the view on the relationship between foreign trade and the environment. The GATT and other trade agreements have not been explicit on this issue. However, the ruling interpretation of these agreements has given priority to free trade over environmental

---

[32] See Koppen (1993) on the role of the European Court of Justice in the formation of European environmental regulation.

[33] For a more detailed discussion of NAFTA's environmental rules and their meaning, see Audley (1993), Wilkinson (1993), and Esty (1994*b*).

concerns. This has been reversed in NAFTA—at least for the case where the trade measures are imposed in the framework of an international environmental agreement.

There is an additional difference between GATT and NAFTA. GATT Article XX does not mention the environment explicitly. NAFTA Article 904 fills this gap:

Each Party may in accordance with this Agreement, adopt, maintain or apply any standards-related measure, including any such measure relating to safety, the protection of human, animal or plant life or health, the environment or consumers, and any measure to ensure its enforcement or implementation. Such measures include those to prohibit the importation of a good of another Party (. . .) that fails to comply with the applicable requirement of those measures.

Another difference between this Article and GATT Article XX is the explicit mention of the fact that these measures may involve trade restrictions. As in the GATT the application of these measures is restricted: they should not result in arbitrary or unjustifiable discrimination of imported goods or constitute disguised barriers to trade (NAFTA Article 907(2)).

NAFTA Article 1114 refers to environmental measures that affect foreign direct investments. Besides acknowledging national sovereignty in environmental policy issues,

The Parties recognize that it is inappropriate to encourage investment by relaxing domestic health, safety or environmental measures. . . . If a Party considers that another Party has offered such an encouragement, it may request consultations with the other Party and the two Parties shall consult with a view of avoiding such an encouragement.

This Article is meant to prevent the downward competition of national environmental regulations. None the less, it remains to be seen whether this remains a mere declaration of will or becomes an enforceable agreement. In practice, it is hard to decide why lax environmental standards have been implemented.

NAFTA contains a number of provisions for conflict resolution (Chapter 20). A Trilateral Trade Commission is created which regularly reviews the performance of trade relations within NAFTA. To resolve trade disputes, it may establish multilateral panels of trade experts. In the case of conflicts concerning environmental and health issues, a party may call on scientific and environmental experts to support its point (Articles 2007 and 2015). This is an extension to what other trade agreements Esty (1994b) argues that environmental experts will have greater weight in the dispute settlement process at the expense of trade lawyers.

Moreover, there exists an Environmental Side Agreement to the NAFTA, which establishes a Commission for Environmental Co-operation (see Esty (1994b) for details).

NAFTA is a prototype of a trade agreement which (i) involves a highly developed and an industrializing country and (ii) takes account of environmental issues in a way hitherto unknown. Therefore, it may serve as an example of a legal framework for an amendment of the world trading system which takes environmental issues into account more explicitly than the original GATT.

9.4.4 Environmental Issues and the Future of the World Trading System

Environmentalists have argued that the GATT and the world trading system should be changed in a way which acknowledges the prevalence of environmental preservation over free trade. Moreover, many advocates of free trade as well see the necessity of a change, be it only for the reason that some of the GATT Articles be clarified. Before we go into the details of which regulations may be subject to changes, we will review the main objectives of a world trading system.

The quintessential goal of a world trading system is the efficiency of the international division of labour and of the use of the world's resources. The efficient use of resources should include the efficient use of environmental resources. Up to here, there is no disagreement between most environmentalists and trade liberals. The conflict arises at the point where national and global rationality diverge.

Why do individual countries choose environmental policy instruments that distort international trade? First of all, there is policy failure. However, no one argues that this should be a reason to refuse the free-trade principle in general.[34] On the contrary, a binding international agreement on trade helps to reduce these distortions since it raises the costs of using distorting policies.[35] The other reason for environmental policies that reduce trade is extraterritorialism. A country uses its environmental policy to exert some influence on a foreign country's environmental policy, emissions, or environmentally intensive production. Here, one has to distinguish between national and international environmental problems. In the case of purely national environmental problems, the motivation for trade-distorting policies is environmental dumping by another country, i.e. too lax environmental standards. In this respect, there tends to be a coalition of supergreens, who suffer from psychic spillovers of foreign pollution on the one hand, and protectionist lobbyists, who want to save their rents, on the other. There are, however, good economic arguments that neither protectionist nor green eco-imperialist interests should be granted an influence on the world trading system. There remain the problems of transboundary pollution and global environmental resources including biodiversity. This will probably be the core issue in debates on free trade and environmental preservation in the near future.

[34] It has been shown above that trade restrictions can be beneficial in circumstances of mistaken environmental policies. And in situations where no better instruments are available, trade restrictions are justifiable. The example used was that of toxic-waste trade.

[35] The costs of distorted environmental policies are raised because an international trade agreement reduces the set of second-best policies that can be used to correct the original policy failure.

In my view, the central problem with global environmental externalities and free international trade is a distributional one. It concerns the distribution of property rights to environmental resources.[36] If countries are sovereign, each of them can decide on its own policy without taking care of the implications for the rest of the world. Thus, sovereignty requires that the property right to the global commons be assigned to the polluting countries. The logical consequence is that polluting countries receive compensation if they reduce their emissions, i.e. that the pollutee-pays principle be applied in international environmental agreements. In contrast, standard morality argues that the polluter should pay. The property-rights distribution implicit in this value-judgement is that the pollutee has the right to enjoy an unpolluted environment. Although the resource allocation can be independent of the initial property-rights distribution as Coase (1960) has shown, the distribution of wealth is not. Property rights are valuable since their owners are eligible to receive compensation. Thus, there are diverging interests and I think that these are essential for the trade-vs.-environment conflict. If there are economic linkages between countries like trade or factor movements, then the initial distribution of property rights is not completely determined. By using trade-policy instruments, polluted countries can force the polluting country to give up its property right claims to environmental resources and change its environmental policy and/or emissions without receiving compensation. This is the idea behind the trade provisions of the Montreal Protocol. Since only a few countries are large and powerful enough to use trade restrictions for environmental purposes, this tends to add another dimension to existing North–South conflicts.[37] The free-trade principle, in contrast, requires that the trade weapon should not be used and, therefore, the property right to environmental resources cannot be shifted.

The main questions concerning an amendment of the GATT and the world trading system are:

1. Should the GATT include environmental preservation or sustainability in its set of objectives?
2. Should the GATT treaty mention environmental issues explicitly?
3. Should there be an 'environmental window' like NAFTA Article 104 which assigns prevalence of international environmental agreements over the free-trade principle?
4. Should trade measures for environmental reasons be allowed if the resources to be protected are outside the territory of the country taking these measures?
5. Should anti-dumping duties be allowed in the case of environmental dumping?
6. What should be done about the environmental impact of international transport?

[36] A similar argument has been used by Subramanian (1992).
[37] It is not coincidence that the most prominent dispute, the US–Mexican tuna case, was between a developed and a developing country.

7. Should the conflict-resolution mechanisms be changed in the light of potential future trade-environment conflicts?
8. If changes are made, how should they be made?

The answer to the first question is clearly: no. A trade agreement is not an environmental agreement and the World Trade Organization is not a World Environmental Organization. I think that the GATT has functioned quite well since it went into force and has been a useful device in promoting freer trade and a better division of labour. Adding additional policy objectives could dilute the original functions of the GATT. Esty (1994a) suggests the creation of a World Environmental Organization for that purpose.

As regards the second question, I think that an extension of GATT Article XX to explicitly cover 'the environment' is not problematic. It may not even be necessary since a wide interpretation of 'human, animal or plant life or health' could already include the environment. But even if the value of an amendment of the GATT is mainly cosmetic, it could signal the public that the GATT is taking environmental issues seriously—without going as far as adding environmental preservation to the GATT's set of objectives.

The third question whether or not to introduce an environmental escape clause is more difficult to answer than the other two. On the one hand, it is rather unsatisfactory for the GATT to have as its signatory parties countries which have signed environmental agreements that erode what is still being viewed as the spirit of the GATT. One possibility would be to argue that the spirit of the GATT may be subject to a change and to introduce an environmental escape clause like NAFTA Article 104. On the other hand, even if a trade intervention is launched on a multilateral basis by the signatory parties of an international environmental agreement, this does not automatically mean that its purpose is purely philanthropic and that it has no protectionist content.[38] Therefore, a country affected by such a measure should have the opportunity to ask for a GATT Panel deciding the issue. This would be impossible if prevalence were assigned to international environmental agreements over GATT principles. Finally, such a clause in the GATT would perhaps even create incentives to introduce trade restrictions as instruments into international environmental agreements. Thus, it appears to be better not to introduce an environmental escape clause which exempts multilaterally agreed trade barriers from the GATT's rules.

The fourth issue is extraterritorialism. This is a core issue. Currently Article XX is not explicit about the location of the humans, animals, plants, and resources to be protected. I think that problems would be aggravated if the Article were made more explicit in one way or the other. On the one hand, one

---

[38] As an example, it is not surprising that the signatory parties of the Montreal Protocol have been predominantly industrial nations. These countries are the first ones to be able to implement CFC-free technologies. An embargo of CFC-intensive goods then also serves the purposes of market closure and rent appropriation. Although these countries have been the main polluters of the atmosphere in past, they deny the same right to late-comers.

could argue that Article XX should be changed such that the use of trade restrictions to protect environmental resources outside a country's own jurisdiction is prohibited explicitly. Then there would be an obvious inconsistency between the GATT and environmental agreements like the Montreal Protocol and the Basle Convention. Given that a substantial number of countries which are GATT parties have signed these agreements, an explicit prohibition of such policies would not be enforceable. And probably the position of the GATT would be weakened by *ex ante* non-enforceability. On the other hand, one could argue that the GATT should explicitly allow these instruments. But, in my view, this is problematic as well. One reason is that the right to adopt green trade interventions could be used as a pretext for disguised protectionist policies and, therefore, could in the end undermine free trade. Moreover, and perhaps more importantly, the legality of trade interventions is an incentive to use them instead of more efficient instruments of environmental policy. A similar view is taken in Article 12 of the Rio Declaration. Finally, extraterritorialism could be introduced through the back door by narrowing down the definition of 'like products' in GATT Article III(4). This would make it possible to distinguish goods by the way in which they have been produced. If this were done, importing countries could treat goods that have been produced abroad by less environmentally sound methods differently from domestic goods. This, however, would probably open a Pandora's box of green protectionism because domestic producers would complain even more than environmentalists about unfair competition from abroad. Given that there are good economic reasons for differences in environmental regulation, unequal treatment of foreign goods based on this criterion would result in welfare losses.[39,40]

Fifth, we have the problem how the GATT should deal with ecological dumping, and similar considerations apply here. If ecological dumping is defined as laxer environmental regulation in the exporting than in the importing country, then there is no reason for the GATT to care about it. Cross-country differences in environmental regulation are simply a result of diversity. However, if ecological dumping is defined as hidden subsidization by too lax environmental standards, then there is an issue. Direct subsidization can be used as a justification to impose countervailing duties. Why not indirect subsidization?

[39] A similar view has been taken by the German Council of Economic Advisors Sachverstädigenrat (1994: 245), who argue that the origin principle should be applied in this context.

[40] It has been argued, *inter alia* by the GATT in its US–Mexican Tuna Panel, that eco-labelling could be used as a substitute for unequal treatment. In cases of global environmental pollution, however, this works only if consumers act irrationally to some extent. A consumer buying a good that she knows has been produced without CFCs at a higher price than an alternative good which may have used ozone-depleting substances in its production has to share the environmental benefits of his action with billions of other people. Thus, if she is rational, she will buy the cheaper good. Matters may be different in the case of psychic spillovers. If someone just likes dolphins even if they are not threatened by extinction, she may be willing to pay more for dolphin-friendly tuna products than for conventional ones because each dolphin saved adds to her personal utility. Of course, there are many implementation problems with eco-labelling, but they will not be discussed here (see Esty (1994*a*: 135, 171–2, and 251–2)).

The big problem is that in the case of environmental regulation no one knows what the true costs of environmental disruption are—in particular in another country. And if the environmental damage is unknown, there is no point of reference to which observed environmental taxes and standards can be compared. Given that countervailing duties have become one of the means of last resort for protectionist forces in a world that has abolished the traditional barriers to trade, it would be unwise to create additional pretexts for their use.

International trade requires transportation and transportation is environmentally intensive. Many of the problems can be dealt with on the national, regional, or even community levels. However, there are still some issues that require supranational regulation, i.e. those transport activities which are performed in extraterritorial environmental media like international waters and air space. Unilateral action like national taxation of aviation fuels or safety requirements for cargo vessels can have undesirable dislocation effects and result in detours that raise environmental and trade costs.[41] However, this is not an issue that the World Trade Organization should put on its agenda with a high priority. There exist multilateral agreements for different means of international transport and these should be amended if necessary to cover the environmental costs of transportation.[42]

Seventh, there is the issue of conflict resolution. It should be noted that the procedures favour the environmentalist position to some extent since the party which has to take first step is the country whose trade interests are affected by environmental policies and not vice versa.[43] Environmentalists have argued frequently that GATT Panels have been biased by the facts that they have been composed mainly of trade lawyers and that outsiders like environmental experts have been underrepresented. The Draft Understanding on Rules and Procedures Governing the Settlement of Disputes which emerged from the Uruguay Round negotiations contains significant refinements of the former GATT dispute settlement mechanism but does not take up this claim explicitly (see Kohona (1994) for an overview). Basic ingredients of the Understanding are the introduction of strict time-scales in the dispute-settlement procedures, automatic processes that can only be stopped by a consensus agreement of the parties involved, and a more detailed specification of the procedures to be adopted and of the criteria for the nomination of Panel members. The Under-

[41] With strict regulations that are not enforced on a global level, convenient-flag problems known from international merchant shipping could spread to other means of transport and become more severe. Some regulations like national taxes on aviation fuels would become inefficient or even counter-productive since their major effect would be to change the location of refuelling rather than to signal environmental scarcity (see Alamdari and Brewer (1994)).

[42] e.g. with the International Maritime Organization there exists an international body dedicated to issues of maritime transport and several safety conventions including one on the prevention of pollution from ships have been in force for several years or even decades (see Blanco-Bazán (1992)).

[43] See Esty (1994a: 211). The alternative procedure favouring free trade would be to have the country wishing to implement environmental policies ask for permission by the GATT or the WTO.

standing states that a panel can ask for the advice, and make use of the expertise, of any individual or body, but there is no requirement to include environmental experts in trade–environment conflicts. Still this is an amendment in which environmentalist concerns have been taken into account (see Kohona (1994: 36)). Finally, one could argue that panels should be more public than they have been in the past. The Understanding takes this into account by granting third parties access to the panel process. Environmentalists wish that this right, which is exclusive to WTO members at the moment, be extended to outsiders like non-governmental organizations. However, one may expect that the party defending its environmental policy in front of a panel has sufficient incentives to stress the importance of environmental issues.

Finally, the question arises of how the changes in the world trading system can be implemented. The extreme scenario to abolish the old GATT and draft a new General Agreement on Trade and Environment is probably not a serious option. Thus, one relies on changing single GATT Articles. GATT Article XXX defines the requirements of such changes. The basic principles, Articles I and II require unanimous decisions, but they are not subject to changes any way. The other articles can be changed by a majority of two-thirds of the GATT parties. Given that many environmental issues involve North–South differences in their perception, it is rather unlikely that major changes in one direction or the other can be made. What may be agreeable to a large majority of countries, however, is the inclusion of the protection of the environment in Article XX in addition to that of human, animal or plant life or health. An additional possibility to change the GATT is the use of waivers (Article XXV). GATT obligations can be waived by a two-thirds vote which must represent a simple majority of all GATT parties. According to Esty (1994a: 216), however, the right to waive GATT obligations is not meant to be an alternative way to change the GATT if the two-thirds majority of total membership cannot be achieved. Thus, in case this qualified majority is impossible, there seems to be no alternative but to leave the GATT basically as it is. The interpretation of the ambiguous GATT rules is then left to panels that have to consider special trade–environment disputes. Of course, it is not satisfying to leave such fundamental decisions to panels which decide on a case-by-case basis and whose composition (three or five members) is by no means representative of the diversity of interests of GATT signatory parties or WTO members.[44] However, in the past the GATT council had the choice whether or not to adopt such panel decisions and in case of adoption they were usable as precedents. A similar procedure could be implemented for the WTO. This would perhaps provide an institutional framework which generates more legal security than the former one, but without giving up the flexibility an international organization needs to balance the interests of a heterogeneous world community.

---

[44] Still another possibility is to agree on a side agreement or code like the dumping code established during the Tokyo Round. However, such agreements and codes are binding only to the parties that accept them (see Esty (1994a: 217)).

9.5 Epilogue

To conclude, the conflict between trade and the environment is a difficult one to solve. The general policy implication of this study—sound environmental policies plus free trade—should be agreeable to everyone because it maximizes the pie that is to be shared. But unanimity vanishes when a decision is to be made on how to implement this rule. There are incentives to free-ride both in the fields of environmental and trade policies. And the property rights to global environmental resources are not defined. Thus, it is unclear who should pay and who should receive compensation. Hence there is a conflict between countries wishing to use their power in international markets as a weapon for the worldwide implementation of sound environmental policies, and other countries arguing that global environmental problems can better be solved with free trade and side payments that allow them to introduce environmentally friendly production technologies. Both arguments are rational and understandable from the corresponding national points of view. From a more global perspective, however, both of them are deficient. Compensation payments to polluters may induce strategic behaviour aiming at the entitlement to receive such payments, e.g. by means of increased emissions. Green trade restrictions are likely to be captured by protectionist interests and their availability as a second-best option may deter governments from going the difficult way to achieve the first best. Thus, given the entrenchment of governments and people behind their individually rational points of view, the reconciliation of international trade and the environment is a utopian perspective. None the less, we should keep on working for it.

Appendix: List of Variables

Usually, lower-case letters denote variables of the home country, upper-case letters denote variables of the foreign country

a, a^i, A, A^i	pollution impact parameters production
b, b^i, B, B^i	pollution impact parameters consumption
c, c^i, C, C^i	consumption
$\tilde{c}, \tilde{c}^i, \tilde{C}, \tilde{C}^i$	cost function
$\hat{c}, \hat{c}^i, \hat{C}, \hat{C}^i$	unit cost function
d, D	demand function
e, e^i, E, E^i	input of environmental resources, emissions
e^o, E^o	quantity of toxic waste deposited in a country
f, f^i, F, F^i	production function
g, g^i, G, G^i	function representing the external effect of environmental disruption on output
h	interest payment function
$\tilde{h}, \tilde{H}$	Hamiltonian function
i	index of good and sector
k, k^i, K, K^i	capital stock
k^e	production capital
m, m^i, M, M^i	imports
n	number of goods or firms
$p, p^i, P, P^i, \tilde{p}$	prices of final goods
q, q^i, Q, Q^i	supply of final good
r, r^i, R, R^i	capital remuneration, interest rate
$\check{r}, \check{R}$	reaction function
s, S	own-country pollution coefficient
t	time
$t^c, t^{c,i}, T^c, T^{c,i}$	consumption tax rate
$t^e, t^{e,i}, T^e, T^{e,i}$	emission tax rate
t^k, T^K	capital income tax rate
$t^t, t^{t,i}, T^t, T^{t,i}$	trade tax rate (tariff)
u, U	utility function
v	foreign-assets position
w, W	welfare level
x, X	exports
z, Z	environmental pollution
β	perceived pollution impact parameter
γ, γ^i	pollution impact parameter transportation
δ	discount rate
Δ	value of a determinant of a matrix (used for different matrices)
ε	expenditure function for given level of environmental quality
ϕ	production function

ζ	used for different purposes
θ, Θ	used for different purposes
χ, X	used for different purposed
κ	capital used for abatement
λ, Λ	shadow price of state variable in dynamic optimisation problems
σ	side payment, subsidy
ζ	intertemporal elasticity of substitution
ψ	abatement function (Ch. 2), saddle-path function (Ch. 8)
ξ	used for different purposes
υ	level of utility derived from consumption
ω, Ω	environmental friendliness of consumption goods

References

ADAMS, P., 1991, *Odious Debts: Loose Lending, Corruption, and the Third World's Environmental Legacy*, London, Toronto: Earthscan.

ALAMDARI, F. E., and D. BREWER, 1994, 'Taxation Policy for Aircraft Emissions', *Transport Policy* 1: 149–59.

ALEXANDER, D. C., 1993, 'The North American Free Trade Agreement: An Overview', *International Tax and Business Lawyer* 11: 48–70.

AMELUNG, T., and M. DIEHL, 1992, *Deforestation of Tropical Rain Forests: Economic Causes and Impact on Development*, Tübingen: Mohr.

ANDERSON, K., 1992a, 'Effects on the Environment and Welfare of Liberalizing World Trade: The Cases of Coal and Food', in K. Anderson and R. Blackhurst, *The Greening of World Trade Issues*, New York: Harvester Wheatsheaf, 145–72.

—— 1992b, 'Agricultural Trade Liberalisation and the Environment: A Global Perspective', *The World Economy* 15: 153–71.

—— 1992c, 'The Standard Welfare Economics of Policies Affecting Trade and the Environment', in K. Anderson and R. Blackhurst, *The Greening of World Trade Issues*, New York: Harvester Wheatsheaf, 25–48.

ANDERSON, S., A. DE PALMA, and J.-F. THISSE, 1992, *Discrete Choice Theory of Product Differentiation*, Cambridge, Mass.: MIT Press.

ANONYMOUS, 1992, 'Let Them Eat Pollution', *Economist,* 8 Feb. 1992, 66.

ARDEN- LARKE, C., 1991, *The General Agreement on Tariffs and Trade, Environmental Protection and Sustainable Develpoment*, Gland: World Wildlife Fund.

—— 1992, 'South-North Terms of Trade: Environmental Protection and Sustainable Development', *International Environmental Affairs* 4: 122–38.

ASAKO, K., 1979, 'Environmental Pollution in an Open Economy', *Economic Record* 55: 359–66.

AUDLEY, J. J., 1993, 'The "Greening" of Trade Agreements: Environmental "Window Dressing" and NAFTA', in K. Fatemi (ed.), *North Americal Free Trade Agreement: Opportunities and Challenges*, New York: St Martin's Press, 252–68.

BARBERA, A. J., and V. D. McCONNELL, 1986, 'Effects of Pollution Control on Industry Productivity: A Factor Demand Approach', *Journal of Industrial Economics* 35: 161–72.

BARBIER, E. B., 1991, 'Managing Trade and the Environment: The Demand for Raw Ivory in Japan and Hong Kong', *World Economy* 14: 407–30.

—— M. RAUSCHER, 1994, 'Trade, Tropical Deforestation and Policy Interventions', *Environmental and Resource Economics* 4: 75–90.

BARDHAN, P. K., 1967, Optimum Foreign Borrowing, in K. Shell (ed.), *Essays on the Theory of Economic Growth*, Cambridge, Mass.: MIT Press, 117–28.

BARNETT, A. H., 1980, 'The Pigouvian Tax Rule under Monopoly', *American Economic Review* 70: 1037–41.

BARRETT, S., 1994a 'Self-Enforcing International Environmental Agreements', *Oxford Economic Papers* 46: 878–94.

—— 1994*b*, 'Strategic Environmental Policy and International Trade', *Journal of Public Economics* 54: 325–38.

BARTIK, T. J., 1988, 'The Effects of Environmental Regulation on Business Location in the United States', *Growth and Change* 19: 22–44.

BARTSCH, E., M. RAUSCHER and I. THOMAS, 1993, *Environmental Legislation and the Impact of Lobbying Activities*, Kiel: Institute of World Economics Working Paper No. 556.

BATRA, R., 1993, *The Myth of Free Trade: A Plan for America's Economic Revival*, New York: Macmillan.

BAUMOL, W. J., 1971, *Environmental Protection, International Spillovers, and Trade*, Stockholm: Almkvist & Wicksell.

—— W. E. OATES, 1988, *The Theory of Environmental Policy*, 2nd edn., Cambridge: Cambridge University Press.

BEAVIS, B. and M. Walker, 1979, 'Interactive Pollutants and Joint Abatement Costs: Achieving Water Quality Standards with Effluent Charges', *Journal of Environmental Economics and Management*, 6, 275–86.

BECKER, G. S., 1983, 'A Theory of Competition among Pressure Groups for Political Influence', *Quarterly Journal of Economics* 98: 371–400.

BEGG, D., J. CREMER, J.-P. DEMTHINE, J. Edwards, V. GRILLI, D. NEVEN, P. SEABRIGHT, H.-W. SINN, A. VENABLES and C. WYPLOSZ, 1993, *Making Sense of Subsidiarity: How Much Centralization for Europe?*, London: Centre of Economic Policy Research.

BENSEL, T., and B. T. ELMSLIE, 1992, 'Rethinking International Trade Theory: A Methodological Appraisal', *Weltwirtschaftliches Archiv* 128: 249–65.

BHAGWATI, J. H., 1972, 'The Heckscher-Ohlin Theorem in the Multi-Commodity Case', *Journal of Political Economy* 80: 1052–55.

BIRDSALL, N., and D. WHEELER, 1992, 'Trade Policy and Industrial Pollution in Latin America: Where Are the Pollution Havens?', in P. Low (ed.), *International Trade and the Environment*, New York: World Bank Discussion Paper No. 159: 159–67.

BLACK, J., M. D. LEVI, and D. DE MEZA, 1993, 'Creating a Good Atmosphere: Minimum Participation for Tackling the Greenhouse Effect', *Economica* 60: 281–93.

BLANCO-BAZÁN, A., 1992, 'The Role of the International Maritime Organization (IMO) in the Management of Maritime Risks', *Geneva Papers on Risk and Insurance* 17: 244–56.

BLAZEJCZAK, J., 1993, *Umweltschutz und Industriestandort: Der Einfluss umweltbezogener Standortfaktoren auf Investitionsentscheidungen*, Berlin: Schmidt.

BOHM, P., and C. S. RUSSELL, 1985, 'Comparative Analysis of Alternative Policy Instruments', in A. V. Kneese and J. L. Sweeney (eds.), *Handbook of Natural Resource and Energy Economics, Vol.1*, Amsterdam: North-Holland, 395–460.

BORREGAARD, N., and H. MEYER, 1988, *Debt-for-Nature Swaps: A Control Theoretical Approach to Compensation Payments*, Kiel: Institute of World Economics Advanced Studies Working Paper No. 137.

BRANDER, J. A., 1981, 'Intra-Industry Trade in Identical Commodities', *Journal of International Economics* 11: 1–14.

—— 1995, *Strategic Trade Policy*, Cambridge, Mass.: NBER Working Paper No. 5020.

——and P. R. KRUGMAN, 1983, 'A Reciprocal Dumping Model of International Trade', *Journal of International Economics* 15: 313–21.

—— and B. SPENCER, 1984, 'Trade Warfare: Tariffs and Cartels', *Journal of International Economics* 16: 227–42.

—— —— 1985, 'Export Subsidies and International Market Share Rivalry', *Journal of International Economics* 18: 83–100.

——and M. S. TAYLOR, 1995*a*, *International Trade and Open Access Renewable Resources: The Small Open Economy Case*, Cambridge, Mass.: NBER Working Paper No. 5021.

—— —— 1995*b*, *Open Access Renewable Resources: Trade and Trade Policy in a Two-Country Model*, Paper Presented at the NBER Summer Institute.

BRENNAN, G. and J. M. BUCHANAN, 1980, *The Power to Tax: Analytical Foundations of a Fiscal Constitution*, Cambridge: Cambridge University Press.

BROOKS, M. and B. HEIJDRA, 1989, 'An Exploration of Rent Seeking', *Economic Record* 65: 32–50.

BUCHANAN, J. M., 1969, 'External Diseconomies, Corrective Taxes, and Market Structure', *American Economic Review* 59: 174–77.

——and G. TULLOCK, 1975, 'Polluters' Profits and Political Response: Direct Controls Vs. Taxes', *American Economic Review* 65: 139–47.

BULOW, J. I., J. D. GEANAKOPLOS, and P. D. KLEMPERER, 1985, 'Multimarket Oligopoly: Strategic Substitutes and Complements', *Journal of Political Economy* 93: 488–511.

BURMEISTER, E., and A. R. DOBELL, 1970, *Mathematical Theories of Economic Growth*, New York: Macmillan.

BURNIAUX, J. M., J. P. MARTIN, and J. OLIVEIRA-MARTINS, 1992, 'The Effect of Existing Distorsions in the Energy Markets on the Cost of Policies to Reduce CO_2 Emissions', *OECD Economic Studies* 19: 141–65.

CARBAUGH, R. and D. WASSINK, 1992, 'Environmental Standards and International Competitiveness', *World Competition* 16: 81–91.

CASS, D. Z., 1992, 'The Word that Saves Maastricht? The Principle of Subsidiarity and the Division of Powers within the European Community', *Common Market Law Review* 29: 1107–36.

CHAMBERLIN, E., 1933, *The Theory of Monopolistic Competition*, Cambridge, Mass.: *Harvard University Press.*

CHARNOVITZ, S., 1991, 'Exploring the Environmental Exceptions under GATT Article XX', *Journal of World Trade* 15(5): 37–55.

—— 1992, 'Environmental and Labour Standards in Trade', *World Economy* 15: 335–56.

—— 1993, 'Environmentalism Confronts GATT Rules: Recent Developments and New Opportunities', *Journal of World Trade* 27(2): 37–53.

CHIANG, A. C., 1992, *Elements of Dynamic Optimization*, New York: McGraw-Hill.

CHICHILNISKY, G., 1994*a*, 'Global Environment and North-South Trade', *American Economic Review* 84: 851–74.

—— 1994*b*, 'Property Rights and the Dynamics of Renewable Resources in North-South Trade', in C. Carraro (ed.), *Trade, Innovation, Environment*, Dordrecht: Kluwer, 15–54.

COASE, R. H., 1960, 'The Problem of Social Cost', *Journal of Law and Economics* 3: 1–44.

COBB, J. B. Jr., and H. E. DALY, 1989, *For the Common Good: Redirecting the Economy toward Community, the Environment, and a Sustainable Future*, Boston: Beacon Press.

Commission of the European Communities, 1993, *Growth, Competitiveness, Employment: The Challenges and Ways forward into the 21st Century: White Paper*, Luxembourg: Office for the Official Publications of the European Communities.

CONRAD, K., 1993a, 'Taxes and Subsidies for Pollution-Intensive Industries', *Journal of Environmental Economics and Management* 25: 121–35.

—— 1993b, *Optimal Environmental Policy for Oligopolistic Industries in an Open Economy*, Mannheim: Faculty of Economics and Statistics of the University, Discussion Paper 476–93.

——and C. J. MORRISON, 1989, 'The Impact of Pollution Abatement Investment on Productivity Change: An Empirical Comparison of the US, Germany, and Canada', *Southern Economic Journal* 55: 684–98.

COPELAND, B. R., 1991, 'International Trade in Waste Products in the Presence of Illegal Disposal', *Journal of Environmental Economics and Management* 20: 143–62.

—— 1994, International Trade and the Environment: Policy Reform in a Small Open Economy, *Journal of Environmental Economics and Management* 26: 44–65.

——and M. S. TAYLOR, 1993, *Trade and Transboundary Pollution*, Vancouver: University of British Columbia Discussion Paper 93–46.

—— —— 1994, North-South Trade and the Environment, *Quarterly Journal of Economics* 109, 755–87.

—— —— 1995, *Trade, Non-Convexities and the Environment*, Paper Presented at the NBER Summer Institute.

CORBETT, R., 1993, *The Treaty of Maastricht: From Conception to Ratification: A Comprehensive Reference Guide*, Harlow: Longman.

CORNES, R. and T. SANDLER, 1985a, *The Theory of Externalities, Public Goods, and Club Goods*, Cambridge: Cambridge University Press.

—— —— 1985b, 'Externalities, Expectations and Pigouvian Taxes', *Journal of Environmental Economics and Management* 12: 1–13.

COUGHLIN, P. J., D. C MUELLER, and P. MURRELL, 1990, 'A Model of Electoral Competition with Interest Groups', *Economics Letters* 32: 307–11.

CROPPER, L., and W. C. OATES, 1992, 'Environmental Economics: A Survey', *Journal of Economic Literature* 30: 675–740.

DALY, H. E., and R. GOODLAND 1994, 'An Ecological-Economic Assessment of Deregulation of International Commerce under GATT', *Ecological Economics* 9: 73–92.

DAVIES, S. W., and A. J. MCGUINNESS, 1982, 'Dumping at Less than Marginal Cost', *Journal of International Economics* 12: 169–82.

DEAN, J. M., 1992, 'Trade and the Environment: A Survey of the Literature', in P. Low (ed.), *International Trade and the Environment*, New York: World Bank Discussion Paper No. 159: 15–28.

DEBELLEVUE, E. B., E. HITZEL, K. CLINE, J. A. BENITEZ, J. RAMOS-MIRANDA, and O. SEGURA, 1994, 'The North American Free Trade Agreement: An Ecological-Economic Synthesis for the United States and Mexico', *Ecological Economics* 9: 53–71.

DEARDORFF, A. V., 1979, 'Weak Links in the Chain of Comparative Advantage', *Journal of International Economics* 9: 197–209.

—— 1982, 'The General Validity of the Heckscher-Ohlin Theorem', *American Economic Review* 72, 683–94.

DEWEES, D. N., 1983, 'Instrument Choice in Environmental Policy', *Economic Inquiry* 21: 53–71.

DIWAN, I., and N. SHAFIK, 1992, 'Investment, Technology and the Global Environment: Towards International Agreement in a World of Disparities', in P. Low (ed.), *International Trade and the Environment*, New York: World Bank Discussion Paper No. 159: 263–85.

DIXIT, A., 1985, 'Tax Policy in Open Economies', in A. J. Auerbach and M. Feldstein, eds., *Handbook of Public Economics*, Amsterdam: North-Holland, 313–74.

—— 1986, 'Comparative Statics for Oligopoly', *International Economic Review* 27: 107–22.

—— 1987, 'Strategic Aspects of Trade Policy', in T. Bewley (ed.), *Advances in Economic Theory*, Cambridge: Cambridge Unviersity Press, 329–62.

——and G. M. GROSSMAN, 1986, 'Targeted Export Promotion with Several Oligopolistic Industries', *Journal of International Economics* 21: 233–49.

—— and V. NORMAN, 1980, *Theory of International Trade*, Welwyn: Nisbet.

—— and J. E. STIGLITZ, 1977, 'Monopolistic Competition and Optimum Product Diversity', *American Economic Review* 67: 297–308.

DOUMA, W. T., 1991, *International Regulations on the Export of Hazardous Waste: The Evolution of a New Piece of International Environmental Law*, Groningen: Rijksuniversiteit Papers on Development and Security No. 33.

DOWNS, A., 1957, *An Economic Theory of Democracy*, New York: Harper & Row.

EATON, J., and G. M. GROSSMAN, 1986, 'Optimal Trade and Industrial Policy under Oligopoly', *Quarterly Journal of Economics* 102: 383–406.

EBERT, U., 1991, 'Pigouvian Tax and Market Structure: The Case of Oligopoly and Different Abatement Technologies', *Finanzarchiv* 49: 154–66.

EDWARDS, J. and M. KEEN, 1994, *Tax Competition and Leviathan*, London: Institute of Fiscal Studies Discussion Paper 94,7.

EKINS, P., 1989, 'Trade and Self-Reliance', *The Ecologist* 19: 186–90.

—— C. FOLKE and R. COSTANZA, 1994, 'Trade, Environment and Development: The Issues in Perspective', *Ecological Economics* 9: 1–12.

ENDERS, A., and A. PORGES, 1992, 'Successful Conventions and Conventional Success', in K. Anderson and R. Blackhurst (eds.), *The Greening of World Trade Issues*, New York: Harvester Wheatsheaf, 130–44.

ENDRES, A., 1986, 'Charges, Permits and Pollutant Interactions', *Eastern Economic Journal* 12: 327–36.

ESTY, D. C., 1994a, *Greening the GATT: Trade, Environment, and the Future*, Washington, DC: Institute for International Economics.

—— 1994b, 'Making Trade and Environmental Policies Work Together: Lessons from NAFTA', *Aussenwirtschaft* 49: 59–79.

ETHIER, W. J., 1982, 'Dumping', *Journal of Political Economy* 90: 487–506.

—— 1984, 'Higher Dimensional Issues in Trade Theory', in R. W. Jones and P. B. Kenen (eds.), *Handbook of International Economics, Vol. 1*, Amsterdam: North-Holland, 131–84.

FEICHTINGER, G., and R. HARTL, 1986, *Optimale Kontrolle ökonomischer Prozesse: Anwendungen des Maximumprinzips in den Wirtschaftswissenschaften*, Berlin, New York: De Gruyter.

—— and A. NOVAK, 1991, 'A Note on the Use of Environmental Resources by an Indebted Country', *Journal of Institutional and Theoretical Economics* 147: 547–55.

FELDER, S., and T. F. RUTHERFORD, 1993, 'Unilateral CO_2 Reductions and Carbon Leakage: The Consequences of International Trade in Oil and Basic Materials', *Journal of Environmental Economics and Management* 25: 162–76.

FOLMER, H., and C. H. HOWE, 1991, 'Environmental Problems and Policy in the Single Market', *Environmental and Resource Economics* 1: 17–42.

—— P. V. MOUCHE, and S. RAGLAND, 1993, Interconnected Games and International Environmental Problems, *Environmental and Resource Economics* 3, 313–35.

FRANTZ, R., 1989, *X-Efficiency: Theory, Evidence and Applications*, Boston: Kluwer.

FRASER, G. A., 1989, 'The Potential Benefits to Canada from Long Range Air Pollution Control', in H. A. Jöbstl (ed.), *Economic Assessment of the Damage Caused to Forests by Air Pollutants*, Wien: Agrarverlag, 143–56.

FRIEDMAN, J. W., 1989, *Game Theory with Applications to Economics*, Oxford: Oxford University Press.

FUDENBERG, D., J. TIROLE, 1991, *Game Theory*, Cambridge, Mass.: MIT Press.

GABEL, H. L., and L.-H. RÖLLER, 1992, 'Trade Liberalization, Transportation, and the Environment', *Energy Journal* 13(3): 185–206.

GALE, D., and H. NIKAIDÔ, 1965, 'The Jacobian Matrix and the Univalence of Mappings', *Mathematische Annalen* 159: 81–93.

GANDOLFO, G., 1986, *International Economics*, Berlin: Springer.

GATT, 1961, *The General Agreement of Tariffs and Trade*, Washington, DC: Departments of State Publication 7182.

—— 1992, *International Trade 1990–91*, Geneva: GATT.

—— 1993, 'United States: Restrictions on Tuna. Report of the Panel (DS 21/R)', *GATT Basic Instruments and Selected Documents Supplement* 39: 155–205.

GEORGE, S., 1992, *The Debt Boomerang: How Third World Debt Harms Us All*, London: Pluto.

GOLDSMITH, E., 1990, 'The Uruguay Round: Gunboat Diplomacy by Another Name', *Ecologist* 20: 202–4.

GRAY, W. B., and R. J. SHADBEGIAN, 1993, *Environmental Regulation and Manufacturing Productivity at the Plant Level*, Cambridge, Mass.: NBER Working Paper No. 4321.

GREENAWAY, D., and S. MILNER, 1986, *The Economics of Intra-Industry Trade*, Oxford: Blackwell.

GRONYCH, R., 1980, *Allokationseffekte und Aussenhandelswirkungen der Umweltpolitik: Eine komparativ-statische Zwei-Sektor-Analyse*, Tübingen: Mohr.

GROS, D., 1987a, 'A Note on the Optimal Tariff, Retaliation and the Welfare Loss from Tariff Wars in a Framework with Intra-Industry Trade', *Journal of International Economics* 23: 357–67.

—— 1987b, 'Protectionism in a Framework with Intra-Industry Trade', *IMF Staff Papers* 34: 86–114.

GROSSMAN, G. M., 1986, 'Strategic Export Promotion: A Critique', in P. R. Krugman (ed.), *Strategic Trade Policy and the New International Economics*, Cambridge, Mass.: MIT Press, 47–66.

——and E. HELPMAN, 1994, 'Protection for Sale', *American Economic Review* 84, 833–50.

——and A. B. KRUEGER, 1993, 'Environmental Impacts of a North American Free Trade Agreement', in P. M. Garber, (ed.), *The Mexico-US Free Trade Agreement*, Cambridge, Mass.: MIT Press, 13–56.

GUTOWSKI, A., 1986, 'From Recycling to Indebtedness: What Went Wrong?', in H. Giersch (ed.), *The International Debt Problem: Lessons for the Future*, Tübingen: Mohr, 1–14.

HABERLER, G. V., 1936, *The Theory of International Trade with Its Applications to Commercial Policy*, London: Hodge.

HAHN, R. W., 1989, 'Economic Presriptions for Environmental Problems: How the

Patient Followed the Doctor's Orders', *Journal of Economic Perspectives* 3(2): 95–114.

HANSEN, S., 1989, 'Debt for Nature Swaps: Overview and Discussion of Key Issues', *Ecological Economics* 1: 77–93.

HANSSON, G., 1990, *Harmonization and International Trade*, London: Routledge.

HARDIN, G., 1968, 'The Tragedy of the Commons', *Science* 162: 1243–8.

HAROLD, C., and C. F. RUNGE, 1993, 'GATT and the Environment: Policy Research Needs', *American Journal of Agricultural Economics* 75: 789–93.

HECKSCHER, E. F., 1919, 'Utrikeshandelsns Verkan på Inkomstfördelningen: Några Teoretiska Grundlinjer', *Economisk Tidskrift* 21: 497–512. Eng. trans. 'The Effect of Foreign Trade on the Distribution of Income: A Theoretical Outline', in H. Flam and M. J. Flanders (eds.), 1991, *Heckscher-Ohlin Trade Theory*, Cambridge, Mass.: MIT Press, 39–69.

HEIJDRA, B. J., and X. YANG, 1993, 'Imperfect Competition and Product Differentiation: Some Further Results', *Mathematical Social Sciences* 25: 157–71.

HELPMAN, E., 1981, 'International Trade in the Presence of Product Differentiation; Economies of Scale ad Monopolistic Competition; A Chamberlin-Heckscher-Ohlin Approach', *Journal of International Economics* 11: 305–40.

—— 1984, 'Increasing Returns, Imperfect Markets, and Trade Theory', in R. W. Jones and P. B. Kenen (eds.), *Handbook of International Economics*, Amsterdam: North-Holland, 325–65.

—— 1987, 'Imperfect Competition and International Trade: Evidence from Fourteen Industrial Countries', *Journal of Japanese and International Economics* 1: 62–81.

——and P. R. KRUGMAN, 1985 *Market Structure and Foreign Trade: Increasing Returns, Imperfect Competition, and the International Economy*, Cambridge, Mass.: MIT Press.

—— ——1989 *Trade Policy and Market Structure*, Cambridge, Mass.: MIT Press.

HERBERG, H. and M. C. KEMP, 1969, 'Some Implications of Variable Returns to Scale, *Canadian Journal of Ecnomics* 2: 403–15.

—— —— and M. TAWADA, 1982, 'More on Variable Returns to Scale', *Journal of International Economics* 13: 65–84.

HETTIGE, H., R. E. B. LUCAS, and D. WHEELER, 1992, 'The Toxic Intensity of Industrial Production: Global Patterns, Trends, and Trade Policy', *American Economic Review (Papers and Proeedings)* 82: 478–81.

HILLMAN, A. L., 1989, *The Political Economy of Protection*, Chur, Switzerland: Harwood.

——and H. W. Ursprung, 1988, 'Domestic Politics, Foreign Interests, and International Trade Policy', *American Economic Review* 78: 729–45.

—— —— 1992, 'The Influence of Environmental Concerns on the Political Determination of International Trade Policy', in K. Anderson and R. Blackhurst (eds.), *The Greening of World Trade Issues*, New York: Harvester Wheatsheaf, 195–220.

—— —— 1994, 'Greens, Supergreens and International Trade Policy: Environmental Concerns and Protectionism', in C. Carraro (ed.), *Trade, Innovation, Environment*, Dordrecht: Kluwer, 75–108.

HILZ, C., and J. R. EHRENFELD, 1991, 'Transboundary Movements of Toxic Wastes: A Comparative Analysis of Policy Options to Control the International Waste Trade', *International Environmental Affairs* 3: 26–63.

HOEKMAN, B., and M. LEIDY, 1992, 'Environmental Policy Formation in a Trading Economy: A Public Choice Perspective', in K. Anderson and R. Blackhurst (eds.), *The Greening of World Trade Issues*, New York: Harvester Wheatsheaf, 221–46.

HOEL, M., 1994, *Environmental Policy as a Game between Governments when Plant Locations Are Endogenous*, Oslo: Dept. of Economics, Memorandum No. 1994, 21.

HOLTZ-EAKIN, D., and T. SELDEN, 1993, *Stoking the Fires? CO_2 Emissions and Economic Growth*, Cambridge, Mass.: NBER discussion paper 4248.

HORSTMAN, I. J., and J. R. MARKUSEN, 1986, 'Up Your Average Cost Curve: Inefficient Entry and the New Protectionism', *Journal of International Economics* 20: 225–49.

—— —— 1992, 'Endogenous Market Structures in International Trade (Natura Facit Saltum)', *Journal of International Economics* 32: 109–29.

HOTELLING, H., 1929, 'Stability in Competition', *Economic Journal* 39: 41–57.

JASAY, A. E., 1960, 'The Social Choice between Home and Overseas Investments', *Economic Journal* 70: 105–13.

JOHNSON, H. G., 1953/4, 'Optimum Tariffs and Retaliation', *Review of Economic Studies* 21: 142–53.

JONES, R. W., 1971, 'A Three-Factor Model in Theory, Trade and History', in J. Bhagwati (ed.), *Trade, Balance of Payments, and Growth*, Amsterdam: North-Holland, 3–21.

—— 1974, 'Trade with Non-traded Goods: The Anatomy of Interconnected Markets', *Economica* 41: 121–38.

KAMIEN, M. I., and N. L. SCHWARTZ, 1991, *Dynamic Optimization: The Calculus of Variation and Optimal Control in Economics and Management*, Amsterdam: North-Holland.

KATRAK, H., 1977, 'Multi-National Monopolies and Trade Policies', *Oxford Economic Papers* 29: 283–91.

KATSOULACOS, Y., and A. XEPAPADEAS, 1994, *Emission Taxes and Market Structure*, Milan: Fondazione ENI Enrico Mattei Working Paper No. 23.

KEMP, M. C., 1964, *The Pure Theory of International Trade*, Englewood Cliffs: Prentice-Hall.

——and R. W. JONES, 1962, 'Variable Labor Supply and the Theory of International Trade', *Journal of Political Economy* 70: 30–6.

——and N. V. LONG, 1984, 'The Role of Natural Resources in Trade Models', in R. W. Jones and P. B. Kenen (eds.), *Handbook of International Economics, Vol. 1*, Amsterdam: North-Holland, 367–417.

KENNEDY, P. W., 1994, 'Equilibrium Pollution Taxes in Open Economies with Imperfect Competition', *Journal of Environmental Economics and Management* 27: 49–63.

KIERZKOWSKI, H., 1987, 'Recent Advances in International Trade Theory: A Selective Survey', *Oxford Review of Economic Policy* 3: 1–19.

KIM, I.-C., 1990, 'An Estimation of the Pollution Content of Trade in Korea', *Seoul Journal of Economics* 3: 205–18.

KISIRI, M. J., 1992, International Trade and the Environment: An Additional Non-Tariff Barrier against the Developing Countries' Trade?', *World Competition Law and Economics Review* 15(3): 75–92.

KLEPPER, G., 1994, 'Industrial Policy in the Transport Aircraft Industry', in P. R. Krugman and A. Smith (eds.), *Empirical Studies of Strategic Trade Policy*, Chicago: University of Chicago Press, 101–26.

——and P. MICHAELIS, 1995, *The Economics of Cadmium Control: An Industrial Metabolism Approach*, Tübingen: Mohr.

References 323

KLETTE, T. J., 1994, 'Strategic Trade Policy for Exporting Industries: More General Results in the Oligopolistic Case', *Oxford Economic Papers* 46: 296–310.

KOHONA, P. T. B., 1994, 'Dispute Resolution under the World Trade Organization', *Journal of World Trade* 28(2): 23–47.

KOPPEN, I., 1993, 'The Role of the European Court of Justice in the Development of the European Community Environmental Policy', in J. D. Liefferink, P. D. Lowe, and A. P. J. Mol (eds.), *European Integration and Environmental Policy*, London: Belhaven Press.

KOWALCZYK, C., 1994, 'Monopoly and Trade Policy', *Journal of International Economics* 36: 177–86.

——and T. SJÖSTRÖM, 1994, 'Bringing GATT into the Core', *Economica* 61: 301–17.

KRISTRÖM, B., and P. RIERA, 1994, 'Is the Income Elasticity of Environmental Improvements Less than One?', *Environmental and Resource Economics* 7: 45–55.

KRUEGER, A. O., 1987, 'Origins of the Developing Countries' Debt Crisis 1970–1982', *Journal of Development Economics*, 27: 165–87.

KRUGMAN, P. R., 1979, 'Increasing Returns, Monopolistic Competition, and International Trade', *Journal of International Economics* 9: 469–79.

—— 1980, 'Scale Economies, Product Differentiation and the Pattern of Trade', *American Economic Review* 67: 298–307.

—— 1987, 'Is Free Trade Passé?', *Journal of Economic Perspectives* 1: 131–44.

—— 1988a, 'Industrial Organization and International Trade', in R. Schmalensee and R. Willig (eds.), *Handbook of Industrial Organisation*, Amsterdam: North-Holland, 1179–223.

—— 1988b, 'Financing vs. Forgiving a Debt Overhang', *Journal of Development Economics* 29: 253–68.

—— 1991, 'History versus Expectations', *Quarterly Journal of Economics* 106: 651–67.

——and A. SMITH (eds.) 1994, *Empirical Studies of Strategic Trade Policy*, Chicago: University of Chicago Press.

KRUTILLA, K. 1991, 'Environmental Regulation in an Open Economy', *Journal of Environmental Economics and Management* 10: 127–42.

LAFFONT, J.-J., and J. TIROLE, 1991, 'The Politics of Government Decision Making: A Theory of Regulatory Capture', *Quarterly Journal of Economics*, 106: 1089–127.

LANCASTER, K., 1979, 'Intra-Industry Trade under Perfect Monopolistic Competition', *Journal of International Economics* 10: 151–75.

—— 1984, 'Protection and Product Differentiation', in H. Kierzkowski (ed.), *Monopolistic Competition and International Trade*, Oxford: Clarendon Press, 137–56.

LEAMER, E. E., 1984, *Sources of Comparative Advantage: Theory and Evidence*, Cambridge, Mass.: MIT Press.

LEE, D. R., 1975, 'Efficiency of Pollution Taxation and Market Structure', *Journal of Environmental Economics and Management* 2: 69–72.

LEIBENSTEIN, H., 1966, 'Allocative Efficiency vs "X-efficiency"', *American Economic Review* 56: 392–415.

LEIDY, M. P., and B. M. HOEKMAN, 1994, '"Cleaning up' while Cleaning up? Pollution Abatement, Interest Groups and Contingent Trade Policies', *Public Choice* 78: 241–58.

LÉONARD, D., and N. V. LONG, 1992, *Optimal Control Theory and Static Optimization in Economics*, Cambridge: Cambridge University Press.

LEONARD, H. J., 1988, *Pollution and the Struggle for the World Product: Multinational Corporations, Environment and International Comparative Advantage*, Cambridge: Cambridge University Press.

LEONTIEF, W., 1954, 'Domestic Production and Foreign Trade: The American Capital Position Re-examined', *Economia Internazionale* 7: 9–45.

LEVINSON, A., 1994, *Environmental Regulations and Manufacturers' Location Choices, Evidence from the Census of Manufactures*, Madison, mimeo.

LLOYD, P. J., 1992, 'The Problem of Optimal Environmental Policy Choice', in K. Anderson and R. Blackhurst (eds.), *The Greening of World Trade Issues*, New York: Harvester Wheatsheaf, 49–72.

LOMAX, D. F., 1986, *The Developing Country Debt Crisis*, Basingstoke: Macmillan.

LONG, N. V., and N. VOUSDEN, 1991, 'Protectionist Responses and Declining Industries', *Journal of International Economics* 30: 87–103.

——and H. SIEBERT, 1991, 'Institutional Competition versus Ex-Ante Harmonization: The Case of Environmental Policy', *Journal of Institutional and Theoretical Economics* 147: 296–311.

LOW, P., and A. YEATS, 1992, 'Do Dirty Industries Migrate?', in P. Low (ed.), *International Trade and the Environment*, New York: World Bank Discussion Paper No. 159: 89–103.

LUCAS, R. E. B., D. WHEELER, and H. HETTIGE, 1992, 'Economic Development, Environmental Regulation, and the International Migration of Toxic Industrial Pollution: 1960–1988', in P. Low (ed.), *International Trade and the Environment*, New York: World Bank Discussion Paper No. 159: 159–67.

MACDOUGALL, G. D. A., 1960, 'The Benefits and Costs of Investment from Abroad. A Theoretical Approach', *Economic Record* 36: 13–35.

MAGEE, S., 1980, 'Three Simple Tests of the Stolper-Samuelson Theorem', in P. Oppenheimer (ed.), *Issues in International Economics*, London: Oriel Press, 138–53.

——, W. A. BROCK, and L. YOUNG, 1989, *Black Hole Tariffs and Endogenous Policy Theory: Political Economy in General Equilibrium*, Cambridge: Cambridge University Press.

MCGUIRE, M. C., 1982, 'Regulation, Factor Rewards, and International Trade', *Journal of Public Economics* 17: 335–54.

MÄLER, K.-G., 1990, 'International Environmental Problems', *Oxford Review of Economic Policy* 6(1): 80–108.

MALONEY, M. T., and R. E. MCCORMICK, 1982, 'A Positive Theory of Environmental Policy Formation', *Journal of Law and Economics* 25: 99–123.

MANNE, A. S., and J. OLIVEIRA MARTINS, 1994, *Comparison of Model Structure and Policy Scenarios: GREEN and 12RT*, Paris: OECD Department of Economics Working Paper No. 146.

MANSER, R., 1983, *The Squandered Dividend: The Free Market and the Environment in Eastern Europe*, London: Earthscan.

MARKUSEN, J. R., 1975, 'International Externalities and Optimal Tax Structures', *Journal of International Economics* 5: 15–29.

—— 1983, 'Factor Movements and Commodity Trade as Complements', *Journal of International Economics* 14: 341–56.

——, E. R. MOREY, and N. OLEWILER, 1993, Environmental Policy when Market Structure and Plant Locations Are Endogenous, *Journal of Environmental Economics and Mangement* 24: 68–86.

——————— 1995, 'Noncooperative Equilibria in Regional Environmental Policies when Plant Locations are Endogenous', *Journal of Public Economics* 56: 55–77.

MAYER, W., 1984, 'Endogenous Tariff Formation', *American Economic Review* 74: 970–85.

—— 1991, 'Endogenous Labor Supply in International Trade Theory: Two Alternative Models', *Journal of International Economics* 30: 105–20.

MERRI'ELD, 1988, 'The Impact of Abatement Strategies on Transnational Pollution, the Terms of Trade, and Factor Rewards: A General Equilibrium Approach', *Journal of Environmental Economics and Management* 15: 259–84.

MILLER, M., 1991, *Debt and the Environment: Converging Crises*, Geneva: United Nations.

MITCHELL, W., and M. MUNGER, 1991, 'Economic Models of Interest Groups: An Introductory Survey', *American Journal of Political Science* 35: 512–46.

MIXON, F. G., Jr., 'Public Choice and the EPA: Empirical Evidence on Carbon Emission Violations', *Public Choice* 83: 127–37.

MORRIS, D., 1991, 'Free Trade: The Great Destroyer', *Ecologist* 20: 190–5.

MOTTA, M., and J. F. THISSE, 1993, *Minimum Standard as Environmental Policy: Domestic and International Effects*, Milan: Fondazione ENI Enrico Mattei Working Paper No. 20.93.

—— —— 1994, 'Does Environmental Dumping Lead to Delocation?', *European Economic Review* 38, 563–76.

MOYERS, B.,1990, *Global Dumping Ground: The International Traffic in Hazardous Waste*, Washington, DC: Seven Locks Press.

MUELLER, D. C., 1989, *Public Choice II*, Cambridge: Cambridge University Press.

MURRELL, P., and R, RYTERMAN, 1991, 'A Methodology for Testing Comparative Economic Theories: Theory and Application to East-West Environmental Problems', *Journal of Comparative Economics* 15: 582–601.

NASH, J. F., Jr., 1951, 'Non-Cooperative Games', *Annals of Mathematics* 54: 286–95.

NISKANEN, W., 1977, *Bureaucracy and Representative Government*, Chicago: Aldine Atherton.

NITZAN, S., 1994, 'Modelling Rent-Seeking Contests', *European Journal of Political Economy* 10: 41–60.

OECD, 1990, *Pollution Control and Abatement Expenditure in OECD Countries: A Statistical Compendium*, Paris: OECD Environment Monographs No. 38.

—— 1995, *Global Warming: Economic Dimensions and Policy Reponses*, Paris: OECD.

OATES, W. E., and R. M. SCHWAB, 1988, 'Economic Competition among Jurisdictions: Efficiency Enhancing or Distortion Inducing?', *Journal of Public Economics* 35: 333–54.

—— K. PALMER, and P. PORTNEY, 1993, *Environmental Regulation and International Competitiveness*, College Park, Md: University of Maryland Working Paper 93–11.

OHLIN, B., 1933, *Interregional and International Trade*, Cambridge, Mass.: Harvard University Press.

OLIVEIRA-MARTINS, J., J.-M. BURNIAUX, and J. P. MARTIN, 1992, 'Trade and the Effectiveness of Unilateral CO_2 Abatement Policies: Evidence from GREEN', *OECD Economic Studies* 19: 123–40.

OLSON, M., 1965, *The Logic of Collective Action*, Cambridge, Mass.: Harvard University Press.

PAGE, D., 1989, 'Debt-for-Nature Swaps: Experience Gained, Lessons Learned', *International Environmental Affairs*, 274–88.

PATTERSON, E., 1992, 'GATT and the Environment: Rules to Minimize Adverse Trade and Environmental Effects', *Journal of World Trade* 26(3): 99–109.

PEARCE, D. W., 1993, *The Greening of the GATT: Some Theoretical Considerations*, Norwich: University of East Anglia, mimeo.

——and R. K. Turner, 1990, *Economics of Natural Resources and the Environment*, New York: Harvester Wheatsheaf.

PEIRCE, W. S., 1991, 'Unanimous Decisions in a Redistributive Context: The Council of Ministers of the European Communities', in R. Vaubel, T. D. Willett, (eds.), *The Political Economy of International Organizations: A Public Choice Approach*, Boulder, Colo.: Westview, 267–85.

PELTZMAN, S., 1976, 'Toward a More General Theory of Regulatory Capture', *Journal of Law and Economics* 19: 211–40.

PETHIG, R., 1975, 'Umweltverschmutzung, Wohlfahrt und Umweltpolitik in einem Zwei-Sektoren-Gleichgewichtsmodell', *Zeitschrift für Nationalökonomie* 35: 99–124.

—— 1976, 'Pollution, Welfare, and Environmental Policy in the Theory of Comparative Advantage', *Journal of Environmental Economics and Management* 2: 160–9.

PHILLIPS, T. P., and B. A. FORSTER, 1987, 'Economic Impacts of Acid Rain on Forest, Aquatic, and Agricultural Ecosystems in Canada', *American Journal of Agricultural Economics* 69: 963–9.

PIGOU, A. C., 1920, *The Economics of Welfare*, New York: Macmillan.

PILLARISETTI, J. R., 'Three Essays on Optimal External Borrowing, Debt-for-Nature Swaps, and the Impaxt of Distortions on Country Risk of the Developing Countries', Manhattan, Kan.: Kansas State University Diss.

PORTER, M. E., 1990, *The Comparative Advantage of Nations*, London: Macmillan.

—— 1991, 'America's Green Strategy', *Scientific American* 264(4): 96.

RAMSEY, F. P, 1928, 'A Mathematical Theory of Saving', *Economic Journal* 38: 543–59.

RAUSCHER, M., 1989, 'Foreign Debt and Renewable Resources' *Metroeconomica* 40: 57–66.

—— 1990a, 'The Optimal Use of Environmental Resources by an Indebted Country', *Journal of Institutional and Theoretical Economics* 146: 500–17.

—— 1990b, 'Can Cartelisation Solve the Problem of Tropical Deforestation?' *Weltwirtschaftliches Archiv* 126: 378–87.

—— 1991a, 'Foreign Trade and the Environment', in H. Siebert (ed.), *Environmental Scarcity: The International Dimension*, Tübingen: Mohr, 17–31.

—— 1991b, 'National Environmental Policies and the Effects of Economic Integration', *European Journal of Political Economy* 7: 313–29.

—— 1992a, 'Economic Integration and the Environment: Effects on Members and Non-members', *Environmental and Resource Economics.* 2: 221–36.

—— 1992b, 'International Economic Integration and the Environment: The Case of Europe', in K. Anderson and R. Blackhurst (eds.), *The Greening of World Trade Issues*, New York: Harvester Wheatsheaf, 173–91.

—— 1994a, 'On Ecological Dumping', *Oxford Economic Papers*, 46: 822–40.

—— 1994b, 'Foreign Trade and Renewable Resources', in C. Carraro (ed.), *Trade, Innovation, Environment*, Dordrecht: Kluwer, 109–21.

—— 1995a, 'Environmental Policy and International Capital Movements', forthcoming in K.-G. Mäler, *International Environmental Problems: An Economic Perspective*, Amsterdam: Kluwer.

—— 1995b, 'Environmental Legislation as a Tool of Trade Policy', in G. Boero and Z. A. Silberston (eds.), *Environmental Economics: Proceedings of a Conference held by the Confederation of European Economic Associations at Oxford, 1993 CEEA Conference*, Basingstoke: Macmillan, 73–90.

—— 1995c, 'Environmental Regulation and the Location of Polluting Industries', *International Tax and Public Finance* 2: 229–44.

—— 1995(d), Trade Law and Environmental Issues in Central and East European Countries, in L.A. Winters, ed., *Foundations of an Open Economy: Trade Laws and Institutions for Eastern Europe*, London: CEPR, 178–217.

REGE, V., 1994, 'GATT Law and Environment-Related Issues affecting the Trade of Developing Countries', *Journal of World Trade* 10(3): 95–169.

REINGANUM, J. F., 1981, Dynamic Games of Innovation, *Journal of Economic Theory* 25: 21–42.

REITZES, J. D., 1992, 'Quality Choice, Trade Policy, and Firm Incentives', *International Economic Review* 33: 817–35.

ROBISON, H. D., 1988, 'Industrial Pollution Abatement: The Impact on the Balance of Trade', *Canadian Journal of Economics* 30: 187–99.

RODRIK, D., 1994, *What Does the Political Economy Literature on Trade Policy (not) Tell Us that We Ought to Know*, London: CEPR Discussion Paper No. 1039.

ROMER, P. M., 1983, 'Dynamic Competitive Equilibria with Externalities, Increasing Returns and Unbounded Growth', Chicago: University of Chicago Ph.D. Diss.

—— 1986, 'Increasing Returns and Long-Run Growth', *Journal of Political Economy* 94, 1002–37.

—— 1994, 'New Goods, Old Theory, and the Welfare Costs of Trade Restrictions', *Journal of Development Economics* 43: 5–38.

ROWLAND, C. K., and R. FEIOCK, 1991, 'Environmental Regulation and Economic Development: The Movement of Chemical Production among States', in M. J. Dubnick and A. R. Gitelson (eds.), *Public Policy and Economic Institutions*, Greenwich, Conn: JAI Press, 205–18.

RUFFIN, R. J., 1984, 'International Factor Movemens', in R. W. Jones, and P. B. Kenen (eds.), *Handbook of International Economics, Vol. 1*, Amsterdam: North-Holland, 237–88.

RUNGE, C. F., 1990, 'Trade Protection and Environmental Regulations: New Nontariff Barriers', *Northwestern Journal of International Law and Business* 2(1): 47–61.

RØPKE, I., 1994, 'Trade, Development, and Sustainability: A Critical Assessment of the "Free Trade Dogma" ', *Ecological Economics* 9: 13–22.

SACHS, J. D., 1989a, Introduction, in J. D. Sachs, *Developing Country Debt and the World Economy*, Chicago: University of Chicago Press, 1–33.

—— 1989b, 'The Debt Overhang of Developing Countries', in G. Calvo and R. Findlay, *Debt, Growth, and Stabilization: Essays in the Memory of Carlos Diaz Alejandro*, Oxford: Blackwell, 80–102.

Sachverständigenrat zur Begutachtung der wirtschaftlichen Lage, 1994, *Jahresgutachten 1994/95*, Bonn: Bundesanzeiger Verlagsgesellschaft.

SAMUELSON, P. A., 1948, 'International Trade and Equalisation of Factor Prices', *Economic Journal* 58: 163–84.

—— 1949, 'International Factor-Price Equalisation once again', *Economic Journal* 59: 181–97.

—— 1971, 'Ohlin Was Right', *Swedish Journal of Economics*, 73: 365–84.

SARKAR, A. U., and K. L. EBBS, 1992, 'A Possible Solution to Tropical Troubles? Debt-for-Nature Swaps', *Futures* 24: 653–68.

SEIERSTAD, A., and SYDSAETER, K., 1987, *Optimal Control with Economic Applications*, Amsterdam: North-Holland.

SHAPIRO, C., 1989, 'Theories of Oligopoly Behavior', in R. Schmalensee and R. D. Willig (eds.), *Handbook of Industrial Organization*, Amsterdam: North-Holland, 329–414.

SHRYBMAN, S., 1991, 'International Trade and the Environment: An Environmental Assessment of the General Agreement on Tarriffs and Trade', *Ecologist*, 20: 30–4.

—— 1991/92, 'Trading Away the Environment', *World Policy Journal*, 93–110.

SHUBIK, M., 1982, *Game Theory in the Social Sciences: Concepts and Solutions*, Cambridge, Mass.: MIT Press.

SIDGWICK, H., 1883, *The Principles of Political Economy*, London: Macmillan.

SIEBERT, H., 1977, 'Environmental Quality and the Gains from Trade', *Kyklos* 30: 657–73.

—— 1979, 'Environmental Policy in the Two-Country Case', *Zeitschrift für Nationalökonomie* 39: 259–74.

—— 1985*a*, 'Spatial Aspects of Environmental Economics', in A. V. Kneese and J. L. Sweeney (eds.), *Handbook of Natural Resource and Energy Economics, Vol.1*, Amsterdam: North-Holland, 125–64.

—— 1985*b*, *The Economics of the Resource-Exporting Country: Intertemporal Theory of Supply and Trade*, Greenwich: JAI Press.

—— 1987, 'Foreign Debt and Capital Accumulation', *Weltwirtschaftliches Archiv* 123: 618–30.

—— 1988, 'Strategische Handelspolitik: Theoretische Ansätze und wirtschaftspolitische Empfehlungen', *Aussenwirtschaft* 43: 549–85.

—— 1990, 'The Harmonization Issue in Europe: Prior Agreement or a Competitive Process?', in H. Siebert (ed.), *The Completion of the Internal Market*, Tübingen: Mohr, 53–75.

—— 1991, 'Environmental Policy and European Integration', in H. Siebert (ed.), *Environmental Scarcity: The International Dimension*, Tübingen: Mohr, 57–70.

—— 1995, *Economics of the Environment*, 4th edn., Berlin Springer.

—— J. EICHBERGER, R. GRONYCH, and R. PETHIG, 1980, *Trade and the Environment: A Theoretical Enquiry*, Amsterdam: North-Holland.

SINN, H.-W., 1987, *Capital Income Taxation and Resource Allocation*, Amsterdam: North-Holland.

—— 1994, 'How Much Europe? Subsidiarity, Centralization and Fiscal Competition', *Scottish Journal of Political Economy* 41: 85–107.

SINN, S., 1992, 'The Taming of Leviathan', *Constitutional Political Economy* 3: 177–96.

SMITH, ADAM, 1776, *An Inquiry into the Nature and the Causes of the Wealth of Nations*. London: Strahan & Cadell.

SMITH, ALASDAIR, 1994, 'Strategic Trade Policy in the European Car Market', in P. R. Krugman and A. Smith (eds.), *Empirical Studies of Strategic Trade Policy*, Chicago: University of Chicago Press, 67–81.

SMITH, T. T., 1993, *Understanding European Environmental Regulation*, New York: Conference Board.

SNAPE, R. H., 1992, 'The Environment, International Trade and Competitiveness', in K. Anderson and R. Blackhurst (eds.), *The Greening of World Trade Issues*, New York: Harvester Wheatsheaf, 73–92.

SOLOW, R. M., 1974, 'The Economics of Resources or the Resources of Economics', *American Economic Review (Papers and Proceedings)* 64: 1–14.

SORSA, P., 1992a, 'GATT and the Environment', *World Economy* 15(1): 115–33.

—— 1992b, *The Environment: A New Challenge to GATT*, Washington, DC; World Bank Policy Research Working Paper 980.

—— 1994, *Competitiveness and Environmental Standards: Some Exploratory Results*, Washington, DC; World Bank Policy Research Working Paper 1249.

SPENCE, A. M., 1976, 'Product Selection, Fixed Costs and Monopolistic Competition', *Review of Economic Studies* 43, 217–35.

SPENCER, B. and J. A. BRANDER, 1983, 'International R&D Rivalry and Industrial Stategy', *Review of Economic Studies* 50, 707–22.

STEININGER, K., 1994a, *Trade and the Environment: The Regulatory Controversy and a Theoretical and Empirical Assessment of Unilateral Environmental Action*, Heidelberg: Physica.

—— 1994b, 'Reconciling Trade and the Environment: Towards a Comparative Advantage for Long-term Policy Goals', *Ecological Economics* 9: 23–42.

STIGLER, G. J., 1971, 'The Theory of Economic Regulation', *Bell Journal of Economics and Management Science* 3: 137–46.

STOLPER, W. S., and P. A. SAMUELSON, 1941, 'Protection and Real Wages', *Review of Economic Studies* 9: 58–73.

STRAND, J., 1990, *Lending Terms, Debt Recessions, and Developing Countries' Resource Extraction*, Oslo: University, Department of Economics Research Memorandum 1990, 5.

—— 1994, *Developing Country Resource Extraction with Asymmetric Information and Sovereign Debt: A Theoretical Analysis*, Oslo: Oslo University, Dept. of Economics Research Memorandum 1994, 17.

SUBRAMANIAN, A., 1992, 'Trade Measures for the Environment: A Nearly Empty Box?', *World Economy* 15(1): 135–52.

SVEDBERG, P., 1979, 'Optimal Tariff Policy on Imports from Multinationals', *Economic Record* 55: 64–7.

SWANEY, J. A., 1994, 'So What's Wrong with Dumping on Africa?', *Journal of Economic Issues* 28: 367–77.

TAYLOR, L., 1992, 'Infrastructural Competition among Jurisdicitions', *Journal of Public Economics* 49: 241–59.

TIROLE, J., 1988, *The Theory of Industrial Organization*, Cambridge, Mass.: MIT Press.

TOBEY, J. A., 1989, 'The Impact of Domestic Environmental Policies on International Trade', Ph.D. Diss., Dept. of Economics, University of Maryland, College Park.

—— 1990, 'The Effects of Domestic Environmental Policies on Patterns of World Trade: An Empirical Test', *Kyklos* 43: 191–209.

TOWER, E., 1983, 'On the Best Use of Trade Controls in the Presence of Foreign Market Power', *Journal of International Economics* 15: 349–65.

TULLOCK, G., 1980, 'Efficient Rent Seeking', in J. M. Buchanan, P. D. Tollison, and G. Tullock, (eds.), *Toward a Theory of the Rent-Seeking Society*, College Station, Tex: Texas A.&M. University Press, 97–112.

UGELOW, J. L., 1982, 'A Survey on Recent Studies on Costs of Pollution Control and the Effects on Trade', in S. J. Rubin and T. R. Graham, eds., *Environment and Trade: The Relation of International Trade and Environmental Policy*, Totowa, NJ: Allanheld & Osmun, 167–90.

ULPH, A., 1992, 'The Choice of Environmental Policy Instruments and Strategic

International Trade', in R. Pethig, *Conflicts and Cooperation in Managing Environmental Resources*, Berlin Springer, 111–29.

—— 1994*a*, 'Environmental Policy, Plant Location and Government Protection', in C. Carraro (ed.), *Trade, Innovation, Environment* Dordrecht: Kluwer, 123–63.

—— 1994*b*, *Environmental Policy and International Trade: A Survey of Recent Economic Analysis*, Milan: Fondazione ENI Enrico Mattei Discussion Paper 94,53.

——and D. ULPH, 1994, *Trade, Strategic Innovation and Startegic Envtronmental Policy: A General Analysis*, Southampton: Discussion Paper in Economics and Econometrics 9416.

ULPH, D., 1994, 'Strategic Innovation and Strategic Environmental Policy', in C. Carraro (ed.), *Trade, Innovation, Environment* Dordrecht: Kluwer, 205–28.

URSPRUNG, H. W., 1991, 'Economic Policies and Political Competition', in A. L. Hillman (ed.), *Markets and Politicians: Politicized Economic Choice*, Boston: Kluwer, 1–25.

VAN BERGEIJK, P. A. G., 1991, 'International Trade and the Environmental Challenge', *Journal of World Trade* 25(6): 105–15.

VARIAN, H. R., 1992, *Microeconomic Analysis*, New York: Norton.

VENABLES, A. J., 1985, 'Trade and Trade Policy with Imperfect Compettion: The Case of Identical Products and Free Entry', *Journal of International Economics* 19: 1–20.

—— 1994, 'Trade Policy under Imperfect Competition: A Numerical Assessment', in P. R. Krugman and A. Smith, (eds.), *Empirical Studies of Strategic Trade Policy*, Chicago: University of Chicago Press, 41–63.

VERDIER, T. 1993, 'Strategic Trade and the Regulation of Pollution by Performance or Design Standards', Milan: Fondazione ENI Enrico Mattei Working Paper No. 58.

VERNON, R., 1966, 'International Investment and International Trade in the Product Cycle', *Quarterly Journal of Economics* 80: 191–207.

VINER, J., 1923, *Dumping: A Problem in International Trade*, Chicago: University of Chicago Press.

VOUSDEN, N, 1990, *The Economics of Trade Protection*, Cambridge: Cambridge University Press.

WALSH, V., 1956, Leisure and International Trade, *Economica* 23: 253–60.

WALTER, I., 1973, 'The Pollution Content of American Trade', *Western Economic Journal* 11: 61–70.

—— 1975, *The International Economics of Pollution*, London, Basingstoke: Macmillan.

—— 1982, 'Environmentally Induced Industrial Relocation to Developing Countries', in S. J. Rubin and T. R. Graham (eds.), *Environment and Trade: The Relation of International Trade and Environmental Policy*, Totowa, NJ: Allanheld & Osmun, 67–101.

—— and J. L. UGELOW, 1979, Environmental Policies in Developing Countries, *Ambio* 8 (2–3): 102–109.

WANG, L.-J., 1995, 'Environmental Capital Flight and Pollution Tax', *Environmental and Resource Economics* 4: 273–86.

WEITZMAN, M. L., 1974, 'Prices vs. Quantities', *Review of Economic Studies* 41: 477–91.

WELLISCH, D., 1995, 'Locational Choice of Firms and Decentralized Environmental Policy with Various Instruments', *Journal of Urban Economics* 37, 290-310.

WHEELER, D. and P. MARTIN, 1992, 'Prices, Policies, and the International Diffusion of Clean Technology: The Case of Wood Pulp Production', in P. Low (ed.), *International Trade and the Environment*, New York: World Bank Discussion Paper No. 159: 197–224.

WILDASIN, D. A., 1988, Nash Equilibria in Fiscal Competition, *Journal of Public Economics* 35: 229–40.

—— 1991, 'Some Rudimentary "Duopolity" Theory, *Regional Science and Urban Economics* 21: 393–421.

—— and J. D. WILSON, 1991, 'Theoretical Issues in Local Public Economics: An Overview', *Regional Science and Urban Economics* 21: 317–31.

WHALLEY, J., 1991, 'The Interface between Environmental and Trade Policies', *Economic Journal* 101, 180–89.

WILKINSON, D. G., 1994, 'NAFTA and the Environment: Some Lessons for the Next Round of GATT Negotiations', *World Economy* 17: 395–412.

WILSON, J. D., 1986, 'A Theory of Interregional Tax Competition', *Journal of Urban Economics* 19: 296–315.

—— 1987, 'Trade, Capital Mobility, and Tax Competition', *Journal of Political Economy 95: 835–56.*

WITHAGEN, C., 1985, Economic Theory and International Trade in Natural Exhaustible Resources, *Berlin Springer.*

WONG, K. Y., 1986, 'Are International Trade and Factor Movements Substitutes?', *Journal of International Economics* 21: 25–43.

WOODLAND, A. D., 1982, *International Trade and Resource Allocation, Amsterdam: North-Holland.*

WYNNE, B., 1989, 'The Toxic Waste Trade: International Regulatory Issues and Options', *Third World Quarterly* 11(3): 120–46.

XEPAPADEAS, A., and Y. KATSOULACOS, 1994, *Environmental Policy under Oligopoly with Endogenous Market Structure, Milan: Fondazione ENI Enrico Mattei Working Paper No. 22.94.*

YANG, X., and B. N. HEIJDRA, 1993, 'Monopolistic Competition and Optimum Product Diversity: Comment', *American Economic Review 83: 295–301.*

YOUNG, L., and S. P. MAGEE, 1986, 'Endogenous Protection, Factor Returns and Resource Allocation', *Review of Economic Studies* 53: 407–19.

YOUNG, M. D., 1994, 'Ecologically Accelerated Trade Liberalisation: A Set of Disciples for Environment and Trade Agreements', *Ecological Economics 9: 43–51.*

ZODROW, G. R., and P. M. Mieszkowski, 1986, 'Pigou, Tiebout, Property Taxation, and the Underprovision of Public Goods', *Journal of Urban Economics* 19: 356–70.

ZYLICZ, T., 1993, *Pollution and Natural Resource Taxes in Poland*, Warsaw: Warsaw University Economics Dept. Discussion Paper.

Legal Materials

Basel Convention on the Control of Transboundary Movements of Hazardous Wastes and Their Disposal (with Annexes), 1992, *Canada: Treaty Series 1992/19, Ottawa: Queen's Printer for Canada.*

Commission of the European Communities DG XI, 1992, *European Environment Legislation*, Luxembourg: Office for Official Publications of the European Communities.

Convention on International Trade in Endangered Species of Wild Fauna and Flora, 1975, *Bundesgesetzblatt Teil II 1975*, 777–833.

The General Agreement of Tariffs and Trade, 1961, Washington, DC: Dept. of State Publication 7182.

European Communities, 1973, *Treaties Establishing the European Communities*, Luxembourg: Centre for Official Publications of the European Communities.

Ministerial Decisions Adopted by Ministers at the Meeting of the Trade Negotioantions Commitee in Marakesh on 14 April 1994: Decision on Trade and the Environment, 1995, repr. in C. Helm, *Handel und Umwelt: Für eine ökologische Reform des GATT*, Berlin Wissenschaftszentrum Papers FS II 95–402, 118–21.

Montreal Protocol on Substances that Deplete the Ozone Layer (including the 1990 Adjustment and Amendment), 1991, repr. in I. Rummel-Bulska and S. Osafo (eds.), *Selected Multilateral Treaties in the Field of the Environment, Vol. 2*, Cambridge: Grotius, 309–23.

North American Free Trade Agreement, 1993, *International Legal Materials* 32: 289–456 and 605–99.

Treaty of the European Union (The Treaty of Maastricht), 1993, in R. Corbett, *The Treaty of Maastricht—From Conception to Ratification: A Comprehensive Reference Guide*, Harlow: Longman, 382–481.

United Nations Conference on Environment and Develoment, 1992, *The Rio Declaration on Environment and Development*, Rio de Janeiro.

United States: Restrictions on Tuna. Report of the Panel (DS 21/R), 1993, *GATT Basic Instruments and Selected Documents Supplement* 39: 155–205.

Index